Louisiana: The Energy State

A HISTORY OF LOUISIANA'S OIL & GAS INDUSTRY

by William D. Reeves

A publication of the Louisiana Oil & Gas Association

HPNbooks
A division of Lammert Incorporated
San Antonio, Texas

Richard Clague and salt solution mining. Before the oil well was the water well and salt well. This painting, Louisiana Rigs in the Marsh *by Richard Clague shows an early (1870) salt solution mining operation adjacent to the just perceptible slope of a hidden salt dome.*
PHOTOGRAPH COURTESY OF NEAL AUCTION.

First Edition

Copyright © 2013 HPNbooks

Printed in China

ISBN: 978-1-939300-14-0
Library of Congress Card Catalog Number: 2013943396

Louisiana: The Energy State

author:	William D. Reeves
dustjacket design:	Calvin Ulery, Ulery Design
contributing writer for sharing the heritage:	Garnette Bane

HPNbooks

president:	Ron Lammert
project manager:	Curtis Courtney
administration:	Donna M. Mata, Melissa G. Quinn
book sales:	Dee Steidle
production:	Colin Hart, Evelyn Hart, Glenda Tarazon Krouse, Tony Quinn

CONTENTS

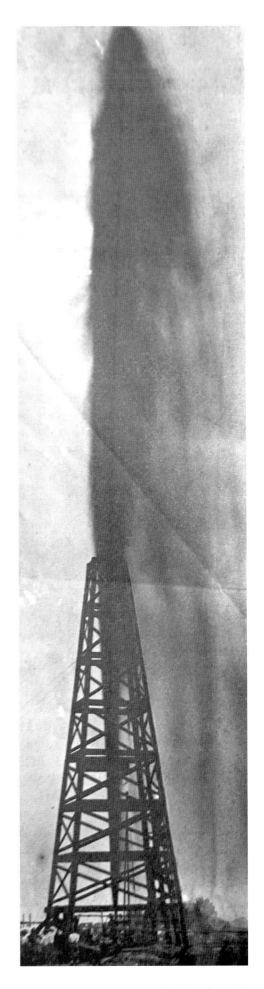

LOGA

LOUISIANA OIL & GAS ASSOCIATION

DON G. BRIGGS, *President*

By Don Briggs
President, Louisiana Oil & Gas Association

The oil and gas industry of Louisiana has impacted the nation's infrastructure and energy supply in a profound manner. From the coastal waters of the Gulf of Mexico, deep in the swamps of Cajun country, or far to the northwest corner of our state in the Haynesville Shale, Louisiana's resources directly power America. Men and women from Louisiana and surrounding states are to be thanked for investing their time and efforts into developing our abundant resources that benefit our state and country. This book offers a reminder of how entrepreneurs, wildcatters and roughnecks have been the pillars of THE energy state, Louisiana. The enclosed information does not cover each event, nor does it name every person that has served in the industry, but it outlines the past, present and future of Louisiana's role in establishing our nation's energy security for years to come. Photos and stories of this book will jar some old memories, create new ideas and serve as a recap of how the oil and gas industry of Louisiana truly is the major contributor to our creating a better tomorrow for our country. The oil and gas industry of Louisiana is not the only show in town, but it serves as the backbone for our state's future success.

LOGA is Louisiana's Oil & Gas Industry

PO BOX 4069   BATON ROUGE, LA 70821-4069   225.388.9525   800.443.1433   FAX:225.388.9561

LOUISIANA - *The Energy State*

4

ACKNOWLEDGEMENTS

I wish to thank particularly those individuals who have exerted themselves on behalf of this book. First, I want to thank Kjel C. Brothen of the Office of Conservation, Louisiana Department of Natural Resources, for creating the comprehensive well permit data base. Jack Holden of Pointe Coupee provided valuable commentary on salt solution mining. Michelle LeBlanc Leckert, of Neal Auction, provided a fine image of Richard Clague's 1870 painting.

Carroll Bertaut, formerly manager of Kerr-McGee's material and transportation for the Oil and Gas Division's Gulf Coast District, took me around Morgan City at the commencement of this project. As always, Irene Wainwright, director of the Louisiana Division, New Orleans Public Library, has taken time to provide sources and images. Jeff Spencer of Midstates Petroleum Company, Inc., has already written extensively on Louisiana oil and gas. He shared everything with me. Ms. Coe McKenzie, director of the Louisiana Oil & Gas Museum at Oil City, provided access to the wonderful image collection there. Henry Goodrich, former president of Goodrich Petroleum of Shreveport and Houston, offered important insights into the business. Dr. Laura Lyons McLemore of the archives division of the Noel Memorial Library at LSU Shreveport uncovered many fine collections pertaining to the oil business in the North. I. Bruce Turner, Head of Special Collections at the Edith Garland Dupre Library, University of Louisiana at Lafayette, found several taped interviews that were useful. Bruce Kirkpatrick of the Stream Companies provided a fine image of Ged Gray. Al Petrie of Investor + Media Relations, LLC, helped with particular oil and gas companies. Cyndy Robertson, assistant dean of the Library, University of Louisiana at Monroe, found several images for this book. Charlene Bonnette, preservation librarian of the State Library of Louisiana, likewise provided several images for this work. Paul Lawless of Helis Oil & Gas Company gave advice. John Laborde, first president of Tidewater Marine, provided images and advice.

Thank you,
William D. Reeves

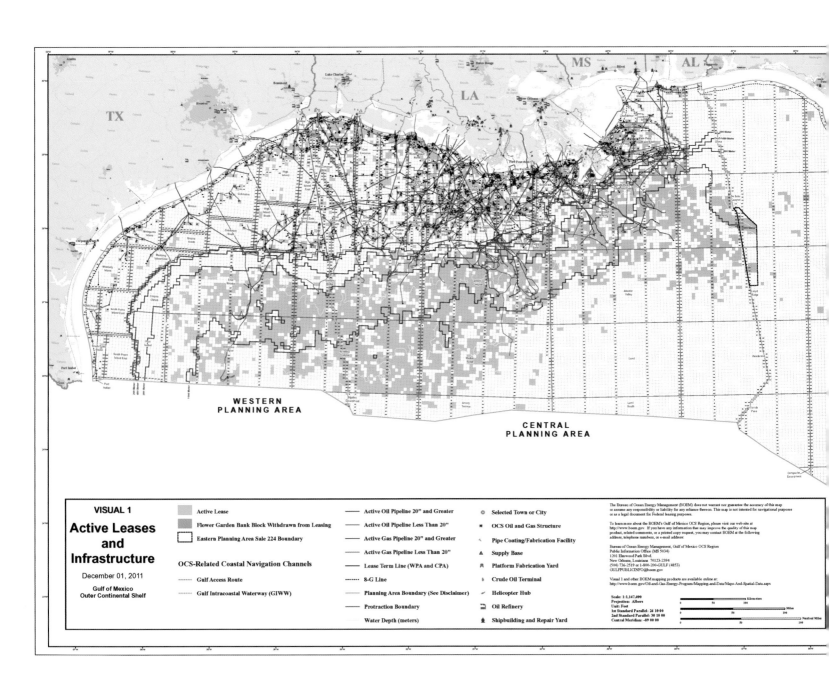

Active leases and infrastructure, December 1, 2011.

MAP COURTESY OF THE BUREAU OF OCEAN ENERGY MANAGEMENT.

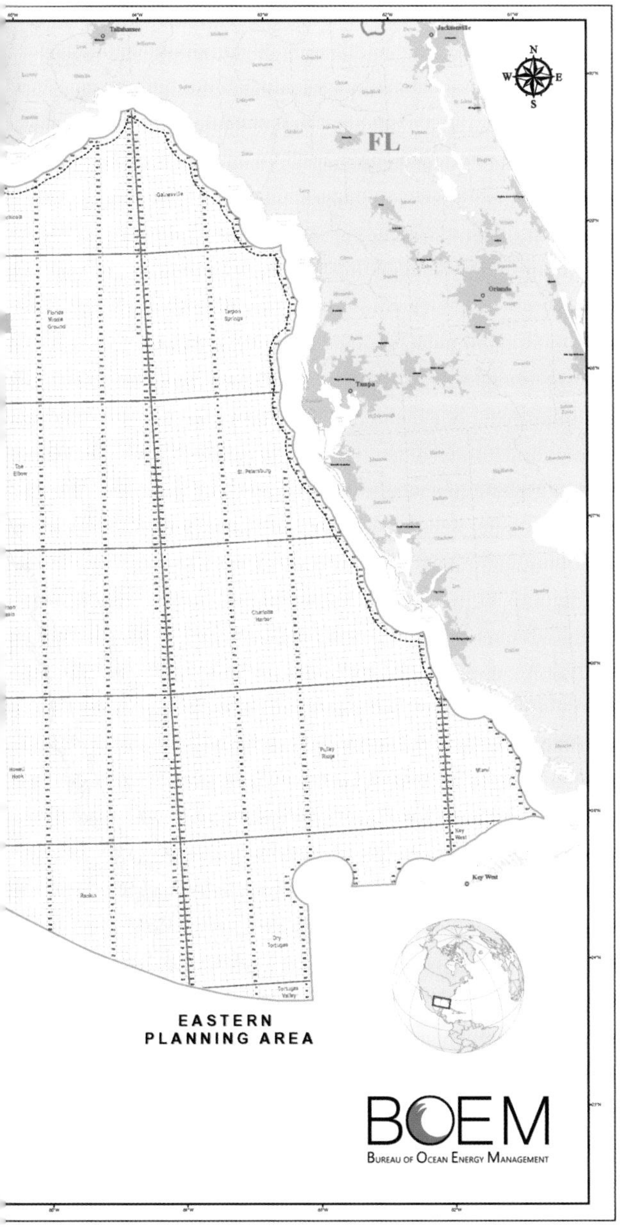

EASTERN PLANNING AREA

BOEM
Bureau of Ocean Energy Management

CHAPTER 1

INTRODUCTION

Louisiana is the energy state. Louisiana produces more energy per square mile than any other State in the Union. It refines more barrels of oil than any state but Texas. Louisiana has more wells off its coast than any state. It has more important offshore support industries than any state. Geography has also conspired to make Louisiana the energy state. It sits atop a great salt pan that extends from north to south and east to west and that has been covered over the millennia by the organic refuse of the greatest river on the continent.

The energy output of a state is best measured in British Thermal Units. BTU incorporates all forms of energy production in one meaningful scale. In gross production Texas is first with 12,000 trillion BTU for the last available year—2009. Louisiana is third in gross output with 7,000 trillion BTU. But, if the number is compared to the square miles of the states, Louisiana ranks first in BTU per square mile with 141 billion BTU per mile. Second is Wyoming at 106 billion BTU per square mile.

Louisiana is a refining state. In the twenty-first century Louisiana has moved to second in refining barrels per day of all the states. Thirty years ago Louisiana ranked third. Louisiana is the third highest state in consumption of natural gas. Texas is first, California is second. But on a per capita basis Louisiana far exceeds the other states. Certainly part of the reason is the strong national chemical industry in the state.

Louisiana's importance to the oil and gas industry continues offshore. The Bureau of Ocean Energy Management (BOEM) distributed a map of Active Leases as of December 1, 2011, shown on the left. The BOEM divided the Gulf of Mexico into three planning zones. These zones correspond to the adjoining states. The Western Planning Zone lies off the Texas shores. The Central Planning Zone lies off of Louisiana. The remainder of the Gulf belongs to the Eastern Planning Zone. Inspection of this map shows an overwhelming number of the Gulf of Mexico leases are off Louisiana's shore in the Central Planning Zone. Of the proved reserves in the Gulf of Mexico at the end of 2005, 87 percent of the gas and 92 percent of the oil were in the Central Planning Area off the Louisiana Coast.[1]

Energy Production in British Thermal Units (BTU) by State by Square Miles, 2009.

Rank Total BTU	State	Total BTU (trillions)	Square Miles	BTU Square Miles (billions)
3	Louisiana	7,302	51,840	141
2	Wyoming	10,337	97,813	106
5	Kentucky	2,819	40,410	70
6	Pennsylvania	2,674	46,056	58
1	Texas	11,915	268,580	44
8	Oklahoma	2,571	69,899	37
9	Colorado	2,483	104,093	24
10	New Mexico	2,412	121,589	20
7	California	2,605	163,695	16

U.S. Energy Information Administration. http://205.254.135.7/state/

Energy production in BTU by state by square miles. Based on state ranking. Total energy production, 2009.

COURTESY OF THE U.S. ENERGY
INFORMATION ADMINISTRATION.

This BOEM map also shows Louisiana's dominant role in the offshore support industries. The two most important are shipbuilding and rig fabrication. The map identifies 32 Platform fabrication facilities in Louisiana, and only 2 in Texas. It identifies five shipbuilding facilities in Louisiana, and only 1 in Texas. In short, Louisiana is vital to the offshore oil and gas industry, and it is vital to Louisiana.

Geography almost made Louisiana's role as the energy state inevitable. Louisiana occupies the center of a great salt shelf extending from central Texas to central Mississippi, from the Arkansas line to the deep water of the Gulf of Mexico. Then, the structure of the North American continent conveniently demanded a river to drain the area between the Appalachian Mountains on the east and the Rocky Mountains on the west. The Mississippi River had to flow south where it emptied into a drying bed of the sea. Steadily, through millions of years it deposited soil over the salt and organic debris settling from the sea. Sand and shale accumulated layer by layer weighing down the salt pan and its oil.

Pressure on the salt pan rose and squeezed the salt like a tube of toothpaste. The salt migrated, some of it upwards in giant domes. The pressure that squeezed the salt also squeezed and heated the organics transforming them particle by particle into oil and gas. It, too, flowed slowly upwards towards areas of less pressure. Over the eons it moved as droplets inching along until it ran into a wall. The wall occurred where the sands and shale broke or sheared, creating the fault or trap that stopped the oil, forcing it to pool within adjacent sands. The salt domes, earlier arrivals, also blocked both the lateral and upward movement of the oil, and so became for later explorers signals of the presence of oil. The result was oil and gas at some depth practically everywhere in Louisiana.

The twentieth century made Louisiana the energy state. Its principal towns became energy towns. In the north Shreveport put on a cloak of oil wells and was the first town to have natural gas piped in. Shreveport on the Red River was simply the northwestern port town for Louisiana, gathering cotton and timber, then shipping them south to

Table 1. Number and Capacity of Operable Petroleum Refineries by PAD District and State as of January 1, 2011.

State	Number of Refineries	Capacity per day January 1, 2011
Texas	26	4,717,199
Louisiana	19	3,219,520
California	20	1,959,271
Illinois	4	973,600
Pennsylvania	5	773,000
Washington	5	628,800
New Jersey	5	548,000
Ohio	4	524,400
Oklahoma	6	520,700
Indiana	2	431,500

U.S. Energy Information Administration.

Table 16. Natural Gas Deliveries to Consumers.

Natural Gas Delivered to Consumers	Trillion Cubic Feet
Texas	2.95
California	2.2
Louisiana	1.2
New York	1.2

U.S. Energy Information Administration. Natural Gas Monthly, February 2012.

New Orleans and west to Texas. The Texas and Pacific Railroad helped this process and welcomed oil shipments from the new fields surrounding the town.

Monroe in the northeast sat atop a giant gas field. Both Shreveport and Monroe profit today from a new wave of shale oil exploration. Monroe, dominating the Ouachita River, did not see great prosperity until the twentieth century. It serviced farms of the Louisiana hill country and welcomed two new inventions partially developed by its residents—Coca-Cola

and Delta Airlines. But the Monroe Gas Field turned it into the energy source for the middle South, with gas pipelines stretching as far as Tennessee and Georgia. Hard scrabble farmers of north Louisiana earned another generation of self-sufficiency from oil and gas beneath their worn-out lands.

Timber made the town of Lake Charles, but oil refining made it happy. The Cities Service Refinery established in the 1940s is the second largest in the state. A ship channel permits exporting refined products. Lafayette was a

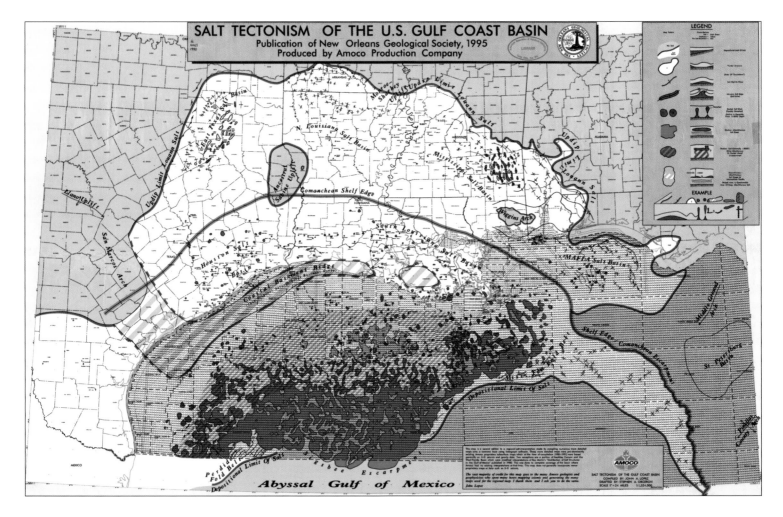

Salt Tectonism of the U.S. Gulf Coast Basin. Key: Red = salt sheet; white = salt basin, green = no salt; darkgreen circles = salt domes; green and red stripes = shallow salt less 8,000 feet. No other state has the equivalent underlay of salt.

MAP COURTESY OF THE NEW ORLEANS GEOLOGICAL SOCIETY.

sleepy town that was well placed to communicate with operations along the Gulf coast. Its bayou and highway to Morgan City and its branch of Louisiana State University enabled it to be the white collar headquarters for the local oil companies. The creation at the end of the thirties of the Layette Oil business park provided a fine piece of infrastructure for new businesses. Lafayette was where the Cajun culture met the English. The great growth of the Cajun population and its inventiveness contributed to Lafayette's success.

Morgan City, still destined for greatness as a port because of its place at the mouth of the Atchafalaya River, took another direction. It used its web of deep water channels to welcome the grand McDermott fabrication plant and the miles of offshore support industries. From Morgan City it is just a short jump into the Gulf of Mexico yet it is tied into a solid state highway network that extends to New Orleans in the east and Lafayette on the west. Morgan City is a town of gaps and holes defined by mysterious channels, not the least of which is the Atchafalaya River. Once crossed the visitor is on the edges of the great Cajun prairie extending northwest past Lafayette to Lake Charles.

New Orleans made its fortune with the development of the offshore oil industry. Downtown, the majors built a dozen high rise office buildings that revolutionized her look and welcomed professional football. But, it was not to be. Like a herd of buffalo, in the 1990s the majors abandoned their new buildings and marched to Houston, always the home of their financial heart. There limitless Texas plains stretched out to the north and west permitting endless sprawl on practically free land. So different in New Orleans, so walled in by her gentle waters, the Mississippi River on the west and Lake Pontchartrain on the north and east. To the south, marsh. Still, the march of the majors west hardly touched the grand town of support businesses that had sprung up along the Harvey Canal on New Orleans' west bank. There, along roads like Industrial

Avenue, hundreds of oil support business plied their trade, their owners racing down the Mississippi or west into the Barataria Bay and out to the Gulf past Shell's outpost on the western tip of Grand Isle. On the west bank of the Mississippi River Avondale shipyards contributed to the oil boom.

As early as 1950 it was estimated that 25,000 Louisiana residents collected lease payments. The total payout had been $100,000,000, including $20,000,000 to the State of Louisiana for rental of state lands.[2] But the best years were about to begin. The great wildcatter Jimmy Owen observed that the boom years started after World War II. "The years from the forties through the sixties were golden years for oil exploration...."[3] Those were the years when Louisiana's Department of Natural Resources classified as many as seventeen percent of the wells drilled as "wildcat."

The oil industry has a vocabulary that still rings familiar in the ears of Louisiana citizens. There are the roughneck and the roustabout, the royalty and the overriding royalty, the Tcf, Bcf, MMcf, Mcf, and just plain cubic feet. Landmen are so ubiquitous as to hardly need an introduction. Anyone who has been in a rural courthouse has met a landman. Because the roughneck works on the drill floor, connecting and disconnecting drillpipe, the public seldom meets him. It seems like nearly all young men worked as roustabouts for one summer. They were the rig's unskilled labor that moved equipment and pipe.

One of the most remarkable misconceptions about the oil and gas business is its permanence. The average citizen thinks that hitting an oil well is income for life, a bed of roses ever after. This history shows that the oil business is first and foremost transitory. Oil wells last a few weeks or a few years and then they are dry. How then does oil keep flowing? The answer is continual drilling, finding new oil. In short, wildcatting.

The central personality of this volume is the wildcatter. He risks all for a new oil or gas

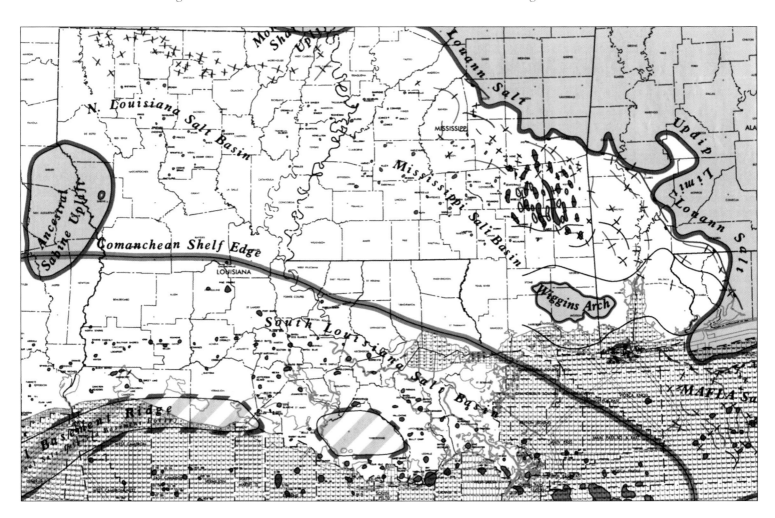

Salt Tectonism detail.

field. And then, and here is the rub, he sells everything and risks it all again for the next field. The wildcatter instinctively knows that oilfields are temporary, and more importantly, he does not wish to be tied to one field. Exploration is his most important quality. This is an unusual quality in most people. Stability and predictability are a major value in the laborer or the banker, the attorney or the teacher. But not for the oil man, or his cousins in the risky support industries.

The following chapters illustrate the wildcatter in action. Oil exploration came to Louisiana in the southwest around the town of Jennings. Scott Heywood embodied the qualities central to the early oil and gas business. In chapter 3 the story moves to northwest Louisiana where risk takers like Mike Benedum developed the gas and oilfields surrounding Shreveport. A decade later the Monroe Gas Field in the northeastern part of Louisiana just blew into Louisiana's oil picture. Chapter 5 chronicles the development in subsequent decades of southeastern Louisiana. Here was a bold mix of wildcatter and oil company. Finally, the oil industry moved offshore, led by the large oil companies but embodied in the thousands of companies and individuals who risked their savings to make the modern offshore—the jewel in the crown of the oil industry.

This story of oil and gas in Louisiana ends happily. In 2012 the prospects for American natural gas skyrocketed. The favorable prospects for the world-wide use of natural gas has heightened the prospects for the export of natural gas as Liquefied Natural Gas or LNG. Two independent studies contracted by the U.S. Energy Information Administration appeared online. A major study by NERA Economic Consulting dated December 2012 and titled "Macroeconomic Impacts of LNG Exports from the United States" looks to the implications of abundant natural gas in the United States. The study pointed not only to energy sufficiency in the U.S. but to a major role for the United States in world energy supply. Not since the Texas Railroad Commission set the world crude oil prices has the United States been so dominant. Another study by the U.S. Energy Information Administration dated January 2012 pointed out that U.S. natural gas prices are best represented at Louisiana's Henry Hub. But those prices are quite variable, moving between $12 and $3 MMBtu over the past five years.[4] But the NERA study concluded that "Across all…scenarios, the United States was projected to gain net economic benefits from allowing LNG exports." If NERA's projections are accepted, Louisiana and the nation's natural gas producers are looking at a bright future.

PARISHES OF LOUISIANA

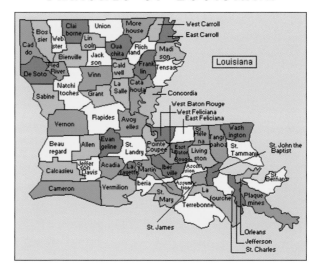

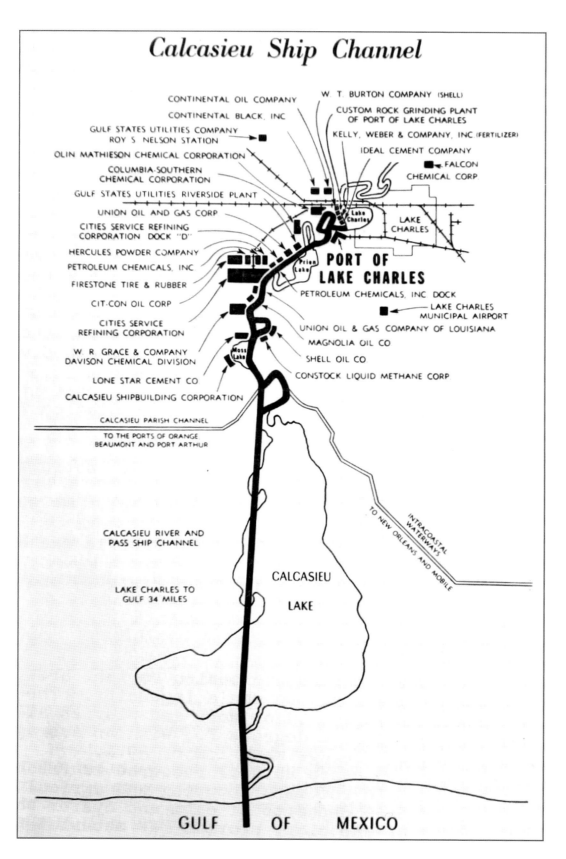

Calcasieu Ship Channel

CONTINENTAL OIL COMPANY

CONTINENTAL BLACK, INC.

GULF STATES UTILITIES COMPANY
ROY S NELSON STATION

OLIN MATHIESON CHEMICAL CORPORATION

COLUMBIA-SOUTHERN
CHEMICAL CORPORATION

GULF STATES UTILITIES RIVERSIDE PLANT

UNION OIL AND GAS CORP

CITIES SERVICE REFINING
CORPORATION DOCK "D"

HERCULES POWDER COMPANY

PETROLEUM CHEMICALS, INC

FIRESTONE TIRE & RUBBER

CIT-CON OIL CORP

CITIES SERVICE
REFINING CORPORATION

W. R. GRACE & COMPANY
DAVISON CHEMICAL DIVISION

LONE STAR CEMENT CO

CALCASIEU SHIPBUILDING CORPORATION

W. T. BURTON COMPANY (SHELL)

CUSTOM ROCK GRINDING PLANT
OF PORT OF LAKE CHARLES

KELLY, WEBER & COMPANY, INC (FERTILIZER)

IDEAL CEMENT COMPANY

FALCON
CHEMICAL CORP.

Lake
Charles

LAKE
CHARLES

PORT OF
LAKE CHARLES

Prien
Lake

PETROLEUM CHEMICALS, INC. DOCK

LAKE CHARLES
MUNICIPAL AIRPORT

UNION OIL & GAS COMPANY OF LOUISIANA

MAGNOLIA OIL CO

SHELL OIL CO

CONSTOCK LIQUID METHANE CORP.

Moss
Lake

CALCASIEU PARISH CHANNEL

TO THE PORTS OF ORANGE,
BEAUMONT AND PORT ARTHUR

CALCASIEU RIVER AND
PASS SHIP CHANNEL

CALCASIEU
LAKE

LAKE CHARLES TO
GULF 34 MILES

TO NEW ORLEANS AND MOBILE

INTRACOASTAL WATERWAYS

GULF   OF   MEXICO

Calcasieu Ship Channel and Port of Lake Charles [1990s] is a major shipping center poised to export natural gas. Calcasieu Parish, Louisiana, Oil and Gas Review: A Resume of the Oil and Gas Development in Calcasieu Parish, South Louisiana and the Industrial Picture as Depicted by the Lake Charles Association of Commerce Along the Port of Lake Charles (n.d.: n.p.), pamphlet in the Hill Library, Louisiana State University.

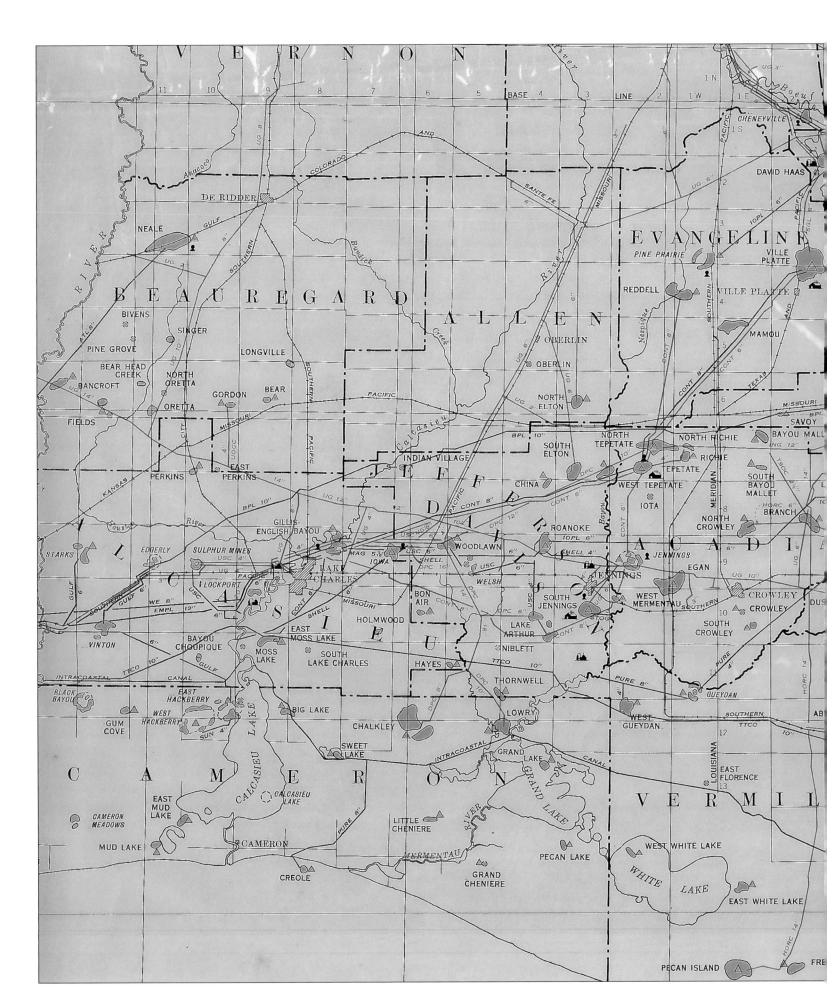

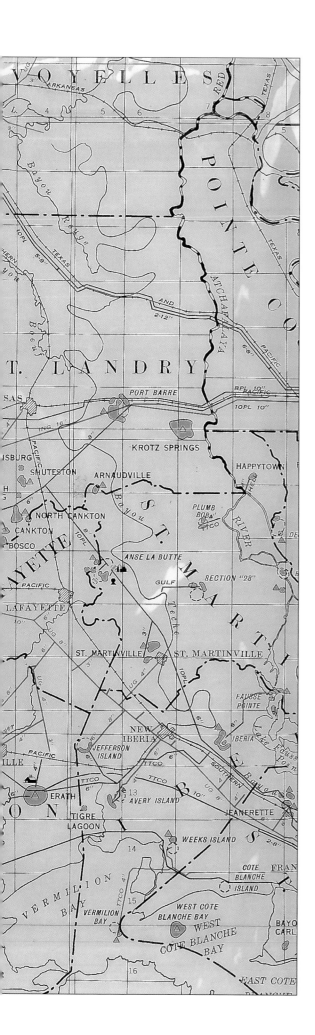

CHAPTER 2

JENNINGS AND THE SOUTHWEST

Louisiana's earliest oilfields dot its thirteen southwestern parishes like beads along the string that is the Southern Pacific Railroad. From Lafayette to Houston high flat lands unroll in welcome relief from the marsh around New Orleans. In the 1880s the railroad persuaded thousands of Midwestern farmers to come to its lands. They discovered it was ideally suited to rice farming because of its unusual impermeability. Jennings became one of the railroad depots for shipping the rice to market.

Though the land looked flat, bulges and marshes often surprised the visitor. Oil seepages had been common. In 1839 a Dr. William M. Carpenter reported in the *American Journal of Science* that the low lands bordering on the Calcasieu River had numerous springs of petroleum. In 1899 the Louisiana Geological Survey reported that just after the Civil War the Louisiana Petroleum and Coal Co. had drilled an oil well in Calcasieu Parish. The well was at the head of Bayou Choupique fifteen miles west of Lake Charles. This same report also mentioned oil springs at Belle Isle in St. Mary Parish, the site of the 1941 Belle Isle Oilfield find. In 1893 Jennings businessman Tom Mahaffey learned of a gas spring near Jennings on the property of a German homesteader. Even before Spindletop Captain A. F. Lucas, its discoverer, was drilling for gas near Breaux Bridge because of gas flares that would spring up from pipes just pushed into the ground.[1]

Oil and Gas Map of Louisiana. Detail of Southwest Louisiana.

Published by the Department of Conservation, Jos. L. McHugh, commissioner.

Compiled by Louisiana Geological Survey, Leo W. Hough, state geologist.

Compilation and cartography by G. O. Coignet, October 1947.

Hereafter Oil and Gas Map, 1947.

GREEN = oil and oil pipeline. RED = gas and gas pipeline.

But it was wildcatter Scott Heywood who led the way in the development of the Jennings Field, the first in Louisiana. He chronicled this development in his autobiography in successive issues of *Oil* magazine, commencing in February, 1941. Scott Heywood was a visionary, "…nothing pleased me better than the drilling of a wildcat well…together with the anticipation of discovering a new field."[2] Heywood introduced Louisiana to the personality of the wildcatter, the risk taker and path breaker. His story was repeated across Louisiana in the coming decades.

Heywood had set out from his hometown of Cleveland in 1893 for the new California oilfields. He was a musician like his brothers, unlike them he was an adventurer. Some early oil wells were being drilled and Heywood,

W. SCOTT HEYWOOD.

Right: W. Scott Heywood. Kerr's Reports, San Francisco, California, August 1902.

Below: Stock certificate for one share in Covington Sulphur, Oil & Mineral Co. Ltd. September 19, 1906. The mountainous terrain portrayed in the engraving betrays little knowledge of the Covington landscape.
PHOTOGRAPH COURTESY OF RANDY HENO AND RUSTY BURNS.

Above: Jennings Oilfield. On the reverse: "Louis Clement, 725 East Plaquemine Street, Jennings, Louisiana" The wooden drilling rig was the most characteristic feature of the early oilfields. Rig builders operated in gangs who usually stayed together. They were among the most sought after workers in the oilfield, so much so that occasionally the rig builders succeeded in unionizing.

Left: In the southwest they used yellow pine such as that supplied by J. A. Bel Lumber Company, Ltd., of Lake Charles. An early invoice from 1902 paid by the Southern Oil Company of Jennings was for 231 pieces and totaled $141. But the extraordinary dimensions are hard to comprehend in the twenty-first century. The first piece was 14 x 14" and 28' long. Most of the pieces were 1"x12" with lengths of 14', 16', and 18'. Surprisingly, the invoice showed a considerable variety of individual sizes such as a 24' long 6"x8" and one 12"x12" 20' long.

who had some funds, invested. He did well. Hearing of the gold strike in the Klondike, he left for Alaska, where again he had only moderate success. Returning to California he brought in several successful wells. But Heywood was ambitious. His three brothers were rather more artistic than anything else. "Alba was a good gambler and was pretty game in staying with me on these wildcats, while my brother Dewey was inclined to be timid…. My brother O. W. was ultra-conservative, and played the game against his desire."

Tribute to the Oil Pioneers:
1. Doug Phelps; 2. Charlie Noble, contractor;
3. Elmer Dobbins, co-contractor;
4. Sank Hendricks; 5. Scott Heywood.
Others asserted that Elmer Dobbins invented the oil well screen. Born in 1876 in Alabama, he attended mechanical school in Poughkeepsie, New York, before turning to artesian well drilling. He early mastered the rotary drilling system and became the king of the drillers after his success at Spindletop. Later he owned businesses in Minnesota and Oregon. This sculpture can be found at the Jennings Oil & Gas Park.

In January 1901 when Heywood heard of the Spindletop discovery he instantly left California for Beaumont where he took a lease on fifteen acres 750 feet from the Lucas Spindletop Well. His dealing in this situation exemplified thousands of subsequent wildcat negotiations. He found the fifteen acres, but had to pay a $2,500 cash bonus and a $2,500 bonus in oil if discovered. Then the fifty percent royalty to the owner kicked in. But Heywood did not have the first $2,500. So he went to the bar of his Beaumont hotel to negotiate. He uncovered a prosperous investor named Captain W. C. Tyrell, who was looking for an oil deal. A series of quick negotiations closed the deal. That night Tyrell

was to put up $1,000 in cash, returnable if a deal was not closed for drilling the next day. The following morning after inspecting the lease hold, Tyrell agreed to pay an additional $9,000, with the Heywoods agreeing to make up any shortfall in the well's cost. Characteristic of this early age in the oil industry, Heywood then had to give driller Elmore Dobbins funds to purchase a rotary drill from a firm in Corsicana, Texas. He paid a bill for derrick lumber and engaged a rig builder.[3]

The center of the Spindletop oil boom soon became the Heywood No. 1 and No. 2 wells on Spindletop, both of which were gushers at initial flows of 15,000 barrels per day. Speculators crowded Heywood's tract. Ex-governor Jim Hogg of Texas and Judge James Swayne purchased fifteen acres to the east of Heywood's and sold it off in parcels as small as twenty square feet. The speculative rush was all about getting rights to some attractive parcel, irrespective of the size, and organizing a stock company.[4] The shares of stock then were pedaled to New Yorkers long familiar with the Pennsylvania and West Virginia oilfields. In his autobiography Heywood took the trouble to note the absence of conservation laws— "…any time anyone wanted to see a well flow, all they had to do was to open the valve and let the oil go into the air while a picture was taken. In other words, the law of the jungle prevailed." Heywood's gift was to be a complete optimist.

Yet, at Spindletop Heywood was always right. Not content with promising just oil, he introduced selling stock on a "guaranteed gusher basis." He tested it first with a diamond salesman who had purchased 1/32 of an acre, a tiny piece of land that had no pipelines, loading rack or room for a settling tank, much less a boiler. So the salesman and Heywood agreed on a split of the costs and profits. Away went the salesman to New York where he disposed of $75,000 worth of stock. With oil selling around 3 or 4 cents a barrel, this was a lot of oil, namely 1,850,000 barrels from just 1/32 of an acre. This preposterous number amply illustrates the speculative nature of the times. Of course,

Heywood took his costs and probably profits right out of the $75,000 stock sales. He recounts that the little well did come in a gusher, but it hardly paid for the organization costs. Heywood concluded his account with "I don't know of anyone who ever lost money guaranteeing gushers in the Spindletop Field."

Heywood was a restless sort and looking east he could see the prairies of western Louisiana rife with bubbling oil and gas. He wanted to take a position where he controlled a giant field. A visit to the nearest site, Hackberry Island, left him with nothing but thoughts about the backwardness of Louisiana land owners. Yet, within days two Louisiana businessmen, I. D. L. Williams and S. A. Spencer, came to Heywood's office with an offer to drill near Jennings, Louisiana. Heywood was "elated." So on April 29, 1901, just four months after Spindletop, Heywood signed a contract to organize the Jennings Oil Company. S. A. Spencer & Co. donated forty acres, to be selected by Heywood. The drillers were to be the Heywood Brothers & Dobbins and the intended depth was to be 1,000 feet on two separate wells. The brothers sent the drilling equipment over from Spindletop consisting of "a small draw-works, a small gripping rotary, two swivels, two Smithvale pumps, ordinary fish-tail bits and one 40 horsepower boiler." One dry hole later, Heywood again went into wildcatter mode, and proposed a new agreement with Spencer. Confident about the well location, Heywood persuaded the partners to let the second well be simply an extension or deepening of the current 1,000 foot dry well. Heywood brought along his brothers and Jennings Oil Co. At 1,700 feet the well hit an oil sand. He recalled, "Casing was set with gate valve for protection, and after running the bailer the second time [ie, removing debris from the hole] the well came in, flowing a solid four inch stream of pipe line oil over 100 feet high." A gusher![5]

But soon a major difficulty appeared. The soft sands began to cave in and plug the well, closing off the flow. Heywood tried various bailing methods, but none worked. He then started Clement No. 2 hoping the problem would not reappear, but it did. He recounts that one night he had the inspiration to place a screen around the casing permitting the oil to flow while supporting the walls of the hole. Meanwhile another group of Jennings men had organized the Southern Oil Company and they had started a well nearby that was sure to fail just as Clement No. 1 had failed.[6] It was also further in the ground than Clement No. 2. Heywood consulted his brothers and offered the competing group the screen idea, thinking that if it worked everybody in the field would be better off. The Southern Well came in at 7,000 barrels a day, and when the screen was placed on Heywood's shortly after it flowed at the same rate. "Within twenty-four hours Heywood Brothers' pipe line had run 7,000 barrels of oil to the loading station on Bayou Nezpique and to our storage tank on the Southern Pacific Railroad near Jennings." In 1902, just a year later, five producing wells yielded 548,617 barrels.

Just a few months later an inventor showed up in Heywood's office with a screen device far better than the one Heywood had "dreamed" up a few months earlier. As Heywood described it, the inventor F. I. Getty, "invented a tool which fastened on to a lathe, and as the round wire was wrapped on the perforated pipe, this tool squeezed the wire into a "V" shapes, with different size lugs left on the wire to keep the wires any distance apart desired...." Heywood stated that he used the Getty screen ever since this first demonstration.

Storage of oil flowing in the Jennings Field remained a major problem. At Beaumont Heywood had proposed earthen surface storage ponds. But his business partner and financier just wanted sell out the oil at the market. When Heywood looked back he lamented that he could have made many millions in Beaumont but ended up only with a million dollars. The lesson he learned in Beaumont he tried to apply to the Jennings Field. Shortly after the first Jennings discovery he had five rigs running night and day and a forty percent royalty from unleased land pushing so much oil that he began building earthen tanks around the Jennings

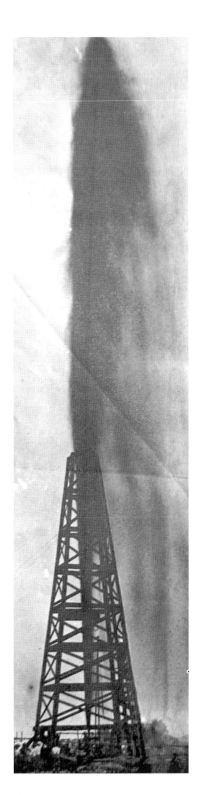

The famous Southern #3. From stationary of the Southern Oil Company.

Right: Mealtime at a boarding house.

Below: Table detail of
Wells Permitted by Parish by Year.
Prepared by Kjel C. Brothen, P. E.,
Office of Conservation, Louisiana
Department of Natural Resources.

Wells Permitted by Decade and Parish

	1910s	1920s	1930s	1940s	1950s	1960s	1970s	1980s	1990s	2000s	2010s	Totals
ACADIA	39	196	402	515	1,035	897	762	1,119	299	184	29	5,477
ALLEN		5	7	18	303	183	134	227	95	87	24	1,083
BEAUREGARD	1	6	56	320	531	313	318	454	138	168	66	2,371
CALCASIEU	72	583	558	489	1,233	854	719	839	377	445	81	6,250
CAMERON	2	210	495	438	1,119	1,520	1,380	1,288	450	393	87	7,382
EVANGELINE		24	109	379	160	181	195	169	55	126	45	1,443
IBERIA	1	46	575	296	725	630	626	520	281	209	16	3,925
JEFFERSON DAVIS	7	81	168	268	441	589	517	519	225	227	26	3,068
LAFAYETTE		1	5	22	113	184	168	211	131	92	15	942
SAINT LANDRY		16	136	249	587	599	505	388	88	99	18	2,685
SAINT MARTIN	9	89	88	467	819	833	693	645	164	123	9	3,939
TERREBONNE	8	51	298	470	2,190	2,712	1,884	1,144	698	553	30	10,038
VERMILION		5	66	321	673	1,009	906	1,018	434	390	46	4,868
Total Southwest	139	1,313	2,963	4,252	9,929	10,504	8,807	8,541	3,435	3,096	492	53,471
% Louisiana	11%	14%	31%	26%	27%	24%	26%	19%	25%	18%	13%	23%
Totals Louisiana	1,314	9,130	9,707	16,264	36,425	44,155	34,007	45,683	13,539	17,566	3,733	231,523

Field. By the time the field started to go dry he had stored seven million barrels of oil in ponds as large as one million barrels. He estimated the cost of the ponds at six cents per barrel and the loss to seepage and evaporation another six cents. But he was able to sell the oil later for fifty to ninety cents per barrel. The 1901 gold-backed dollar was worth fifty or more times the value of the modern dollar. Heywood's ninety-cent oil adjusted for inflation comes out to the average cost of a barrel of oil in the twentieth century.

Replica of the derrick at Clement #1, now standing next to the Jennings Oil & Gas Museum.

Comparison of Oil Production from Four Fields.
Thousands of Barrels of Forty-two Gallons.

Year	Jennings	Welsh	Anse La Butte	Spindletop
1901				3,593
1902	548			17,420
1903	892	25		8,600
1904	6,683	36		3,433
1905	8,891	10	9	1,652
1906	9,025	24	23	1,077
1907	4,895	47	76	1,699
1908	4,856	43	219	1,741
Totals	35,794	186	329	24,788

Harris, Oil and Gas in Louisiana 1910, p. 26.

Above: Comparison of Oil Production from four wells. Harris, Oil and Gas in Louisiana 1910, p. 26.

Right: Oilfield fire at No. 3. This shows the water/steam cannon commonly used to extinguish oil well fires.
PHOTOGRAPH COURTESY OF THE EDITH GARLAND DUPRÉ LIBRARY, SPECIAL COLLECTIONS, UNIVERSITY OF LOUISIANA AT LAFAYETTE.

Opposite, top: This 1907 photograph from the Jennings Oilfield shows two oilfield workers. It also shows a respectable row of oil storage tanks.
PHOTOGRAPH COURTESY OF THE CARNEGIE LIBRARY, SPECIAL COLLECTIONS, JENNINGS.

Opposite, center: Oilfield fire at No. 2.
PHOTOGRAPH COURTESY OF THE EDITH GARLAND DUPRÉ LIBRARY, SPECIAL COLLECTIONS, UNIVERSITY OF LOUISIANA AT LAFAYETTE.

Opposite, bottom: Oilfield fire at the Evangeline Oilfield (also known as Jennings) 1901.
PHOTOGRAPH BY DUNCAN AND ELKINGTON.
PHOTOGRAPH COURTESY OF THE CARNEGIE LIBRARY, SPECIAL COLLECTIONS, JENNINGS.

Duncan & Elkinton

The Royal Refining Company. Considered the first refinery in Louisiana.

His great lakes of oil were always in danger from vandals who might break a levee or ignite the oil. The town of Jennings had become "a wild boom and conglomeration consisting of saloons, dance halls, honkey-tonks, gambling houses, boarding houses, restaurants and lodging houses and all classes of people, with fights, murders and everything that usually goes on in a boom of that kind."[7] Heywood built guard towers with searchlights and armed guards to oversee the ponds. Purchasers were hard to find. But when found, the oil was shipped out in oil tank cars on the Southern Pacific. Archives hold an invoice that documents oil shipments to The Sterling Sugar and Railway Co., Limited, at Franklin, Louisiana.[8]

In just a few years the new Louisiana fields in the Southwest eclipsed Spindletop. The table on page 22 shows production from Jennings, two other small southwestern Louisiana fields, and Spindletop. While Spindletop production early on surpassed other domes, after eight years Jennings had produced fifty percent more oil. Jumping ahead a century, another comparison is to daily consumption in the United States in the twenty-first century. Jennings' thirty-five million barrels over eight years is not two days consumption of oil in the current economy.

Heywood operated at Jennings from 1901 to 1908 when he leased all of his property to the Gulf Oil Refining Company. Gulf paid a royalty of twenty percent on small wells and up to over forty percent on the larger wells. Heywood Bros. sold the pipeline and other hard assets for $330,000. Ten years later Gulf Oil Company returned some of Heywood's leases, ones it thought unprofitable. But, on a little seven-and-a-half acre tract abandoned by Gulf, Heywood drilled a well that brought in 264 barrels a day from only 1,800 feet. Then he turned to two wells that had been capped for years. "I decided to sidetrack some tubing left in the well and my second well on this little lease was made by sidetracking and it resulted in getting a two hundred forty bbl. well." Then he drilled a third well that yielded eighty barrels a day.[9] Heywood's punishment for tweaking Gulf's nose was a cut in the price Gulf would pay for the oil from $1.10 a barrel to 80 cents a barrel. It was the only customer because it owned the only pipeline to the site. Heywood responded to Gulf by building a 10,000 bbl. steel storage tank and trucking the oil to nearby fertilizer companies that paid a good price for oil.

In 1928 Heywood got enthusiastic for Huey Long. "I was impressed with his program of good roads, free school books, and free ferries and bridges.... I sent him some pamphlets which I had written and had published." Long and Heywood met and Long said he intended to raise the $500,000 for school books from a tax on the oil men. Heywood said he would be in favor of a tax for such a worthy cause. The tax on oil had been 3 percent on oil sold by the producer. Long proposed to change it to 7 cents a barrel, regardless of gravity. Heywood then had to explain that high gravity oil was more valuable than low gravity and a flat tax would be discriminatory. Some oil brought $1.50 a barrel while lighter brought only $1.10 a bbl. Long was impressed enough with the argument to charge Heywood to come up with a fair percentage tax plan. Heywood then discovered that the oil men led by the majors opposed any tax. In fact, however, the industry would go along with a flat tax on the theory they could get the courts to knock it out. But Long held to a modified 7 cents flat tax and it passed the legislature and the courts. "Of course, the oil men blamed me for helping pass the law, but I told them if they would run their own business and not listen to attorneys of the major oil companies...they would be much better off."[10]

Heywood's views epitomized the eternal divide between the small producer wildcatter and the majors. In a report to Oklahoma Governor William H. Murray dated February 14, 1931, he laid out his concerns for the small producer. The issues have hardly changed. The majors have used conservation and oil imports as excuses to suppress the prices paid for domestic oil. Conservation became proration, the practice of limiting the amount of oil that could be extracted from a field. Since by the law of supply and demand this might increase prices, importation of cheap foreign oil held down prices. On the refiners side, however, there was no link between the cost of oil and the cost of retail gasoline. Heywood charged the major refiners with unfairly profiting from the oil producers of America. He signed this report as the Personal Representative of the Honorable Huey P. Long.[11] His proposal was to put a tariff on imported crude oil and declare crude oil "of public interests." Next the oil producing states should form a compact to make their regulatory laws identical in respect to drilling and in respect to the price to be paid the producers of oil.

With politics in his blood, Heywood decided to run for the State Senate from southwestern Louisiana, pledging to serve only one four-year term. He won and proposed a Tax Reform Commission to consist of members from both houses of the legislature to define a homestead exemption from property taxes. After a two-year struggle with the administration it passed into law. At the end of his autobiography Heywood wrote of his admiration for Long.

In spite of Heywood the southwestern fields did not become a significant factor in oil well drilling until the 1930s. In the first three decades of the twentieth century well permitting in the southwest was far behind the northern parishes such as Caddo. The southwest reached its largest point of influence from the 1930s when it had thirty percent of Louisiana's permitted wells to the 1970s when it still had twenty-six percent.

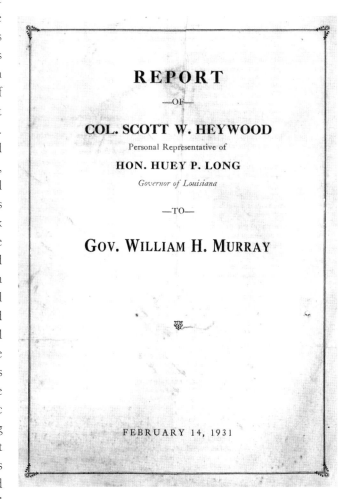

Report to Oklahoma Governor

William H. Murray by Scott Heywood.

PHOTOGRAPH COURTESY OF THE EDITH GARLAND DUPRÉ LIBRARY, SPECIAL COLLECTIONS, UNIVERSITY OF LOUISIANA AT LAFAYETTE.

From the beginning of Louisiana's oil and gas industry outsiders played a disproportionate role. Getty, Dobbins, and Spencer came to Louisiana from elsewhere. Getty was from Chicago, Dobbins from Alabama, and Spencer from Iowa. Two men from Pennsylvania also made an impact on

Group portrait of a roustabout gang with
Robert Shivers's dad, front center with his
legs crossed, 1919.

PHOTOGRAPH COURTESY OF THE
MINERALS MANAGEMENT SERVICE, VOLUME VI
AND ROBERT SHIVERS.

Jennings. T. C. (Uncle Tom) Mahaffey was a free wheeler, the perfect personality for the wildcatter. The other, George Zigler was the opposite, "a quiet, honest, goodly man...." Uncle Tom gambled and speculated. Though as early as 1893 he knew of oil near Jennings, instead he built the Mahaffey Hotel soon after the Jennings oil came in. This four-story hostelry was the fanciest between Houston and New Orleans. But it burned, its replacement burned, and Mafaffey gradually lost his oil money.

Ironically it was the quiet good man who made the fortune. George Zigler had operated a haberdashery in North Dakota until his health gave out. He moved to a South that came to mean the Louisiana rice belt. At first he tended horses in the new oilfields but soon he came to see possibilities in cheap abandoned wells. These sat unused for years

until suddenly new technology made them very valuable. Zigler promoted shipping oil out of the prairies by barge. In 1913 Zigler founded a shipyard and started building wooden barges. After his death in 1936 his son Fred B. Zigler became president of the Zigler Oil Company. Later the Zigler fortune funded McNeese State University, along with the fortune of another southwest oil family— the Streams. Fred Zigler's widow donated her home to serve as a serious art museum for the town of Jennings.

The Zigler Shipyard continued into the offshore era. It employed about 300 persons to build and repair barges, tugs, towboats, menhaden vessels, offshore supply vessels and seismographic vessels. Shipbuilding grew rapidly in the 1960s and 1970s. At the beginning of the 1970s, the yard was building simple 150-foot supply vessels for

Undoubtedly roughnecks had it rough,
look at the roustabouts building this bog log
structure, a horizontal reinforcement of
vertical poles in the marsh. C. J. Christ in
the sunglasses, Calcasieu Springs.

PHOTOGRAPH COURTESY OF THE
MINERALS MANAGEMENT SERVICE, VOLUME VI
AND CHARLES "C. J." CHRIST.

the Gulf of Mexico at the rate of three to four boats per year. In 1976 the yard designed and built 210-foot offshore tug/supply vessels for North Sea operations at the rate of six to eight ships per year.[12] Today Zigler Shipyard, a Division of Lee-Vac, Ltd., is situated on an 83-acre tract off the Mermentau River in Jennings, Louisiana.

Heywood's success drilling at Jennings soon inspired drilling everywhere across the southwest. Anse la Butte drew a lot of attention, with only modest results. The Moresi Brothers of Jeanerette drilled their Pioneer well during the fall of 1901. The following summer they drilled their well No. 1 close to the "swamp," a local bog. The Moresi Anse La Butte venture is an early example of how successful businesses diversified into the oilfield. In 1885 Swiss immigrant Antoine Moresi founded Moresi's Foundry and Machine Company in Jeanerette, Louisiana. Moresi's Foundry was intended to maintain and develop the machinery needed to harvest the bounty from the Louisiana flood plain, particularly sugar mills. After his death in 1904, the company was known as A. Moresi Company, Limited and managed by his sons Louis Moresi, president; Damas Moresi, general manager; and Albert Moresi, assistant manager.[13]

If there could be a successor to Scott Heywood it would be Jimmie Owen. He, too, wrote an autobiography.[14] Owen grew up in Texas, served in World War I, and went directly into the Texas oilfields. After World War II he wildcatted in Canada and then in Louisiana. He felt that the boom years for Louisiana oil exploration were the two decades after World War II. "The years from the forties through the sixties were golden years for oil exploration...."

He recounted that his "first big lick" was to take over some leases from Atlantic Refining company near Maxie and Crowley in Acadia Parish. In typical wildcatter fashion Owen turned around and sold two-thirds interest to H. L. Hunt, provided they paid all the drilling costs. When the bit reached 10,576 feet they hit the Maxie Sand, about 100 feet of rich gas condensate sand.[15] Owen recounted that along with three of Hunt's landmen he quickly leased about 5,000 more acres. Hunt finally purchased Owen's one third, paying Owen $525,000 cash and two million dollars out of 1/16 of future production. An earlier success had allowed Owen and a partner to start their own drilling firm. With the Maxie money Owen bought out his partner and brought in his son. The new firm took space in the new Lafayette Petroleum Center, the hub of the oil industry in central coastal Louisiana. By 1962 Owen was a small independent operator. He had eleven rigs and 265 employees.[16] Again characteristically of the wildcatter, Owen sold everything to General American Oil Co. for $15 million. This was the first of several sellouts in order to raise the cash needed up front for drilling. The fate of the wildcatter is to spend immense amount of cash long before a well can replenish his coffers. The more a wildcatter drills, the deeper in debt he goes and the more exposed to vagaries in the economy he becomes. For a while Owen was famous for his Owen Drilling Rig #7 on Leo Fontenot #1 near Kaplan in Vermilion Parish. In 1966 Owen drilled this well to a depth of 23,157 feet, at that time the second deepest well in North America. In the 1980s Owen went bankrupt twice before settling down to writing about his experiences.

Another "autobiography" appeared in 1941 when *Oil* magazine published "The Diary of a Roughneck," supposedly written in February 1921. Sam Mims, its author, went to a lot of trouble to capture the slang and difficulties of the oilfield. In this section of the diary the roughneck was "fishing" all night trying to retrieve 400 feet of pipe that had dropped down a hole. Fishing is oilfield lingo for putting a line or pipe down to attach to pipe or tool stuck down a well. After two days, the roughneck recounts that all they had succeeded in accomplishing was to cut the pipe in two places, leaving now three sections of pipe. "Now what we have got to do is to get a steel nipple down in the hole and cut threads on three pipes instead of one." Then this apocryphal roughneck speculated, who cares? "If I thought any of my offsprings was gonna be roughnecks I wouldn't marry Mamie nor nobody else. It's a dog's game. …If you are good air-tight liars, all of you make leasehounds out yourselves. That's all it takes, knowing how to tell hot ones. If you kaint lie good but still aint got no conschience, then make peetrolium ingerneers out yourselves."[17]

South of Jennings at the mouth of the Mermentau River is the town of Lake Arthur. Superior Oil Company, presided over by Howard Keck, provided some 1,900 jobs for many years. Well technician Lawrence Hebert talked to the oral historians for the volume *Jefferson Davis Parish: An Oral History*. "Quite a few families in Jennings and Lake Arthur owned oil companies…." In the wildcatter tradition, Superior took the first flyer offshore in the Creole Field in the late 1930s. "It was a small company and there was kind of a family atmosphere." Mobil bought Superior in 1980, to the disgust of many of its employees.[18]

About ten miles west of Jennings the Welsh Field was profitable for a long time. It runs along the Southern Pacific Railroad northwest of the town of Welsh. Most of its early production came from twenty-one wells drilled into a square of 1,500 feet on a side, about fifty acres. Daily production was measured in the hundreds of barrels.

Much farther to the west near the Texas border is the Vinton Field in Calcasieu Parish. This major field was the only rival to Jennings. As early as the 1860s Dr. W. H. Kirkman had visited the prairies south of Vinton and announced a large oilfield beneath its surface. A landowner Aladin Vincent spent many years trying to prove this statement. But it was Dr. Kirkman's son-in-law John Geddings ("Ged") Gray who purchased 8,000 acres, about fifteen square miles, near the Vinton salt dome who made

A long range photograph from the top of Atlantic Company's No. 5, showing the field, Sinclair Company's big gasser, Orange, Texas.

Proud owners of a well.
PHOTOGRAPH COURTESY OF THE CARNEGIE LIBRARY,
JENNINGS, LOUISIANA.

the discovery. But soon after the first shallow wells were drilled a leasing conflict broke out leaving 5,000 of his acres in a dispute that did not end until 1910. Detroit businessman Frederick Benckenstein organized the Vinton Petroleum Oil Company. Some claim that its No. 1 Gray was the first successful production well in the field. Others dispute it, but it is clear that the Vinton Petroleum Co. drilled 65 wells on a 20-acre tract to such good effect that it claimed the tract was "the most prolific 20-acre oil tract in the United States."[19] About this time John Geddings Gray claimed that "I bought land to run cows on, and found an oil well under every cow." By January 1911 twenty-four rigs were drilling and eight more under construction. Thirty car loads of oil were shipped out every day. Carloads of derrick lumber, machinery and supplies occupied the rail sidings at Vinton. Production in 1911 totaled 2,454,000 barrels of oil, the field's peak until new discoveries after World War II. Thereafter it

ran about 1,000,000 bbl/yr. A characteristic of successful fields was the wide diversity of companies participating in the boom. Harmony Oil Company, Producers Oil Company, Gardiner-Noble Oil Company, Hooks Oil, Lake Arthur Oil Company, Crowley Oil and Mineral Company, and Heywood Oil all had interests.

The evanescent town of Ged was the result. It grew in sixty days to 1,500 people, then reached 3,000. John Geddings Gray donated much of the land in the town of Ged, a stroke that accelerated the town's growth. But the bubble burst, and though the field limped on the town of Ged began to vanish, a process that lasted over two decades. In its brief life it had a school, post office, barbershop, pharmacy, dry goods store, and two machine shops. The giant Texas Transportation Company (pipeline) maintained an office in Ged. The Ged Bath House, for "Ladies & Gentleman," had four stalls with bath tubs. Dr. W. F. Brooks maintained an office next to his Rexall Drug Store. The Vinton Petroleum Company maintained a company store known as the Blue Goose like many of the great plantations. But as soon as the boom moved on, the town of Ged began to disappear. Workers dismantled their houses and moved to the west side of Vinton. Vinton had the good fortune to have become a switching town for the Southern Pacific Railroad and so claimed the right to ship and sell product of the region.

Though Ged withered, the Vinton Field did not. A second boom led by Gulf Oil No. 7 Vincent well in 1917 brought production up, despite damage from a large 1918 hurricane.

A picture of the field in 1930 showed fifty derricks, though production gradually declined to a low of 306 MBO in 1940. Gas did not play a large role at the Vinton Field, leaving one positive result that there were very few blowouts. Natural gas did not come to southwest Louisiana towns until June of 1931 when the United Gas Public Service Company extended a line across the area from the East Texas Field.[20]

Though the town of Ged has vanished, the Gray family has remained large landowners in Calcasieu Parish. Ged Gray left a daughter, Matilda, and two sons, Bill and Henry. They formed the Stream Companies. Their

John Geddings Gray and his daughter Matilda at the Gray Ranch.
PHOTOGRAPH COURTESY OF BRUCE KIRKPATRICK FOR THE STREAM COMPANIES.

Goose Creek Oilfield, renamed Baytown,
Texas, 1940s. The steel rig has arrived.
PHOTOGRAPH COURTESY OF THE
MINERALS MANAGEMENT SERVICE, VOLUME VI
AND ROBERT SHIVERS.

landholdings stretched from Vinton southward to the Gulf of Mexico at Johnson's
Bayou. This Gray Ranch originated as a cattle
ranch and remains one today. The oil wells,
many of which continue to produce, cohabit
nicely with the agriculture. At one time, the
oilfields on the Gray Ranch were the most
productive in the world. Bill Gray's daughter
Matilda Gray Stream eventually came to
manage the family's holdings, followed by
her son Harold H. Stream III, who is still
the CEO of the family's various operations.

South of Vinton the parish of Cameron
defines the southwestern tip of Louisiana.
The town of Hackberry, named many years
ago for the groves of trees that thrive in the
vicinity, is located in Cameron Parish, deep in
the marsh country of Southwest Louisiana.

The first mineral lease in the area was granted in 1886. The Intracoastal Canal now runs
along the north side of the parish. In 1924,
the prolific Miocene oil sands were discovered. The first oil well to become a producer
in Cameron Parish was the Pure Oil Company's
Fount Lee No. 3 of the Sweet Lake Field. The
well was completed on October 12, 1926 and
by 1928 the field's oil output reached 1,000
barrels daily. Hackberry was a unique operation
both above and below the earth's surface.
Above the surface it was water bound.
Transportation was carried out by boats on
an elaborate canal system. Black Lake and
the marshland—little more floating turf—
surrounding it covered the field. Calcasieu
Lake, often called Big Lake, was on the east.
Marshland prevails west to the Sabine River

and south to the Gulf. An inland water operation in every sense, the Hackberry Field is called the "Venice of the oil patch."[21]

In 1956 a famous wildcatter named Michel Halbouty remembered the efforts in the 1930s by Yount-Lee, Stanolind Oil & Gas, then Pan American Petroleum to drill in the area of West Hackberry. Halbouty had known about a log that showed two hundred feet of oil sand, but the explorers had ignored it. He predicted a profitable reservoir there and his prediction came through. In its first twenty years the reservoir turned out 3.1 million barrels of oil and was paying in 1958 $40,000 a month. These kinds of finds made the fortunes of many wildcatters.[22]

In the last decade the Oligocene Trend that includes a Hackberry sand has yielded considerable oil and gas in Cameron Parish. Exxon opened the West Chalkley Field in Cameron Parish in 1988. Exxon #1 Sweet Lake produced 157 BCFE, of which 96 percent was gas, becoming the highest cumulative producer in the Oligocene. Further south independent producer Sam Gary drilled a number of successful wells in the Hackberry sand.[23] The John Geddings Gray Ranch has continued productive to the present day.

But as the plat of 2010 oilfields in South Louisiana shows, the preponderance of drilling and production was on the eastern side of South Louisiana.

Oil and gas fields of South Louisiana, 2010.

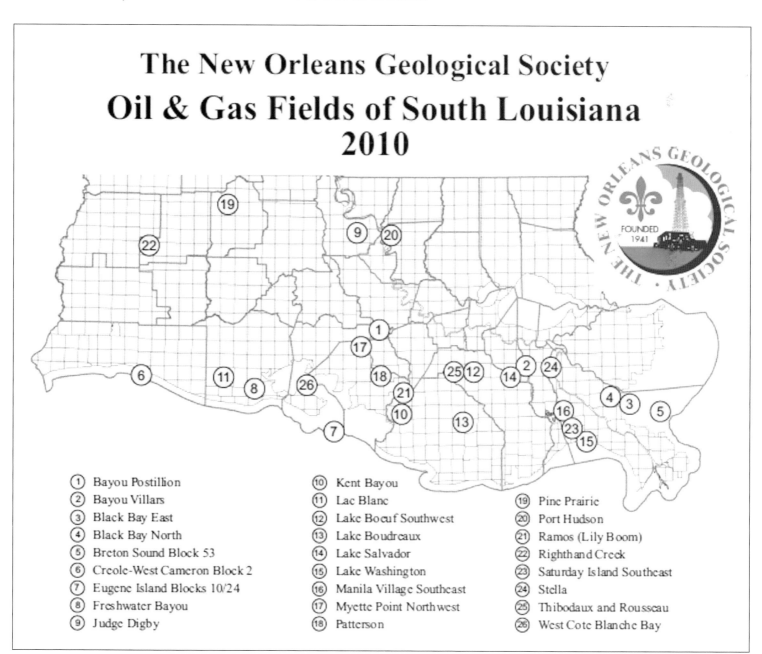

The New Orleans Geological Society
Oil & Gas Fields of South Louisiana
2010

THE NEW ORLEANS GEOLOGICAL SOCIETY · FOUNDED 1941

① Bayou Postillion
② Bayou Villars
③ Black Bay East
④ Black Bay North
⑤ Breton Sound Block 53
⑥ Creole-West Cameron Block 2
⑦ Eugene Island Blocks 10/24
⑧ Freshwater Bayou
⑨ Judge Digby
⑩ Kent Bayou
⑪ Lac Blanc
⑫ Lake Boeuf Southwest
⑬ Lake Boudreaux
⑭ Lake Salvador
⑮ Lake Washington
⑯ Manila Village Southeast
⑰ Myette Point Northwest
⑱ Patterson
⑲ Pine Prairie
⑳ Port Hudson
㉑ Ramos (Lily Boom)
㉒ Righthand Creek
㉓ Saturday Island Southeast
㉔ Stella
㉕ Thibodaux and Rousseau
㉖ West Cote Blanche Bay

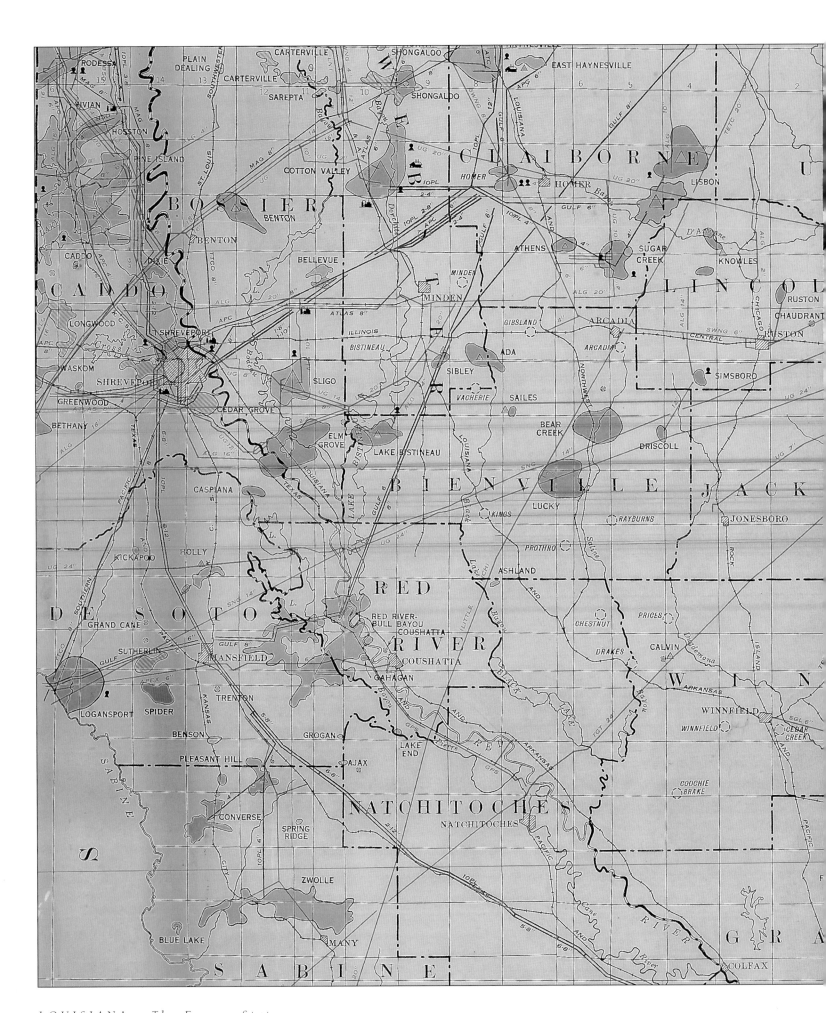

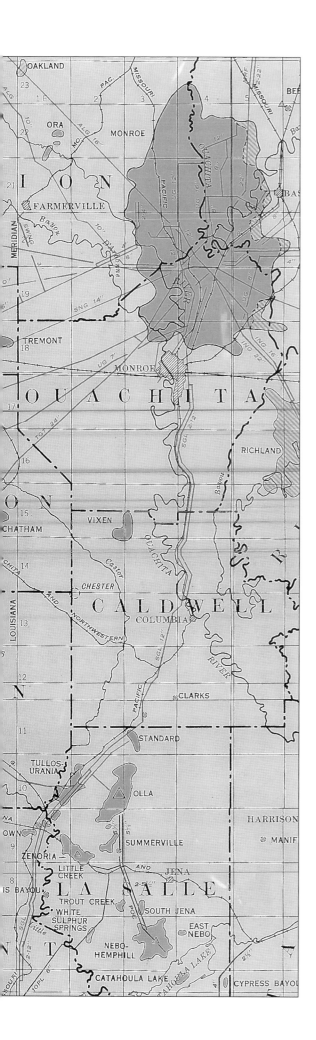

SHREVEPORT

Southwest Louisiana began in oil. Northwest Louisiana began in gas. Much of the early drilling simply followed gas leaks. The watery terrain of the Red River flood plain forced early wells into marshes and pools filled by the over-flowing Red River. Teams of oxen and mules hauled boilers and derrick lumber miles over swampy roads to crazy sites picked out by wildcatters. Of the various parts of Louisiana, Northwest Louisiana was where wildcatters thrived the best.

The nine northwest Louisiana Parishes—Caddo, Bossier, Webster, Claiborne, De Soto, Red River, Bienville, Sabine and Natchitoches—are the only part of Louisiana to dominate the state oil and gas industry at both at the beginning and at the end of the twentieth century. The following table on page 36 illustrates one aspect of Northwest's dominance. In the second decade of the century 88 percent of the permitted wells in the State of Louisiana were in the Northwest. This percentage gradually declined to 21 percent by the 1970s. Then, with the turn of the new century, the proportion of permitted wells in the Northwest has again climbed. In the two years 2010-2011 Northwest had 61 percent of Louisiana's permitted wells.[1]

In 1904 lumberman D. C. Richardson drilled a water well soon contaminated by gas. He mentioned the gas to the Kansas City Southern Railroad chief engineer Ira G. Hedrick who soon drilled three shallow wells in De Soto Parish that produced. Richardson then heard of plentiful gas north of Shreveport near the future Oil City. He leased some land for oil and gas development and is credited with being the first to do so in Caddo Parish. The discovery well for the Caddo/Bossier Fields came in at only five barrels a day on March 28, 1905, from 1,556 feet. Savage Brothers and Morricelli drilled the well, known variously as Offenhauser No. 1, later Caddo Lake No. 1. Carl Jones, an early roughneck whose memories were recorded in an oral history program at LSU Shreveport, visited the well because his brother-in-law [Walter D. George] was the driller. "It was a chalk rock well somewhere in the neighborhood of 1,400 or 1,500 feet." The biggest fire Carl Jones recalled was at the Harold No. 7 by Producers Oil Company, southwest of Vivian. One man died and the driller, Ron Hewitt, was badly burned. The well burned for weeks. The owners sent to El Dorado, Arkansas, for about forty minors to dig a tunnel into the bore hole from the side in order to extinguish it.

Oil and Gas Map of Louisiana, 1947. Detail of Northwest Louisiana.

Wells Permitted by Parish by Decade, Updated 11/1/2011

	1910s	1920s	1930s	1940s	1950s	1960s	1970s	1980s	1990s	2000s	2010-2011	Totals
BIENVILLE	12	56	62	115	271	253	356	415	537	962	163	3,202
BOSSIER	101	825	377	536	864	714	1,325	1,249	595	1,983	128	8,697
CADDO	495	1,923	1,616	2,814	6,791	4,290	2,973	8,709	1,511	2,147	374	33,643
CLAIBORNE	278	1513	299	640	679	419	566	1206	556	331	38	6,525
DE SOTO	46	278	222	310	1,091	809	1,060	1,723	571	2,026	929	9,065
NATCHITOCHES	2	55	33	82	192	211	109	214	43	32	33	1,006
RED RIVER	200	353	85	110	403	279	298	387	94	341	290	2,840
SABINE	10	124	1,190	189	327	3,034	394	1,374	131	263	259	7,295
WEBSTER	8	533	232	155	747	349	219	1,258	395	492	45	4,433
Total Northwest parishes	1,152	5,660	4,116	4,951	11,365	10,358	7,300	16,535	4,433	8,577	2,259	76,706
	88%	62%	42%	30%	31%	23%	21%	36%	33%	49%	61%	33%
All Parishes	1,314	9,130	9,707	16,264	36,425	44,155	34,007	45,683	13,539	17,566	3,733	231,527

RICHARDSON OIL CO.
AYNE NO 2

Opposite, top: Table detail of
Wells Permitted by Parish by Decade.
Prepared by Kjel C. Brothen, P. E.,
Office of Conservation, Louisiana
Department of Natural Resources.

Opposite, bottom: D. C. Richardson played
a major role in the Alamo No. 2 owned by
the Alamo Oil Co. He is in the center of this
picture with A. Deutsch and A. J. Moore.
The well had produced 5,000 barrels a day
for eighteen days. D. C. Richardson died in
1926. The Advocate wrote that he was the
"father of Louisiana Oil Fields." Only two
months before his death at the age of 68 he
had uncovered a new pool in Caddo Parish.
"He had been "a consistant wildcatter and
his last strike was twelve miles from
Shreveport...." April 28, 1926.

PHOTOGRAPH BY GRUETER & GREENE, FEBRUARY 14, 1913,
COURTESY OF THE OIL CITY MUSEUM.

Left: An early D. C. Richardson Oil Co. well
known as Hayne No. 2 after a gas blow-out.

PHOTOGRAPH COURTESY OF THE OIL CITY MUSEUM.

In the next few years numerous unsuccessful oil wells generated vast amounts of gas and the wells were usually capped for lack of distribution. In 1906 the Caddo area produced only 4,560 barrels of oil. In 1907 the J. M. Guffey Petroleum Company and others completed twenty-three wells of which only eight produced oil, but it was substantially more than the preceding year. Most of the wells in 1907-8 were gassers. The U.S. Geological Survey reported in 1908 that 70,000,000 cubic feet of gas was let run daily. David T. Day, geologist for the United States Geological Survey denounced this "most flagrant abuse of natural wealth yet recorded in this industry."[2]

The horrific gas well blowouts in the early years led to a conservation movement aided by state and federal legislation. One other assist came from the construction of pipelines that in 1910 began to take Caddo gas to Shreveport, Texarkana, and Marshall, Texas. Gas at the rate of 15,000,000 cubic feet per day began flowing away from Caddo gas fields. The wild gas waste and the enthusiasm of the speculators led to a flurry of state and federal regulation. One line of attack favored by Washington was to withdraw federal lands from any drilling. However, drilling had already commenced on some of the land, an event that led to a massive federal law suit.[3]

The high pressure of gas in the Caddo Field is legendary. Unlike Jennings, blowouts were common because gas was common. One well burned for five years. An early well by Producers Oil Company drew a visit from the Governor and Major Frank M. Kerr, chief of the Louisiana state engineers. "On the day of this visit, (the) well presented a scene of magnificent energy and surprising spectacular effect. A basin or bowl of water some 250 feet in diameter had resulted from the action of the escaping gas, and the roll of waves from the mouth of the orifice toward the rim of the basin, like waves on a sea beach in stormy weather, from the center of which leaped a flame some thirty feet in diameter and equally high. This, with the monster upheaval of water and leaping of spray, presented a spectacle which might readily have been likened to the display of a prismatic

fountain of unusual magnitude and superb effects."[4] Matson reported that these enormous flares reduced the gas pressure in the field, generally an undesirable feature. The well was kept burning to evaporate the saltwater that also flowed from the well into the pond. Finally, in 1913, the State Conservation Commission with oil company assistance dug a nearby relief well then pumped mud into the bottom of the burning well. The lesson from this well was the need to have the casing cemented at the bottom of the hole so as to prevent gas from rising in the hole and bursting through mud walls.[5]

Natural gas was and is an important part of the north Louisiana economy. But before natural gas was artificial gas, a product sold everywhere and its manufacture was one of the largest industries in the nation. It was coal gas, made by heating coal and capturing the resulting gas, primarily hydrogen with a lessor amount of methane and much less other gasses. The town of Shreveport had artificial gas suppliers, and gas mains in Shreveport for the distribution of artificial gas dated back to 1859. So the advent of natural gas directly from the ground had wide implications. Its cost must be less and its availability greater, especially if the gas is almost free for the taking. Gas bubbles were common throughout western Louisiana, both north and south, but it was in Caddo Parish that the first great use was made of the bubbles.

On October 30, 1905, the Shreveport Gas, Electric Light & Power Co. amended its charter to allow it to distribute natural, rather than artificial, gas. A month earlier the Shreveport City Council had granted a franchise to distribute natural gas to the Citizens Oil & Pipeline Co. The Dawes Brothers of Chicago had built the first manufactured gas distribution system in Shreveport prior to 1910. On May 24, 1906, city officials led by Mayor Andrew Querbes gathered with the officers of the Shreveport Gas, Electric Light and Power Company for a ceremony to mark the turning of natural gas into the company's main pipe lines.[6] The paper noted that the ordinary citizen did not pay much attention to the epoch-making event. The natural gas seemed to come with greater pressure then

Opposite: Tunnel contractor H. H. Hair working on Harrel #9, May 27, 1911.

the old artificial gas. It burned with a bluish light rather than the former yellow light. When used for heating natural gas vastly surpassed the artificial. But it marked a progressive step for Shreveport which was only the third city in the South to use natural gas, following Fort Smith, Arkansas, and Corsicana, Texas.

These two companies cooperated and slowly spread their network of pipelines, first to Bossier City on the other side of the river. Shreveport's population in 1910 was 23,000. In the 1920s the city's pipeline system passed into the hands of the Arkansas Louisiana Gas Co.[7] Gas normally came out of the well at extreme high pressure, enabling the pipe line company to hook up to the well and direct the gas to a customer. But all gas wells experience a gradual reduction of pressure to where the transmission company had to construct compression stations that accelerated the pressure and pushed the gas along.

While Caddo gas caused problems, Caddo oil created opportunities. It was the wildcatter who made the most of those opportunities. "The Greatest Wildcatter" put the Caddo Field on the map, just as difficulties were cooling the interest of the majors in the area. He was Michael Benedum. He grew up in West Virginia, and settled in the town of West Union where he met John Worthington who was the general superintendent of the South Penn Oil Company. At the time (the early 1890s) the oil business in West Virginia was booming. The chief oil-producing area of the state was around Parkersburg where it was known as the Marietta Field. Worthington sent Benedum out to sign leases, especially the difficult leases. Mike proved an excellent landman. By 1892 Benedum had made a firm place for himself in the West Virginia oil regions.

In 1895 Benedum met Joseph Clifton Trees, six-foot three-inches tall, all muscle and trained in engineering. With South Penn's permission Benedum did some lease speculation with Trees in areas that did not interest South Penn. One day Trees came to Benedum with a lease and said they should drill this one. Up to then the pair had just been land speculators. Joe handled the drilling and Mike the financing. Just before noon one day the driller called that he thought a well was coming in. Benedum rushed over. It was a dramatic moment and he remembered every detail. "I can see Joe yet…standing on the floor of the derrick grinning like a schoolboy, scooping the oil up in his hands and letting it trickle through his fingers. I wasn't conscious of doing anything except watching Joe, but he always said that I was doing the same thing I don't doubt that I was. No man who has never had the experience can understand the feeling of exhilaration that comes when you bring in an oil well, especially your first one. There are no words to describe it. This may sound strange, but the thought of the material profit to be derived never crosses your mind.

You are staggered and filled with awe at the realization that you have triumphed over stubborn and unyielding Nature, forcing her to give up some of her treasure."[8] This first well was good for seventy-five barrels a day.

Benedum quit the South Penn Oil company in the autumn of 1896 and became an independent producer. After several years of success in oil his brother convinced him to invest in banking and other ordinary businesses. By 1904 Benedum was virtually bankrupt. But the partnership of Benedum and Trees went forward. Joe was the engineer for the partnership and had the technical training along with high intelligence and good intuition. Joe was the boss of the drilling site. Benedum had terrific foresight and was quick to see possibilities. He was also the dealmaker and could successfully argue his point with the big oil companies. The partnership went into Illinois where they made a million dollars, but Trees could see that Benedum was

not content with a steady success. As a wild-catter he wanted new fields. Trees said that Benedum never cared much for drilling in proven territory.

They went next to Oklahoma, but success did not follow them. They heard about Caddo Parish and near the end of 1907 went over to Shreveport. When Benedum and Trees arrived in Caddo the field was wrapped in controversy. The enormous gas pressure caused repeated blowouts. Benedum and Trees got the distinct impression that the majors, who had been interested in the field, were abandoning it. A technique had to be found that stopped the gas and permitted the oil drilling. The problem was essentially the same facing BP in the Gulf of Mexico in 2010. Trees came up with the idea of blocking the well a few feet above the gas layer, using cement to set a floor. The oil well would then drill through the cement thus keeping control of the well and preventing the gas from caving the well walls. It worked extremely well and has been used in various forms since.[9]

They decided to plunge into Caddo, and instead of buying just a few leases they ended up leasing 130,000 acres. The first big lease in Shreveport was signed on December 2, 1907, with W. P. Stiles, a well-to-do farmer who owned 3,254 acres near the future Oil City a few miles north of Shreveport. His property was not very good for farming, being mainly marsh, but as an oilfield it was spectacular. Their first big well, Stiles No. 1 brought in enormous difficulties and was almost abandoned. Benedum and Trees were in Pittsburgh on the crucial weekend. The site superintendent telegrammed that the well looked bad. Trees responded, "keep drilling until we come down on Monday." Finally it roared in a gusher, a well that produced more than 185 million barrels of oil and as late as 1952 was still producing two million barrels a year.

Benedum and Trees set up headquarters in a Shreveport hotel. They rode up to the fields on the daily train that went north. From the depot they often took the corduroy roads that

Bringing a boiler across on a ferry.
The boiler provided steam for the steam
engines that operated the drill.

LOUISIANA - *The Energy State*

had to be laid out to the well head. However, the time came when Benedum and Trees had to meet the tough and lawless part of the oil-field population. Not surprisingly, the confrontation came over race. One well that had come in was blowing hard. The crew refused to go near it. To stop it, tanks were necessary but the operation required labor. Benedum then had a strong wire fence erected around the well and hired a fearless Irishman to maintain order. He then brought in a crew of Black workers from a neighboring plantation to construct the necessary tanks. The plantation owner insisted that his men be protected. For that the wire fence, its one opening, and the tough Irishman succeeded. A group of the former crew rode up on horses and tried to get through the gate, only to be met by bullets from the guard. Several went to the hospital and the difficulties evaporated.

Twin problems soon clouded Benedum's prospects. First, Standard Oil launched a significant lease program to go along with its giant new pipeline originating in Oklahoma. The pipeline was to move oil from the various Oklahoma fields to Standard's new refinery at Baton Rouge. It soon appeared that Standard would like to have Benedum's leases so the pipeline could pick up oil from the Caddo Field. John D. Rockefeller had organized the Standard Oil trust in 1882. It included the South Penn Oil Company and dozens of companies from Cleveland, New York, Philadelphia, Pittsburgh, and Parkersburg. The great web of pipelines and lubricant companies bought products from producing companies in West Virginia and Ohio. Rockefeller presided along with Henry M. Flagler, William Rockefeller and John D. Archbold. The Standard's business already covered the entire world—Mexico, South America, Canada, Europe, and Asia. It was a formidable adversary.

A second difficulty faced Trees and Benedum. The state authorized the Caddo Parish Levee Board to lease its land. This led to the realization that Benedum and Trees had not leased the water bottoms, especially the land below Caddo Lake and its extension Ferry Lake. The Mellon's Gulf Oil, probably by some prearrangement, soon leased the 8,000 acres of Caddo Lake water bottom. It paid a $30,000 bonus and guaranteed royalties of $70,000. Gulf drilled its 1910 well in the Ferry extension of Caddo Lake from a fixed platform. In the succeeding six years Gulf

Above: "Hauling rig timbers," Ferry Lake Field, c. 1910. Ferry Lake was an extension of Caddo Lake, crossed by a ferry. Wooden rigs were used regularly until after World War I.
PHOTOGRAPH COURTESY OF THE OIL CITY MUSEUM.

Below: Reportedly the world's first offshore well. Drilled in Caddo Lake, completed May 1911, known as Ferry Lake #1.
PHOTOGRAPH COURTESY OF THE OIL CITY MUSEUM.

"The Hardie No. 2 and the Men Who Brought Her In." well after the gusher had slowed considerably.

PHOTOGRAPH BY SIMMS LINDERMAN, COURTESY OF THE OIL CITY MUSEUM.

drilled 56 successful wells out of a total of 58. To service these wells Gulf operated a fleet of three tug boats, ten barges, a floating pile driver, and thirty-six skiffs.

The majors gradually threw a network of oil pipelines around Shreveport. Standard Oil's line ran from Oklahoma to Baton Rouge. Gulf Oil likewise built from Oklahoma, but their refinery was at Port Arthur. The Texas Company's "Oklahoma" pipeline also passed by Shreveport headed for Beaumont. Oilfield worker Carl Jones remembered this line as an 8-inch pipeline. It passed through Gilliam and Belcher. The line was dug by hand by Irish laborers about four feet deep. The pipeline itself was assembled with "dresser couplings." Bolts and rubber packing held the plates together.

Yorke Indestructible Steel Derricks and Drilling Rigs
Letter No. 5

Producers of oil and gas:

Gentlemen—like the "Wedding of Canaan," when the patriarchs of old clinked their glasses and declared, "Verily they have kept the good wine for the last," so have we. We cannot furnish you with this identical beverage, but nevertheless, if you follow us for a fleeting moment, we can at least guarantee you a rare treat.

We start by telling you a secret, viz: That every set of bullwheels, band-wheel, steel tug pulley and steel walking-beam that is used in any metallic complete rig in the oil country is manufactured by our people. If you were going to case a well, you would not use two different makes of casing. Why? Because it wouldn't screw together. You don't use different joints in the same string of tools. Well, then, is it logical to use different kinds of material in your drilling rigs? We think not, especially when by sticking to our kind, which is structural steel—admitted by the engineers of the world to be the best material for any and every class of structure.

Just here we beg to submit some figures on drilling rigs: When a well is completed with one of our rigs, ten two-horse wagon loads on a reasonable road moves it to the next location. Thirty wagon loads are required to move a wood rig, with one third waste when you get it there. But we think we hear someone exclaiming in a far-away sepulchral voice, "We don't move wood rigs if we get a well." Now, this is the very question that we wish to bring up. Very well—leave your wood rig—which means $1,500 inactive, and subject to decadence, fire and wind.

We can furnish you a sixty-foot steel pumping derrick that the additions to it will make a pumping outfit cost about $500, and it won't rot, burn or blow down.

Ten teams at $6.66 per day makes our steel rig cost $60 for moving; thirty teams for wood rig makes a cost of $180; difference, $120. Add $1,000 for your wood rig standing at completed well, makes a credit in favor of the steel rig of $1,120. Let us place the number of wells that a steel rig will drill at a minimum— say thirty. We know for certain that it will do this, for we have some very close to this number right now.

Now, Mr. Mathematician, carry the $1,120 along and add another $1,120 for each well drilled, provided you use wood rigs and leave them at the wells, until thirty wells are drilled. It amounts in round numbers to $33,600. Add interest at four percent for four years on this amount and you will see what can be saved by using structural steel drilling equipment. In a word, by using steel you save enough, compared with using ,wood, so that you not only get the steel outfit for nothing, but make money by using it, after deducting $1,800 for moving the steel rig.

Yorke Derrick Company
Washington, Pennsylvania

from *The Oil and Gas Journal*. March 29, 1917, p. 23

Wood verses steel rigs.

Standard Oil was Benedum's strongest adversary. The constant threat to the wildcatter was success. If the wells came in too fast or the competition forced him to drill too swiftly his financial position would deteriorate. Money went out faster than the oil could bring it in. Everyone knew this, especially Standard Oil. Deep pockets and owning all elements of the business kept it in cash. In Shreveport, however, Benedum and Trees had neglected the watery lakes, especially Caddo Lake. Derricks were appearing in the lakes and draining oil from the reserves of Benedum and Trees. The traditional response to this attack was to counter attack by digging more wells on the boundary lines so as to keep the oil from moving across it. But, digging more wells in an already large venture threatened Benedum's financial stability. They had to sell more oil. For that they needed pipelines, which were owned by Standard. Joe Trees decided he had to have a deal with Standard, so began selling his half of the oil for 39 cents a barrel, far

Below: Cypress storage tanks and boilers on the shore of Caddo Lake. The men are Billy Daniel, John Miller, and W. E. Martin, the surveyor who has just located the post on the Cochran lease across from Trees, Louisiana.

Caddo Lake.
PHOTOGRAPH COURTESY OF THE NOEL LIBRARY,
LOUISIANA STATE UNIVERSITY IN SHREVEPORT.

below what Standard usually paid. Benedum, in Pittsburgh, heard of this and reacted strongly. He went to Louisiana and began selling truckloads of oil to cotton mills and elsewhere for 70 cents a barrel. Standard objected. The flow of oil to Standard from the large Benedum and Trees leases slowed. Then Benedum constructed a pipeline to a nearby railroad and began to move oil that way.

Standard responded. Suddenly it appeared that the railroad no longer had tank cars to haul the partners' oil. The pipeline and the 800,000 barrels of oil in pits was threatened with obsolescence. Benedum surveyed the railroad and figured out that Standard had put pressure on the railroad to deny him cars. Theodore Roosevelt was in the White House and was a progressive crusader against monopoly. Benedum went to Washington where he explained the situation to Roosevelt and suddenly the railroad's problem disappeared and the Trees and Benedum oil began to move again.

But they realized that war with the Standard was not profitable. Standard wanted the property. The only remaining issue was

how to make it pay a fair price. Benedum threatened and actually took steps to build his own refinery that would soak up his oil and that of his neighbors. Standard's supply would diminish more. This led to an overture from Standard for a meeting in New York at 26 Broadway. Benedum met with a Standard vice-president and three lessor officers and began dealing. But Benedum could see that every step of the way one of the Standard men would leave the room, quietly to report to John D. Archbold, president of Standard of New Jersey, and the principal in the dealings. The partners had previously agreed that $3,000,000 would make them happy, but Benedum felt otherwise. The $3,000,000 price passed, then Benedum got Standard up to $5,000,000. Whereupon Benedum protested that he would no longer deal with a subordinate, he was a principal and expected to deal with a principal. Archbold came into the room and Benedum laid out his prepared scientific assay of the oil property. Benedum then said, I want another million based on these numbers, and here is how to pay it. You pay

Above: If more power was needed than could be supplied by the mule team, oxen were called in. Here are oxen pulling a wagon loaded with three giant logs.
PHOTOGRAPH COURTESY OF THE OIL CITY MUSEUM.

Below: Here is a mule team stuck in either snow or mud, possibly at Homer, Louisiana.
PHOTOGRAPH COURTESY OF THE OIL CITY MUSEUM.

the $5,000,000 up front. After you have collected enough revenue from the property to offset the $5,000,000 then you will owe the $1,000,000. After a query to a Standard engineer to verify the quality of the oil, Archbold took the deal.[10] Trees and Benedum walked away from the Louisiana oil business, never to return. But it soon developed that Benedum had not sold Standard the gas from the 130,000 acres. That became another story.

The settlement between Benedum and Standard Oil enabled the oil and royalty payments to flow. Leases on Caddo good oil land paid out for decades. Over their life the leases yielded to their various owners over a billion dollars.[11] Records in the archives of LSU Shreveport document how one landowner prospered. The W. P. Stiles collection preserves records of many years of Standard Oil payments to Stiles. They

covered three different products—light oil, Caddo Hy, and Ex. Heavy. Nearly all of it was light oil and Standard Oil paid during the month of December 1914 eighty cents a barrel for it. Stiles' interest was 1/8, so of the 90,000 barrels produced he was credited with about 11,000 barrels that brought in $9,000. But from his 1/8th interest Stiles had sold off almost 5/6, leaving him with a handsome monthly check for $2,276.[12]

Benedum and Trees tried to leave a legacy in Louisiana—the town of Trees, named after Joe Trees who conceived the idea for the town. Curiously, it was a reaction to the wild west scenario being experienced at Oil City. Burning gas wells illuminated warrens of tents and shacks housing thousands of oilfield workers and speculators. Bars and houses of prostitution ensured that the work force would be unreliable. Muggings were common. Along with some oil companies, Trees and Benedum developed a new town that would be orderly, with a grid plan, and real houses suitable for men to bring their families into. Churches, schools, a bank and a post office appeared. The latter still stands, now most ironically in Oil City where it forms the focus of the Oil City Petroleum Museum.

Left and below: The Bank of Trees and its post office, now the focus of the Oil City Museum.

PHOTOGRAPH COURTESY OF WILLIAM D. REEVES, 2011.

15 cords every 24 hours

Electric lighting system

GRABILL 1936

Boiler pit — 3 days water supply.

Another one of the thousands who crowded the Oil City Fields was Howard Hughes, Sr.[13] An oral interview with Carl Jones, early oil man, shed some light on Hughes' marketing methods. He made his fortune by designing a drill bit that could drill through hard rock. Before this new bit, oil drillers were not able to reach the large pockets of oil lying beneath the hard rock. Howard Hughes, Sr., and a colleague established the Sharp-Hughes Tool Company which held the patent for the new drill bit, manufactured the bit, and leased the bit to oil companies. He filed the basic patents for the Sharp-Hughes Rock Bit in 1908, and a year later was granted U.S. Patent 930,758 and U.S. Patent 930,759 for this rock drill. Hughes' two-cone rotary drill bit penetrated medium and hard rock with ten times the speed of any former bit, and its development revolutionized oil well drilling.

Jones recounted that when he was a rough-neck he saw Howard Hughes, Sr., several times. In 1909 Hughes patented his dual cone drill bit that cut through rock quickly. It was the foundation of the Hughes Tool Company fortune. "He'd make the oilfields and try to get people interested in using his bit and he carried it in a "croaker" sack over his shoulder." Jones continued, "...he would make the oil-field and walk—that was about the only way you could get around in Oil City. The town was known as Ananias in those days. And he would finally get somebody, after they had hit that hard rock at about 1,800 feet—they called it the sand rock. And he would get someone, maybe the field manager, to run his bit in the hole and that's where the Hughes tool started, right there." But, many of the workers were scared of trying Hughes' bit because they might leave it in the hole. Hughes did not live out at Oil City, only the roughnecks did, they had to stay on the job. The supervisors and men like Hughes lived in Shreveport, a hotel on Texas Street, and took the "plug" up to Oil City. That train left Shreveport in the morning, arrived at Oil City, waited a few hours, and came back.

Life in the early oilfields for the rough neck or roustabout was busy. Initially animals were the principal sources of transportation. The mule team was the most common method for bringing timber and boilers to the well site. The ox team moved the heaviest items. A Grabill photograph captures the story of how much needed to be done. This annotated photograph shows the enormous pile of firewood needed by the boilers. The water pit must hold three days supply of water. See photograph on opposite page.

A more enduring and important legacy of the first two decades of oil and gas in the Northwest were the conservation laws of Louisiana. The various acts of the legislature in the first twenty years of the twentieth century amounted to a Progressive agenda that remains as pertinent today as yesterday. The first well blowouts in Caddo led in 1906 to Act 71 that permitted the state to seize and close burning or abandoned wells. The same year the state required, by Act 36, that pipelines shall be common carriers regulated by the Railroad Commission of Louisiana. In return, they were granted the right to use public lands and eventually to expropriate for rights of way. The new Department of Conservation acquired a commissioner to

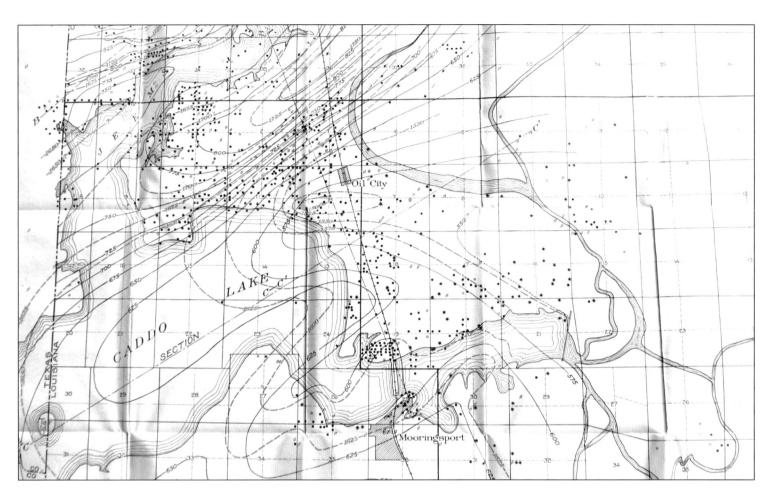

Above: Matson map of Caddo Field. George Charlton Matson, The Caddo Oil and Gas Field, Louisiana and Texas. *Washington: Government Printing Office, 1916.*

Opposite, top: Jeems Bayou opposite Stacey's Landing.
PHOTOGRAPH BY GRUETER & GREENE, COURTESY OF THE OIL CITY MUSEUM.

Opposite, bottom: A well along Jeems Bayou. The photograph shows in the foreground an oil pond being filled, pump station, and housing, along with several derricks.
PHOTOGRAPH COURTESY OF THE PERCY VIOSCA, JR., COLLECTION, LOUISIANA AND LOWER MISSISSIPPI VALLEY COLLECTIONS, LOUISIANA STATE UNIVERSITY LIBRARIES, BATON ROUGE, LOUISIANA.

administer it by Act 66 of 1916. In 1918 by Act 268 new powers were thrust on the commissioner. To stop waste, gas manufacturers were required to report the amount of natural gas consumed, an act aimed at the carbon plants. Another act from that year, Act 170 of 1918, required meters on gas and oil wells and prohibited discrimination in the purchase of gas from common pools. In 1920 a series of acts were signed into law by Governor John Parker, a Progressive. Act 31 leveled the first severance tax on minerals. The act carefully noted that it was to carry into effect Article 229 of the Constitution of 1898, as amended in 1910, and repeated in the Constitution of 1913. This two percent tax on the value of minerals taken from the ground was an extraordinary extension of the state's regulatory and taxing power, an extension that underlies nearly all state regulation today. The Louisiana Civil Code had long held that minerals did not belong to the surface owner. He only had the right to remove them. The following year the legislature passed Act 81 of 1921 imposing a sales tax of

one cent per gallon on all gasoline sold for domestic consumption in Louisiana. Both of these acts created reporting requirements that gave the state oversight of every aspect of the business. Act 73 of 1920 aimed at discrimination by pipelines and others when buying from a group of wells drawing from the same pool. Underlying this and other acts was the concept of proration, a centerpiece of later oil and gas legislation. Finally, in 1921, by Act 70, the legislature authorized municipalities and parishes to acquire or expropriate gas plants and pipelines.

The various conservation laws of the Progressive era had beneficial consequences for the land. Jeems Bayou, just to the west of Oil City and Trees, is a broad estuary running south into Caddo Lake. Like the lake, it was extensively drilled early in the century. Today it has become a scenic forested fishing spot just along the Texas border.

In the decades after World War 1 wildcatters played the key role in expanding the oil lands of Northwest Louisiana. A venturesome wildcatter discovered the Pine Island Oilfield.

The Elton Oil Company completed the first well for the Pine Island Oilfield during 1917. This field was a northeast extension of the Oil City Field. It took in over 7,600 acres, about eleven square miles. The Dixie Oil Company was the pioneer in deep well drilling in the Pine Island Field. During 1929 the Dixie Oil Company completed its Dillion #92 well at a total depth of 6,357 feet, which was then the deepest well in Northern Louisiana.[14]

R. W. Norton-Hill became the #1 gas discovery well in the Rodessa Field on August 3, 1930. This field stretched northwest from the Caddo to the Arkansas and Texas borders and beyond.

Right: One of many W. P. Stiles wells, No. 5, J. J. Simmonds, driller.
PHOTOGRAPH BY GREENE, APRIL 8, 1912, COURTESY OF THE OIL CITY MUSEUM.

Opposite, top: Wonderpool of the World *is the title of a Grabill photograph of an oilfield, possibly the Homer Field. It shows several camps, notably the Standard Oil Camp, and identifies several drilling rigs.*
PHOTOGRAPH COURTESY OF THE LIBRARY OF CONGRESS.

Opposite, center: Wonderpool of the World *a closer view of the same photograph above.*
PHOTOGRAPH COURTESY OF THE LIBRARY OF CONGRESS.

Opposite, bottom: Aerial view of part of Homer Field.
GRABILL PHOTOGRAPH COURTESY OF THE NOEL LIBRARY, LOUISIANA STATE UNIVERSITY IN SHREVEPORT.

Above: Oil City was still booming in 1922.
Automobiles line the street and people stand
around talking excitedly.

Right: In 1912 horses and carriages
dominated Oil City's main street.

A series of gas wells followed before United Gas Public Service Company brought in Young #1 July 7, 1935. In the 1930s approximately 1,100 wells were dug in Rodessa.[15] Another wildcatter, E. P. Kilgore from Oklahoma, brought in the Zwolle Field in 1932.[16] E. T. (Reb) Oakes, wildcatter, discovered the Lisbon Field in Claiborne Parish about 1936.[17]

Personal information about wildcatters is spotty. But occasionally it is possible to find financial statements for wildcatters. One such comes from the Tom Bell Collection at LSU Shreveport. It is a semi-annual statement for the first half of 1945. The receipts are not broken out. They are merely identified as deposits totaling $10,940. But his expenses

make a long list. Repayment of a note and personal cash account for $2,100. Then comes a payment of $757 for the Thigpen & Harold #1 and #2 wells. Drilling rig expenses were $681, trucking and hauling $754 and derrick construction $152. The Willis Well #2 cost $512, liability insurance $186, income tax $84 and state and parish taxes of $213. These and other expenses totaled $8,253 leaving cash of $1,655. Twenty years earlier he filed a federal tax return for which he kept a draft. For the year 1926 it showed income of $11,000 and expenses of $6,889. His tax bill came out to $160. In short, Tom Bell was not making a great fortune.

Wildcatter R. O. Roy discovered the most unusual field in Louisiana—the Bellevue Oil-field in Bossier Parish sixteen miles northeast of Shreveport. On November 14, 1921, Roy's discovery well began flowing at 5,000 barrels a day. What was amazing is that the strikes were all at depths of only four hundred feet. It was such a surprise that there were no pipelines or storage tanks nearby. It was so promising after the discovery well that Standard Oil began spending substantial sums to build pipelines to the field. The Louisiana Oil and Refining Corporation came in behind Standard on three forty-acre tracts in its possession. It planned to build a pipe

Above: The tent city was the very first attempt to keep workers at their job.
PHOTOGRAPH COURTESY OF THE OIL CITY MUSEUM.

Below: Interior view of Trees City Pool Hall, c. 1916. Could Joe Trees have approved of this?
PHOTOGRAPH COURTESY OF THE OIL CITY MUSEUM.

Top: Tom Bell plowing.

Center: Tom Bell's first truck.

Bottom, left: Tom Bell.

Bottom, right: Tom Bell at Grey #1.

line to the main track of the Louisiana & Arkansas Railroad.[18] The Shreveport Chamber of Commerce oozed eloquence over the "importance of this great shallow field to Shreveport.... It perpetuates for an indefinite time the already strong position of this city...."

R. O. Roy and his associate John Y. Snyder were well-known for being among the most secretive of wildcatters. Their most famous coup was keeping their discovery of the shallow Bellevue Field a secret for a week. The secrecy, so hard to achieve in the competitive landmen economy, enabled Roy's syndicate to lease many additional acres in the vicinity. Epitomizing Roy's success was another of his discoveries, the Sligo Gas Field twelve miles due east of Shreveport in the forest of southern Bossier Parish. "Hidden deep in the pine woods, remote from any highway, it is a typical wildcat for location..." said The *Shreveport Times* on May 31, 1925. But, besides its location, the well produced lots of liquid gasoline that became a bonanza for local farmers who "blazed a trail to it by repeated trips in quest of free gasoline...." Only one other well in the northwest was known for free gasoline, Dixie Oil Company's Robertshaw #43 in Pine Island Field.

While R. O. Roy began his exploratory work in South Bossier in 1915, he was not alone. Also drilling in the Elm Grove Field were Texaco and Gulf. It was Gulf Refining that brought in the first oil producer. But the local media credited Roy with discovering the field. "Hats off to Mr. R. O. Roy, the first oil man to begin operations in the Elm Grove Field.... It was a lucky day for Bossier Parish when Mr. Roy headed this way...."[19] Roy's luck extended to De Soto Parish. De Soto got its first big "gasser" in 1928 with the completion of R. O. Roy's Jesse Fuller No. 1, thirty miles south of Shreveport. The well opened up an entirely new gas field. Even before the gauges were installed oil men estimated the flow of gas at 40,000,000 cubic feet of gas a day.[20]

As the twentieth century went by, a new type of oil man appeared, not wildcatter, and not a major. These were the field extenders. This was the oldest basic technique for finding oil—go first where it is. Recently *Oil and Gas Investor* interviewed Shreveport-based

Oil soaked roughnecks work on the drill floor in Pine Island Field, c. 1920.
PHOTOGRAPH COURTESY OF THE OIL CITY MUSEUM.

Rutledge Deas. For Deas, geology was "the key to success in the oil and gas business." He has been both a discoverer and extender in LaSalle and Ouchita Parishes. He praised Prentis Boatner for his "superb subsurface geology," that permitted him to drill discovery wells in the Smackover formation in Union Parish and development wells in the Valentine and Lapeyrouse Fields.

Henry Goodrich lived the life of a successful oil man and he considered himself an extender. Born at Shreveport, he graduated from LSU in 1951.[21] He went to work scouting in Tyler, Texas, and returned to Shreveport in 1960. He found a businessman and a geologist in Charles T. McCord. They formed a partnership in 1971 called McCord-Goodrich. Prosperity permitted Goodrich to sell his interest and form a new company called Goodrich Oil Co. The company drilled in Texas and Louisiana. He explored the Rodena Oilfield near Vivian. Eventually he started drilling in south Louisiana maintaining an office in Lafayette with four geologists. It prospered until 1995 when Goodrich merged with Patrick Petroleum out of Michigan, creating a new company with a New York stock exchange listing. His geologist son, Gill, joined the company and in 2002 Henry became Chairman Emeritus. Henry was a

fighter for the oil industry. From 1980 to 1982 he was president of LAPro. He spoke throughout Louisiana on behalf of the industry, quarreling with Governor Dave Treen over his proposal for a 12 and a half percent Louisiana severance tax. He spoke to the various landmen associations. He felt that on balance Texas and Louisiana treated oil companies about the same. In 2012 the company's headquarters are in Houston, though some staff occupy offices in Shreveport.

Henry Goodrich thought Louisiana's biggest step forward was the formation of the Conservation Commission in line with the Natural Gas Act of 1938. The Natural Gas Act (NGA) of 1938 was the first instance of direct Federal regulation of the natural gas industry. It came as a result of the tremendous market power of the gas transmission companies who often discriminated between different purchasers and communities in their pricing and availability. Eventually the Federal Energy Regulatory Commission came to set "just and reasonable rates" for the transmission or sale of natural gas in interstate commerce. A "certificate of public convenience and necessity" is issued under Section 7 of the NGA, and permits pipeline companies to charge customers for some of the expenses incurred in pipeline construction and operation. The NGA also

R. O. Roy and W. H. Fromme March 14, 1930, in Holly, Louisiana, seven miles north of Mansfield, De Soto Parish. Roy and Fromme are showing off their new well that produces 2,500 barrels a day.
PHOTOGRAPH COURTESY OF EUREKA STUDIO, MANSFIELD, LOUISIANA.

requires Commission approval prior to abandonment of any pipeline facility or services. Louisiana led the states in forced pooling, an important conservation measure that limited the ability to drill repeatedly in specific sites. In Louisiana the state, aided by professional geologists, formed the unit, whereas in Texas the individual leaseholders formed it for their own convenience.

Stories of wildcatters pop out of life histories. Attorney Robert Stacy, Jr., came out of World War II, got his degree, and went to law school. He talked about his father. In 1931 the elder Stacy worked for a pipeline company, but he wanted to get into oil. So he raised some money from California and elsewhere, bought some used drilling equipment from a junk yard, and began drilling just as the East Texas Field was opening. The Rodessa Field (1936) was even closer to Shreveport. Stacy's father became quite prosperous and sold out at the end of the 1930s. He took with him some fine production, but within a year his wells had turned to salt water.[22]

According to Robert Stacy, Shreveport did very well in the early to mid-1920s. The East Texas Field brought some prosperity in the early 1930s. Stacy felt Shreveport should have been a big town. It was surrounded by production in Mississippi, South Arkansas, South Louisiana, and Texas. The *Shreveport Times* reported at the fiftieth anniversary of the first gas transmission line that "Nearly every major (and minor) oil company has an important office in Shreveport and many of the leading gas transmitting and distributing companies are headquartered here."[23] But, continued Stacy, Shreveport did not make it for two reasons. First, banks in Shreveport were ultra-conservative. "The oil business lived on borrowed money. They could get it in Dallas…" Second, Louisiana politicians thought only about raising taxes, not growth. The big oil companies left Shreveport for Texas because that's where they got their money. All the big companies once had division headquarters in Shreveport and they all vanished.

In the 1930s prosperity gave Shreveport its watering holes and eating places. The Columbia Restaurant on Market Street was the "prime congregation place…." In the 1930s, 1940s, and 1950s the oil men gathered there after 4:00 to drink and swap tales. Not surprisingly the old line society of Shreveport, the landed farmers or planters, did not take well to the oil men. "The early oil men were less than polished. A lot of them were pretty rough characters. Pioneers were you know like the gold miners, they were hustling a quick buck, with little education."[24]

In the 1950s Shreveport was still operating like the old days, but gradually everything changed. The year 1954 was probably the peak of Shreveport's influence in the national gas business. Companies with headquarters in Shreveport operated 36,000 miles of pipeline and transmitted thirty-two percent of the total volume of U.S. gas. The twenty-two Caddo/Bossier Oil and Gas Fields produced 93 billion cubic feet of gas and 10,200,000 barrels of oil annually.[25] Deals on a handshake disappeared. The final blow was OPEC that suddenly jacked the price of oil up. "The business from then on changed, it was no longer a good buddy business…. You never do anything unless its contractional, because of lawsuits. I don't sell deals anymore. But if I did you'd have to have a lawyer in your pocket."[26]

Workers had to repair their ordinary bits regularly as shown in this photograph *"Dressing a Fish tail Bit"* by Jack Darnell and crew, 1925.

PHOTOGRAPH COURTESY OF THE OIL CITY MUSEUM.

In 1930 the independent gas line companies of North Louisiana consolidated into the United Gas Corporation. Wildcatters Benedum and Trees organized their gas production on their early leases into Arkansas Natural Gas Company. It built pipelines from Oil City Fields to Little Rock, Hot Springs, and Pine Bluff Arkansas. Trees became the first president of Arkansas Natural Gas Company. T. N. Barnsdall's large holdings in northwest Louisiana were incorporated into the new gas

company. Dr. M. P. Cullinan of Houston constructed gas pipe lines from the Caddo Field to Marshall, Texas. In 1911 Honore and Potter Palmer, Jr., like the Dawes also from Chicago, created the Atlas Oil Company that took a major position in the gas business. In the 1920s the most important gas pipelines stretched across Texas and became, with Louisiana properties, the heart of the United Gas Corporation.[27] Its first president was Norris Cochran McGowan, a Chicagoan who came to Shreveport in 1913. He remained president for thirty years. In 1938 he served as president of the American Gas Association. In 1940, in an unusual reverse move, McGowen brought the corporate headquarters for United Gas Corporation back to Shreveport from Houston. United Gas introduced the concept of "restricted take." and early proration.[28] In the thirty years from 1930 to 1960 United Gas had revenues of $3.6 billion. Expenses of $2.1 billion and taxes of $400 million (11 percent) left a net profit of $661 million.[29]

But in 1965 Pennzoil got control of the company with 42 percent of the stock and immediately merged all of United's production into Pennzoil. Hugh and Bill Liedtke controlled Pennzoil and their plan was to move unregulated assets from United Gas into Pennzoil. These were primarily gas reserves and production facilities. Without sufficient reserves and production capacity United was forced to raise prices, an increase the Federal Power Commission was forced to approve because even then some companies were too large to fail. The bill for rescuing United thus fell on its customers while Pennzoil's shareholders did very well from the profits on United's gas reserves.[30] In 1975 Pennzoil moved all the companies to Houston, a move that cost Shreveport many jobs. The United Gas Building was sold to the State of Louisiana. In 1985 the Liedtkes spun off United Gas. It then began a journey through a series of owners that by the mid 1995 witnessed the disappearance of the name into Koch Gateway Pipe Line Company.[31]

Board Road.

PHOTOGRAPH COURTESY OF THE
MINERALS MANAGEMENT SERVICE, VOLUME VI,
AND PEGGY WURZLOW.

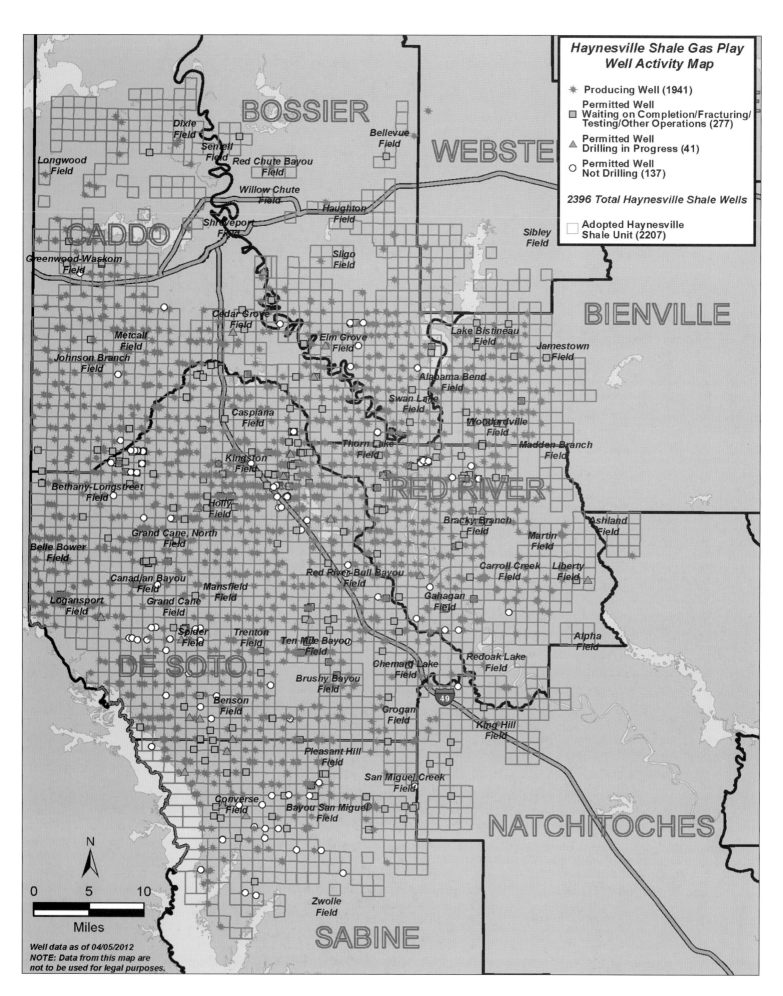

Haynesville Shale Gas Play
Well Activity Map

☀ Producing Well (1941)

▢ Permitted Well
Waiting on Completion/Fracturing/
Testing/Other Operations (277)

▲ Permitted Well
Drilling in Progress (41)

○ Permitted Well
Not Drilling (137)

2396 Total Haynesville Shale Wells

▢ Adopted Haynesville
Shale Unit (2207)

N

0   5   10
Miles

Well data as of 04/05/2012
NOTE: Data from this map are
not to be used for legal purposes.

One of the amazing features of oil and gas is its layered nature. Land that would not produce oil and gas from one layer, might from another. Shreveport and the Northwest is now undergoing an enormous oil and gas boom because of the discovery and technical development of the Haynesville Shale layer. The 9,000 square miles that make up the Haynesville Shale Gas Play stretch across extreme northern Louisiana almost to Monroe. Haynesville is not a location but a geologic strata. Porous shale rock comprises the strata. It is distinctive because unlike other oil bearing strata, the oil within the shale rock is fixed within small pores that practically stop the migration of oil. An oil drill that penetrates the shale layer unlocks a tiny amount of oil in the rock knocked around by the drill, but nothing that flows. To make the oil or gas flow the shale must be fractured. At eleven thousand feet in depth, the average depth of the Haynesville/Bossier shale, it takes a powerful jet of water and sand pumped into the well at high pressure. The water breaks the cell walls of the shale and the small amount of sand props the cells open, allowing the oil to flow. The early Caddo/Bossier Fields tended towards the northern half of the northwest section, while the Haynesville centers on De Soto Parish in the southern half. A 2008 study of the Haynesville estimated 74.7 trillion cubic feet of gas was technically recoverable. This compares favorably with the total offshore production of dry natural gas in 2006 in the amount of 2.7 trillion cubic feet.[32] The shale layer is from 200 to 300 feet in depth. The average well extracts 80 percent of the technically recoverable oil or gas within ten years.[33] Louisiana Geological Survey director David E. Dismukes "estimates the reserve potential for this emerging resource play at some seven billion barrels (BBbls). To put this resource into perspective, current estimates for the offshore Gulf of Mexico are 3.8 BBbls in proved reserves out of a total of some 20.6 BBbls (proven reserves) for the entire U.S."[34]

Horizontal drilling along with the fracturing technique has dramatically increased the efficiency of oil and gas recovery. Horizontal drilling reduces the number of oil well structures that dot the landscape. At the beginning of the oil and gas age derricks stood fifty feet apart. After unitization the derricks moved to

500 or more feet apart. With horizontal drilling one per square mile is hardly necessary.

The largest producer in the Haynesville, Chesapeake Energy Corp., paid De Soto Parish tax agencies $7.3 million in 2011. Bossier Parish was next with $675,000, followed by Sabine Parish at $597,000. Bienville, Natchitoches, Red River and Webster Parishes received lessor amounts.[35] In 1980 De Soto Parish produced 36MMcf of natural gas. In 2010 it produced 644 MMcf of gas, more than a ten-fold increase.

Northwest Louisiana had nurtured many wildcatters over its century of glory. Today the most successful wildcatter to strike in Louisiana is Floyd Wilson. An army brat, Wilson studied at the University of Houston to become an oilfield engineer. Going independent and moving to Kansas, he formed and nurtured Hugoton Energy Corp. In the 1990s he sold it to Chesapeake Energy Corp; founded 3TEC in 1999 and sold it to Plains Exploration & Production Co. All the time he was busy adopting and having children, eventually reaching nine in his Austin, Texas, family. He had prospered, but the biggest stroke was next. In 2004 he founded Petrohawk Energy Corp. and spent $60 million buying leases and drilling in lands that soon became known as Eagle Ford Fields, in Louisiana as the Haynesville Shale. Flat-out success came in 2008 when his Haynesville well hit the shale. "The well spewed enough natural gas in a single day to power 84,000 typical U.S. homes, marking the discovery of one of the largest natural-gas fields in the world."[36] Wilson, an experienced fund solicitor on Wall Street, went back to New York where he raised the billions of dollars needed to develop the field. Wells cost $10,000,000 each, but they had to be drilled to protect Wilson's suddenly valuable leases around Shreveport. In 2012 Wilson sold Petrohawk to BHP Billiton Ltd. for $12.1 billion.

Because of its oil and gas dominance at both the beginning and end of the twentieth century the Northwest deserves the crown as the most active oil and gas region of the century. The proximity of the Louisiana coastline to the great offshore fields promises to reinforce Louisiana's role as the energy state.

Opposite: This plan shows the Haynesville Shale Gas Play Well Activity Map in Louisiana as of 2012. The small boxes are the individual shale unit of which there are 2,207. Of these units there are 1,941 producing wells. The play extends around Shreveport almost to Caddo Lake. State of Louisiana, Haynesville Activity Map. April 6, 2012.

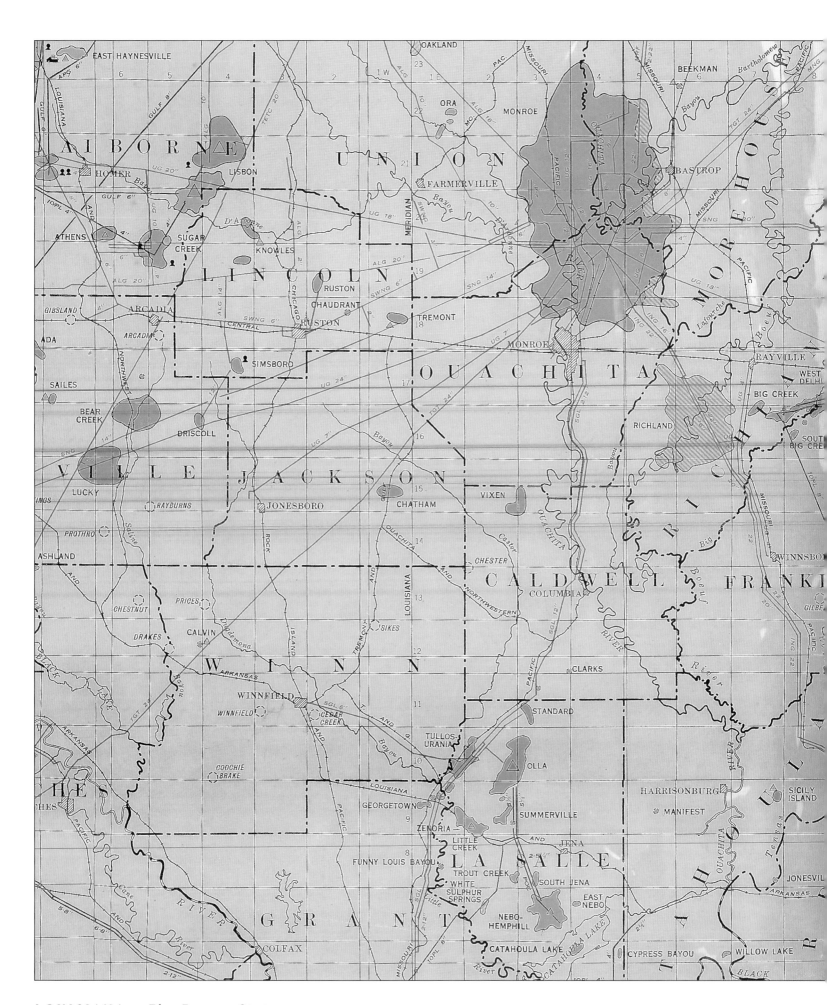

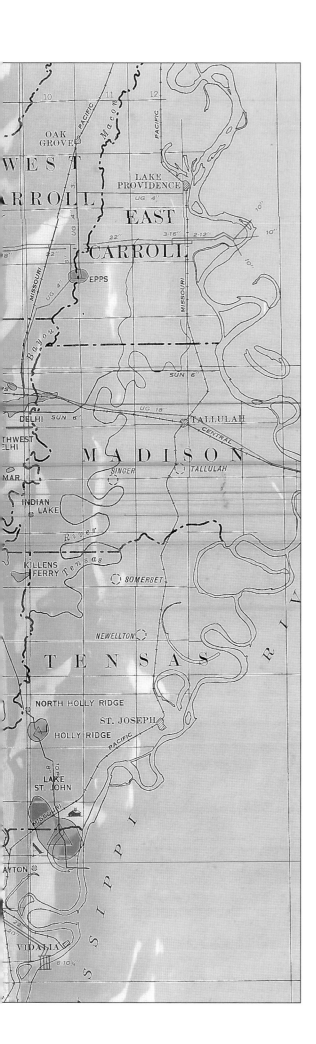

MONROE

Northeast Louisiana is all about the Monroe Gas Field, the greatest gas field in Louisiana and once one of the largest in the world. It did not explode on the consciousness of Louisiana. Much like Shreveport's Caddo Field, it started out like a lamb with a water-well drilled in Monroe's City Park in 1909. Instead of water, however, it turned out a little bit of gas and lots of saltwater. The latter is a strong harbinger of oil and gas. In 1913 the Consolidated Ice Company, seeking water, found gas and saltwater. In 1916 wildcatters searching for oil drilled just north of Monroe and turned up commercial quantities of gas. To this day oil has remained a scarce commodity in the Northeast. Not until 1957 was oil found in the Monroe Gas Field.[1]

But, slowly, others became interested in the gas near Monroe. Wildcatters like Fred Stovall took portable rigs into the field, an early technique that had been used in Caddo Parish. By 1920 the major players—gas line companies and the carbon black companies—were firmly in place. The earliest surveys of gas holdings in the Northeast estimated 2.345 trillion cubic feet (2.345 Tcf) of gas was recoverable from the field.[2] The field, however, had not been discovered in its full extent. By 1960 the Monroe Field had produced 5.776 Tcf, four times the amount of the second ranked field in Louisiana. By 2012 the Monroe Field had produced 7.5 Tcf of gas.[3] The largest producer in the Gulf of Mexico today, the Shell Mars Project, would take about ninety-four years to produce the same quantity if its reserves were large enough. Of course, the Monroe Field did take that long.

Oil and Gas Map of Louisiana, 1947. Detail of Northeast Louisiana.
It shows the spider web of pipelines radiating from the Monroe Field.
In the southwest is Tullos, an important junction.
On the east side the Interstate Pipeline extends south to Vidalia.

Fred Stovall's portable pole rig pulled and

powered by a tractor.

While the Monroe Field was a giant for its time, offshore reserves are vastly greater today. A study of proved reserves as of December 2005 showed 181 Tcf of gas in the Gulf of Mexico.[4] The largest fields, West Cameron and Eugene Island, have reserves of 20 Tcf each. Annual offshore gas production peaked in 1970 at about ½ Tcf.[5]

The first and most important chapter in the story of the Monroe Gas Field is the story of the carbon black industry. Thirty-three different owners had dug wells in the field as of 1921. Southern Carbon Co. had the most wells, followed by Ouachita Natural Gas & Oil Co., The Texas Co., Sterling Oil & Gas Co., United Oil & Natural Gas Products Corp., and H. C. Morris, Trustee.[6] As soon as the Monroe Gas Field reached a critical mass

about 1919, the West Virginia carbon black industry began to leave that state for the cheaper gas in Louisiana.

The carbon black business was nasty and wasteful. In its simplest form carbon black was produced by holding a metal plate over a candle or jet of burning gas. The carbon black is the black soot deposited on the plate. By 1921 there were nine carbon black plants in operation. Carbon black was used in automobile tires, rubber goods, printers' ink, stove polish, phonograph records and paint. It was essential for printers. About 43,500,000 lbs. were made annually.[7] But the success of the business depended on cheap gas. Ten cents per thousand cubic feet (Mcf) was the tipping point over which the carbon plants could not make money.

The principal political problem of the carbon black industry was the realization of its waste of the heat content of natural gas. Using average numbers, 31 lbs. of carbon are found in 1,000 cf of natural gas. However, the plants could not extract even a pound from 1,000 cf of gas. This means an efficiency of three percent. The heat of the gas was all lost.

The Monroe Gas Field rapidly expanded to about 425 square miles in area when it ranked third in area in the United States. Developers kept drilling out from the field's center near Monroe. For example, on September 7, 1922, the Windsor Oil and Gas Company brought in its Windsor Pipes Well. The well was nine miles due north of Monroe in southeastern Morehouse Parish. The well was expected to bring in an additional 50,000,000 cf/d.[8]

Gas was produced from two separate reservoir zones known as the "gas rock" and the "second sand." The gas rock, or upper zone, occurred at shallow depths ranging from 2,050 to 2,300 feet. The second sand, or lower reservoir zone, occurred 100-250 feet below the gas rock horizon. As of December 1932, 876 gas wells were completed in the field. Of approximately 70 wells testing the second sand, only 23 were commercially successful. The initial well-head pressure of each of the reservoirs was 1,020 pounds per square inch, an extremely favorable number. The initial open-flow volumes from both the gas rock and second sand ranged as high as 50 MMcf/d. By 1932 the pipeline and carbon black companies had taken approximately 1.59 Tcf of gas from the reservoirs.[9]

Stovall crew with Fred Stovall, the drilling contractor, third from right.

Table 15. Historic Gas Production by Region

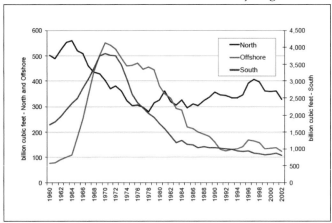

Table 15. Historic Gas Production by Region. See endnote 6.

Almost from the discovery of the field it came to fascinate Louisiana, and especially Louisiana businessmen. As early as 1921 the *Times-Picayune* learned of an engineering study to bring Monroe natural gas to Baton Rouge and New Orleans. The projected cost was $15,000,000 for two 18" adjoining pipes. The cost was heightened because for much of the route they would have to be insulated because of the deleterious effect of swamp soils on the pipe.[10] The following year Major Frank T. Payne, engineer for the Louisiana Department of Conservation, spoke to the American Association of Engineers meeting at the Cabildo in New Orleans.[11] While the cost of the pipelines was large, Major Payne argued that natural gas would be economic because natural gas delivers two to three times the heat of manufactured gas for a given aperture. He had surveyed three possible routes for a pipeline to New Orleans. The two feasible ones were each about 280 miles long. One went through Alexandria; the other towards Mississippi thence south in the high land on the east side of the river.

The roaring new field drew national investors, including or according to rumor, Henry Ford and associates. According to a breathless article in September 1921 the "Ford interests" were trying to get a lease on Muscle Shoals over in Alabama to generate electricity. This would open the way for industry that would use natural gas from the Monroe Field. The center of this new industry was to be Memphis.[12] Meanwhile R. A. Deming invented a new process for making carbon used in the refining of sugar.

Locally Henry Pharr introduced the process to the Monroe Field.[13]

Alongside the national interest in the Monroe Field, local businessmen in the three parishes of Ouachita, Union and Morehouse each organized Chambers of Commerce. In September 1923 the Monroe chamber met with the Monroe Rotary, Kiwanis and Lions Clubs for a banquet at Hotel Monroe designed to raise as much as $50,000 for an advertising budget to promote industry to the northeast gas belt.[14]

From the discovery of the Monroe Gas Field enormous wastage had been a constant issue for the state's conservation department. It was the principal subject of a comprehensive report by the Department of Conservation in 1921. Wastage was staggering. The engineers at the Louisiana Department of Conservation estimated ten million cubic feet of gas was wasted every day underground due to poor casing.[15] Poor regulation permitted the flow rate of individual wells to vary dramatically. When the flow rate was high, the pressure inside the well that pushed gas up tended to drop. If it got too low, nearby saltwater would flow into the gas field, creating the expense of removal and threatening equipment. At this early date in the history of the field the authors were very concerned with the accuracy or even presence of meters to measure the amount of gas removed from a well. The regulations of the Department of Conservation required a meter on each well.

The new meters showed that over 1920 daily production from the field doubled. Average daily production of the Monroe Field increased from 37.6 MMcf/d in January 1920 to 76 MMcf/d in January 1921. The carbon plants received ninety-one percent of the gas. The 1921 estimated consumption capacity of the carbon plants was 108 MMcf/d yielding 95,000 pounds of carbon black per day. This could supply two-thirds of the annual United States consumption of carbon black.

A decade earlier the State Legislature had given the Conservation Commission the power to require the filing of drilling permits with maps of well locations, to require the use of surface casing and cement, and to require that abandoned wells be plugged. In early 1925 the Department of Conservation released a study of the 335 producing wells that were metered by the state in 1921. From 1922 to January 1, 1925, the field produced 290 billion cubic feet of gas. The biggest producer was the Guthrie No. 1 owned by the United Oil and Gas Company that over its life generated 8 billion cf of gas. The second place well (Smith No. 2 of the Ouachita Oil and Natural Gas Company) produced almost 7 billion cubic feet in the period.

Cheap natural gas led directly to the wastage inherent in the carbon black industry. It also led to an experiment in West Virginia with disappointing results. A 1918 study of per capita natural gas consumption looked at the West Virginia experiment of providing free natural gas to households. It found that average annual consumption for each domestic customer was 480,000 cf. In the United States as a whole average annual consumption was 100,000 cf and in the town of Louisville 53,000 cf. The lesson was that free gas led to dramatic wastage even in domestic consumption.[16]

In the spring of 1923 the Ouachita Parish grand jury spent ten days studying allegations that carbon black companies, particularly the Southern Carbon Company, had failed to safeguard the gas. It was alleged that Southern had dodged the meters by using "by passes." The grand jury indicted a number of company officials, but ultimately little immediate relief appeared.[17] The following year outgoing State Attorney General Adolphe V. Coco blasted the Department of Conservation for permitting the Monroe Field to become chaotic. The state's position was that the carbon black companies operated by specific franchises and were limited as to the amount of gas they could pull from their wells.

Saltwater gusher. In South Louisiana oil and salt were entwined. At Monroe, saltwater was ubiquitous and dangerous. Without care, the saltwater could get into the field, damaging its recovery prospects. Here saltwater is dumped onto a field, an environmentally disastrous step soon prohibited and closely monitored.

Right: Map of the heart of the Monroe Gas Field, 1921. Sterlington was later the home of a giant electrical generation plant; down the central corridor is the Peerless Carbon Company, the Southern Carbon Company, and the Louisiana Carbon Company.

MAP COURTESY OF H. W. BELL AND R. A. CATTELL, DEPARTMENT OF CONSERVATION *BULLETIN NO. 9.*

Below: Wild gas crater near Shongaloo, Louisiana. This romantic spot lies along the Arkansas border between Homer and Plain Dealing, Louisiana.

PHOTOGRAPH COURTESY OF THE PERCY VIOSCA, JR., COLLECTION, LOUISIANA AND LOWER MISSISSIPPI VALLEY COLLECTIONS, LOUISIANA STATE UNIVERSITY LIBRARIES, BATON ROUGE, LOUISIANA.

*The Tullos Oilfield. All oilfields have their
bleak side. This image from the Tullos Field
shows a stream of oil or water, a jumble of
trees and parts of a rig following a gusher.*

An enormous public discussion of the carbon black companies erupted. The Department of Conservation reacted to the public pressure by refusing to issue a new carbon black license to a company led by J. Smylie Herkness and represented by Esmond Phelps, a prominent New Orleans attorney. Herkness went into Federal Court to compel the state to issue the license. Wood H. Thompson, first assistant attorney-general for Louisiana, argued "the efficiency of operation in manufacturing carbon black from natural gas is far below the efficiency of using natural gas for fuel purposes, either industrial or domestic. When based on heat units the efficiency of operation in manufacturing carbon black is not over 1.75 percent."[18] The communities that used natural gas, such as Monroe, had an interest in preventing the wastage from such a use. He argued that nearly every other state prohibited carbon black manufacturing from natural gas. "The owners of land do not own the gas lying below it. Such gas is not susceptible of ownership until reduced to possession. Its extraction and use is subject to regulation, or even complete restriction or suppression, by the state."[19] The court came down squarely for the state, putting an end to new carbon black plants in Louisiana. The business had already begun moving to Texas where it was welcomed and remained a significant user of natural gas for fifty years.

The other side of the argument soon appeared as the three parishes involved let it be known that the vast quantity of gas consumed by the carbon black companies still put a large amount of money in the treasuries of the local communities. Many public projects would be halted by the cutback in carbon black companies without more profitable uses. It was then leaked out that the City of Memphis was contemplating a gas line 216 miles to its environs, while a similar one was under construction to New Orleans by the Southern Carbon Company and Standard Oil. The Tullos Oilfield became a three-way intersection for the Southern Gas Line Co. It had a 12-inch pipeline from Monroe to the Tullos Oilfield. From Tullos a line branched west towards Shreveport, and

south towards Alexandria. Standard Oil financed the Interstate line southward. Meanwhile, the Texas Company grabbed part of the action, not content with its role in the south and northwest.

It was thought that this new demand would by itself jack up prices so as to make carbon black manufacturing unfeasible. However a reporter noted that extreme doubt about the New Orleans line existed among professionals. Demand in New Orleans was so variable and cheap Mexican fuel oil delivered to New Orleans satisfied much of the industrial demand.[20]

A speech in July 1926 by State Representative Thomas Davis Berry extolled Monroe's new prosperity based on gas and carbon black. Monroe's population had increased from 12,000 to 20,000 over the past six years. Seven hundred thousand dollars had been spent on public schools.[21] The number of automobiles in the northeast part of the state had tripled in the three years from 1922 to 1925.[22] Louisiana politicians generally endorsed the status quo by backing the existing regulations of the Conservation Commission. Two weeks later Louisiana Senator T. L. Hood

spoke to a luncheon meeting in Monroe. His point was that the legislature was not likely to act against the carbon black industry. He felt the Department of Conservation had successfully reduced waste and consumption. The allowable was then at 275 MMcf/d, just slightly more than that projected for the later giant offshore Mars Field. He predicted the demise of the carbon black industry once the price of gas rose because other more profitable uses appeared. West Virginia, he pointed out, had once suffered from those companies, but a price rise quickly drove them out. They landed in Louisiana and Texas. The carbon black industry pumped $300,000 into the three parishes, along with $100,000 in severance taxes to the state.[23] Another use for the gas was to drive the Louisiana Power and Light generating station at Sterlington that opened in 1925. It became a major electrical source for the region. About this time, too, the size of the Monroe Field was extended yet again with the completion of S. D. Hunter's well to the southwest of Monroe.[24]

Later in 1926 United States senator from Louisiana Joseph E. Ransdell painted another picture of the carbon black industry. A study of the gas usage "provides but meager grounds for complimenting either the state or the Monroe District for its stewardship." Part of the problem, he said, was that once out of the ground the gas belonged to the individual land owner and it was hard to persuade them to conserve. The accounting showed that 18 percent of the gas brought up was completely wasted into the air. Seventy-five percent was used in the carbon black industry, a process that wasted virtually all of the heat potential of the gas. Only seven percent went to the production of light and heat. The only bright spot he found was that the allowable for the carbon black industry had been reduced over the previous year and a half from 300 million cubic feet a day to 243 MMcf/d.[25] He felt that one major interstate pipe line could drive the price of gas high enough to suppress completely the carbon black industry.

The *Times-Picayune* reported in the fall of 1925 that a 16-inch pipe had been started from Bastrop, apparently headed for Baton Rouge. H. C. Morris, trustee, was the mastermind.[26] The following spring brought confirmation of the rumored Standard Oil line to compete with the Morris line. The New York firm of Ford, Bacon and Davis, Inc., was to start the project about April 1, 1926. Both it and the Morris line were to cross the Mississippi at Natchez, turn south through two Mississippi counties, then proceed to Baton Rouge. At the same time unnamed investors announced two gas lines to be built from the Monroe Field to Pine Bluff, Arkansas. The town was then getting its gas from Arkansas Gas Company, but the Monroe Field gas was to be used for a $5 million dollar paper mill at Camden, Arkansas.[27]

The battle over gas wastage continued through the 1920s. Legislators made several attempts to increase the severance tax on gas already at three percent of gross value at the well head. This rate was the highest in the nation, followed by Oklahoma at three percent of net value at the well head (less royalty). Though the local businessmen tended to support the carbon black industry, the newspapers remained distinctly critical. The *Monroe News-Star* ran a column in November 1928 calling attention to the three cratered wells in

Richland Parish Field as well as an incipient problem of leaky pipelines that waste gas.[28]

From the first discovery well in the Monroe Gas Field everyone dreamed of a pipeline extending 250 miles south to the state's largest city—New Orleans. The city had recently come out of a reform phase that saw the rebuilding of the port, the public schools, and city government. New Orleans had rapidly become important to the Gulf Coast oil industry. In 1921 it was the nation's largest oil port in total exports and imports of petroleum products. Its rival at the time was Lake Charles, or as the *New Orleans Item* put it, the Sabine District which included Galveston, Texas. By 1921 New Orleans had seven refineries with a daily capacity of 65,050 barrels. Before 1911 there were no refineries in Louisiana; by 1922 there were twenty. Refinery capacity in the United States had increased to 2.3 million barrels per day. New Orleans' share was three percent and growing. Besides refining, the New Orleans area had enormous storage or bunkerage warehouses. In 1921 Louisiana produced five percent of the nation's oil equaling twenty-six million barrels. New Orleans' exports of oil soared after World War I, rising from 8.1 million barrels in 1919 to 22.5 million barrels in 1921. That year New Orleans was the second largest oil importer with 15 million barrels, Galveston was first at 16.1 million barrels. The United States imported 105 million barrels of crude oil then. In the twenty-first century that number grew to 20 billion barrels.[29]

By 1922 the refineries were:

- Mexican Petroleum Corporation, Destrehan, value $2 million, capacity 25,000 barrels/day
- New Orleans Refining Company, Norco, value $2.5 million, capacity 30,000 barrels/day
- Island Refining Corporation, Good Hope, value $2 million, capacity 20,000 barrels/day
- Sinclair Oil Company, Mereaux, value $1.5 million, 5,000 barrels/day
- Pelican Oil Refining Company, Chalmette, value $225 thousand, 1,200 barrels/day
- Liberty Oil Refining Company, New Orleans, value $100,000, 1,200 barrels/day
- Chalmette Oil and Refining Company, Chalmette, value $1 million, 650 barrels/day

*Above: Huey Long and outgoing Governor
O. H. Simpson, 1928.*
PHOTOGRAPH COURTESY OF THE NEW ORLEANS
PUBLIC LIBRARY.

Below: Picture in Times-Picayune *August
23, 1928, showing Miss Esther Hall turning
the valve at the "city gate" allowing natural
gas to flow to 8,000 NOPSI customers.*

City's Natural Gas Turned On

A turn of a valve in the pipeline at the "city gate" sent natural
gas through mains in the Carrollton section and into the homes
of more than 8000 customers of New Orleans Public Service
Inc. Wednesday afternoon. Miss Esther Hall, daughter of
Utilities Commissioner William T. Hall, is shown as she turned
the valve, with W. P. Simpson, a director of Public Service, on
her right, and T. Semmes Walmsley, acting mayor, and Colonel
Marcel Garsaud, general manager of the dock board, on her left.

The United States remained a net exporter of oil products until 1949, and did not return to that category until 2011.

Another New Orleans reform was the combination of some of the principal public franchises into the hands of one company. A hodgepodge of gas, electricity, and transit companies competed against one another and after World War I most were in receivership. In 1922 the city council created a new private company, the New Orleans Public Service, Inc. (NOPSI), into which it forced the consolidation of those services. The company soon branched out into power generation, even as water and sewerage remained firmly municipal. Monroe's cheap natural gas soon had New Orleans clamoring for the transition from artificial gas to natural gas, much as towns across the northern part of the state had successfully accomplished.

This juncture presented a major opportunity for bold actions on NOPSI's part. The reverse transpired. NOPSI took out five quarter-page advertisements to show why it was not feasible for the company to provide domestic natural gas. The first ad began with the conclusion: "Our directors have felt that it was beyond the scope of the company's operations to embark upon the hazardous enterprise of attempting to acquire gas holdings and to pipe gas from the Monroe Field (the only dependable source) to this city...."[30] NOPSI did have a plan. They proposed to buy gas (25 MMcf/d) from the Ford, Bacon and Davis pipeline that had been built with Standard Oil money from the Monroe Field to Baton Rouge and then to Destrehan. This pipeline was completed on September 1, 1927. NOPSI proposed to link up with the pipeline there and supply gas to industry, with any remainder going into the artificial gas network. The proposed quantity of gas purchased by NOPSI was half the output of one large well in the field. The ads were fulsome in detailing the difficulties of supplying gas to the city. The City of Chicago needed seven times as much gas overall as New Orleans, but New Orleans' peak demand often equaled Chicago's peak demand. The resulting tremendous variation in demand would require a large capacity gas plant to be used comparatively seldom. This ad noted that New Orleans was not rated a "Good Gas City" like Chicago. A related problem was the unfavorable load factor that would mean, if NOPSI built another line, much of the time the line would not be used to capacity, making it difficult to regain its investment. Industrial use appealed to NOPSI. Industrial use was much more even and predictable, so that it was what the company would provide.[31]

In response to the negative attitude of New Orleans Public Service, Inc. the city council employed experts J. W. Billingsley of New Orleans and the firm of Forstall, Robinson and Luqueer of New York to study the possibilities for natural gas in New Orleans.[32] Besides NOPSI's plan, it was to be expected that the Old Regular political ring would put a plan into play. Recorder of Mortgages Augustus Williams proposed a plan to supply both domestic and industrial natural gas. Perhaps here is where the idea for a municipal gas company originated. The city council had charged its hired experts to study the feasibility of municipal ownership of its power.

The city's experts, Billingsley and associates, proposed to have their report on April 5, 1928. However, in the interim NOPSI began laying gas mains in the streets of New Orleans. The city fathers immediately reacted, crying injunction and other moans, to prevent NOPSI from preempting the struggle for cheap natural gas by tying up the streets with their own mains. Under the heading "Collision" the *Times-Picayune* editorialized begging for a non-legal solution. The editors thought it likely that "there are belligerents on one or both sides who would like nothing better than to sew up in the courts for an indefinite period this whole question of natural gas.... That might mean months—or possibly years—of inaction, with the city officials parading their injunction-tied hands as proof that the delay was not their fault, and Public Service blandly sitting tight and marking time...."[33]

The outcome of the drive for inexpensive natural gas was, not surprisingly, the entry of Huey Long into the fray. From a seat on the Public Service Commission, in 1928 Long moved into the governor's office. In June 1928 he held a conference in the "Gold Room" of the Roosevelt Hotel where he twisted arms. For almost a year NOPSI and the city council had been battling over what NOPSI would charge its customers. NOPSI wanted $1.15 per Mcf plus a 50 cents a month meter charge. Long persuaded NOPSI to accept a price of 90 cents a Mcf plus a 25 cents a month meter charge. Meanwhile Commissioner of Finance T. Semmes Walmsley demanded a lower rate and introduced ordinances to slash electric

rates and modify NOPSI's franchise. An "Indignation Meeting" called by labor, probably with the consent of the Old Regular political organization, drew a thousand participants backing lower rates. A main grievance was Long's interference in New Orleans' affairs. Long's influence stemmed from his ability to stop some key bills sought by the city to permit it to municipalize public services.

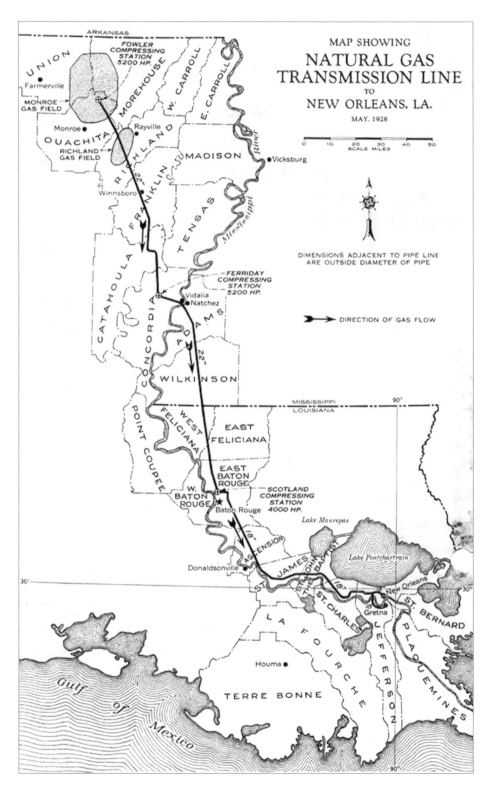

Natural Gas line from Monroe to New Orleans. Beginning at the Fowler Compressing Station, northeast of Monroe, a 22-inch line goes south…to Baton Rouge, then an 18-inch runs southeast to New Orleans. NOPSI, Study of Natural Gas Situation at New Orleans (May 1928).
PAMPHLET COURTESY OF THE NOEL LIBRARY, LOUISIANA STATE UNIVERSITY SHREVEPORT.

MAP SHOWING
NATURAL GAS
TRANSMISSION LINE
TO
NEW ORLEANS, LA.
MAY, 1928

The Gold Room conference then led to Long's legislative package that featured increased severance taxes on natural resources and a special tax on the carbon black industry dedicated to pay for free text books for public school children. With the council acceptance of the NOPSI offer, it quickly appeared that state permission for the city purchase of gas properties would fly through.[34]

Meanwhile, NOPSI was busy urging citizens to purchase electric refrigerators by Frigidaire, Copeland, Superior, General Electric, Kelvinator, Electrolux, Majestic and Bohn.

The big gas pipeline into New Orleans deserved to be famous for another feature.[35] By 1920 welding technology had reached a stage at which safe welds could be reliably produced and as a consequence continuously welded transmission pipeline could be constructed. Randomly generated soil electrical currents routinely damaged pipelines. Engineers had been searching for a practical form of cathodic protection. New Orleanian Robert J. Kuhn installed the first cathodic protection rectifier in 1928 on a long-distance gas pipeline in New Orleans, and thus inaugurated the first practical application of cathodic protection of pipelines. At the Washington Conference for Corrosion Protection held by the National Bureau of Standards in 1928, Kuhn reported on the significant value of his experiments, on which the entire modern technology of cathodic protection is founded.

The Monroe Gas Field thus had an amazing effect on Louisiana. Reliable and plentiful natural gas reached the major towns of the state. The parasitical carbon black industry helped to finance a center piece of the Long legislative program—free textbooks. Another surprise was the transformation of the carbon

black companies into pipeline companies. The carbon black companies had acquired large holdings in the Monroe Field. Once the price equations changed, it was an easy matter to redirect their gas from their own carbon black plants to interstate pipelines. In early 1929, for example, the Columbians Carbon Company announced it was promoting several pipeline projects. The Interstate Natural Gas Pipeline Company reported that it secured much of its gas from Columbian.[36]

Interstate Natural Gas Company ran a 20-inch and a 22-inch pipeline south from the Monroe Field to Vidalia. This was part of the system that resulted in an important test case of the power of the Federal Power Commission.[37] Interstate claimed that it gathered gas from various wells or sellers in the Monroe Field, moved it at well pressure to compressor stations of three purchasing companies (one of which was an affiliate of United Gas), then at the higher pressure the gas moved in pipelines across state lines. But, the sales of the gas had already taken place before the gas moved into the interstate pipelines of the three purchasers. So Interstate argued it was not involved in the interstate transmission of gas.

The U.S. Supreme Court disagreed. It found that virtually all of Interstate's gas was actually in the interstate business. Based on 1941 gas sales, the U.S. Supreme Court found that Interstate owed over a half a million dollars back to the purchasers. Furthermore, it appeared that one of the purchasers was an affiliate of Interstate. The excessive charges had been passed on by the purchasing companies to their buyers in several states as far away as Illinois. These excessive costs thus ended up in the consumer rate base.

One of the sources of the National Gas Act of 1938 was a series of Supreme Court decisions denying states the power to regulate the sale of gas intended for interstate use. The Interstate Natural Gas Company used these decisions to avoid regulation by the State of Louisiana. The U.S. Supreme Court went on to compliment the State of Louisiana. "The state, in a series of enactments, has made elaborate provision

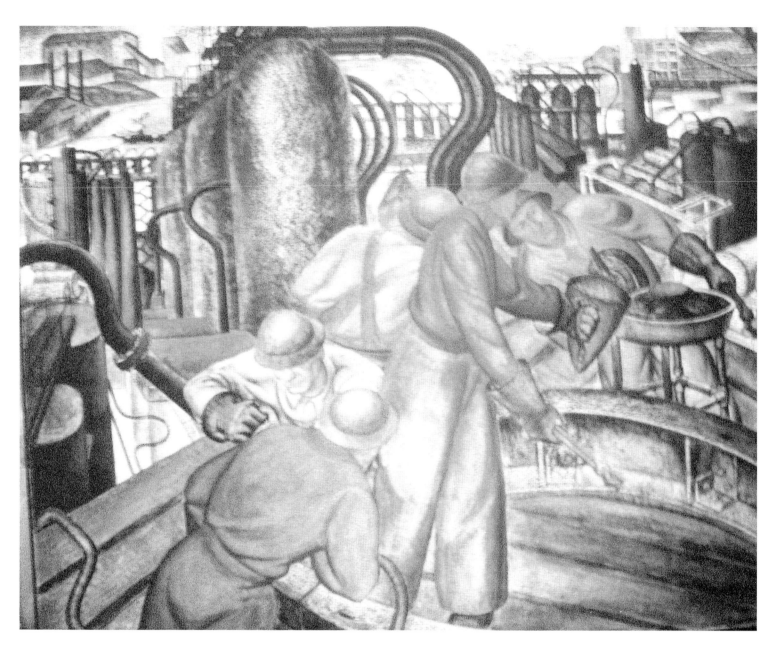

for the conservation of its natural gas resources, and has established various rules and regulations relating to the production and gathering process."

Monroe's Gas Field played a major role in Louisiana natural gas for two more decades and it is still producing. In the 1930s the city of Monroe was bubbling with prosperity. In 1937 Monroe's State Representative Thomas Davis Berry wrote again of Monroe's greatness. Ten natural gas companies, led by the Southern Carbon Company and the United Carbon Company, supplied gas to its 35,000 residents and the entire state. The town had two parks, including the famous Salt Water Natatorium that Monroe had dug looking for gas back in 1909. Three railroad

lines passed through Monroe, the Missouri Pacific, Arkansas & Louisiana Railroad, and the Illinois Central. Its municipal airport was the home of Delta Airlines, soon to move to Atlanta. Joseph A. Bidenharn, the first Coca-Cola bottler in the nation, moved to Monroe in 1912. His two sons Malcolm and Bernard joined the new crop dusting firm that soon became Delta Airlines. Fifty years later they were the largest stockholders in the company. The Monroe Hardware Company was one of the largest in the South.[38] In 1925 Louisiana Power Co. had opened Sterlington, the largest electrical generation plant south of St. Louis, fueled by natural gas. It supplied power to Arkansas, Mississippi as well as Louisiana.

Conrad Albrizio painting of chemical plant workers (probably the great Standard Oil Refinery) at the State Capital Annex, 1938. Oil and gas also made chemicals and plastics.

PHOTOGRAPH COURTESY OF SHAINA POTTS.

Heavy withdrawals from the Monroe Field during World War II paved the way for an important hearing in 1944 before the Federal Power Commission. United Gas Pipeline Company, besides being the major player in North Louisiana, also supplied gas to Memphis. It sought to more than double its pipeline capacity to Memphis so proposed a line with a capacity of 100,000,000 cubic feet a day on top of its large existing lines. The State of Louisiana intervened to protect the integrity of the Monroe Field that had suffered a loss of 229 Bcf in the previous year. United replied that it was also planning to supply its new pipeline from fields along the route, such as Carthage and Rodessa. Testimony then showed that Rodessa was nearing depletion. The witnesses argued over

Below: Map of the United Gas Pipeline system. It shows the presence across the north, as well as the line from Texas along the southern parishes. The company missed the line leading from Monroe to Vidalia and on to New Orleans.

MAP COURTESY OF THE NOEL LIBRARY,
LOUISIANA STATE UNIVERSITY SHREVEPORT.

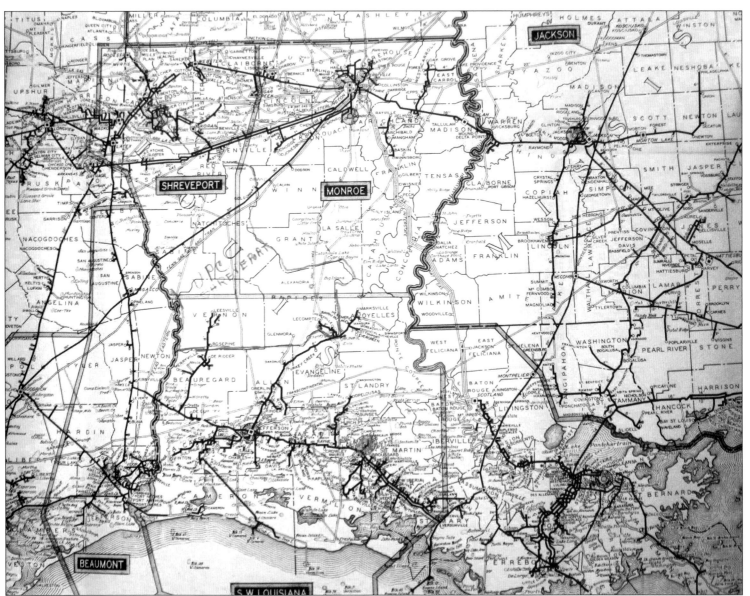

Above: The Richland Field with a well in the distance. Nearby water or gas is being vented.
PHOTOGRAPH COURTESY OF THE STATE LIBRARY OF LOUISIANA.

the reserves remaining in the Monroe Field. It transpired that United had abandoned the Richland section of the field. Some months earlier the geologist for United Gas, John T. Scopes, had testified that Monroe's reserves were down to 2.1 Tcf. Louisiana felt this number justified slowing down withdrawals from the field. United's position, in spite of its geologist's numbers, was that whatever the number was in Monroe, it could get gas from other fields so should be granted the pipeline.[39]

The Monroe Gas Field has continued to produce over the past sixty years. The field remains leased up due to continued production. However, new horizontal drilling technologies breathed new life into the old field. In 2003 Louisiana For Energy 2000 NGC, Inc., awarded a contract to Verdisys, Inc., to drill abandoned wells horizontally. The incredible efficiency of horizontal drilling was expected to yield commercially successful gas production. Verdisys began work on forty-five old wells. But the company's efforts collapsed for lack of capital.

In 2006 the Tulane Environmental Law Clinic and other conservation groups threatened to sue EnerVest Operating LLC, a major operator of natural gas wells in the Monroe Gas Field, to force clean-up of mercury-contaminated wetlands and other soils at gas fields in Ouachita, Union and Morehouse Parishes in North Louisiana. The difficulty went back to the beginning of the field when meters that depended on liquid mercury were installed in the field. Over the decades some had leaked mercury into the ground and streams. Most places, such as federal lands, had banned that type of meter, but the age of Monroe Field worked against replacement. Enervest controlled more than 3,000 producing gas wells in the field.

In migration to Monroe and West Monroe from farms impacted the city most in the 1960s when its population increased from 67,000 to 82,000. The average price of natural gas sold to customers in Louisiana in 2011 was 12 cents Mcf. Considering the tremendous inflation of the past century the 90 cents Long secured looks wildly expensive. But of all the states in the union in 2010 Louisiana ranked behind only Texas and California in natural gas delivered to all consumers— 1.095 Tcf.[40] But the Monroe Field continued to decline from the 1960s. In 1980 Ouachita, Morehouse and Union Parishes were only average producers of gas. Most of Louisiana's gas came from the southern coastal parishes. By 2010 the Monroe Field had dropped further behind. The leading fields were now all in the Northwest in the Haynesville Shale area of Desoto, Caddo, and Bossier Parishes. That year Ouachita Parish produced 4 MMcf; while De Soto produced 644 MMcf.

A meter in the Richland Field.
PHOTOGRAPH COURTESY OF THE STATE LIBRARY
OF LOUISIANA.

A solid wooden drilling rig gushing gas in the Richland Field, c. 1929.

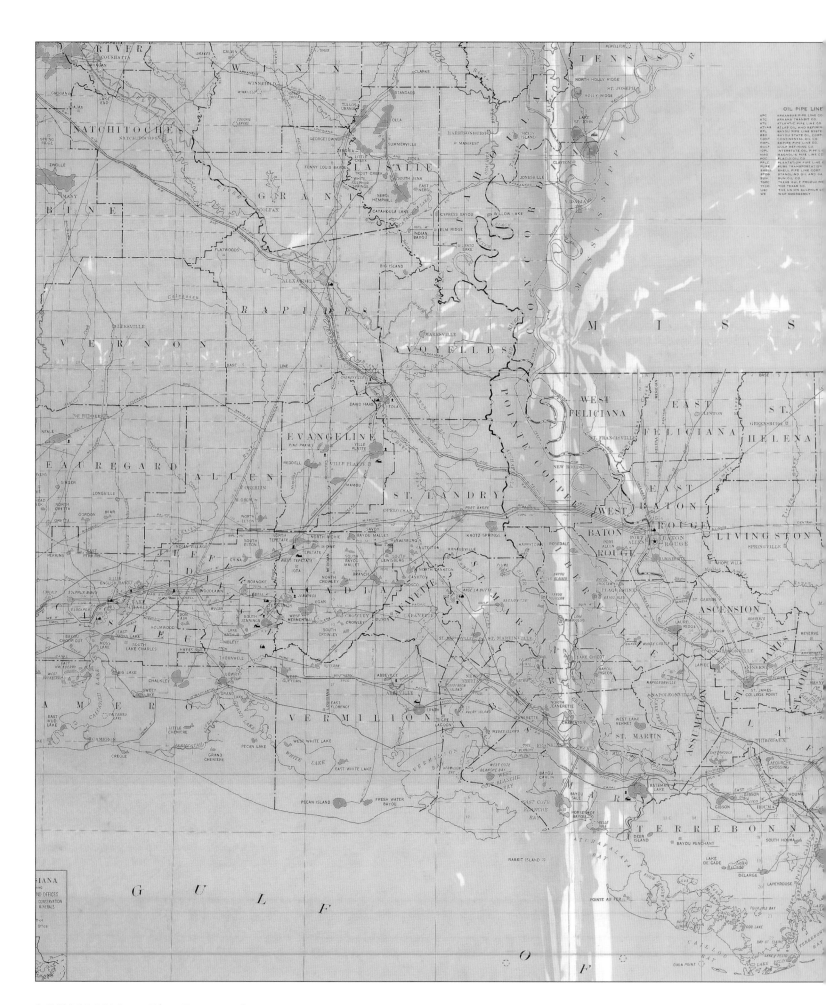

LOUISIANA - *The Energy State*

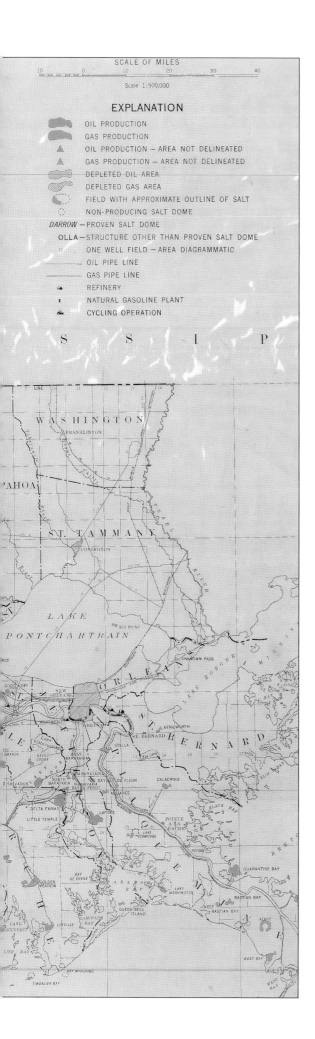

CHAPTER 5

SOUTHEAST LOUISIANA

The grand sequence of oil in Louisiana follows the clockwise rotation of discovery that began in the Southwest, moved to Shreveport and Monroe in the north, and in the 1950s settled in Southeast Louisiana. In the 1950s and 1960s the Southeast accounted for almost a third of the oil well permits in Louisiana. But by the first decade of the twenty-first century Southeast's share of well permits had dropped to a mere sixteen percent. In 2010 these parishes produced 32 million barrels of oil, but it was only about twice the production of just one offshore well, Petronius.

The Southeast has a large block of parishes that contributed little to Louisiana's oil and gas. Well permits in Orleans Parish and its northern neighbors the Floridas have been scarce. From the beginning of the oil industry to today only 1,365 wells have been permitted in Orleans and the Florida Parishes—St. Tammany, Washington, Tangiahoa, Livingston, St. Helena, and East and West Feliciana. By way of comparison, Jefferson Parish alone had 2,995 wells permitted. Leaving out Livingston and St. Helena, impacted by the Tuscaloosa Shale Trend, production in the remaining six Florida Parishes totaled 20,000 barrels in 2010 compared to Jefferson's 1.4 million barrels of oil. In Orleans Parish over the two decades 1980 to 2000 only two organizations produced any significant amount of oil, Apache Corporation and Florida Exploration Company, but the amount was only 60,000 barrels for the twenty years. For natural gas, the story is similar.

Oil and Gas Map of Louisiana, 1947. Detail of Southeast Louisiana.

Well Permits in Southeast Louisiana Parishes with Significant Oil & Gas Production

	1910s	1920s	1930s	1940s	1950s	1960s	1970s	1980s	1990s	2000s	2010s	Totals
SAINT BERNARD		3	29	13	83	391	280	594	121	242		1,756
SAINT CHARLES			8	227	345	433	364	192	56	62	9	1,696
SAINT JAMES		2	8	87	98	123	196	78	23	30	2	647
SAINT JOHN THE BAPTIST			2	13	76	82	66	38	12	7		296
SAINT MARY		35	258	500	948	1,514	988	738	402	372	60	5,815
ASSUMPTION		8	14	65	288	267	246	180	62	59	11	1,200
JEFFERSON			52	250	569	900	467	404	155	190	8	2,995
IBERVILLE	1	17	96	294	498	636	542	450	97	113	15	2,759
LAFOURCHE		34	436	817	2,406	2,248	1,458	1,045	483	392	94	9,413
PLAQUEMINES	2	9	339	920	4,364	5,471	2,643	1,778	923	972	88	17,510
TERREBONNE	8	51	298	470	2,190	2,712	1,884	1,144	698	553	30	10,038
Total Southeast	11	159	1,540	3,656	11,865	14,777	9,134	6,641	3,032	2,992	317	54,124
Percent SE of All	1%	2%	16%	22%	33%	33%	27%	15%	22%	17%	8%	23%
Totals Statewide	1,314	9,130	9,707	16,264	36,425	44,155	34,007	45,683	13,539	17,566	3,733	231,523

🛢️

Above: Table detail of Wells permitted by Parish by Year. Prepared by Kjel C. Brothen, P. E., Office of Conservation, Louisiana Department of Natural Resources.

Opposite, top, left: Table from the Times-Picayune October 22, 1961.

Opposite, top, right: Table detail of Historic Fields of the Southeast Before Offshore.

Opposite, bottom: Geography of the New Orleans area about 3,500-4,000 years ago, showing barrier islands (in black) being covered by the advancing Cocodrie Delta (from Saucier, 1963). This image is found in J. C. Snowden, W. C. Ward, and J. R. J. Studlick, Geology of Greater New Orleans: Its Relationship to Land Subsidence and Flooding (New Orleans Geological Society, 1980) p. 9.

By the process of elimination then, the only interesting part of Southeast Louisiana consists of the parishes of Jefferson, St. Bernard, Plaquemines, Lafourche, Terrebonne, Assumption, St. Charles, St. James, St. John the Baptist, and St. Mary Parish (though on the west side of the Atchafalaya it remains closer to the eastern marsh). Soil type distinguishes the marshes of Southeast Louisiana from those of Southwest Louisiana. The Southeast marshes consist of sediment from the Mississippi River. The Southwest marshes owe their origin to the western rivers that brought different soil to the coast.[1] An early map of Louisiana oilfields dating from 1920 makes the point that there were comparatively few oilfields in Southeast Louisiana. The map on page 88 created by the F. E. Gallup Map Company shows the great fields of the Southwest, the Caddo Fields, and even the incipient Monroe Field, but the Southeast had only oil springs.

The following ranking of oilfields in 1960 demonstrates the new dominance of Southeast Louisiana. Caddo is ninth in millions of barrels of oil. The Louisiana state lands along the coast line are now the leading fields—Callou Island, South Pass Block 24 as shown on the detail table at the top, left of page 87. It already points to the dominance of offshore production, though not the outer continental shelf.

In the Southeast lumbermen and reclamation investors were precursors of the oil and gas industry. At the commencement of the twentieth century the nation-wide demand for farm lands sent hundreds of mid-western farmers to Southwest Louisiana where they fanned out across the prairies on railroad bounty land. In the Southeast, however, the farmers ran into swamp and marsh. So northern developers appeared with an idea—the marsh could be drained. After drying out, they felt that marsh would make splendid farm land. The swamps appealed to northern lumbermen who had already clear cut the forests of Wisconsin and Michigan. They moved to Louisiana and began clearing the swamp of its oak and cypresses.

For thirty years from 1890 to 1920 the most important business along the Harvey Canal was the Louisiana Cypress Lumber Company, founded by Joseph Rathborne. He immigrated to Chicago from Ireland in the

Rank	Field	Year 1960
1	Callou Island	16.7 MMb
2	South Pass Block 24	16.5 MMb
3	Lake Washington	10.7 MMb
4	Bay Marchand Block 2	10.3 MMb
5	West Delta Block 30	7.6 MMb
6	South Pass Block 277	7.4 MMb
7	Main Pass Block 68	7.3 MMb
8	Weeks Island	7.0 MMb
9	Caddo-Pine Island	6.0 MMb
10	Lake Barre	5.3 MMb

Historic Fields of the Southeast Before Offshore

Moving southwest from New Orleans	Moving west from New Orleans, up the river
Paradis	Small fields at every town
Lafitte	Good Hope
Delta Farms	LaPlace
Lake Salvador	Convent
Raceland	Darrow
Golden Meadow	Laurel Ridge
Leeville	University
Gibson	Rosedale
Bateman Lake GAS	Krotz Springs
Bayou Sale	Port Barre
West Cote Blanche	Ville Platte
Weeks Island GAS	
Avery Island OIL	
Erath GAS	

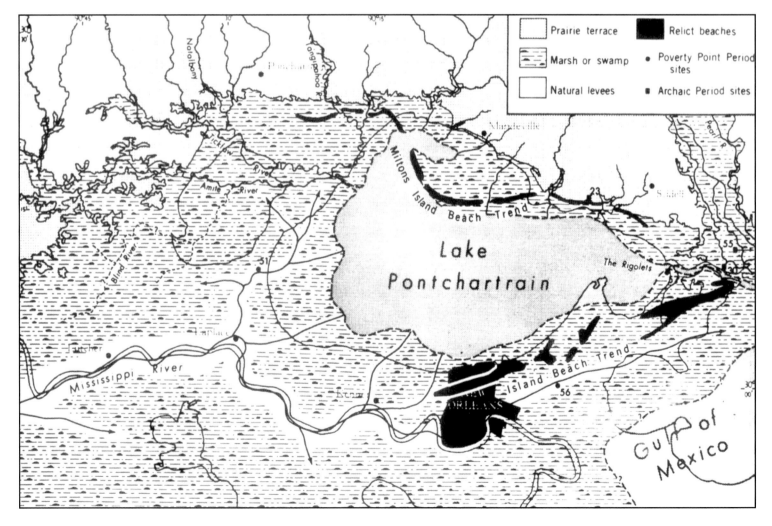

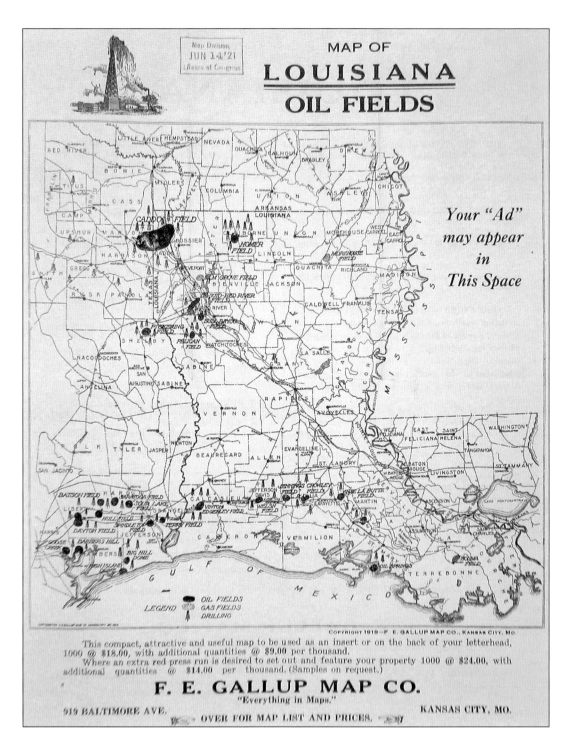

Above: Map of Louisiana oilfields, 1920.

Opposite, top: Four field boilers.

Opposite, bottom: Swivel in the mousehole.

The next length of pipe is prepared for

adding to the drill string.

1870s and went to work for a northern lumber company.[2] In the late 1880s Rathborne heard of the lumber in Louisiana. In 1889 levee districts across the southern part of the state began auctioning swamp lands so as to use the proceeds to erect levees around the developed communities. That year Rathborne purchased the land adjacent to the east bank of the canal to erect the Louisiana Cypress Lumber Company. The Harvey Canal was valuable to it because logs for the mill were floated to the mill from deep in the Barataria Country.

The Louisiana Cypress Lumber Company started slowly, but by 1898 business was booming.[3] Unlike swamp land, timber prices were substantial. The Rathborne Company tried unsuccessfully to purchase for $270,000 a tract in St. Martin Parish estimated to contain 40,000,000 board feet of cypress and 40,000,000 board feet of hardwoods. But the Williams Brothers sawmill at Patterson, Louisiana, got the tract. Nevertheless, as late as 1997 Rathborne enterprises owned 45,000 acres of land in southeastern Louisiana.[4]

Rathborne's heirs acquired his then-cleared lands after his death in 1923. They launched an aggressive oil leasing program over the decades on denuded lands. For example, in 1952, the Joseph Rathborne Land & Lumber Company, Inc., granted an oil, gas, and mineral lease to the California Company for large acreage in St. Charles Parish, Louisiana. The leasing revenues (bonus payment plus rental payment) on the entire 5,834 acres, totaled $2,916,000.[5]

Another lumber baron whose heirs made a second fortune from oil was Frank B. Williams. Beginning in the 1870s at Patterson, Louisiana, he purchased saw mills, developed new logging systems, and acquired land. His biographer asserted that the family never disposed of cutover land. Williams died in 1929.[6] H. L. Lutcher formed the Lutcher and Moore Cypress Lumber Company and came to own 500,000 acres. In the 1890s it made a name for itself selling cypress to the Pennsylvania oilfields for barrels.[7] Just before World War I cypress made Louisiana the number one lumber producer in the United States, surpassing Washington State. Louisiana produced almost four billion board feet, a little over ten percent of the nation's lumber.[8] By 1929 the disappearance of cypress trees forced the cypress lumber mills to close.

Top: Joe Tassin developed the marsh buggy
in the 1930s near Westwego.
PHOTOGRAPH COURTESY OF THE
MINERALS MANAGEMENT SERVICE, VOLUME VI,
AND RUSSELL POIENCOT.

Above: A Model A Ford modified as a
marsh buggy.
PHOTOGRAPH COURTESY OF THE
MINERALS MANAGEMENT SERVICE, VOLUME VI,
AND PETE ROGERS.

Right: Closer look at a marsh buggy.
PHOTOGRAPH COURTESY OF THE
MINERALS MANAGEMENT SERVICE, VOLUME VI,
AND RUSSELL POIENCOT.

Map showing the vast acreage in Southeast Louisiana claimed by Edward Wisner, his successors, and others.

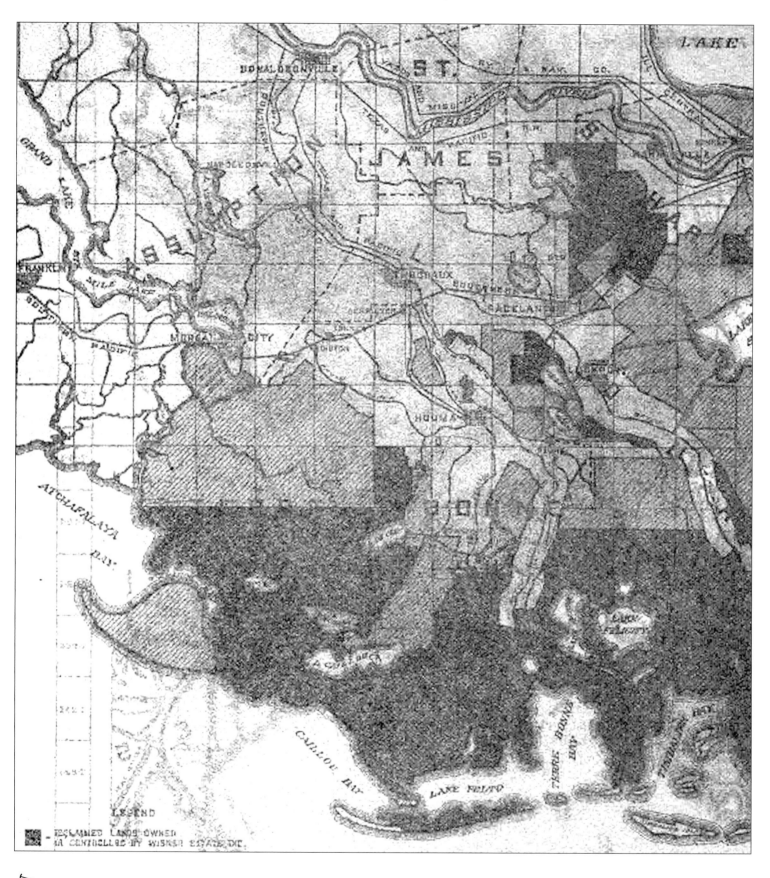

Above and opposite: Slanted hatching means land has been reclaimed. Dark full hatching indicates unreclaimed marsh.

Edward Wisner lands. John A. Fox, The Wisner Estates Incorporated *(New Orleans: Wisner Estates Inc., 1917), attachment.*

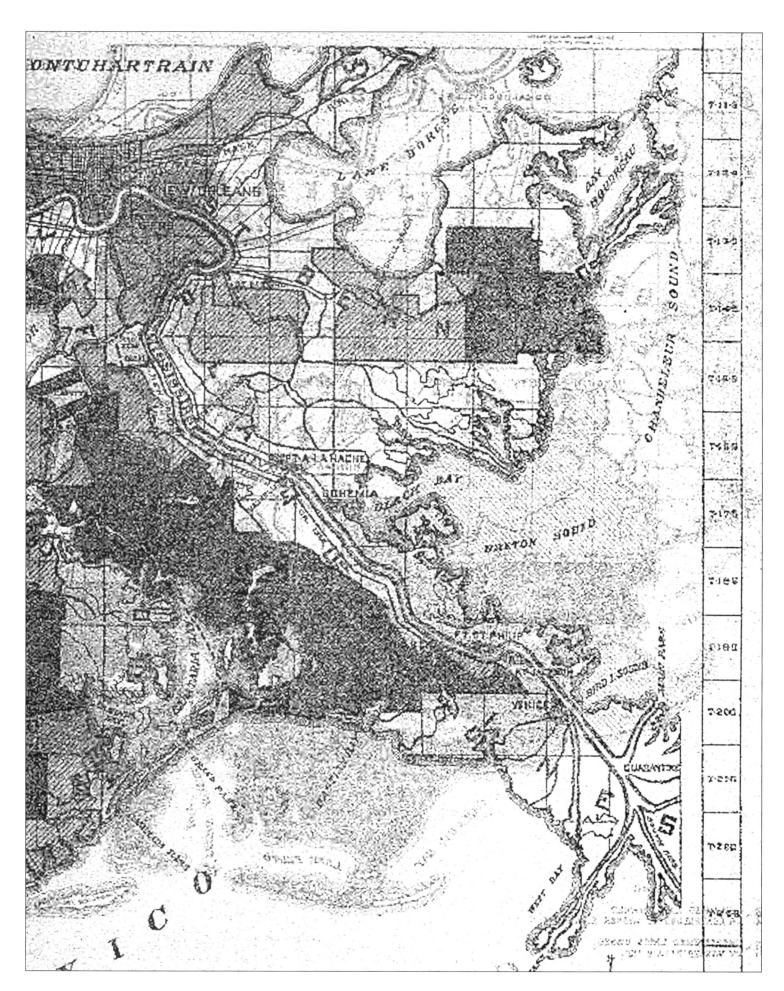

The final clearing of timber from the marshes of Southeast Louisiana about 1930 forced the timber barons into oil and gas exploration. Simultaneously, the would-be reclamation investors turned to oil and gas. Michigan native Edward Wisner was the biggest and in every respect but one the luckiest investor. He died in 1915 just before he could learn the real lesson of reclamation. His heirs had all the luck. Like dozens of northerners in the late nineteenth century, Wisner saw Louisiana's marsh lands as incipient farm land.[9] In an interview in 1909 he predicted Louisiana's marshes would become home to three million people. The reclamation would not be cheap—he thought it would cost $15 an acre. From 1900 until his death in 1915 Wisner acquired a million acres of Louisiana land, or about three percent of the total acreage in the state. Louisiana parish levee boards considered most of it waste land that they sold for as low as 12.5 cents per acre. Wisner reclaimed forty-five sites totaling about 250,000 acres. To make farms, he had to build levees and install steam powered pumping stations to drain each of the sites. The idea for this type of reclamation gathered strength after 1900 when railroads, the new Office of Experiment Stations in the U.S. Department of Agriculture, and Professor W. Gregory of Tulane University joined in proving its feasibility. But by World War I the reclamation idea was dead, killed by its own flaws. Farm land could not be built in marshes.

Wisner's death led to the disposal of 400,000 acres for debts and 600,000 went to H. H. Timken, owner of the Timken Roller Bearing Company in Cincinnati. In the late 1920s the Timkens joined up with Colonel E. F. Simms, a Houston oil man who had acquired leases on a million acres of Louisiana State-owned land along the coast. The two were a natural fit and they formed the Louisiana Land & Exploration Company. At the same time they began using a new technique for locating salt domes—the torsion balance and seismograph method. Applied to the L. L. & E. Co., lands, within a year it located nine new salt domes. Finding oil was a different matter. A string of failed wildcats ran up a debt of $3,000,000. To save the company, the owners made a deal with Texaco. Texaco would put up cash, and agree to drill at least four wells on each of the domes within ten years. A second round of seismic search in 1934 using refraction technology yielded L. L. & E. Co., and its partner Amerada Petroleum Corporation three

Right: A steam rig owned by Saltana Drilling working for Texaco near Paradis.
PHOTOGRAPH COURTESY OF THE MINERALS MANAGEMENT SERVICE, VOLUME VI, AND DONALD NAQUIN.

Below: Crew houseboat on coastal canal at White Lake, Louisiana. The houseboat is built on a cypress barge, 1936.
History of the Offshore Oil and Gas Industry in Southern Louisiana *by Diane Austin and Justin Gaines.*
PHOTOGRAPH COURTESY OF THE MINERALS MANAGEMENT SERVICE, VOLUME VI, AND JERRY CUNNINGHAM.

Opposite: The Phillips 66 drilling barge J. P. Stephens *as a marsh rig.*
PHOTOGRAPH COURTESY OF THE MINERALS MANAGEMENT SERVICE, VOLUME VI, AND MERRILL UTLEY, SR., AND MERRILL UTLEY, JR.

more domes: Bayou des Allemands, Raceland, and Lake Chicot. In 1938 L. L. & E. Co., located the Golden Meadow Dome.

Despite setbacks, by the 1970s L. L. & E. Co., was reaping $40,000,000 a year from these domes. The ownership of L. L. & E. Co., passed to Burlington Resources, Inc., and then to Conoco Phillips. It remains headquartered in New Orleans though it operates worldwide.

Other Midwestern investors in Louisiana land did not fare so well. Early in the twentieth century Frederick Scully of Lincoln, Illinois, acquired thousands of acres on the east bank of Bayou Lafourche. Clovelly Farms, a 2,500 acre tract diked with pumps, hosted many houses, a school, and a store. For several decades hired hands grew corn, potatoes and other vegetables. Scully probably invested more than $500,000 in the project over the years. By the 1960s the danger of subsidence drove everyone from Clovelly. The Clovelly Salt Dome is now used for Louisiana Offshore Oil Port storage. LOOP injected fresh water to create eight caverns 230 feet in diameter and 750 feet in height, each with a capacity of about 4,000,000 barrels of oil. Salt dissolves in water, but not in oil. Oil and water do not mix. Thus oil in a salt dome will remain trapped. Saturated saltwater injected into the dome, being heavier, will go directly to the bottom, forcing oil in the dome upwards to the delivery pipelines. The terminal consists of eight caverns with a total capacity of 50 million barrels, a pump station with four 6,000-horsepower pumps, meters to measure the crude oil receipts and deliveries, and a 25-million-barrel brine storage reservoir. The brine reservoir is supersaturated with salts to prevent further degradation of the massive salt dome.

Below: Panorama of the Standard Oil Company of Louisiana refinery. In 1916, the refinery covered some 500 acres on the east bank of the Mississippi River near Baton Rouge and employed more than 2,000 men producing products under the "Stanocola" trade name. Their sales office in New Orleans took up most of the twelfth floor of the Whitney Central Bank Building. Standard had founded its refinery in 1909 and by the 1920s it was at the center of Louisiana gasoline production. In 1914 cracking of oil led to the production of gasoline, though the initial yield was only 18 percent. By the 1920s that number had risen to 40 percent. At the end of the decade Standard Oil Louisiana played an important role in the merging of some German and American patents to produce the process of hydrogenation of petroleum. This high temperature, high pressure process, yielded almost 100 percent of the gasoline. The first test plant began operation at Baton Rouge in 1928. Times-Picayune June 17, 1929. At the end of World War II the Standard refinery again made history with enormous improvements in the cracking of oil and production of gasoline.

Above: Golden Meadow in the 1940s.

PHOTOGRAPH COURTESY OF THE
MINERALS MANAGEMENT SERVICE, VOLUME VI,
AND MELVIN BERNARD

Clarence Cheramie at the site of the
Golden Meadow blowout next to the
Texas Company Canal. It was said that
neighbors could not put their wash on the
line for months afterward because the
airborne droplets continued to fall and
coat everything, 1937.

Other reclamation projects foundered similarly. In 1908 Henry L. Doherty, the founder of Cities Service Oil Company, purchased 46,000 acres south of Lake Salvador. The levees around Delta Farms, his centerpiece, broke in 1928, and for the last time in 1971 when the place was abandoned.[10] Chicago attorney Cornelius Jon Ton purchased a section of land northwest of Lake Cataouatche in 1910. After spending $500,000 of mainly Dutch money, the Hurricane of 1915 finished it off. Chicago investor, John Cruise, founded Churchill Farms, another diked community that eventually filled with water. Failed reclamation projects across southeast Louisiana proved to be excellent oil leasing prospects.

Southeastern Louisiana did not come into its own for oil and gas production until the late 1930s. The successes in the late 1930s were all around the Bayou Lafourche area with good fields at Des Allemands, Raceland, and Golden Meadow.[11] The new prominence was aided not by just the number of new fields opened, but by the arrival of a new writer on the staff of the *Times-Picayune*. William H. Weathersby wrote weekly of drilling across the state, but 1939 saw the biggest new wells in the Southeast. "Unprecedented success in wildcat operations in the past few weeks in the Southeast Louisiana oil producing area has brought with enrichment of the section additional problems for the department of conservation in proration."[12] This was the year that Paradis became a success having failed as a community, reclamation area, and farm land. The Texas Company was the leading driller in both the Paradis and Lafitte finds. "Leasing and royalty purchasing at Paradis has been active in the past few weeks, and the interests held by independent operators probably will lead to rapid expansion," reported the *Times-Picayune* on December 13, 1939. An independent, D. D. Feldman of Houston, paid $15,000 for a lease with the burdensome clause that drilling must commence within ninety days. The principal landholder in the area was Louisiana Land & Exploration Company, allied with the Texas Company. From the inception of the field until 1977 it produced 155 million barrels of oil and 760 million cubic feet of gas. Shortly after 1977 it withered away and produced only another 25 million barrels till 2012.[13]

Along with Paradis, finds at Barataria, Laplace, Lafourche Crossing, all contributed to the new feeling that the Southeast had arrived. "All of these have helped to bring the oil boom to New Orleans and its surrounding area. They have also served to shift the principal scene of oil exploration work in Louisiana and to cause more problems…in proration." The difficulty was that Louisiana was already producing over its national allotment of 259,000 barrels daily. How the Commissioner of Conservation would fit in the new fields was not solved until the demands of war intervened.

The difficulties of oil exploration common to the other parts of Louisiana also plagued the Southeast. In 1938 several efforts were made in Orleans Parish, notably New Orleans East near the Chef Menteur on a large tract owned by the Louisville & Nashville Railroad. The wildcatter was W. T. Burton, independent oil operator of Lake Charles, who launched two more wells to go with the two he had previously drilled. By the end of 1938 seven sites were being drilled or explored in Orleans and St. Bernard Parishes. Besides the four Burton wells, William Helis was preparing to drill No. 1 Mereaux and Nunez in the rear of Chalmette. Vendome Petroleum was preparing to drill several miles east of Poydras in St. Bernard. Gulf Oil was also drilling in Lake Borgne with nothing to show for it. In 1941 Gulf Oil Refining drilled a well in Plaquemines Parish that blew out, destroying the derrick and rig. It took several days to cap. While it was blowing it sent 150,000,000 cf of gas a day into the atmosphere. In early 1941 the California Company drilled a wildcat in East Lake Borgne in St. Bernard Parish while simultaneously drilling in the Stella Field in Plaquemines Parish. Point au Fer in Southwest Terrebonne

This reclamation map of Louisiana was prepared in 1917, just two years after the great hurricane of 1915. The map shows the path of the 1909 and 1915 storms. The storms flooded the reclamation projects and ended the dream of new farmland.

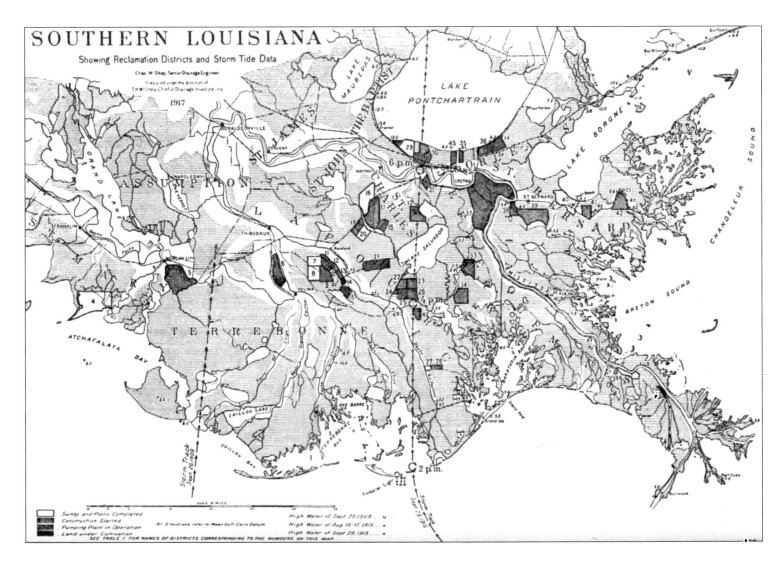

was thrown into confusion by the sudden abandonment of a deep well by the Barnsdall Oil Company. In Iberville Parish the Titanic Oil Company drilled a wildcat into the St. Gabriel prospect at more than 9,000 feet. "The St. Gabriel prospect is another area which has survived the discouraging effects of several dry holes to attract the attention of wildcatters again...."[14] Two years earlier the Texas Company had launched a wildcat in Vermillion Bay in Iberia Parish and taken it down to 10,240 feet where an electrical log showed only some oil. Vermillion Bay had been noted for its gas.[15] These dry holes and blowouts evoked the difficulties already experienced in the western part of the state.

In the later 1930s the Southeast witnessed the first steps offshore Louisiana. Gulf Oil discovered and developed the West Bay Field ten miles south of Venice along the shore just west of "Head of Passes." It illustrates a feature of the oil industry that should not be forgotten. Many fields produce for decades or more. The West Bay Field produced 219 MMB of oil by 1982. Though its rate declined, in 2010 it still produced just under a million barrels. The field also yielded gas, and is still ranked thirtieth among gas fields in the Southern part of the state. The highest yielding field in South Louisiana in 2010 was Lake Washington in Plaquemines Parish, just north and inland from West Bay. Lake Washington produced more than four times as much oil as West Bay. It was a major field in the 1960s ranking of fields in Louisiana. Its operator, Swift Energy Company, described the field as "an inland-water field that produces from multiple stacked Miocene sand layers that radiate outward and downward from the surface of a centrally located salt dome. The salt dome itself has surface depths that vary from 1,200 feet at its peak down to about 14,000 feet, and the water covering the field varies in depth from about 2 feet to 12 feet."[16]

In the Southeast a Greek immigrant, who had arrived in the United States in 1904, settled in Dallas and invested in Louisiana. William G. Helis founded a family of exploration and production companies that created a substantial empire. He invested and drilled in many places in the Southeast, such as the eastern end of Orleans Parish,

By State Lease 00318 dated 1935. William T. Burton acquired the bottoms of Lakes Maurepas, Ponchartrain, and St. Catherine, as well as all streams and bayous that flow into them, but only up to a distance of one mile from the lake. The Mineral Board cancelled the lease in 1975 from SONRIS. Burton helped organize the Win or Lose Oil Company. In 1936 State Lease 340 granted Burton virtually all of the state lands off of Terrebonne, Vermilion, Iberia and St. Mary Parishes.

SL 340   340
Baton Rouge, Louisiana
_Jn_ _4th_ 1936.

TO THE HONORABLE JAMES A. NOE, GOVERNOR OF THE STATE OF LOUISIANA:

        In conformity with your Notice for Publication dated January 9th, 1936, published in the official journal of the State, advertising that sealed bids will be received at your office on or before the 4th day of February, 1936, at eleven o'clock, A. M., for the lease of the oil, gas and other mineral rights in and to the following described property in Vermilion, Iberia, St. Mary, and Terrebonne Parishes, State of Louisiana, to-wit:

        "All of the property now or formerly constituting the beds and other bottoms of lagoons, lakes, gulfs, bays, coves, sounds, inlets and other water bodies, and also all islands and other lands belonging to the State of Louisiana and not under lease from the State on the date of application, namely, Jan. 8th, 1936, and being situated or included within the following described boundaries:

        "Beginning on the mean high water line at the most westerly tip of Terrebonne Parish, La., known as Pointe au Fer, and running along said mean high water line as it follows the shores of Atchafalaya Bay, Four League Bay, East Bay, Morrison's Cut-off, Bayou Sale Bay, East Cote Blanche Bay, West Cote Blanche Bay, Jaws or Litte Bay, Vermilion Bay, Weeks Bay, and of all lagoons, lakes, bays, coves, sounds, inlets, and other water bodies adjoining or forming arms of said named bays, excluding, however, all rivers, creeks, streams or bayous tributary thereto, said mean high water line, with the exception of that part bordering Four League Bay or arms thereof, following the shores of Terrebonne, St. Mary, Iberia and Vermilion Parishes, to the most eastern point on that promentory of land forming the west side of Southwest Pass; thence in a general westerly direction along the short of the Gulf of Mexico to the dividing line between Cameron and Vermilion Parishes; thence south along said dividing line into the marginal or maritime belt of the Gulf of Mexico to the extreme limit or boundary of the domain, territory, and sovereignty of the State of Louisiana; thence easterly along said limit or boundary to a point due south of place of beginning; thence north to place of beginning, including in particular the beds and bottoms of Vermilion Bay, Weeks Bay, West Cote Blanche Bay, Jaws or Litte Bay, East Cote Blanche Bay, Bayou Sale Bay, Morrison's Cut-off, East Bay, Atchafalaya Bay and Four League Bay, Southwest Pass and part of the Gulf of Mexico; this particularization, however, not being or intended to be all-inclusive.

the LSU campus in Baton Rouge, and various water bottoms. He got mixed up in one proto scandal that seems to prefigure the dealings of the Win or Lose Oil Company. The dispute was almost an inevitable consequence of the complex regulations governing oil drilling. Early on Helis had invested in Leeville, and by 1934 seven companies were drilling the pool subject to a very restrictive proration decree from the state of 17,000 barrels a month. Helis' lease had originally gone to A. Guidry for $500 and the normal 1/8 royalty to the state. Instead of drilling, Guidry quickly sold the lease to Helis at a substantial markup. In a familiar form of oilfield payment, Helis agreed to pay Guidry the first $200,000 he made from just 1/8 of the 7/8 he owned. If drilling did not pay, Guidry would get virtually nothing. The number $200,000 then went around with the claim that Helis had bribed the administration with that sum. To this claim was added the charge that Helis had been given 1/3 of the entire proration for the Leeville pool.

The bribery claim was then sent to Washington where Roosevelt's New Deal had inaugurated a vast extension of federal power over oil and gas. The enmity between the Huey Long government in Louisiana and the Roosevelt administration threatened to bring down the lease. Helis responded vigorously, denying everything, including any connection with Long. He had never met Long. "This company is owned and controlled by me," said Mr. Helis. "I am not a politician and have no partisan interest in politics. I am engaged in the oil business and brought in the first real oil well in the Leesville Field." Dr. J. A. Shaw, the respected head of the Minerals Division of the Office of Conservation, was also quoted as saying the allotment had been handled in a professional way. The upshot of the dispute was nothing. However, Helis must have learned something about politics. In January 1937 Helis, now described as an oil magnate, was one of the seventy-six men who took the train to Washington for Roosevelt's second inauguration. Other members of this train ride were W. H. McFadden, millionaire oil man, New Orleans; Ulic J. Burke, secretary and manager of the Choctaw Club; Captain William A. Bisso, Old Regular political leader; Alfred D. Danziger; R. L. Gay of Zwolle, Louisiana, oil man; Harry Jacobs, state engineer; and Judge Leander Perez, district attorney for St. Bernard and Plaquemines Parishes.[17]

The four decades after Roosevelt's death were the boom years for southeast Louisiana. Four wildcatters epitomized the era—Earl Burke, "Doc" Pennington, Louis J. Roussel, and J. Michael Poole. Earl Burke made a splash in the marshes of South Louisiana. A graduate of New Orleans' St. Aloysius High School he joined Chevron's Bay Marchand staff as a roughneck just before the offshore exploration moratorium. After more education and new discoveries in 1974 he drilled a deep well for his own account in what came to be the Kaplan Field in Vermilion Parish.[18] He went on to drill 127 wells below 15,000 feet, a characteristic depth for South Louisiana.

Claude ("Doc") Pennington started in optometry, but quit to develop lands that he felt had the potential for large energy production. After drilling in the Darrow and Lobdell Fields, the Port Hudson structure north of Baton Rouge captured his interest. The president of a Chicago bank owned a thousand acres there. Instead of leasing it to

Above: Louis J. Roussel, Jr.

Below: The front door to Roussel's offices in the American Bank Building, fifteenth floor.

Pennington, he sold it. Pennington then approached Amoco with the idea of a Tuscaloosa test. Georgia Pacific No. 1, as the well was named, became the discovery well for the original Tuscaloosa Trend that stretched across the middle of the state and ended at the Rigolets. Chevron had drilled the first Tuscaloosa well on Alma Plantation near White Castle in May of 1975. The heart of the Tuscaloosa was a giant structure north of Baton Rouge with outliers named the Judge Digby Field and the Port Hudson Field. The most famous well was the Chevron #1 Parlange that blew out on August 13, 1977. When it was controlled, for sixty days it pumped 140 million cubic feet of gas a day into the Florida sales line. The Tuscaloosa Trend has had other dramatic and beneficial effects. The income from the Chevron blowout well led to the restoration of Parlange Plantation. This icon of Creole country houses in Pointe Coupee Parish has been in the hands of the Parlange family for a century or more. By the 1980s it was tired and needed significant restoration.

Also in 1977 Amoco's #1 Georgia Pacific opened the Port Hudson Field with 161 feet of new gas sand. Pennington, the land owner, saw the field produce 103 BCF and 9,250,168 barrels of condensate.[19] The land itself has yielded a large part of its projected $4 billion worth of minerals. Pennington went on to become one of the richest men in the United States. One of his charities was Pennington Biomedical Research Center at LSU that he funded with $125,000,000.[20]

Louis J. Roussel was the classic Southeast Louisiana wildcatter. He fought and scratched. He grabbed opportunities as they came along. He didn't have any cash, so he learned to take small parts in large projects that made other people rich. Then, they made him rich. Roussel was born in 1906 and in his early teens was helping his father with potato farming. He got into the oil business through Jacques Blevins, who asked Louis to convince a Bayou Lafourche farmer to lease his oil rights for $1 an acre. Louis succeeded and Blevins got the lease. Next week Louis went to the courthouse and looked up the transaction, discovering that Blevins had resold

the lease for $55 an acre. Louis' response was "Man, I thought to myself, how long has this been going on?"[21]

STELLA FIELD SONRIS Field ID 8703		
Year	Oil Total	Gas Total
1960-77	10,793,240	31,250,120
1977	62,837	382,526
1978	47,384	216,386
1979	62,056	196,428
1980	64,233	229,039
1981	67,235	376,491
1982	150,050	469,070
1983	190,762	374,784
1984	169,524	1,378,262
1985	145,167	1,807,608
1986	119,232	1,610,960
1987	121,586	831,335
1988	140,205	657,393
1989	140,816	686,000
1990	121,751	587,078
1991	116,428	405,284
1992	108,699	380,520
1993	122,214	361,533
1994	103,322	248,520
1995	80,491	247,361
1996	107,866	191,189
1997	108,241	165,350
1998	87,269	156,066
1999	75,946	116,861
2000	66,923	106,656
2001	58,809	112,204
2002	56,421	165,129
2003	59,250	939,800
2004	157,076	7,473,607
2005	246,975	11,296,928
2006	207,063	11,840,247
2007	137,523	9,861,380
2008	89,221	6,725,370
2009	85,819	4,069,910

So Roussel became an oil patch translator for the majors whose people could not understand the local French. He helped the Southeastern farmers negotiate for mineral rights. At age nineteen, he decided to make a break from the farm. He found a good lease

Right and opposite: Stella is the closest confirmed salt dome to the City of New Orleans. It has seen extensive surface development. In addition to the Mississippi River, there is a major highway, a railroad, a large chemical plant and numerous commercial and residential buildings. The biggest single surface feature is the Belle Chasse Naval Air Station. Operators on the Stella Dome have been forced to use extensive directional drilling. As recently as 2003 new developments have come to the Stella Field more than a half century old. Nearly all of the oil produced from the field has come from 6,300 to 7,700 feet depth. From essay by Louis E. Lemarié in Oil and Gas Fields of South Louisiana, issued by the New Orleans Geological Society, 2010.

Stella Field Annual Oil Production

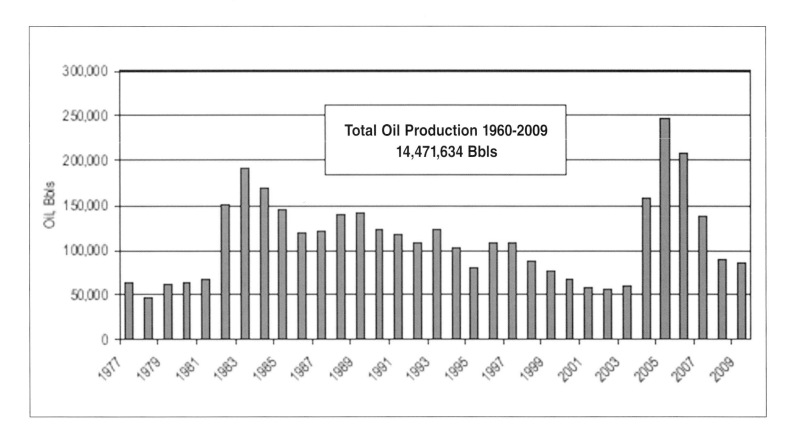

Total Oil Production 1960-2009
14,471,634 Bbls

Stella Field Annual Gas Production

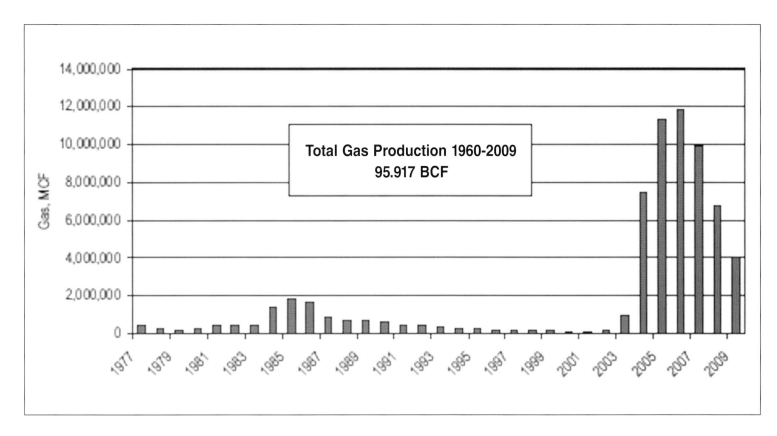

Total Gas Production 1960-2009
95.917 BCF

for $500; then he went to his doctor and borrowed some bonds. He loaned the bonds to a bank for cash, bought the lease, and then sold it for $1,700 to a Houston dealer with whom he had already made a deal. Louis felt rich.

Roussel then left the farm permanently. He went to New Orleans and became a streetcar/ bus driver. But he was always thinking oil. He would hitch rides to Raceland, the beginning of the Southeast oil patch, and watch along the roads for the oil company pennants that signaled exploration work nearby. Explorers were using dynamite to record waves on seismographs to get the underground shapes. Roussel spent five years in New Orleans as a bus driver, going to accounting school at night. But he was always late getting to the leases. He realized he had to get into the country.

In 1930 he bought his first lease at Paradis on credit, resold it but kept a 1/16 interest. It wound up with Texaco, the well hit,

"I was finally in the oil business." But the first million came from the Willie and Inez Pierce property. Roussel saw that it was in litigation. A surveyor had fudged a line separating the two parcels. Roussel got a lease from Willie with cash down and a note, resold the lease and retained 1/16. He then went to Texaco. It had drilled successfully on the disputed line so he negotiated a settlement giving him an interest in the entire property. When it hit he and his backer each were making $20,000 a month. Later he formed a syndicate with twenty-seven members, including his doctor. Six wells hit in a row. Everybody was paid off. He sold two of the wells for the entire cost of the project and the syndicate ended up with four wells entirely free.[22] From its inception to 1977 the Paradis Field produced 155 million barrels of oil.

An improper land description on a valuable 400-acre tract led to another series of disputes. A company in Baltimore had bought some land from Wisner Estates, then sold a lease to Humble Oil. The error in the property description gave Roussel and his partner the opportunity to go to Wisner and buy its interest in the property based on the theory that the sale of the lease was improper. They sued in 1943 and not until 1959, after two Supreme Court hearings, did they finally win. "Nothing attracts litigation like oil." Roussel went on to win several other litigious rights law cases where enemies sold an interest acquired from Roussel to third parties without giving him the first right to purchase as specified in the lease.

In 1955 Roussel began construction of a natural gas processing plant in the heart of Caddo Parish's Pine Island Oilfield. It covered 15 acres and was connected to 2,200 individual oil wells and had a daily capacity of 27 million cubic feet of natural gas. The total Chalk Zone gas reserves from the wells were 167 billion cubic feet.

Roussel got interested in how jack-up rigs were designed. It led to the Roussel jack, utilizing four hydraulic cylinders which alternate to jack up the barge. That the cylinders

opened and closed alternately gave the jack positive lock. It was impossible for it to slip. In 1957 he started building it. It cost $4.8 million and Roussel had it patented for seventeen years. The barge had twelve legs and a width of 133 feet and a length of 204 feet. It was designed to drill to 20,000 feet and work in waters up to 120 feet deep, with the main platform 40 foot above water. It had a single-hull and a self-elevating platform. The rig could drill nine wells at a time with a crew of forty-six. The Roussel's, father and son, went on to become large patrons of the Catholic Church and Loyola University, to name only two recipients of their generosity.

A more recent oil explorer is J. Michael Poole, Sr. In 1978 he formed Sunbelt Energy, Ltd. to generate, evaluate, and develop oil and gas prospects throughout the Gulf Basin. Sunbelt has operated as both an independent oil and gas company and as a joint venture partner. The company partnered with many companies like L. L. & E. Co., Devon Energy, and Texaco. The company has always emphasized the use of seismic tools, especially 3-D.

Index Map, Salt Domes of South Louisiana, New Orleans Geological Society 1962, Atlas of Oil and Gas Fields, vol. 1, disk 1 of Publications of the New Orleans Geological Society (3CD-ROMS, issued 2002).

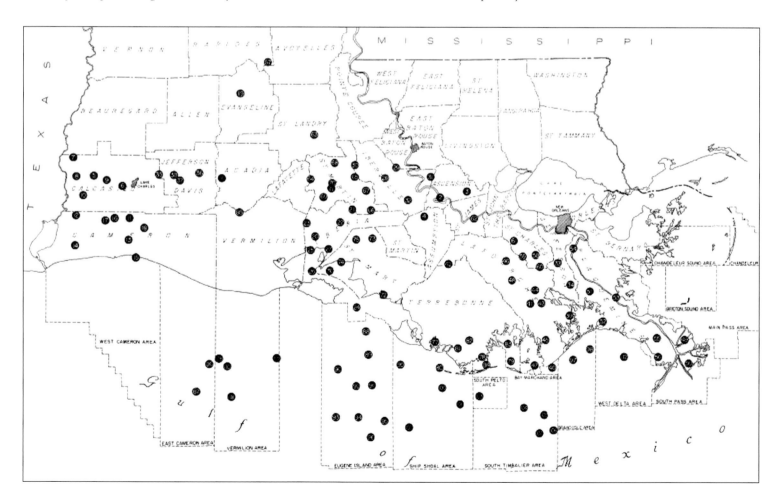

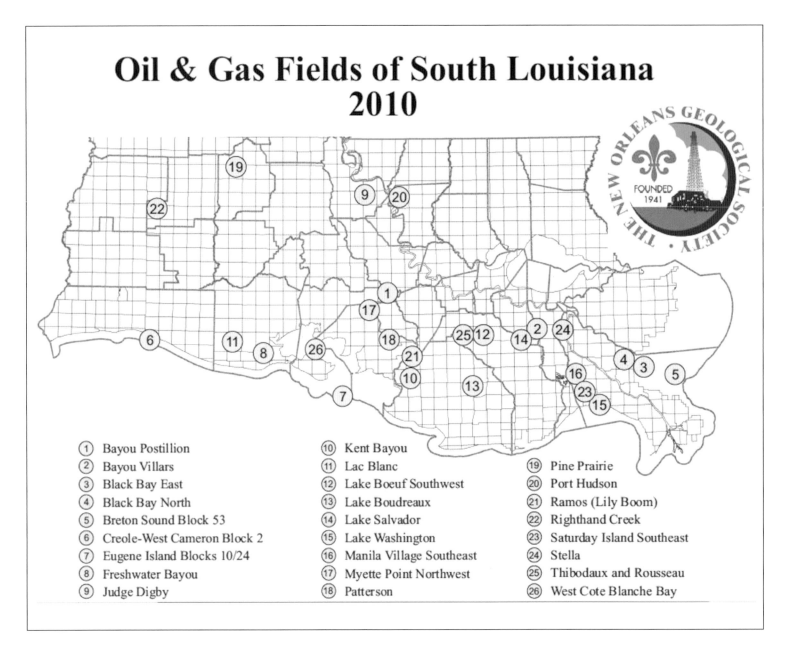

Oil & Gas Fields of South Louisiana
2010

THE NEW ORLEANS GEOLOGICAL SOCIETY
FOUNDED 1941

① Bayou Postillion
② Bayou Villars
③ Black Bay East
④ Black Bay North
⑤ Breton Sound Block 53
⑥ Creole-West Cameron Block 2
⑦ Eugene Island Blocks 10/24
⑧ Freshwater Bayou
⑨ Judge Digby

⑩ Kent Bayou
⑪ Lac Blanc
⑫ Lake Boeuf Southwest
⑬ Lake Boudreaux
⑭ Lake Salvador
⑮ Lake Washington
⑯ Manila Village Southeast
⑰ Myette Point Northwest
⑱ Patterson

⑲ Pine Prairie
⑳ Port Hudson
㉑ Ramos (Lily Boom)
㉒ Righthand Creek
㉓ Saturday Island Southeast
㉔ Stella
㉕ Thibodaux and Rousseau
㉖ West Cote Blanche Bay

Above: Issued by the New Orleans Geological Society, CD, 2010, p. 5.

Opposite: The stratigraphic column shows the layers mentioned in the text—Lower Miocene, Tuscaloosa, Middle Miocene, Oligocene, Eocene. U.S. Department of the Interior, Bureau of Land Management, Eastern States, Jackson Field Office, Louisiana: Reasonably Foreseeable Development Scenario for Fluid Minerals, 2008.

Poole's north shore roots led him to join up with LLOG, another north shore oil and gas exploration company. Using a 3-D program they generated over fifty prospects in the Black Bay, Breton Sound and Main Pass Areas. Thirty of the thirty-six wells drilled on the prospects were completed as either oil or gas wells (an 83 percent success rate). Amerada Hess later purchased the tracts for $300,000,000. With Manti Operating Company and an un-named major, Sunbelt used 3-D to shoot one of last un-shot salt domes in South Louisiana.

Thanks to the New Orleans Geological Society, oil exploration to the east of the Atchafalaya has been well documented. The Society devoted itself to salt domes,

the tectonics of salt, the Mississippi River sediment courses, and even New Orleans' geology. The departure of the majors from New Orleans decimated the ranks of geologists in New Orleans. Fortunately, in 2003 the American Association of Petroleum Geologists got together with the New Orleans Geological Society to produce a three-cd set of the maps and papers produced by the Society over the preceding forty years. In 2010 the New Orleans Geological Society produced a follow-up volume to their earlier work. In the later twentieth century *Times-Picayune* writer W. Jeff Davis continued the *Picayune*'s coverage of the oil and gas industry that had started in the 1930s. His regular columns frequently considered wildcatting.

In 1964 he noted "South Louisiana's most active wildcatter, Pan American Petroleum Corp., is also probing deeper levels in a search for new reserves." He discussed new wells in Vermillion, Iberia, and St. Bernard Parish. "In Cameron Parish the No. 1 state lease 4079, section 1-16s-5w, was initially planned for 16,500 feet. It is now to be deepened to 17,500 feet, and the crews were drilling ahead at 17,377 feet Tuesday. This location is on the Rockefeller Game Preserve."[23] While he did not cover developments in Washington, he saw to it that reports from the *Congressional Quarterly* appeared frequently.

Five geological trends have dominated the southeast Louisiana story over the last twenty years. The first in importance is the Lower Miocene zone of South Louisiana. It is a hydrocarbon-prolific, sand-rich zone that is up to several thousand feet thick. Salt domes, basins, and fault systems have created numerous producing sandstone reservoirs. The Lower Miocene extends from lower Cameron, Vermilion, Iberia, St. Mary, southern St. Martin, Assumption, northern Terrebonne, Lafourche, southern St. James and St. John the Baptist, and northern St. Charles and Jefferson Parishes. The largest Lower Miocene wildcat discovery was the Union Oil of California's (UNOCal) Freshwater Bayou Deep DPT discovery in Vermilion Parish in 1994. Ironically it was made with 2-D seismic and subsurface data.

In the last twenty years a new expanded Tuscaloosa Trend has played an important role in Louisiana gas and oil. It has added 1,724 billion cubic feet oil equivalent to Louisiana's production, a number second only to the Lower Miocene Trend.[24] The original Tuscaloosa stretched across the middle of the state. New 3-D seismic work was primarily responsible for the expansion of the trend from Point Coupee Parish southeastward to Baton Rouge, the Felicianas, and Livingston Parishes.

The Middle Miocene Trend contributed 914 BCFE in new field discovery production and 321 BCFE production from the redevelopment of Stella, Kent Bayou, Mound Point, Golden Meadow, Lapeyrouse, Cutoff, and Humphries Fields. From 1999 through 2001,

Cenozoic	Tertiary	Quat.	Pleist. — Undifferentiated
		Tertiary	Pliocene — Undifferentiated
		Miocene	Upper
		Miocene	Middle
		Miocene	Lower
		Oligocene	Anahuac Formation
		Oligocene	Frio Formation ⟩ Hackberry
		Oligocene	Vicksburg Group
		Eocene	Jackson Group
		Eocene	Upper Claiborne Group
		Eocene	Lower Claiborne Group
		Paleocene	Wilcox Group
		Paleocene	Midway Group

Industries along the Lower Mississippi River Corridor

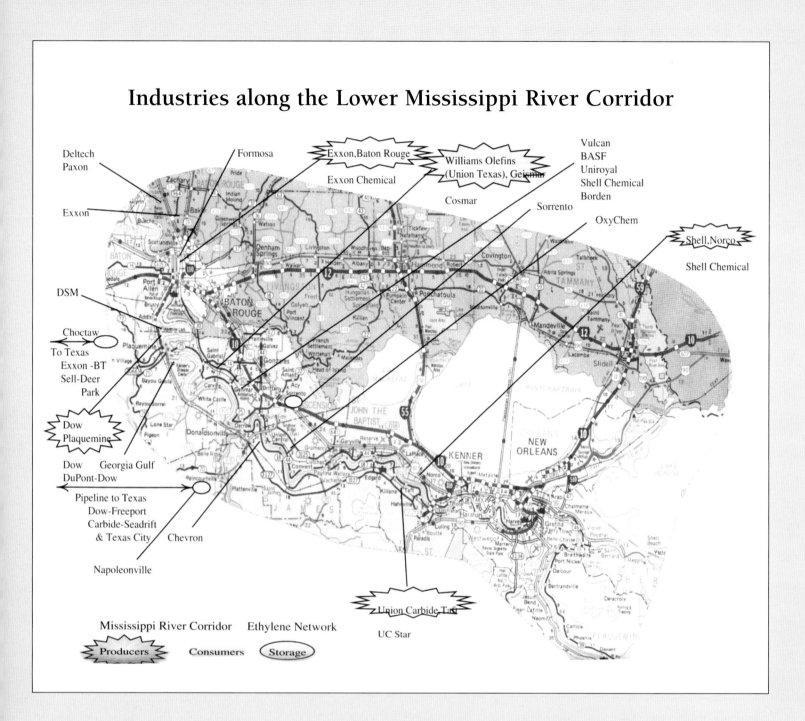

Deltech
Paxon

Formosa

Exxon, Baton Rouge

Exxon Chemical

Williams Olefins
(Union Texas), Geismar

Cosmar

Vulcan
BASF
Uniroyal
Shell Chemical
Borden

Sorrento

OxyChem

Shell, Norco

Shell Chemical

Exxon

DSM

Choctaw

To Texas
Exxon -BT
Sell-Deer
Park

Dow
Plaquemine

Dow   Georgia Gulf
DuPont-Dow

Pipeline to Texas
Dow-Freeport
Carbide-Seadrift
& Texas City   Chevron

Napoleonville

Union Carbide, Taft

UC Star

Mississippi River Corridor   Ethylene Network

Producers   Consumers   Storage

*Above: Map of the Industries along the
lower Mississippi River Corridor.*

*Right: The ubiquitous helicopter unloading
on Grand Chenier.*

PHOTOGRAPH COURTESY OF THE
MINERALS MANAGEMENT SERVICE, VOLUME VI,
AND JOHN RYAN.

Chemical Industry

Standard Oil opened the first great refinery along the Mississippi River Corridor in 1909. Initially using hydrocracking to produce more gasoline from crude, in 1927 Standard Oil decided to locate a new process development laboratory in Baton Rouge. Standard paid $35 million for the patents and embarked on catalytic cracking. Standard had a close relationship with the Massachusetts Institute of Technology. Engineers there introduced the idea of a powdered catalyst. The first pilot plant came on line in 1941 and became the forerunner for the immense Baton Rouge gasoline production during World War II.

The eight refineries along the Mississippi River Corridor all differ. Marathon and Texaco were built as complete or "grass roots" refineries to operate exclusively on heavy foreign crude. The Texaco refinery is now Motiva. Dow's first large chemical plant was at Freeport, Texas. But in 1956 it opened a giant plant on 3,000 acres near Plaquemine, Louisiana.

In 1940 Shell opened an alkylate plant that contributed to high-octane gasoline, important for airplanes. In 1935 Standard's Baton Rouge plant provided the military with the first tank car of 100 percent octane gasoline. In 1940 many refineries were producing 100 percent, the total for the year was 33,000 barrels per day. By the middle of the war, 1943, refineries were producing 507,000 barrels per day of 100 percent octane gasoline.

General Motors got the patents on anti-knock additives to gasoline and Standard Oil had the best process for producing it. In 1924 the two formed the Ethyl Corporation. It employed Dupont to construct a plant at Baton Rouge in the 1930s, getting needed ethylene from the adjacent Standard refinery.

Ethylene is another component of petroleum that has made a big name in the late twentieth century. A billion pounds are produced every year for use in plastics and rubber. Union Carbide was the first large company to make ethylene. Dow got into the business in Louisiana in 1958. Shell entered the field in 1964 at NORCO. Ethylene is used everywhere along the river and in east Texas. It is stored in salt domes as a gas and moved to customers over a pipeline network.

Until Pearl Harbor tires for automobiles and all rubber products were made from natural rubber from the Far East. Many strands of research on synthetic rubber came together after December 7, 1941. Congress exempted the big petroleum companies from anti-trust laws so patent and research sharing proceeded quickly. A company known as Copolymer built the first synthetic rubber plant at Baton Rouge and in 1943 the first bale of commercial synthetic rubber went on to the market. Many rubber factories appeared in the decades after the War, notably at Exxon, Uniroyal in Geismar, Dow in Plaquemine and Copoylmer at Addis. These plants depended on a large supply of petroleum products, notably ethylene and propylene.

Many plants along the river produce chlorine, essential to a variety of products notably aluminum, paper, PVC, and polyurethane foams. Dow, Ethyl, BASF, Kaiser, Hooker were among the plants that developed the business in the 1940s and subsequently.

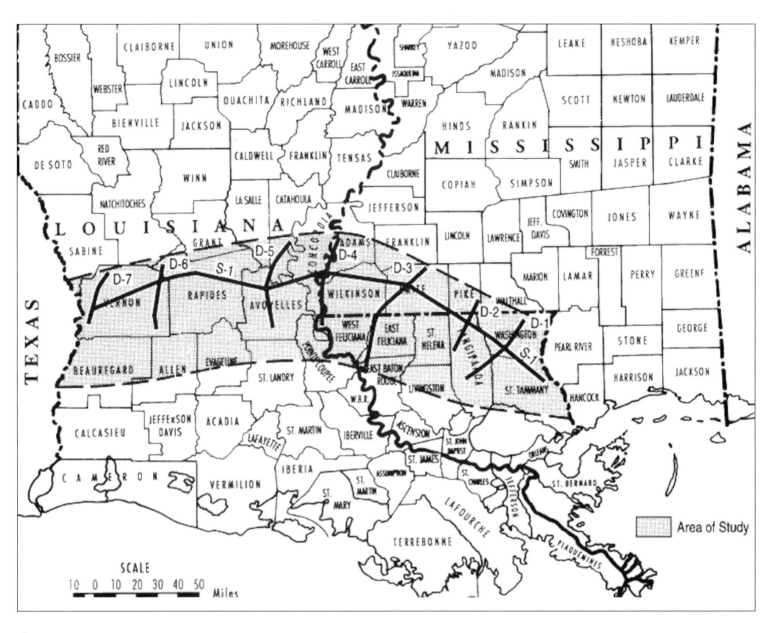

Tuscaloosa Marine Shale Play.

approximately 450 BCFE were discovered as the result of 3-D acquisition east of the Mississippi River out into Louisiana State Waters. From 2003 through 2005, new field discovery additions slowed until the large Contango discovery in Eugene Island 10 in 2006. This site straddles the boundary line between state and federal waters just off Iberia Parish.[25] The Contango discovery was the largest in the Middle Miocene Trend in the last twenty years and has produced 150 BCFE (132 BCFE and 2.86 MMBO) to date and may produce in excess of 350 BCFE. The highest average daily rate for a Middle Miocene well was the Contango #2 SL 19266 (EI 10) which produced at the average rate of 95,972 MCFE/D (87,050 MCF/D and 1,487 BO/D) in July 2008.

The Oligocene Trend follows a path similar to the Lower Miocene. It extends from Calcasieu and Jefferson Davis Parishes on the west to Lafayette, West Baton Rouge and Ascension, Livingston, St. James and St. John Parishes. Exxon made the largest and almost the earliest discovery in the Oligocene using 2-D seismic and subsurface data about 1988. It alone has produced 530 BCFE to date (2010). Three-D seismic added many features and developed interest in the Hackberry play. Sam Gary made the largest Hackberry discovery in 2001 now called Marceaux Island near the eastern edge of Cameron Lake. In 1983 Sam Gary had founded the integrated energy company bearing his name Sam Gary, Jr., Exploration headquartered in Denver.

The Eocene Trend is the smallest of the new finds in the past twenty years. It extends through Beauregard, Allen, Evangeline, St. Landry and Point Coupee Parishes. The largest wildcat discovery was the Buxton Creek Field in Calcasieu Parish with 18 BCFE. The largest redevelopment was in the Pine Prairie Field in Evangeline Parish with 27 BCFE.

Another small trend discovered in the last twenty years is the Austin Chalk. Initially discovered in Texas, it follows the Cretaceous shelf edge in south Louisiana from Beauregard Parish through Vernon, Rapides, Avoyelles and St. Landry Parishes. Discovered in 1996 and 1997, this oil play came on line at the beginning of a great drop in oil prices. Most of the reserves in the play were recovered at the bottom of the market. The entire trend ended up unprofitable.

Wildcat discoveries in South Louisiana have totaled 3,567 BCFE over the past two decades. While large, it did not equal the amount produced by development of existing fields. Six wells produced 58 percent of the wildcat production: West Chalkley (1998); Freshwater Bayou Deep (1994); Taylor Point/ Myette Point Northwest (1994); Kent Bayou (1999); Ramos (1999) and Eugene Island 10 (2006). After 1995 small independent oil and gas companies took the lead in the development of new production. The transfer of existing fields from the majors to the independents facilitated this fundamental shift in onshore south Louisiana gas and oil.[26]

After the peak of oil and gas production just prior to the Arab oil embargo, production has generally declined in south Louisiana fields. The current low price for gas has aggravated the problem for the independent producer because most of the wells in south Louisiana have ended up as gas wells. But at least two plays offer the possibility of a large boom in south Louisiana oil and gas. The previously-mentioned Tuscaloosa marine shale belt across central and southern Louisiana offers some hope provided the fracking problems can be surmounted. Another exciting possibility is ultra-deep gas play McMoran has pioneered. The simple idea is that the productive sands on shore have gradually sloped down as they have moved south. But more than that, the sands have cut under the salt layer, so drilling requires great depth. The technical challenges are great, but so would be the rewards.

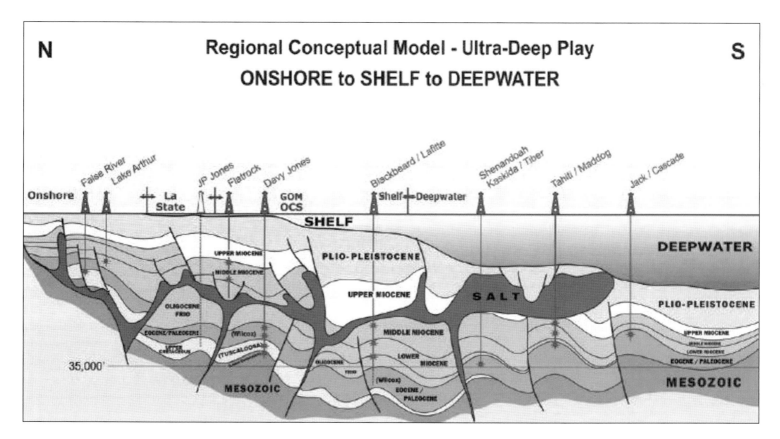

McMoran Ultra Deep Gas Play.

CHAPTER 6
OFFSHORE

From the present perspective it is not surprising that Louisiana's oil and gas industry has shifted its center from the northern reaches of the state southward. But in the first four decades of the twentieth century Shreveport and Monroe were the epicenter of oil and gas production. This, even though the first wells were in the Southwest. After World War II oil and gas production shifted southward to the coastal parishes where the Acadians shrimp, crab, fish and hunt. This shift followed the tilt in the continental shelf beneath Louisiana. In the 1940s, even with onshore production soaring, the first intrepid spirits began locating oil and gas formations offshore, a logical continuation of the watery Louisiana Coast. Chester Cheramie observed,[1]

> And the Golden Meadow area was one of the prime sections of the oil field
> besides Morgan City. They started drilling right in Golden Meadow, then they went
> to Leeville and then to Bay Marchand right out of Fourchon just a little offshore.

The effort to drill deeper and further off the coast of Louisiana has defined a new Louisiana oil & gas industry. It is not about oilfields. It is about the businesses that run men out to the rigs, supply the food and the mud, maintain and build rigs, feed and support thousands of Louisiana families. The oilfield may be invisible, but the businesses that make it work line the Louisiana Coast. Since 1947, more than 50,000 wells have been drilled in the U.S. Gulf of Mexico. The United States Outer Continental Shelf extends out from the three coasts of the United States. But only the continental shelf in the Gulf of Mexico has seen major exploration. Approximately 97 percent of the oil produced on the U.S. Outer Continental Shelf is produced in the U.S. Gulf of Mexico. There are currently nearly 7,000 active leases (see map on page 117) in the Gulf of Mexico, 64 percent of which are in deepwater.[2] Since 1995, deepwater drilling activity has increased significantly in the Gulf. In 2001, U.S. deepwater offshore oil production surpassed shallow water offshore oil production for the first time. As of May 2010, operators had drilled approximately 700 wells in water depths equal to or greater than 5,000 feet, the approximate depth of the Macondo Well that blew out that April.

Rig in the Gulf of Mexico with storm coming in. Used on the cover of Offshore *magazine 1973.*

PHOTOGRAPH COURTESY OF THE MINERALS MANAGEMENT SERVICE, VOLUME VI, AND LYNDA MILLER.

Central Planning Area, Gulf of Mexico, Outer Continental Shelf.

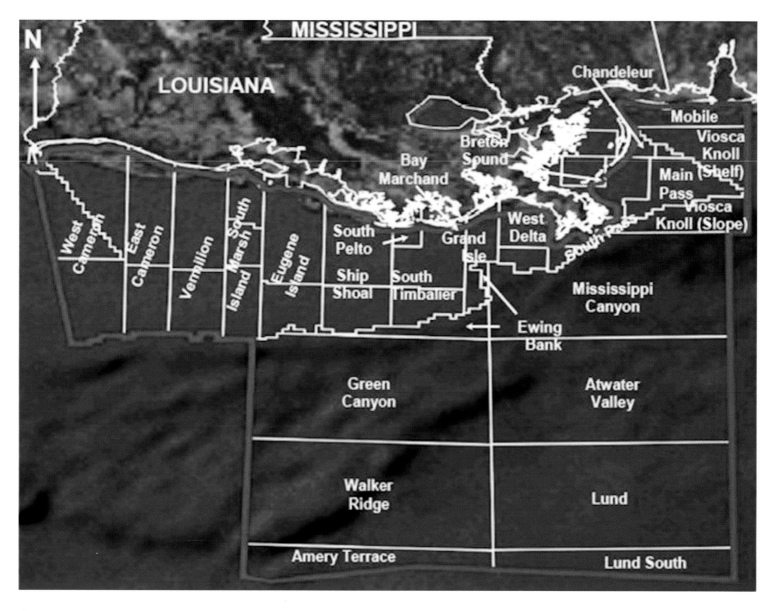

Zones in the Central Planning Area, Gulf of Mexico, and the Outer Continental Shelf, 2011. These names have become familiar to Louisiana residents.

MAP COURTESY OF THE BUREAU OF OCEAN ENERGY MANAGEMENT.

Then, once off shore, exploration continued to move southward into deeper and deeper water and formations. The deepest wells now extend seven miles into the earth. The drilling rigs and production platforms are among the tallest manmade structures in the world. Despite massive production, proved reserves continue to increase from the 2007 level of twenty billion barrels of oil and 183.7 trillion cubic feet of gas in 1,229 proved fields.[3] This proven oil reserve amounts to three years of oil consumption at twenty million barrels a day for the American economy.

For the working population of south Louisiana, the offshore oil and gas industry was a logical continuation of their watery nautical life. While the major oil companies quickly dominated the business, it rested on the shoulders of thousands of risk-taking individuals. Cajun fishermen and oystermen along Bayou Lafourche and the other Louisiana waterways turned their crafts to service the new businesses opening in the Gulf. They steadily developed new boat designs and opened new supply companies that made the giant rigs and explorations possible. Louisiana's state government initially helped the business, but state politics cost the state its role offshore beyond three miles. Fortunately, federal control made leasing large tracts feasible and set the fundamental financial parameter for the enormously expensive drilling rigs to follow.

But early on the majors decided to stay out of the supply business. Subcontracting this skilled profession out of the company ensured the best performance because of the highly competitive atmosphere along the Cajun coast. It also limited liability. The supply business involved dozens of different industries. Local independent companies, for example, represented the fabricators of valve actuators. Their local proprietors cruised oil company offices looking for rig managers in need of valve actuators. Anchor handling for the great rigs was a remarkably skillful occupation that a variety of businesses along the Louisiana coast entered. The basic supply boat evolved from Louisiana roots and soon became the trademark of a major company still headquartered in New Orleans—Tidewater, Inc. Lynn Dean invented the liftboat in the 1950s with the capability of servicing rigs and seismographic projects. Much of this new business was invented along Louisiana's Gulf Coast. Rigs evolved from fixed platforms, to submersibles, to jackup rigs, to ship drilling units, and today to semi-submersibles floating in the deepwaters of

the Gulf and worldwide. Offshore exploration made sleepy villages into vibrant towns like Golden Meadow that added in the 1950s a town hall, a telephone company, a solid bank, and a radio station. From Lafayette offshore enterprises dispatched their management personnel to the new on-site towns of Morgan City and Port Fourchon.

Offshore exploration has a much longer history than is usually recognized. In the late 1890s drillers constructed piers out from the California coast line and installed drilling rigs at the end of them. It was successful and in 1908 the technique was adapted to the coast of Texas. It spread rapidly along the Gulf Coast. Meanwhile, the oil boom in Caddo Parish led the Levee Board to lease its Caddo Lake. The biggest purchaser was Gulf Oil. The Ferry Lake No. 1 well was completely offshore, though hardly in the same sense as Gulf of Mexico wells. In the next decade oil men introduced slant drilling along the shore line but extending under the adjoining water. Meanwhile, at the U.S. Geological Survey geologist David White had written in 1927 that the undersea continental shelf

A NOAA graphic shows various types of offshore drilling platforms, including:

1, 2 Conventional fixed platforms

3 Compliant tower

4, 5 Vertically moored tension leg and mini-tension leg platform

6 Spar

7, 8 Semi-submersibles

9 Floating production, storage, and offloading facility

10 sub-sea completion and tie-back to host facility

must contain undersea oil-rich salt domes just as the adjacent dry land did. Platforms then appeared in the shallowest waters of the Gulf Coast. Extremely low prices and demand discouraged expensive oil exploration offshore during the 1920s and 1930s.

But as the 1930s progressed and World War II loomed interest in the offshore increased. In 1937 Pure Oil Company and Superior Oil Company jointly drilled from an offshore platform over a mile from the shore of Cameron Parish. The salt dome below yielded oil. This "Creole" Field, a complex of eleven wells, came to produce 1,500 to 2,000 barrels a day and over its thirty-year career produced four million barrels of oil. But, simultaneously many other efforts were dry holes. Despite spiraling demand, World War II stopped expensive drilling because the federal government did not allocate steel to the industry. For the duration the industry expanded its existing fields. But, in the view of the authors of a history of the engineering giant Brown & Root, the biggest problem was that there were "no dependable supply or service companies." Brown & Root could design and construct offshore rigs, but how did workers and supplies get to the rigs efficiently? It was not until the late 1940s that the competitive business world began producing solutions.[4]

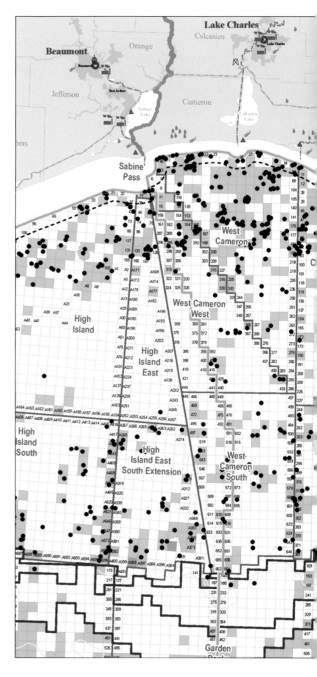

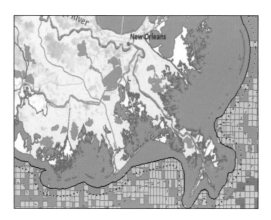

Right: Detail Map of Active Oil and Gas Leases, showing submerged lands act boundary. March 3, 2012.

MAP COURTESY OF THE BUREAU OF OCEAN ENERGY MANAGEMENT.

Once steel was again available for drilling rigs, the State of Louisiana responded to the offshore interest by holding its first offshore lease sale. On August 14, 1945, Louisiana offered leases on 129,025 acres that extended thirty miles offshore. Exxon's Magnolia Petroleum Company bid $660,597, more than five times the bids of Superior Oil and Pure Oil Company. Magnolia was to pay 1/8 royalty and a small overriding royalty. Magnolia took three months to complete a giant platform rising twenty feet above water level on a lease just off Terrebonne Parish. Though Magnolia proved to be a dry hole, the Creole Field continued to spit out oil. In 1946 platform drilling in state-protected waters resumed.

The complexity of ending the war initially prevented the federal government from involvement in the offshore. But Louisiana's offshore lease raised alarms in the Executive branch. It was not at all certain that Louisiana

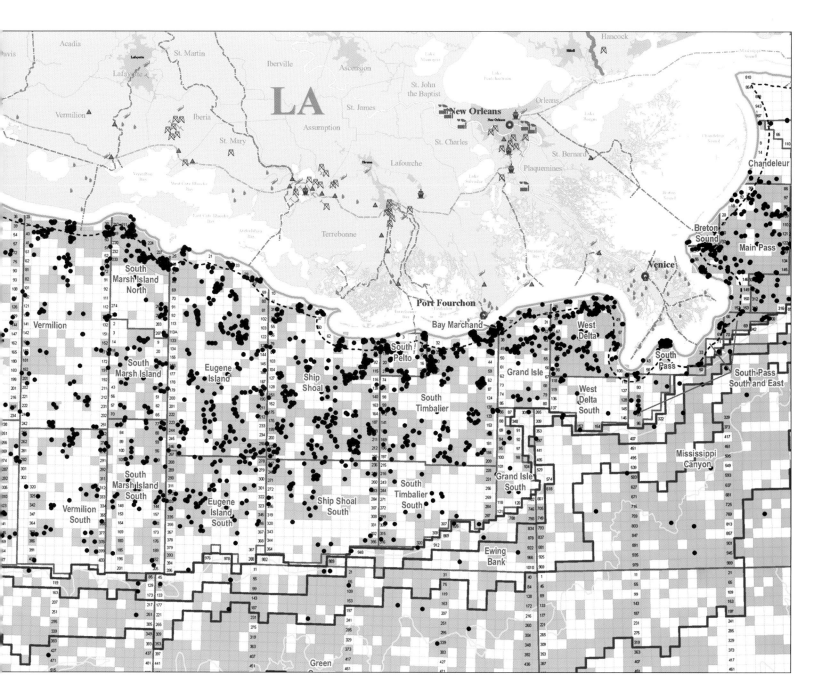

owned water bottoms in the Gulf of Mexico. On September 20, 1945, coastal states representatives successfully persuaded the U.S. House of Representatives to pass a resolution by an 108 to 11 vote: "The United States of America hereby renounces…any right, title…to all lands beneath tidewaters and navigable waters within the boundaries of each of the respective states." This resolution woke up the Truman administration. President Harry Truman issued an executive order putting the marine resources of the submerged lands on the continental shelf in the hands of Secretary of the Interior Harold Ickes.

Above: Detail Map of Active Leases and Infrastructure, November 1, 2012.

The active leases are in green; gas pipelines in red, oil pipelines in blue.

Platform fabrication facilities are represented:		*Shipbuilding facilities are represented:*	
They are located at New Iberia and St. Mary: 8; Morgan City: 8; Houma: 7; New Orleans: 8; and Lake Charles: 1.		*They are located at Morgan City:1; Lafourche: 1; and New Orleans: 3.*	

Texas has a shipbuilding facility at Beaumont and a platform fabrication facility at Houston and Corpus Christi.
http://www.boem.gov/uploadedFiles/BOEM/Oil_and_Gas_Energy_Program/Mapping_and_Data/visual1.pdf

MAP COURTESY OF THE BUREAU OF OCEAN ENERGY MANAGEMENT.

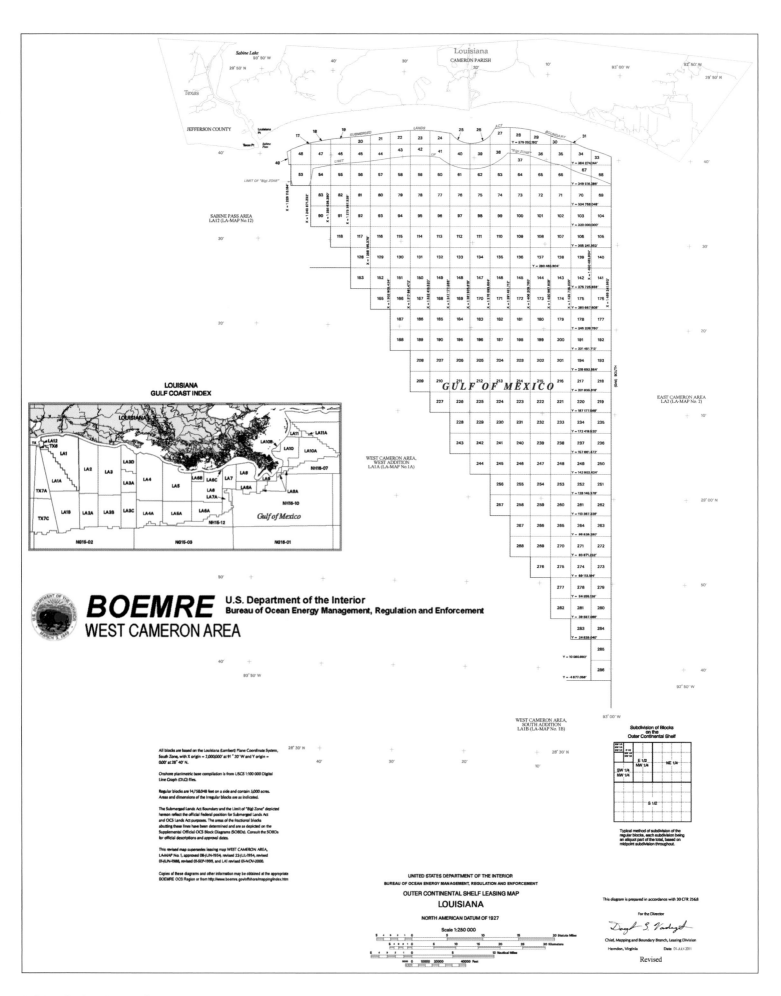

Opposite: Block 192 in the West Cameron area is the site of the first offshore well fully equipped with blowout preventer. Higgins Fabrication Company of New Orleans produced the production platform for Shell in 1955. Notice the Submerged Lands Act boundary. Block 192 is the tenth block on the eastern boundary line of West Cameron. Water depth of fifty-five feet.
BUREAU OF OCEAN ENERGY MANAGEMENT, REGULATION AND ENFORCEMENT.

Left: Shell production platform in Block 192 of the West Cameron area.
PHOTOGRAPH COURTESY OF THE MINERALS MANAGEMENT SERVICE, VOLUME VI, AND JAKE GIROIR.

Below: Contour map of "Top of Salt", Hackberry West Field, Cameron Parish.
PHOTOGRAPH COURTESY OF THE NEW ORLEANS GEOLOGICAL SOCIETY.

Contour Map of "Top of Salt," Hackberry West Field, Cameron Parish, Louisiana

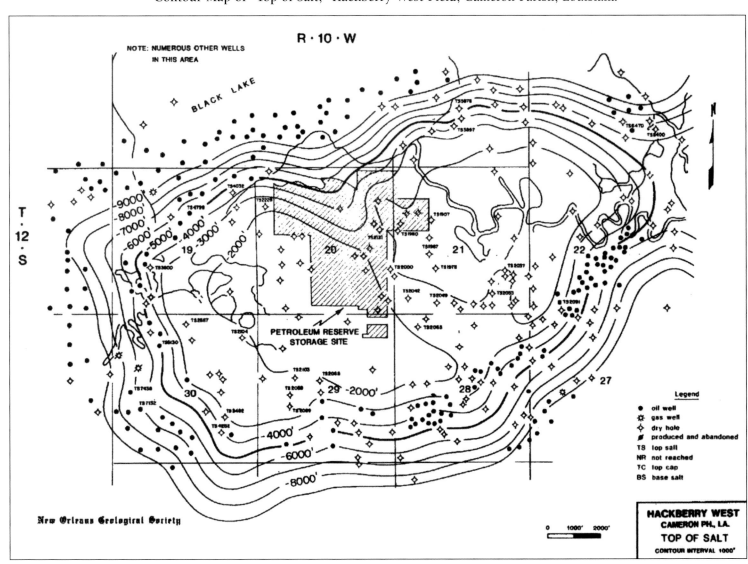

Right: First offshore well out of sight of land. Kerr-McGee, 1947.

Below: Kerr-McGee Rig 63 loaded on a ship and being transported.

Above: Kerr-McGee Rig 45 almost capsizing in Breton Sound, 1974.

PHOTOGRAPH COURTESY OF THE MINERALS MANAGEMENT SERVICE, VOLUME VI, AND CHESTER PISPSAIR.

Left: Kerr-McGee Rig 45 almost capsizing, showing pontoons.

PHOTOGRAPH COURTESY OF THE MINERALS MANAGEMENT SERVICE, VOLUME VI, AND CHESTER PISPSAIR.

CHAPTER 6

Above: Shell developed this East Bay production facility in 1957. The adjacent structures are satellites, www.bsee.gov.

Below: Kerr-McGee Rig 39, the Frank Phillips, a drilling tender in Ship Shoal Block 32, Navy yard facility barge converted after WWII.

President Truman's executive order launched the "Tidelands" dispute, a dispute that has not yet been put to bed. Everyone could see that the State of Louisiana owned coastal waters, but it was not clear where the coast began or how far out the state's claim extended. The marshy estuaries ebbed and flowed, so determining Louisiana's boundary was subject to much haggling. The administration claimed the offshore royalties for the federal government and defined offshore as beyond the three-mile line from the coast. Drawing this line was a challenge. Truman's proposal was for the state to receive two-thirds of the inshore royalties, but only three-eighths of the royalties from drilling beyond the three miles. Inshore the state would issue leases, offshore the federal government would do the issuing. Secretary of the Interior Harold Chapman defined a shoreline that decided the actual coastline from which the three miles would be measured.[5] Adding spice to the controversy was the discovery of large offshore fields beyond the three mile limit. Already Shell had leased South Pass Blocks 24 and 27 and Eugene Island 18; California Company had leased Bay Marchand Blocks 2 and Main Pass 69; and Humble Oil had leased Grand Isle 18.

Unfortunately for the state, Leander Perez, district attorney of the large shoreline parish of Plaquemines, led the power brokers in the Louisiana Democratic party of the era. Perez was heavily involved in the oil business by virtue of his office. He controlled access to nearby offshore and onshore rigs. Only his friends could supply companies. He coerced the oil companies into giving him a hidden royalty on oil from parish lands. Hating the national Democratic Party, Perez persuaded the state to oppose Truman's offer to Louisiana. The state decided to wait until the expected Republican victory in 1952. But, as more and more drilling took place offshore the federal government decided to keep all of the off-shore royalty money, leaving the state with the dwindling inshore income. A moratorium in the early 1950s prevented any drilling offshore. But for the next sixty years Louisiana lost out on hundreds of millions of dollars in oil revenue while Perez and his allies basked in secret oil royalties. Only after Hurricane Katrina did Congress agree to share offshore revenue and by 2017 Louisiana will be receiving 37.5 percent of the income.

Some idea of the cost to Louisiana of bad government can be found in the statistics of how much the federal government made from the offshore lands. From 1953 through 2000, the leasing of federal lands in the U.S. Outer Continental Shelf, primarily in the Gulf of Mexico, led to a total commercial production of 13.1 billion barrels of oil and 140.5 trillion cubic feet of natural gas. Lease payments and royalties were a major source of revenue for the United States, the second largest behind taxes. From 1954 to 2002, the federal government collected a total of $49.5 billion in cash bonuses and $67.3 billion in royalties from offshore oil and gas leases.[7] In constant dollars, according to a former Interior official, the U.S. offshore program has been the largest non-financial auction in the world.[8]

Louisiana's first offshore leases had drawn the interest of Dean A. McGee the head of Kerr-McGee, who was looking for new fields for the Oklahoma oil company that had generally avoided Louisiana until that point. The principals wanted the company to become a major oil company rather than

TIDELANDS BATTLE

In fighting the Tidelands Battle the State of Louisiana strove to show that its citizens and only its citizens had used the coastal waters off of Louisiana. Furthermore, that the State of Louisiana had carefully regulated that use since the nineteenth century. One of the witnesses in the struggle was J. C. De Armas, Jr., engineer for the parish of Plaquemines. His father, John Carlos De Armas, Sr., had operated an oyster schooner named the *John Eugene* since 1894 and owned oyster license No. 1 issued by the Louisiana Department of Conservation. De Armas, Jr., served as deputy oyster surveyor for the Oyster Commission of Louisiana from 1904 to 1908. In 1902 the Louisiana legislature approved Act 153 to protect, regulate and develop the oyster industry in the state. De Armas was well qualified to describe the use of the coastal waters.

Statement of Mr. J. C. De Armas, Jr.:

> Breton Sound and Chandeleur Sound and all the coastal waters surrounding the Delta of the Mississippi River were under the regulation and control of the Oyster Commission prior to the creation of the Conservation Commission and the Wildlife and Fisheries Commission, and have been so regulated and controlled for more than fifty years to my knowledge. This is true with reference to all the bays and coastal waters off Plaquemines and St. Bernard Parishes. The bays and coastal waters lying offshore from Louisiana, referred to above, have never been used in interstate or foreign commerce, (with the exception of the Mississippi River Passes) and cannot be so used because of the shallowness of the waters and the existence of reefs, shoals and sand bars.
>
> It has always been the belief of the people of Louisiana, and particularly of those engaged in public works in the coastal parishes that all of the coastal waters and submerged lands adjoining the coast of Louisiana belonged to and were a part of this state.[6]

remain a minor one. They decided there was plenty of oil offshore, but another new technology was needed to make it economically feasible to drill. Their first step was to lease two twenty-thousand-acre tracts from the Louisiana Mineral Lease Board in the Ship Shoal area off Point au Fer in Terrebonne Parish. Much of the lease territory was out of sight of land even though the water was shallow. The first rigs were simple platforms on piles standing in the water. One of the first derrick fitters on this platform was Loulan Pitre who left memoirs fifty years later. An interview with Pitre in 2002 described how the derrick fitters discovered and surmounted the problem that the bolts were too thick for the pre-drilled holes. It developed that the bolts had been galvanized and thus were thicker than expected.[9]

Crew boat the Viator family had built in
1963 for offshore work.

Another of Kerr-McGee's employees at the time was Alden Laborde, a true Louisiana entrepreneur, part wildcatter, but part builder. During World War II, this West Point graduate served as a Navy Captain escorting supply ships to Europe. Jobless after the war, he joined a seismic crew hauling cables and clearing brush for a "shooting crew" doing seismic exploration.

But with a characteristic wildcat mentality, by keeping his ear to the ground Laborde soon moved into the marine branch of the oil industry with a job to maintain and manage the construction of a drilling barge at Orange, Texas. He had been trained as an engineer at West Point and his navy career had given him considerable experience in steam engineering. The drilling barge moved to Plaquemines Parish where Laborde heard about Kerr-McGee's first offshore wells. Again, he seized an opportunity and headed for the Kerr-McGee division manager at Morgan City. The company had just discovered the many marine difficulties that encumber drilling offshore and Laborde stepped into the position of marine superintendent. Kerr-McGee was the operational manager for a group of oil companies with the earliest finds in the Gulf. They had also found problems that Laborde was perfectly suited to manage—supply vessels, crew boats, oil barges, tugs, radio systems, offshore quartering and catering.

With little to do offshore during the moratorium, in 1951 management at Kerr-McGee found a drilling rig that had worked in Breton Sound for the Barnsdall Oil Company. This rig consisted of two hulls, the lower intended to rest on the sea bottom where it supported vertical posts that lifted the upper deck well above the wave action of the surface. Stability was the problem and Oklahoma engineer John T. Hayward had designed a set of outrigged pontoons moved by hydraulic jacks to remain at the surface level preventing tipping. Haywood's system intrigued Laborde. Soon an opportunity arose to use it on a Sun Oil Company well a mile off the Texas Coast. Its success converted Laborde into an ardent supporter of Haywood and his concept. Laborde brought it to Dean McGee, but Kerr-McKee was not ready to go forward. The election of Dwight Eisenhower, who had promised to lift the moratorium on offshore drilling, incited Laborde to action. He left Kerr-McGee, telling his colleagues "that I was not around for the gold rush, or Spindletop, or the Florida land boom, but for this one, I planned to be right in the middle of it...."[10] These words are echoes of Scott Heywood's when he heard of Spindletop, "I immediately made up my mind to see this strike and try to get in on the ground floor."[11] This is the wildcatter attitude.

Now without a day job, Laborde traveled the oil company circuit looking for backers to construct a new version of the John T. Haywood submersible drilling rig. Haywood was Laborde's first backer, but almost his only one. In his autobiography Laborde discussed the sheep-like tendency of the major oil companies, so unlike the wildcatters and plungers. "If Exxon and Shell are doing it, then others go along, with a feeling of comfort. They do the same in exploring a new area—all going there with one another—then all giving up at once. They similarly copy each other's organizations and techniques...."[12] The great Caddo Parish wildcatter Mike Benedum had said much the same in 1907. After many months of beating the pavement, Laborde's idea reached a set of mid-sized oil companies with no involvement offshore, but a considerable desire to find an innovative technique.

Late one night Burch Williams of the Murphy Oil Company in El Dorado, Arkansas called Laborde to come immediately up to head-quarters, and come in Murphy's plane. The meeting was a complete success, beginning decades of Murphy Oil Company involvement in the Gulf and support for Laborde's projects. Murphy took a half interest in the new company called Ocean Drilling & Exploration Company or ODECO. Their first rig was to be called *Mr. Charlie* after Charles Murphy, Sr., the retired chairman of Murphy Oil. The Hayward concept was soon pressed on Shell Oil Company's regional office in New Orleans that agreed to put the *Mr. Charlie* on some potentially valuable leases in East Bay.

In June 1954 *Mr. Charlie* left the Alexander Shipyards on the east bank of New Orleans Industrial Canal and set sail for East Bay. Its first well for Shell was a stunning success and Shell became Laborde's steady backer. Time showed that Laborde's bottom-sitting submersible worked best in waters up to

forty feet; the jack-up rigs worked best in waters of seventy-five feet to three hundred feet of depth. For deeper water the industry drilled from floating anchored ships. Other new developments cost more and more money and ODECO, which had been private, was forced to go public for additional funds. But by 1970 in the opinion of the authoritative *Oil & Gas Journal* ODECO was "one of the off-shore-drilling giants."[13]

ODECO never lacked competition. SEDCO, an antecedent of Transocean, immediately took up the concept of the submersible and then semi-submersible rigs. After a few years it had more at work than ODECO. SEDCO claims to have launched the first jackup rig to be used offshore as early as 1954.

Louisiana has always played an important role in rig construction and design. Drilling rigs and producing platforms have steadily evolved until today they are among the largest structures in the world. The fixed platform started the evolution that was

Taking the Kelly off to trip the pipe, Kenneth Viator to the left, with Pappy Dupré, center, and George Caisson, the motorman.

PHOTOGRAPH COURTESY OF THE MINERALS MANAGEMENT SERVICE, VOLUME VI, AND KENNETH VIATOR.

Mr. Charlie *sea trials. After operating for thirty years Kerr-McGee donated* Mr. Charlie *to the Morgan City Offshore Oil Museum where it remains open for tours, www.bsee.gov.*

PHOTOGRAPH COURTESY OF OFFSHORE STATS AND FACTS, GULF OF MEXICO REGION, DATA CENTER, AVAILABLE RESOURCES, IMAGE LIBRARY.

initially dictated by water depth. To be able to move the platform soon suggested drilling from a ship and then submersible rigs like the *Mr. Charlie*. These had fixed legs and the platform moved up and down by filling and emptying tanks that gave the rig stability. The next logical step was the jack-up rig that propelled itself to the drilling site and ratcheted down long legs to the ocean floor.

The evolution of drilling rigs then became revolutionary. Alden Laborde and others figured out that a large structure that floated was very stable provided most of its weight was well below the surface. These rigs did not sink to the ocean floor, they floated and were thus "semi-submersibles." They were kept in place over the drilling site by the same system that anchored ships—large anchors and cables a mile long. This anchoring system was basic, but difficult to manage. Here was one of the most skillful jobs for Louisiana mariners. Shell Oil, from the beginning the leader in offshore leasing, introduced in 1962 its "revolutionary *Bluewater 1* semi-submersible drilling vessel."[14] It was a cargo-carrying ship with drilling deck in which the loaded hull and cargo could be lowered into the water for greater stability.[15] In the 1960s Laborde went on to design the *Ocean-Driller*, the first column-stabilized semi-submersible drilling rig. It actually floated in deepwater, kept in position by anchors. The deck was supported by three large hollow columns that extended into the sea. They provided immense stability to the drilling deck and the entire vessel. The largest semi-submersible drilling and production platform is *Thunder Horse* built for BP in 2008 at 130,000 tons displacement.

Another revolutionary idea was to return to the seabed. It soon occurred to the industry that water 6,000 feet deep could be drilled from fixed or somewhat fixed platforms. The tension-leg platform attached long semi-stiff legs to a rig that floated, but it was held in place horizontally by legs fastened to piles driven in the seabed. The tension leg inevitably was flexible. Stronger materials soon suggested another step, the compliant tower rig. Here a rig tower was placed on the sea floor. It rested on piles. The tower could be built in up to 3,000 feet of water. It was designed to sway, to harmonize with current, wave, and wind forces.

Following up on its successes with *Mr. Charlie*, Shell strengthened its offshore research. Seismic exploration developed steadily in the 1960s and towards the end of the decade Shell geologists developed the "bright spot" technique for locating some types of oil play. It was used successfully by Shell in the 1970 and 1972 offshore auction conducted by the federal government. This particular technique located about 2 billion bbl of oil equivalent on the shelf and more than 4 billion bbl of oil equivalent in the deepwater of the Gulf of Mexico.[16]

Getting supplies and men to the new offshore rigs bedeviled the majors. Initially, they seized on what was at hand—the large shrimping fleet of coastal Louisiana. Ronald Callais, one of six brothers in the shrimp, oil, and tug business, described how the family went offshore. It started with his father Abdon Callais renting the shrimp boat to the oil company after shrimp season was over. But for years it was inshore work. "He'd be working in the lakes, bringing crews, bringing supplies to rigs. In fact, one summer I remember, the state hired his boat…the whole wooden bulkhead that's in Bayou Lafourche down here? My father was the boat that pushed the pile driver the[that] drove all those things in. Mom and I'd go bring him dinner every day."[17] Shrimp boats then morphed into LSTs. World War II had left a legacy of landing craft tank in the Gulf waters, craft that were put to use in the 1940s supplying the first fixed platform rigs.

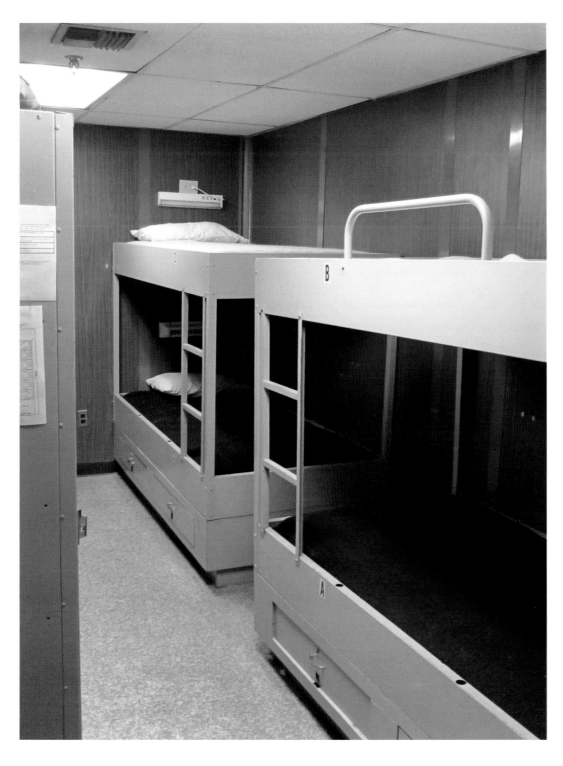

Bunks in the Mr. Charlie, *2011.*

Botruc, *the Rhode Island-designed supply vessel.*

The need for a more specialized craft quickly appeared. Two innovators, Alden Laborde and Luther Blount, developed comparable supply vessels with a pilot house forward and a long open rear deck. Luther Blount, owner of a shipbuilding yard at Warren, Rhode Island, had come to Morgan City in response to a request from Parker Conrad to build a seismographic vessel. His principal business had been constructing ferry boats, but he quickly saw that his ferry boat design had the qualities needed in the offshore oilfields. His design, called the *Botruc*, featured a molded ship-shaped hull. The first *Botruc* measured 65 feet on a 23 foot beam. Conrad encouraged Blount to get financing, and suggested George Engine Company, the principal supplier of Detroit diesels to the offshore market. George agreed to finance two *Botrucs* using his Detroit Diesel 6-110s. Here is an early example of how the support-supply side of the oil industry pushed the industry itself forward. George Engine also sold heavily to Tidewater.

Minor Cheramie, already in the supply boat business, latched onto the *Botruc* and eventually built and owned a fleet of them. Cheramie contracted with American Marine in New Orleans to build them, and to improve them. Using the services of Y. K. Mock, naval architect, he increased the size of the *Botrucs*, keeping their successful deep V bows and molded lines that made them efficient in the rougher waters. Though the oil companies jumped at the chance to lease these durable workhorses, the *Botruc* remained a minor part of the supply fleet.

The major part of the supply boat business, first in the Gulf and then worldwide, went to another company. Tidewater Marine came to own by far the largest fleet of supply vessels. Tidewater originated in a meeting that Alden Laborde called in June 1954. Present were C. E. Laborde, Jr.; J. E. Kyle, Jr., Berwick, Louisiana, contractor, marine operator and lumberyard owner; Burch Williams, financial vice-president of the Murphy Corporation; John T. Hayward, an engineer inventor; Donald W. Durant, operator of a river towing business in New Orleans, brother to Leslie Durant, owner of the Alexander Shipyard; a friend Ralph Hebert; and Sterling Little. Each agreed to put up $10,000 to build a new type of supply boat with a front pilot house and long open rear deck.

Laborde and Murphy immediately recognized there was a conflict of interest between ODECO and Tidewater, so Laborde let Tidewater go. Murphy and Laborde agreed that Laborde's younger brother John had the capacity to run the new enterprise. John Laborde took over as Tidewater's first President. Under John Laborde's leadership within a decade it became the largest supply company to the oil industry worldwide. Alexander Shipyards, Inc. constructed their first three boats, *Ebb Tide*, *Rip Tide*, and *Gulf Tide*.[18] Many more followed over the succeeding decades. Among the largest were two Tidewater commissioned in 1974 from a shipbuilder in Ulsteinvik, Norway. These became the *Mammoth Tide* and the *Goliath Tide*, each 218 foot in length with four engines pushing two props. For their size they made the respectable speed of 13.5 knots.

Submersible and semi-submersible rig building anchored the supply side of the oil business. Boat building spread the oil business through many communities long devoted to

Above: John Laborde, president of Tidewater Marine.

Below: Ebb Tide, first of Tidewater's supply boats.

PHOTOGRAPH COURTESY OF JOHN LABORDE.

Right: Mars Tension leg platform also operates in the Mississippi Canyon, 2006. Shell Offshore.

PHOTOGRAPH COURTESY OF THE BUREAU OF SAFETY AND ENVIRONMENTAL ENFORCEMENT.

Below: Sedimentary Provinces Offshore Louisiana, this remarkable chart shows that mysterious place called the Mississippi Canyon. This was the bed of the Mississippi River eons ago when the sea level was 500 feet lower. U.S. Geological Survey Open-file report, 2006. http://pubs.usgs.gov/of/2006/1195/htmldocs/browse_maps.htm

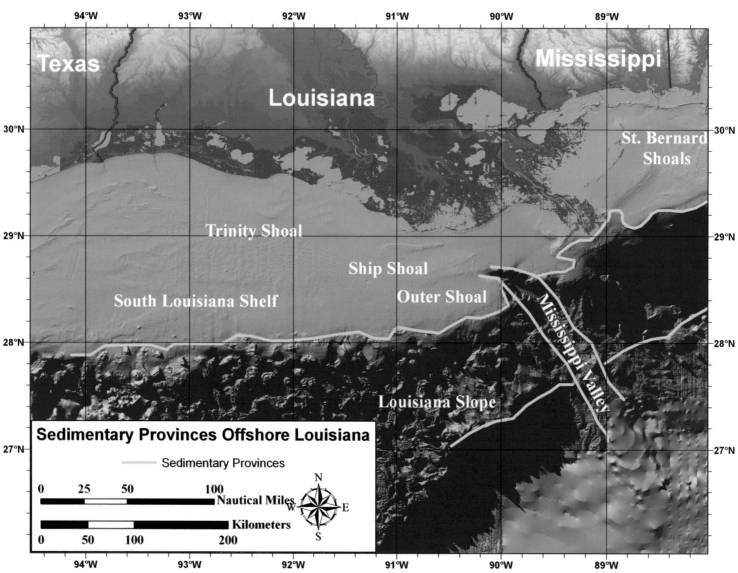

the sea. Alexander, Avondale, and Bollinger Shipyards contributed enormously. Alexander, on the east bank of New Orleans' Industrial Canal, became American Marine Corp. and constructed many of the Tidewater supply boats and early ODECO rigs such as the *Mr. Charlie* and *John Haywood*. Avondale's giant facility just upriver from Westwego mainly did U.S. Naval vessels, but at its Harvey Canal Yard Avondale played an important role in the business. Donald Bollinger's father was a wooden boat builder along Bayou Lafourche. In 1946 Donald inherited $10,000 and purchased additional land along the bayou. He went to New Orleans where he purchased another kind of World War II surplus—an entire machine shop no longer in use. He dismantled it and brought it to Bayou Lafourche where he serviced existing boats. Not until 1953 did he fabricate his first boat,

the *Etiennette Bollinger*. Within a few years the Bollingers were producing dozens of steel workboats that the boatmen, those who purchased the boats in supply companies, were buying to supply the rigs.

Above: Thunder Horse. 2005. *Topsides being loaded by a shore-based crane. It moved to the Mississippi Canyon.*
PHOTOGRAPH COURTESY OF THE BUREAU OF SAFETY AND ENVIRONMENTAL ENFORCEMENT.

Below: Neptune Spar. 1996. *Oryx Energy developed* Neptune, *and was later acquired by Kerr-McGee in 1999. The classic spar hull is basically a cylinder separated into three main sections: 1. Upper section filled with air to provide the buoyancy. 2. Centerwell flooded with seawater. 3. Keel section "soft tank" with ballast.*

THE SHELL KEYS RESERVATION

Records of Assistant Attorney General of Louisiana Oliver Stockwell found now at the Historic New Orleans Collection as MSS492 contain the following representative agreement regarding the environment as of 1955. It concerns the three hundred acres of the Shell Keys Reservation about three-and-a-half miles south of Marsh Island. This applicant, a woman named Miss Tillie Odom, submitted an operating program as an applicant for Federal Oil and Gas Lease under application BLM-041635 (Louisiana).

Specifically applicant agrees that:

1. No part of the Shell Keys Reservation will be used for line of travel to or from drill sites, actual location of drill sites, base of operations, storage of material and equipment, storage of oil, location of pipe line, or otherwise constitute a trespass across or upon the idlets in the Reservation.

2. Development of the area for oil and gas shall be either by slant drilling from water sites located not closer than 500 feet from the mean low tide water mark of any islet in the Reservation, or by participation in a unit area.

3. Drilling mud will be kept at all times in special steel tanks aboard the drilling barge or platform from which drilling is being conducted, and will not be dumped into the water in any way which will pollute the waters or injure aquatic life of the seas or islets of the Reservation.

4. Regulations of the federal government or the State of Louisiana regarding pollution, safety devices, abandonment, plugging and restoration of area will be strictly observed, depending on the location of the drilling site and the particular governmental authority or agency having jurisdiction.

5. An indemnity bond will be provided by applicant in the amount of $100,000 to insure conformance with the lease and operation program.

6. The director of the Fish and Wildlife Service may impose such other conditions and requirements as may be necessary to insure full protection of the particular values for which the Reservation was established.[20]

Opposite: Nolte Theriot advertisement making the point that the North Sea was much rougher than the Gulf of Mexico. Diane Austin and Justin Gaines, authors of History of the Offshore Oil and Gas Industry in Southern Louisiana.

PHOTOGRAPH COURTESY OF THE MINERALS MANAGEMENT SERVICE, VOLUME VI, AND DREW MICHEL.

The pioneers in the Gulf of Mexico oilfield supply business created the industry that subsequently moved worldwide. In 1958 Tidewater opened a business in Venezuela that grew to a fleet of seventy vessels. Many native Louisiana mariners became experts at moving rigs and barges and anchoring them. Nolte Theriot from Bayou Lafourche had been handling anchors for the new rigs for a decade. He was among the best of this specialized skill essential to the barge side of the business and finally to semi-submersibles. Brown and Root developed a field in the North Sea in 1965, but needed skilled captains and tugs to handle the barges laying pipe into England. Conditions in the North Sea were a hundred times worse than in the comparatively placid Gulf. They required specially ice protected tugs, and larger tugs. Theriot, who had a contract with Brown and Root, bid to become the anchor handler and won it. He vowed to bring his entire fleet to England, but discovered that none of his tugs

could handle the weather. So he immediately contracted to build four brand-new tugs at Equitable Shipyard and bring them across the Atlantic rather than experimenting with European shipyards unfamiliar with his tug boat needs. He constructed his first new boat, the *J. V. Alario* in Golden Meadow, and contracted three more to Houma Fabricators. They were much larger than the normal Gulf tug, 100 feet by 27 feet iced class with four 16-71 GM engines. This contract was a perfect example of how the oil and gas industry impacted Louisiana even when the business moved worldwide and how the impact rippled through the related industries.[19] In April 1966 Captain Tommy Vizier took the *J. V. Alario* to England, leaving from the nascent Port Fourchon, accompanied by a competitors tug, the *Gulf Queen*, belonging to Claude Autin. All Theriot's men were from Golden Meadow. They had all started out in the shrimp boat business.

That North Sea is a Rough Mother!

"In Phillips' Ekofisk location, off the Norwegian Coast, the North Sea can grab you like you've seldom been. That old lady can slap your face with gale force 12 wind and make waves up to 65 feet in a matter of minutes. Anyone and anything messing with her then is up to its loadline in one helluva storm, 200 miles from peace and quiet any which way you turn. And, the trouble is, she'll turn you any which way but loose."

But we believe she's up against some even tougher customers. Phillips, ODECO and Brown and Root (the people we work for) are sending men who are ready, willing and able to take on anything she can dish out. Those hands are using some sharp techniques and some really tough tools and heavy equipment.

All in all, it's going to be an expensive proposition getting to that ol' gal. And our customers know in a head-knocking contest like this, they can't afford to come out second best.

That's why they're using rugged Theriot tugs and crews to protect their men, their equipment and their investment.

Nolty J. Theriot, Inc.
1600 Canal St.   New Orleans, La. 70112

Edison Chouest, another successful Acadian shipbuilder, developed a series of repair and fabrication yards. The heart of the operation was North American Shipbuilding (NAS) at Larose on Bayou Lafourche founded in 1974. Winning the contract to provide supply boats for the Louisiana Offshore Oil Port (LOOP) was an important initial boost to the business. Today the company claims to have "built more specialized offshore vessels than any other shipyard in the world. Designing and constructing vessels for ECO has garnered many notable achievements for NAS, including the construction of the first U.S. Antarctic icebreaking research vessel and the largest and most powerful anchor handling vessel in the U.S. fleet."

The Cajun mariners strengthened England's impression of Americans as cowboys, even though they were French speaking. They acted forcefully, without hesitation, and without formality. The Cajun tugs in English waters demonstrated the best of the wild-catter American spirit. Moving 30,000 pound anchors called for immense power which the Cajuns sometimes acquired by using the momentum of the tug itself. "The European captains usually recoiled, as any first-timer would, when a Cajun tug bore down on an anchor and the force drove the deck underwater, with the seas rising up to the deckhands' necks."[21] But the anchor came free. The *J. V. Alario*'s first project was to handle the monster pipe-laying barge the *Hugh W. Gordon*. It carried 5,000 feet of two-inch cable for the ten-line mooring system. The *Hugh W. Gordon* laid the first pipeline carrying North Sea gas into Britain.

The nature of the offshore oil business is clear from the oral histories collected in the early years of the twenty-first century by Tom McGuire for the U.S. Minerals Management Service OCS Region. Chester Theriot high-lighted the risky nature of the business. The majors, he said, "...don't promise you anything. You build and take a chance that, you know, you've been with the company quite a few years and they say, "well we'd like to have a bigger boat." So you build the bigger boat but you might have a job today but if the job depletes, that's it...and you start over

again."[22] Ronald Callais tells the same story. When the oil & gas business collapsed in the mid-1980s "...it just blindsided us. Nobody expected that. Look, I had six boats in those days. I'd just bought this shipyard and I was operating six medium sized offshore boats. I had a company talking to me about building a job, a boat, for a particular job for them. Within three months I had five of my six boats tied up."[23]

While the major oil companies migrated to Houston following the oil bust of 1985, much underlying rig and vessel construction remained in Cajun country. Tidewater kept its headquarters in Louisiana. In 2011 President Dean Taylor and officers resided in the New Orleans area. In the early 1980s Morgan City, the hub of Louisiana's offshore business, was booming. An article in the Kerr-McKee employee newsletter of August 1982 describes this important hub of the offshore oil indus-try. Kerr-McGee operated a large dock with a busy daily routine. "Groaning cranes load

Edison Chouest Offshore C-Port at
Port Fourchon.

supplies on brightly painted work boats. Eighteen-wheelers rumble into the yard by the dock, hauling drill pipe and casing. Nearby, on the new heliport, whirring choppers settle down just long enough to change passengers and take on fuel." To reach an offshore rig may take the supply boat thirteen hours while the helicopter makes the trip in one hour. When a hurricane came along Kerr-McGee evacuated between 500 and 700 workers depending on the drilling activity.

Carroll Bertaut, manager of Kerr-McGee's material and transportation for the Oil and Gas Division's Gulf Coast District, kept his finger on the pulse of the operation. Material expediters, and there were five, supervised the actual shipments. Kerr-McGee's Gulf Coast District operated 400 offshore structures, fifteen of them manned platforms, and varying number of drilling rigs. Kerr-McGee did not own its own boats, but kept fifty-five under contract and busy. "The work boats are the trucks of offshore oilfields. Flat decks

carry pipe, cement and other bulky loads. Tanks below deck hold drinking water, mud, brine and fuel." One of these larger boats rented for $3,100 a day in good times, but by July 1982 the price had dropped to $2,100, an indication of the extreme sensitivity of the supply boat industry to demand.

In 1956 McDermott, Inc., opened its great fabrication yard at Morgan City putting Louisiana solidly in the rig construction business. For many years this was the world's largest offshore fabrication yard. Though a Texas company originally, it opened a New Orleans office in 1937 and became a major part of Louisiana's coming offshore oil business. J. Ray McDermott constructed the earliest pipeline to an offshore well. Like Tidewater, McDermott quickly went worldwide, entering the Venezuela market in 1957 and Arabian market in 1960. Its presence in Morgan City soon led to a housing boom fed by homes constructed by McDermott for its workers.

Above: Petronius compliant tower rig.

McDermott's Louisiana engineering and fabrication played a key role in many of the great offshore fields. In 1978 McDermott installed the 46,000-ton platform for Shell's Cognac Field development in the Gulf of Mexico. The American Society of Civil Engineers awarded McDermott an achievement award for several innovations on this project. Built in three pieces, it was set in more than 1,000 feet of water. McDermott introduced the underwater pile driver, an essential tool for the many fixed and floating rigs yet to come. It constructed and installed topsides for Shell's Auger Tension Leg Platform (TLP), in the Gulf of Mexico, achieving several records such as the largest single-piece structure (26,000 tons) in the Gulf of Mexico, for which it received the American Society of Civil Engineers' Outstanding Civil Engineering Achievement award as "World's Tallest Manmade Structure." McDermott worked on the world's largest and deepest Tension Leg Platform (TLP), the Shell Ursa project in 4,000 feet of water in the Gulf of Mexico. It virtually invented the non-guyed Compliant Tower rig installing the first in 1,800 feet of water for Chevron Texaco's Gulf of Mexico Petronius project. Completed in 2000, it produces

42,000 barrels of oil per day and 70 MMcf/d of gas. Located on the Viosca Reef, it stands twenty miles north of the Macondo Rig. It is a compliant tower designed to sway more than two percent of its height, when a normal skyscraper is limited to one-half percent. Two percent is equivalent to 36 feet. McDermott developed the deep sea pile driving technique. Three piles each 450 feet into the bottom of the sea anchor the four corners of this tower, once the tallest manmade structure in the world.

Soon after McDermott introduced the Spar platform for Chevron Texaco's Genesis project at 2,600 depth in the Gulf of Mexico. A few years later the company introduced the first truss Spars for Kerr-McGee's Gulf of Mexico Boomvang and Nansen Fields in 3,453 and 3,678 feet of water, respectively. In 2001 Morgan City, Louisiana, was the first offshore platform fabrication facility to receive ISO 14001 certification by American Bureau of Shipping Quality Evaluations for its Environmental Management System (No. 36683 December 26, 2001).

Left: The Midnight Crusader, *a Texaco crew boat.*

PHOTOGRAPH COURTESY OF THE MINERALS MANAGEMENT SERVICE, VOLUME VI, AND VINCE GUZZETTA.

Below: The Margaret Lab, *a crew boat to bring workers speedily to the rigs along with equipment.*

PHOTOGRAPH COURTESY OF JOHN LABORDE.

Today McDermott's headquarters are in Houston, but its big fabrication plant continues to produce rigs and part of its engineering group remains in New Orleans. As of the fall of 2011 it has made its first steel cut for the 10,120 ton deck, jacket and piles for the West Delta platform for Shell Offshore.[24]

OPPOSITE, TOP: PHOTOGRAPH COURTESY
OF THE MINERALS MANAGEMENT SERVICE, VOLUME VI,
AND ED HENRY.

OPPOSITE, BOTTOM: PHOTOGRAPH COURTESY
OF THE MINERALS MANAGEMENT SERVICE, VOLUME VI,
AND ROY SMITH.

Above: An old workboat converted from a

shrimp boat.

PHOTOGRAPH COURTESY OF THE MINERALS
MANAGEMENT SERVICE, VOLUME VI,
AND BOB COCKERHAM.

Left: In a strong current, two Nolte Theriot

tugs are holding a pipe laying barge in

position so that the pipe will not buckle.

PHOTOGRAPH COURTESY OF THE MINERALS
MANAGEMENT SERVICE, VOLUME VI, AND JOE SCHOUEST.

CHAPTER 6

Diver working underwater doing burning, wearing wetsuit.

PHOTOGRAPH COURTESY OF THE MINERALS MANAGEMENT SERVICE, VOLUME VI, AND MARY ANN GALLETTI.

Diving bell being brought on board the Pacific Seal.

PHOTOGRAPH COURTESY OF THE MINERALS MANAGEMENT SERVICE, VOLUME VI, AND LYNDA MILLER.

The fortunes of the oilfield offshore service industry can be tracked by the rig count. As oil prices soared in the early 1980s, the number of operating rigs in the United States rose to more than 4,500. The count fell to a post-World War II low of 869 in 1989, but rebounded to 1,010, according to Baker Hughes Inc. Outside the United States, the rig count has been far less volatile. The international average, excluding Canada, was 907 rigs in 1990—the first year since 1985 that the United States has beaten that average.

Modern offshore diving began at the oil rigs off California at the beginning of the twentieth century. Diving then followed the offshore industry to the Gulf Coast. Like much of the oil & gas industry, diving innovations and young businesses founded in Louisiana spread worldwide. Cal Dive, now one of the largest, began in the Gulf of Mexico in 1975. In 1980 it acquired Oil Field Divers of Morgan City and in 2001 acquired New Orleans Professional Divers. A new firm, Legacy Offshore, uses the 300 foot ship *Adams Vision* for rig repair and construction.

Dving helmet made by Walt Daspit.

PHOTOGRAPH COURTESY OF THE MINERALS MANAGEMENT SERVICE, VOLUME VI, AND WALTER DASPIT.

It has offices in Broussard, Louisiana. The most famous local diver was Joe Savoie of Boutte, just west of New Orleans. He was more an inventor than a diver. His most important invention was the first practical lightweight helmet with a rubber neck dam seal developed in the 1960s. Savoie also designed machines to make the helmet components and fabricated them himself at his shop in Boutte.

Offshore diving is a dangerous but necessary branch of the offshore oil industry. The Diver's Forum lists seventy-six divers who have died in accidents over the past couple of decades. Divers and their associations have always pushed for higher safety standards. Since 1990 the U.S. government has been considering and partially adopting a Safety and Environmental Management System (SEMS). But not till after Katrina did it acquire the force of law and not until after the BP oil spill have the regulations been put in force.[25] The editor of the *Offshore Diver*.com welcomed the implementation of SEMS by the Bureau of Ocean Energy Management, Regulation and Enforcement (BOEMRE).[26]

Another Louisiana innovation was the Louisiana Offshore Oil Port (LOOP). The late twentieth century development of the supertanker, the giant oil carrier with drafts of 100 feet or more, has led to the creation of another highly specialized port at the mouth

of Bayou Lafourche. Whereas older and smaller tankers were once able to steam up the river to the refineries near Baton Rouge, the supertanker simply cannot risk trying to enter the river. To meet this, imaginative Louisiana oil men conceived of a plan to extend the Louisiana pipeline network into the Gulf. Tankers offload at LOOP by pumping crude oil through hoses connected to a Single Point Mooring (SPM) base. Three SPMs are located 8,000 feet from the Marine Terminal. The SPMs are designed to handle ships up to 700,000 deadweight tons. The crude oil then moves to the Marine Terminal via a 56-inch diameter submarine pipeline. The Marine Terminal consists of a control platform and a pumping platform. LOOP's onshore facilities, Fourchon Booster Station and Clovelly Dome Storage Terminal, are located just onshore in Fourchon and twenty-five miles inland near Galliano, Louisiana. The pipeline system is a joint project of three major oil companies— Marathon, Murphy, and Shell Oil Companies. Port Fourchon now services about ninety percent of the Gulf's deepwater rigs and platforms. In 2006 it handled an estimated $63.4 billion worth of oil and natural gas, some thirteen percent of the nation's foreign oil, about 1.2 million barrels a day. The system connects by pipeline to thirty-five percent of the refining capability of the country.

Aerial view of Port Fourchon, 2004,
www.bsee.gov.

PHOTOGRAPH COURTESY OF OFFSHORE STATS AND FACTS, GULF OF MEXICO REGION, DATA CENTER, AVAILABLE RESOURCES, IMAGE LIBRARY.

PHOTOGRAPHS THIS PAGE COURTESY OF THE MINERALS
MANAGEMENT SERVICE, VOLUME VI, AND JOE SCHOUEST.

Offshore natural gas comes ashore just south of Lafayette. The Henry Hub near Erath, Louisiana, is the center for the natural gas pipelines bringing offshore gas to shore and depositing it in the interstate lines. United Gas Pipeline Company of Shreveport laid one of the earliest pipelines with a twenty-inch pipe that stretched twenty-five miles from Eugene Island to shore. An armada of derrick barges, laying barges, winch barges, tugboats and crew boats worked to put the pipe beneath five feet of cover. Twenty years later the Stingray line extending for 228 miles between seventeen

offshore blocks and back to Holly Beach, Louisiana, went into service at a cost of $161 million. Today thousands of miles of gas pipeline tie into the Henry Hub owned and operated by Sabine Pipe Line LLC.[27] Further west Lake Charles has become a major hub for liquefied natural gas (LNG).

Along with LOOP, the last thirty years have witnessed the implementation of the Strategic Petroleum Reserve. This multi-million barrel storage system was devised to be both a reserve for true shortages as well as a device for moderating price swings. The Strategic Oil is kept in giant caverns carved from salt domes.

Top: A Nolte J. Theriot tug headquartered at Golden Meadow.

PHOTOGRAPH COURTESY OF THE MINERALS MANAGEMENT SERVICE, VOLUME VI, AND JOE SCHOUEST.

ABOVE: PHOTOGRAPH COURTESY OF THE MINERALS MANAGEMENT SERVICE, VOLUME VI, AND JOE SCHOUEST.

Above: Fabricating an offshore platform in the McDermott Yard at Amelia, Louisiana.

PHOTOGRAPH COURTESY OF THE MINERALS
MANAGEMENT SERVICE, VOLUME VI,
AND DELORES HENDERSON.

Right: Close up to a rig fire.

PHOTOGRAPHS COURTESY OF THE MINERALS
MANAGEMENT SERVICE, VOLUME VI,
AND JAMES BROUSSARD.

Above: Penrod Drilling Company's drill

barge, the Tom Sorrell.

PHOTOGRAPH COURTESY OF THE MINERALS
MANAGEMENT SERVICE, VOLUME VI, AND RUTH CAMP.

Left: Quenching a rig fire.

PHOTOGRAPHS COURTESY OF THE MINERALS
MANAGEMENT SERVICE, VOLUME VI,
AND JAMES BROUSSARD.

Oil is naturally found compressed in sand or gravels from which pressure releases it to a nearby oil well. It would never be feasible to re-inject oil into oil sands on any systematic basic.

The year 2010 was a pivotal year in Gulf of Mexico offshore drilling. The BP Macondo Well explosion shut down exploration and drilling in the Gulf. It threatened to close permanently efforts to develop additional offshore fields. This well discharged an estimated 750,000 tons of oil (five and a quarter million barrels or one quarter of a day's consumption in the United States), a number three times the size of the *Amoco Cadiz* spill.

Chevron wells in Main Pass Field. Interior Secretary Walter Hinckel ordered Chevron to cease operations in Block 41 to permit federal inspectors to review the operation. This decision affected 292 wells with 64,000 barrels of oil per day. The Interior Department postponed a large lease sale of western Louisiana offshore tracts scheduled for later that year.[28] But a later public hearing with 150 participants found only token opposition to renewing lease sales as conservationists asked only that the leases contain protections for the environment. The strongest opposition came from the shrimpers association which protested shallow water damage to shrimp holes.[29]

Unidentified jackup rig in the Gulf of Mexico. The platform ratcheted up and down the three legs.

The offshore industry has never experienced the number of blowouts and accidents as land based drilling. One of the earlier accidents in the offshore business occurred in 1970 when a fire led to the shutdown of

The tension between the oil industry and environmentalists has always been high because of the exceptional nature of Louisiana's delicate coast line. As the twentieth century oil industry rolled over the coastal parishes,

oil drillers cut up the marshes making access and pipeline canals. Windell Curole, former levee board president Lafourche Parish, described the problem:

> It's mostly flood control, but there is no doubt the oil industry has, I guess, exacerbated the situation and made it much worse with the navigation canals, the floatation canals, the location canals, the pipelines canals that have done all this crisscrossing. Where we have all this induced saltwater coming in here. We have a battle between the Mississippi River building land, the Gulf of Mexico taking land back…we tied one hand back and let the gulf start eating. Secondarily though we came in with the oil industry right after and tied the other hand back by helping out the Gulf of Mexico bring in more saltwater. So those two things are tied together. But if we ever get the river going back again, provided we have a

political will to do what we need to do, we can go ahead and get systemic solutions and again heal most of the damage that was done by the oil industry.[30]

One of the consequences of the Deepwater Horizon oil spill was the commitment by BP to spend $30 billion to compensate individuals and businesses hurt by the accident. But equally important is the large sum the company dedicated to restoring Louisiana's coast, an effort that will have long term beneficial consequences for the sensitive marsh of Louisiana.

In the grand scheme the Macondo Well, with its estimated reserves of 50 mmb of oil, is modest compared to the reserves expected much further out and deeper in the Gulf. BP has a Tiber project with expected reserves of 3 billion barrels of oil. This is about two years of America's daily consumption of oil.

Cracien Curole standing on board walks in Golden Meadow, c. 1940.

PHOTOGRAPH COURTESY OF THE MINERALS MANAGEMENT SERVICE, VOLUME VI, AND BERNICE CUROLE.

PHOTOGRAPH COURTESY OF THE MINERALS
MANAGEMENT SERVICE, VOLUME VI, AND LYNDA MILLER.

CHAPTER 6

CONCLUSION

Louisiana, the energy state, remains unrivalled. It has the only off-shore hub for the down-loading of super tankers, its natural gas hub sets the price of natural gas in the United States, its chemical corridor, very much a part of the petroleum industry, is unsurpassed, and its offshore drilling and production eclipses any other coast of the United States. Louisiana ranks number one in many petroleum categories on a per capita basis. But even in absolute terms this middle-range sized state ranks first, second, or third in absolute refining and production.

Louisiana continues to produce wildcatters and risk takers in the petroleum industry. The best jobs in Louisiana, from refinery management to offshore drilling, are thanks to petroleum. Louisiana's contribution to the wealth of the nation both in petroleum and in plastics is large. Louisiana is stellar in other respects. Its petroleum industry, seafood industry, and cultural industry are all practically first in their class among the states.

The petroleum industry is world-wide and because of that Louisianians who have gone into the business have become citizens of the world. They have gone to the North Sea, to Nigeria, and to Saudi Arabia. It ties Louisiana to the rest of the world.

Historians have been impressed. Daniel Yergin's epochal work on the oil industry called *The Prize* set the stage for the optimism of the first years of the twenty-first century.[1] Historians produced works such as *Offshore Pioneers: Brown & Root* by Joseph A. Pratt, Tyler Priest et al; *50 Years Offshore* by Hans E. Veldman and George H. C. Lagers; and *Deep Challenge: The True Epic Story of our Quest for Energy Beneath the Sea* by Clyde W. Burleson.

But, soon enough difficulties appeared and the academic story began to change. In 2007 Tyler Priest produced his article "Extraction Not Creation: The History of Offshore Petroleum in the Gulf of Mexico" published in *Enterprise & Society*. The author argued that all the books about technological inventions and business creativity generating new oil finds in the Gulf of Mexico were beside the point. Simply put, oil was there. It needed only to be extracted and would have been, easily or not. But now, wrote Priest, those "simple, celebratory narratives" mentioned above were inadequate. "The fable of technological-generated abundance belies the fact that the Gulf of Mexico is an oil province in terminal decline." In other words, the end is near. All of the industry's technological and creative wizardry will be for naught because the oil has been used up. For Priest, who had earlier produced a prize-winning book *The Offshore Imperative: Shell Oil's Search for Petroleum in Post War America*, turned to helping the *Journal of American History* produce an entire volume on America's oil industry. Now Priest was writing "Bucking the Odds: Organized Labor in Gulf Coast Oil Refining" and simultaneously moving from the Houston oil environment to a professorship at the ethanol-centered University of Iowa.

As we have seen, however, nature threw a curve at this narrative. The end had not come just yet. Technology and creativity produced the era of natural gas just commencing. Yergin discusses this "Shale gale" in his latest book *The Quest*.[2] But he makes some more fundamental points. The energy infrastructure does not change appreciably from year to year or even decade to decade. He quoted Winston Churchill's aphorism, "variety, and variety alone" is the key to energy sufficiency. Nevertheless, petroleum remains central. The geologists preach "Oil is found in the minds of men."[3] Fortunately, the growth in world demand for energy is now matched by the globalization of innovation. This paean to creativity brings the story back to where it started—in the mind of a wildcatter.

Conrad Albrizio painting of chemical plant workers (probably the great Standard Oil Refinery) at the State Capital Annex, 1938. Oil and gas also made chemicals and plastics.

ENDNOTES

Chapter 1

1. U.S. Department of the Interior, Minerals Management Service Gulf of Mexico OCS Region, Estimated Oil and Gas Reserves as of December 31, 2005. (2009). Table 1. See also Marc Humpries, Robert Pirog, and Gene Whitney, U.S. Offshore Oil and Gas Resources: Prospects and Processes (Congressional Research Service, April 26, 1910), p. 14. www.crs.gov.
2. Mid-Continent Oil and Gas Association, *Louisiana Oil and Gas Facts* (1950).
3. Jimmy Owen, p. 139.
4. U.S. Energy Information Administration. Effect of Increased Natural Gas Exports on Domestic Energy Markets, as requested by the Office of Fossil Energy. January 2012. p. 12.

Chapter 2

1. Mid-Continent Oil and Gas Association. *Louisiana Oil and Gas Facts*. (Baton Rouge: Mid-Continent Oil and Gas Association, 1967).
2. W. Scott Heywood, "The Autobiography of an Oil Man" in *Oil: Pictorial Trade Journal of the Petroleum Industry* (July 1941), p. 23.
3. Heywood, "The Autobiography of an Oil Man" (May 1941), p 33.
4. Heywood, "The Autobiography of an Oil Man" (June 1941), p. 21.
5. Heywood, "The Autobiography of an Oil Man" (June 1941), p. 23.
6. See also *Oil Investors' Journal*, May 24, 1902, p. 3.
7. Heywood, "The Autobiography of an Oil Man" (July 1941), p. 22.
8. Bill of Lading, September 8, 1902, acknowledging the return of an empty Oil Tank Car, Archives, Dupre Library, University of Louisiana at Lafayette.
9. Heywood, "The Autobiography of an Oil Man" (September 1941), p. 15.
10. Heywood, "The Autobiography of an Oil Man" (September 1941), p. 16.
11. Colonel Scott W. Heywood, Report to Governor William H. Murray, February 14, 1931 (pamphlet at the Archives Department, Dupre Library, University of Louisiana at Lafayette).
12. Syed Mohammad, Head of Engineering, Zigler Shipyards, Inc., Jennings, Louisiana, "Use of Prelikon at Zigler Shipyards," in Proceedings of the REAPS Technical Symposium, June 15-16, 1976, Atlanta, Georgia. www.dtic.mil/cgi-bin/GetTRDoc?AD=AdA448261
13. G. D. Harris, *Oil and Gas in Louisiana with a Brief Summary of their Occurrence in Adjacent States*. Bulletin—United States Geological Survey, Issue 429 (Washington: Government Printing Office, 1910), 35-36.
14. James P. Owen, *Let the Eagle Fly…Again!* (Lafayette, Louisiana: Corita Jean Owen Smith, 1989), p. 139.
15. Owen, Let the Eagle, p. 140.
16. Owen, Let the Eagle, p. 175.
17. Sam Mims, "The Diary of a Roughneck" in *Oil* (June 1941), 25.
18. Jack Giovo, I. Bruce Turner, and Linda Parker Langley, *Jefferson Davis Parish: An Oral History* (Jennings, Louisiana: Jeff Davis Arts Council, 2000), 94-96.
19. Jeff A. Spencer, The Vinton (GED) Oil Field, Calcasieu Parish, Louisiana, Oil-Industry History, v. 11, no. 1, 2010, p. 19.
20. *Times-Picayune* June 21, 1931.
21. Ann W. Diamond, "Cameron's Gold: Gas, Oil and Wildlife," a paper submitted to McNeese State University, May 1973.
22. Jack Donahue, *Wildcatter: the Story of Michel T. Halbouty and the Search for Oil* (New York: McGraw-Hill Book Company, 1979), 134-35.
23. New Orleans Geological Society. Paul Lawless, p. 25, 2010.

Chapter 3

1. SONRIS, the online data base of the Office of Conservation in the Department of Natural Resources.
2. Gerald Forbes, "A History of Caddo Oil and Gas Field" in *Louisiana Historical Quarterly* XXIX (January 1946), 61.
3. Forbes, "A History of Caddo Oil and Gas Field," 66-67.
4. *Oil Investor's Journal*, December 18, 1905, p. 11.
5. George Charlton Matson, *The Caddo Oil and Gas Field, Louisiana and Texas* (Washington: Government Printing Office, 1916), p. 10.
6. *The Shreveport Times*, May 25, 1906, Clipping in the Randall Martin Collection, folder 138, LSU Shreveport Archives.
7. *The Shreveport Times*, May 20, 1956. Clipping in the LSU Shreveport Archives.
8. Sam T. Mallison, *The Great Wildcatter* (Charleston, West Virginia: Education Foundation of West Virginia, Inc., 1953), 107-108.
9. The Department of Conservation recommended the use of cement plugs in the Haynesville Oil Field. W. W. Scott and Ben K. Stroud, *The Haynesville Oil Field, Claiborne Parish, Louisiana* (Baton Rouge: Department of Conservation, 1922), Bulletin No. 11, p. 13.
10. Mallison, *The Great Wildcatter*, 204-210.
11. Field Trip Notes, part of The History of the Oil Industry Symposium, March 23-26 at Shreveport, Louisiana.
12. Oil accounting, Standard Oil Company for December 1914 in the W. P. Stiles Collection, folder 53, LSU Shreveport Archives.
13. Typescript of Oral Interview with Carl W. Jones, early Shreveport oil man, by Hubert Humphreys, in Louisiana State University in Shreveport, Archives, Oral History Program.
14. Undated Report by A. F. Crider, Consulting Geologist, in the Randall Martin Collection, folder 421, LSU Shreveport Archives.
15. Undated Report by C. C. Clark in the Randall Marin Collection, folder 422, LSU Shreveport Archives.
16. *Times-Picayune* January 19, 1939.
17. Franks and Lambert, p. 85.
18. Pamphlet, Commercial Review published by the Shreveport Chamber of Commerce, February 1922, in the R. O. Roy Collection, Box 1, LSU Shreveport Archives.
19. Clipping from the *Bossier Banner*, April 27, 1922, in the R. O. Roy Collection, LSU Shreveport Archives.
20. Clipping, *The Shreveport Times*, August 7, 1928 in the R. O. Roy Collection, Box 2, Archives of LSU Shreveport.
21. Interview with Henry Goodrich by author, November 16, 2011, at Goodrich Petroleum, 33 Texas Street, Suite 1375, Shreveport, Louisiana 71101.
22. Interview with Robert Stacy, Jr., by Autumn Grant on November 11, 2001, in Louisiana State University in Shreveport, Archives, Oral History Program.
23. Clipping from *The Shreveport Times*, May 20, 1956, in LSU Shreveport United Gas Collection.
24. Transcript of Interview with Robert Stacy, Jr., by Autumn Grant on November 11, 2001, p. 4, in Louisiana State University in Shreveport, Archives, Oral History Program.
25. Clipping from Oil & Gas Progress Week, October 10-16, [1954], Randall Martin Collection, folder 149, LSU Shreveport Archives.
26. Transcript of Interview with Robert Stacy, Jr., by Autumn Grant on November 11, 2001, p. 6, in Louisiana State University in Shreveport, Archives, Oral History Program.
27. Norris Cochran McGowan, Natural Gas: The Gulf South's Symbol of Progress, an address to the New Orleans meeting December 13, 1951, of The Newcomen Society. United Gas Collection, Archives, LSU Shreveport.

28. Pamphlet, The Story of United Gas, 1930–1960, p. 29, in folder 23, Box 2, United Gas Collection, Archives, Louisiana State University at Shreveport.

29. Pamphlet, The Story of United Gas, 1930–1960, p. 31, in folder 23, Box 2, United Gas Collection, Archives, Louisiana State University at Shreveport.

30. Clipping from Forbes, September 15, 1974, pages 54 and 57, Randall Martin Collection, folder 171, LSU Shreveport Archives.

31. "What Happened to the United Gas Log?", a pamphlet in the United Gas Collection, folder 1, LSU Shreveport Archives.

32. U.S. Energy Information Administration, "Natural Gas" Gulf of Mexico Federal Offshore Production, http://www.eia.gov/dnav/ng/NG_PROD_DEEP_S1_A.htm.

33. U.S. Energy Information Administration, Review of Emerging U.S. Shale Gas and Shale Oil Plays (July 2011), 25-28.

34. *Catalyst* Jan-Apr 2012 p. 19. [http://brac.org/docs/catalyst/BRAC_Catalyst_Jan_Apr_2012_Shale.pdf]

35. http://www.askchesapeake.com/Haynesville-Shale/

36. *Wall Street Journal.* June 15, 2012.

Chapter 4

1. *Times-Picayune* March 20, 1957.

2. H. W. Bell and R. A. Cattell, *Department of Conservation Bulletin No. 9: The Monroe Gas Field, Ouachita, Morehouse, and Union Parishes Louisiana* (Baton Rouge: Department of Conservation, 1921).

3. SONRIS, "Oil and Gas—Inception to Date Field Production by District".

4. U.S. Department of the Interior, Mineral Management Service, Gulf of Mexico OCS Region, Estimated Oil and Gas Reserves (December 31, 2005), Table One.

5. U.S. Department of the Interior, Bureau of Land Management, Eastern States, Jackson Field Office, Reasonably Foreseeable Development Scenario for Fluid Minerals (March 2008), Figure 15.

6. U.S. Bureau of Mines, Map of the Monroe Gas Field: Ouachita, Morehouse and Union Parishes Louisiana, April 1921, insert in Bell and Cattel.

7. Bell and Cattel, p. 77.

8. *Times-Picayune* September 7, 1922.

9. Preston Fergus, Monroe Gas Field, Louisiana AAPG Special Volumes Volume SP 7: Geology of Natural Gas, Pages 741-772 (1935).

10. *Times-Picayune* July 29, 1921.

11. *Times-Picayune* November 25, 1922.

12. *Times-Picayune* September 3, 1921.

13. *Times-Picayune* February 14, 1921.

14. *Times-Picayune* November 11, 1923.

15. Bell and Cattell, p. 43.

16. Bell and Cattell.

17. *Times-Picayune* March 27, 1923.

18. *Times-Picayune* January 22, 1926.

19. Frost-Johnson Lumber Co. v. Salling's Heirs, 91 So.207, 150 La. 756; Herkness v. Irion et al 11 F. 2d 386 (1926), No. 18272 District Court, E. D. Louisiana, March 6, 1926.

20. *Times-Picayune* March 20, 1926.

21. *Times-Picayune* July 1, 1926.

22. *Times-Picayune* July 1, 1926.

23. *Times-Picayune* April 2, 1926.

24. *Times-Picayune* June 5, 1926.

25. *Times-Picayune* October 23, 1926.

26. *Times-Picayune* September 30, 1925.

27. *Times-Picayune* March 7, 1927.

28. *Times-Picayune* November 26, 1928.

29. *New Orleans Item* October 18, 1922.

30. *Times-Picayune* November 22, 1927.

31. *Times-Picayune* November 22, 23, 25, 28, and 30, 1927.

32. *Times-Picayune* December 31, 1926.

33. *Times-Picayune* March 22, 1928.

34. This struggle is also detailed in T. Harry Williams, *Huey Long* (New York: Vintage Books, 1981), 302-310.

35. W. V. Baeckmann, W. Schwenk, W. Prinz. editors, *Handbook of Cathodic Corrosion Protection* third edition (Houston: Gulf Professional Publishing, 1997), "The History of Corrosion Protection." p. 15.

36. *Times-Picayune* March 28, 1928.

37. Interstate Nat. Gas Co., Inc. v. FPC, 331 U.S. 682 (1947).

38. *Times-Picayune* January 25, 1937.

39. *Times-Picayune* September 12, 1944.

40. Energy Information Administration, Natural Gas Monthly, January 2012.

Chapter 5

1. Robert W. Harrison and Walter M. Kollmorgen, "Drainage Reclamation in the Coastal Marshlands of the Mississippi River Delta" in *The Louisiana Historical Quarterly* XXX (April, 1947), 654-5.

2. Obituary of Joseph Rathborne. *The Lumber Trade Journal* (September 1, 1923).

3. Clipping, *The Lumber Trade Journal*, May 7, 1921, in Scrapbook, 1889-1949, Rathborne Company Files, Harvey, Louisiana.

4. John Powers, ed., *Celebrating the Century* (New Orleans: 1997), p. 21.

5. United States Court of Appeals, Fifth Circuit, Rathborne Land Company v. Ascent Energy Inc. and Ascent Energy Louisiana, L.L.C. No. 09-30499, June 23, 2010.

6. Anna C. Burns, "Frank B. Williams, Cypress Lumber King," *Journal of Forest History* (July 1980), 127-133.

7. Rachael Edna Norgress, "The History of the Cypress Lumber Industry in Louisiana," in The Louisiana Historical Quarterly XXX (July 1947), 1013.

8. Norgress, 1038.

9. *New Orleans Item* July 26, 1909, Interview with Edward Wisner.

10. Doherty founded Cities Service Oil Company in 1910 to manage holdings in Oklahoma and later, Kansas. In 1912 the company acquired the oil lands of Theodore N. Barnsdall, a large investor in northwest Louisiana. In 1944 Citgo built its manufacturing complex in Calcasieu Parish at Lake Charles.

11. *Times-Picayune* November 13, 1938.

12. *Times-Picayune* December 3, 1939.

13. SONRIS Production tables.

14. *Times-Picayune* February 16, 1941.

15. *Times-Picayune* July 16, 1939.

16. http://www.swiftenergy.com/menus/OP-Lake-Washington.htm

17. *Times-Picayune* August 25, 1934, and January 18, 1937.

18. Bertie Taylor, "A Century of Pioneers" in Louisiana: Proud Past, Promising Future (http://www.oilandgasinvestor.com/pdf/LASuplement.pdf: Oil and Gas Investor, 2005), p. 57.

19. NOGS CD, Port Hudson Field, p. 237 (2010) CD.

20. Bertie Taylor, "A Century of Pioneers", p. 67.

21. Louis J. Roussel, Jr., *Friends, Enemies & Victims. The Personal Success of a Seventh-Grader: Autobiography of Louis J. Roussel, Jr.,* (New Orleans: Louis J. Roussel, Jr., 1997), p. 13.

22. Roussel, p. 23, 26.

23. *Times-Picayune* February 19, 1964.

24. Paul Lawless, "South Louisiana Exploration Results (1988-2010)" in Oil & Gas Fields of South Louisiana 2010 (CD).

25. Eugene Island Blocks 10/24 Field, p. 105-108, NOGS CD (2010).

26. Paul Lawless, "South Louisiana Exploration Results (1988-2010)."

Chapter 6

1. T. McGuire, *History of the offshore oil and gas industry in southern Louisiana: Interim report; Volume II: Bayou Lafourche—An oral history of the development of the oil and gas industry* (New Orleans: U.S. Department of the Interior, Minerals Management Service, Gulf of Mexico OCS Region, New Orleans, Louisiana, 2004), p. 84.

2. See Department of Interior, *Increased Safety Measures for Energy Development on the Outer Continental Shelf*, (May 27, 2010). Although there is no single accepted definition of "deepwater," a common use of the term is to refer to locations where the water depth is at least 1,000 feet.

3. T. Gerald Crawford, Grant L. Burgess, Steven M. Haley, Peter F. Harrison, Clark J. Kinler, Gregory D. Klocek, Nancy K. Shepard, *Outer Continental Shelf Estimated Oil and Gas Reserves: Gulf of Mexico,* December 31, 1906 (New Orleans: Resource Evaluation Office, Reserves Section, U.S. Department of the Interior. Minerals Management Service, New Orleans, December 2009).

4. Joseph A. Pratt, Tyler Priest, and Christophe J. Castaneda, *Offshore Pioneers: Brown & Root and the History of Offshore Oil and Gas* (Houston: Gulf Publishing Company, 1997), 12-13.

5. In 339 US 699 the United States Supreme Court ruled that the U.S. had a "paramount interest" in the Tidelands beyond Louisiana's three-mile limit.

6. Statement of Mrs. J. C. De Armas, Jr., dated November 20, 1956, found in the Oliver Stockwell Papers, MSS 492, Box 107, Williams Research Center.

7. D. Austin, B. Carriker, T. McGuire, J. Pratt, T. Priest, and A. G. Pulsipher, *History of the offshore oil and gas industry in southern Louisiana: Interim report; Volume I: Papers on the evolving offshore industry* (New Orleans: U.S. Department of the Interior, Minerals Management Service, Gulf of Mexico OCS Region, New Orleans, Louisiana OCS Study MMS 2004-049), p. 30.

8. Ibid., p. 30.

9. McGuire, p. 39.

10. Alden J. Laborde, *My Life and Time* (New Orleans: Laborde Printing Company, [1997]), 157.

11. Heywood, Autobiography in *Oil* (May 1941), p. 33.

12. Laborde, *My Life*, p. 160.

13. *Oil & Gas Journal*, May 4, 1970, p. 107.

14. D. Austin, B. Carriker, T. McGuire, J. Pratt, T. Priest, and A. G. Pulsipher, *History of the offshore oil and gas industry in Southern Louisiana: Interim report*, p. 43.

15. http://www.marineinsight.com/marine/types-of-ships-marine/semi-submersible-ships-and-semi-submersible-rigs-a-general-overview/

16. Michael C. Forrest, "Gulf of Mexico 'Bright Spots:' Early Shell Discoveries" in Charles A. Sternbach, Marlan W. Downey; and Gerald M. Friedman, *Discoverers of the Twentieth Century: Perfecting the Search, A Collection of Stories about Significant Discoveries by those who know them best* (Tulsa, Oklahoma: The American Association of Petroleum Geologists, 2005), 93-108.

17. McGuire, p. 100.

18. Online shipyard database by Tim Colton.

19. Woody Falgoux, *Rise of the Cajun Mariners: The Race for Big Oil.* (Stockard James. 2007).

20. Oliver Stockwell Papers, MSS 492, Box 100, Williams Research Center.

21. Falgoux, *Rise of the Cajun Mariners*, p. 156.

22. McGuire, p. 87.

23. McGuire, p. 100.

24. www.TheStreet.com, August 4, 2011.

25. 30 CFR Part 250 Subpart S—Safety and Environmental Systems (SEMS).

26. www.offshorediver.com.

27. Bertie Taylor, "A Century of Pioneers" in *Louisiana: Proud Past, Promising Future* (http://www.oilandgasinvestor.com/pdf/LASuplement.pdf: Oil and Gas Investor, 2005), p. 54.

28. *Oil & Gas Journal*, March 2, 1970, p. 41.

29. *Oil & Gas Journal*, July 20, 1970, p. 44.

30. McGuire, p. 134.

Conclusion

1. Daniel Yergin, *The Prize: The Epic Quest for Oil, Money & Power* (New York: Free Press, 1991). But by 2009 even Yergin was hesitant. In an epilogue that year he concludes that over the next quarter of a century the world will need at least forty percent more oil. "Perhaps innovation will lower that number. The answers depend upon policy and markets and on technology and the scale and character of research and development." p. 773.

2. Daniel Yergin, *The Quest: Energy, Security, and the Remaking of the Modern World* (New York: The Penguin Press, 2011).

3. Daniel Yergin, *The Quest*, 716-17.

Oilfield work paid well and provided jobs for both white and black workers.

BIBLIOGRAPHY

Primary

Historic New Orleans Collection. Williams Research Center. Oliver Stockwell Papers, MSS 492.

International Petroleum Museum & Exposition, Morgan City, Louisiana.

Jennings Oil and Gas Museum.

Jennings Carnegie Library.

Jennings Public Library.

Louisiana State Oil and Gas Museum, Oil City, Louisiana.

LSU Baton Rouge. Hill Library. Caddo-Pine Island Museum. Governing Board. Minutes / Caddo-Pine Island Museum Governing Board. Publication info: [Oil City, Louisiana]: Caddo-Pine Island Museum, 1998-2001. Physical description: v. 28 cm. Volume/date range: January 12, 1998—April 12, 2001. Continued by: Louisiana State Oil and Gas Museum. Governing Board. Minutes.

LSU Shreveport. Jones, Typescript of Oral Interview with Carl W. Jones, early Shreveport oil man, by Hubert Humphreys, Oral History Program; Martin, Randall Collection; Roy, R. O. Collection; Stacey, Transcript of Interview with Robert Stacy, Jr., by Autumn Grant on November 11, 2001, Oral History Program; Stiles, W. P. Papers; United Gas Collection.

Tulane University. Special Collections Jones Hall. Kuhn Papers. #385. Cathodic protection; Moore, Andre Brown. Papers 1921-1985. Collection # 736.

Published

Giovo, Jack; Turner, I. Bruce; and Langley, Linda Parker. *Jefferson Davis Parish: An Oral History*. Jeff Davis Arts Council, 2000.

Heywood, W. Scott. "The Autobiography of an Oil Man" in *Oil: Pictorial Trade Journal of the Petroleum Industry* (May-September 1941).

Laborde, Alden J. *My Life and Time*. New Orleans: Laborde Printing Company, [1997].

Louisiana Geological Society. *Typical Oil & Gas Fields of Southwestern Louisiana*. Lafayette, Louisiana, 1983.

Owen, James P. (Jimmie). *Let the Eagle Fly…Again!. Memoirs*. Lafayette, Louisiana: Corita Jean Owen Smith, 1989.

Roussel, Jr., Louis J. *Friends, Enemies & Victims. The Personal Success of a Seventh-Grader: Autobiography of Louis J. Roussel, Jr*. New Orleans: Louis J. Roussel, Jr., 1997.

Secondary

Baeckmann, Walter; Schwenk, Wilhelm; and Prinz, W. *Handbook of Cathodic Corrosion Protection: Theory and Practice of Electrochemical Protection Processes*. Houston: Gulf Professional Publishing, 1997. On Robert Kuhn

Barton, Donald C., and R. H. Goodrich, 1926, The Jennings Oil Field, Acadia Parish: American Association of Petroleum Geologists Bulletin, volume 10, p. 72-92. Published:Tulsa, Oklahoma, American Association of Petroleum Geologists. v. 2-50; 1918-1966. Cumulative Index:Vols. 1-6, 1917-22 (issued as v. 7, no. 6, part 2) with v. 7; vols.1-10, 1917-26, 1 v. ORDER THROUGH TULANE Gulf Professional Publishing, 1997.

Bell, H. W. and Cattell, R. A. Department of Conservation Bulletin No. 9: The Monroe Gas Field, Ouachita, Morehouse, and Union Parishes Louisiana. Baton Rouge: Department of Conservation, 1921.

Oilfield near Jennings, Louisiana.
PHOTOGRAPH COURTESY OF THE GEORGE FRANCOIS
MUGNIER COLLECTION, NEW ORLEANS PUBLIC LIBRARY.

Burns, Anna C. "Frank B. Williams, Cypress Lumber King." *Journal of Forest History* (July 1980), 127-133.

Diamond, Ann W. "Cameron's Gold: Gas, Oil and Wildlife," a paper submitted to McNeese State University, May 1973.

Donahue, Jack. *Wildcatter: The Story of Michel T. Halbouty and the Search for Oil.* New York: McGraw-Hill Book Company, 1979.

Dufour, Charles L. *Taken at the Flood: The Story of Tidewater.* 1981.

Ezell, John Samuel. *Innovations in Energy: The Story of Kerr-McGee.* Norman, Oklahoma: University of Oklahoma Press, 1979.

Falgoux, Woody. *Rise of the Cajun Mariners: The Race for Big Oil.* Stockard James. 2007.

Forbes, Gerald. "A History of Caddo Oil and Gas Field" in *Louisiana Historical Quarterly* XXIX (January 1946), 59-72.

_____. "Jennings, First Louisiana Salt Dome Pool" in *Louisiana Historical Quarterly* XXIX (April, 1946), 496-509.

Fox, John A. *The Wisner Estates Incorporated.* New Orleans: Wisner Estates Inc.,1917.

Franks, Kenny A., and Paul F. Lambert, 1982, *Early Louisiana and Arkansas. A Photographic History 1901-1946.* College Station, Texas A & M University Press, 1982.

Hakes, Jay. *A Declaration of Energy Independence: How Freedom from Foreign Oil can Improve National Security, Our Economy, and the Environment.* Hoboken, New Jersey: John Wiley & Sons, Inc., 2008.

Harris, Gilbert D. *Oil and gas in Louisiana, with a brief summary of their occurrence in adjacent states.* Washington: Government Printing Office, 1910.

Harrison, Robert W. and Kollmorgen, Walter M. "Drainage Reclamation in the Coastal Marshlands of the Mississippi River Delta" in *The Louisiana Historical Quarterly* XXX (April, 1947), 654-709.

Heywood, W. Scott. "The Autobiography of an Oil Man" in *Oil, Pictorial Trade Journal of the Petroleum Industry*, v. 1, no. 3-9, June 1941.

Lindstedt, Dianne. History of oil and gas development in coastal Louisiana. Baton Rouge: Louisiana Geological Survey, 1991.

Louisiana Geological Survey. Oil and gas map of Louisiana, index / compiled by C. P. Stanfield. [Baton Rouge, Louisiana]: Department of Natural Resources, Louisiana Geological Survey, 1981.

Louisiana State Mineral Board. A handbook on the duties and responsibilities of the State Mineral Board and its several divisions; Geology of natural gas in south Louisiana. Includes: AAPG memoir, vol. 1, p. 376-413; The lower Tuscaloosa trend of south-central Louisiana, GCAGS, vol. 29, p. 37-38; South Louisiana Tuscaloosa activity, Louisiana Department of Conservation, 1977 / prepared by the staff of the Louisiana Office of Mineral Resources with the cooperation of the American Association of Petroleum Geologists and the Gulf Coast Association of Geological Societies. Baton Rouge, Louisiana: Department of Natural Resources, Office of Mineral Resources (State Mineral Board), [1979].

Mallison, Sam T. *The Great Wildcatter.* Charleston, West Virginia: Education Foundation of West Virginia, Inc., 1953.

Matson, George Charlton. *The Caddo Oil and Gas Field, Louisiana and Texas.* Washington: Government Printing Office, 1916.

Mid-Continent Oil & Gas Association. *Louisiana oil and gas facts.* Baton Rouge, Mid-Continent Oil & Gas Association.

Miles, Ray. *King of the Wildcatters: The Life and Times of Tom Slick, 1883-1930.* College Station: Texas A&M University Press, c. 1996.

NERA Economic Consulting. *Macroeconomic Impacts of LNG Exports from the United States.* December 2012.

New Orleans Geological Society. *Oil & Gas Fields of South Louisiana, 2010.* Tulsa, Oklahoma: AAPG Datapages, 2010. CD.

Norgress, Rachael Edna. "The History of the Cypress Lumber Industry in Louisiana," in *The Louisiana Historical Quarterly* XXX (July 1947), 979-1059.

Owen, Edgar W. *Trek of the Oil Finders: A History of Exploration for Petroleum.* 1975.

Peterson, R. W. *Giants on the River, A Story of Chemistry and the Industrial Development on the Lower Mississippi River Corridor.* Baton Rouge: Homesite Company, 2000

Pratt, Joseph A., Priest, Tyler, and Casteneda, Christophe J. *Offshore Pioneers: Brown & Root and the History of Offshore Oil and Gas.* Houston: Gulf Publishing Company, 1997.

Sarter, C. Lane. Program of the annual meeting Petroleum History Society at Shreveport, Louisiana 2003. "Early History of the Caddo-Pine Island Field, Caddo Parish, Louisiana.

Sarwinski, Nancy J. *Louisiana's Oil and Gas: History, Law and Design.* 1979.

Scott, W. W. and Stroud, Ben K. *The Haynesville Oil Field, Claiborne Parish, Louisiana.* Baton Rouge: Department of Conservation, 1922. Bulletin No. 11.

Sternbach, Charles A.; Downey, Marlan W.; and Friedman, Gerald M. *Discoverers of the Twentieth Century: Perfecting the Search, A Collection of Stories about Significant Discoveries by those who know them best.* Tulsa, Oklahoma,: The American Association of Petroleum Geologists, 2005.

Weaver, Bobby D. *Oilfield Trash: Life and Labor in the Oil Patch.* College Station: Texas A&M University Press, c. 2010.

Williams, T. Harry. *Huey Long.* New York: Vintage Books, 1981.

Yergin, Daniel, *The Prize: The Epic Quest for Oil, Money & Power.* New York: Free Press, 1991.

_____, *The Quest: Energy, Security, and the Remaking of the Modern World.* New York: The Penguin Press, 2011.

United States Government Publications

Humphries, Marc, Pirog, Robert, and Whitney, Gene. U.S. Offshore Oil and Gas Resources: Prospects and Processes. Congressional Research Service, April 26, 2010. www.crs.gov

Department of Interior, Increased Safety Measures for Energy Development on the Outer Continental Shelf, (May 27, 2010).

T. Gerald Crawford, Grant L. Burgess, Steven M. Haley, Peter F. Harrison, Clark J. Kinler, Gregory D. Klocek, Nancy K. Shepard, *Outer Continental Shelf Estimated Oil and Gas Reserves: Gulf of Mexico December 31, 1906* (New Orleans: Resource Evaluation Office, Reserves Section, U.S. Department of the Interior, Minerals Management Service New Orleans, December 2009.

United States, The Bureau of Ocean Energy Management, Regulation and Enforcement. Report Regarding the Causes of the April 20, 2010, Macondo Well Blowout, September 14, 2011.

U.S. Department of the Interior, Bureau of Land Management, Eastern States, Jackson Field Office, *Louisiana: Reasonably Foreseeable Development Scenario for Fluid Minerals* (2008).

U.S. Energy Information Administration. *Effect of Increased Natural Gas Exports on Domestic Energy Markets, as requested by the Office of Fossil Energy*. January 2012.

Mineral Management Volumes

Austin, D., B. Carriker, T. McGuire, J. Pratt, T. Priest, and A. G. Pulsipher. *History of the offshore oil and gas industry in southern Louisiana: Interim report; Volume I: Papers on the evolving offshore industry*. U.S. Department of the Interior, Minerals Management Service, Gulf of Mexico OCS Region, New Orleans, Louisiana. OCS Study MMS 2004-049. 98 pp.

Austin, D. E., T. Priest, L. Penney, J. Pratt, A. G. Pulsipher, J. Abel and J. Taylor. History of the offshore oil and gas industry in southern Louisiana. Volume I: Papers on the evolving offshore industry. U.S. Department of the Interior, Minerals Management Service, Gulf of Mexico OCS Region, New Orleans, Louisiana. OCS Study MMS 2008-042. 264 pp.

McGuire, Tom. History of the offshore oil and gas industry in southern Louisiana: Interim report; Volume II: Bayou Lafourche—An oral history of the development of the oil and gas industry. U.S. Department of the Interior, Minerals Management Service, Gulf of Mexico OCS Region, New Orleans, Louisiana. OCS Study MMS 2004-050. 148 pp. online

Sell, J. L., and T. McGuire. 2008. *History of the offshore oil and gas industry in southern Louisiana. Volume IV: Terrebonne Parish*. U.S. Department of the Interior, Minerals Management Service, Gulf of Mexico OCS Region, New Orleans, Louisiana. OCS Study MMS 2008-045. 90 pp.

Austin, D. E., ed. 2008. *History of the offshore oil and gas industry in southern Louisiana.Volume V: Guide to the Interviews*. U.S. Department of the Interior, Minerals ManagementService, Gulf of Mexico OCS Region, New Orleans, Louisiana. OCS Study MMS 2008-046.1259 pp.

Austin, Diane and Gaines, Justin. 2008. *History of the offshore oil and gas industry in southern Louisiana. Volume VI: A Collection of Photographs*. U.S. Department of the Interior, Minerals Management Service, Gulf of Mexico OCS Region, New Orleans, Louisiana. OCS Study MMS 2008.047. 165 pp.

ABBREVIATIONS

Bibliographical

BOEMRE or just BOEM = Bureau of Ocean Energy Management, Regulation and Enforcement created 2010 replacing MMS, Minerals Management Service

BSEE = Bureau of Safety and Environmental Enforcement. Cited for www.bsee.gov. Offshore stats and facts, Gulf of Mexico region, Data Center, Available Resources, Image Library.

MMS6 = Austin, D. E. and Gaines, J. *History of the Offshore Oil and Gas Industry in Southern Louisiana.* Volume VI: A Collection of photographs. U.S. Department of the Interior, Minerals Management Service, Gulf of Mexico OCS Region, New Orleans, Louisiana, 2008. OCS Study MMS 2008-047, 165 p.

NOGS = New Orleans Geological Society

Oil City Museum = Louisiana State Oil and Gas Museum, 200 South Land Avenue, Oil City, Louisiana

Measurement

Mcf = a thousand cubic feet of natural gas at sixty degrees F and 14.63 psi

MMcf = million cubic feet

Bcf = billion cubic feet

Tcf = trillion cubic feet

MBO = thousand barrels of oil

EUR = Expected Ultimate Recovery

TRR = Technically Recoverable Resource

BCFE = Billion cubic feet equivalent is an artificial number designed to measure the amount of both gas and oil from a well or field. Basically, it translates barrels of oil BO into cubic feet. For example, 7.2 BCFE equates to 3.7 billion cubic feet of gas and 584,000 barrels of oil. The ratio is generally five or six thousand cubic feet of gas (5Mcf) ascribed to every barrel of oil.

1 MCF natural gas = 1.027 million BTU = 1.027MMBTU

OIL AND GAS TERMINOLOGY

Common Abbreviations

bbl. = barrel
b/d = barrels per day
Mcf = thousand cubic feet
MMcf = million cubic feet
Bcf = billion cubic feet
Tcf = trillion cubic feet
BTU = British Thermal Unit
NGL = Natural Gas Liquids
LPG = Liquified Petroleum Gases

Energy Conversions

One barrel of crude oil equals:
    42 gallons
    5,800,000 BTU of energy
    5,614 cubic feet of natural gas
    0.22 ton of bituminous coal

One cubic foot of natural gas equals:
    7.48 gallons
    1,030 BTU of energy
    0.000178 barrel of crude oil
    0.00004 ton of bituminous coal

One short ton of bituminous coal equals:
    2,000 pounds
    26,200,000 BTU of energy
    4.52 barrels of crude oil
    25,314 cubic feet of natural gas

One metric ton of crude oil equals:
    2,204 pounds
    7.46 barrels of domestic crude oil
    6.99 barrels of foreign crude oil

One cubic meter of natural gas equals:
    35.314 cubic feet

"The Hardie No. 2 and the Men Who Brought Her In." well after the gusher had slowed considerably.

SHARING THE HERITAGE

Historic profiles of businesses, organizations, and families that have contributed to the development and continued growth of the Louisiana oil and gas industry

Replica of the derrick at Clement #1,
now standing next to the Jennings Oil &
Gas Museum.

EXPLORATION & PRODUCTION

PLAINS EXPLORATION & PRODUCTION COMPANY

The Inglewood Field was discovered in 1924 and encompasses an approximate one-thousand-acre area of the Baldwin Hills area of Los Angeles. PXP is the fourth largest oil and gas producer in California.

Plains Exploration & Production Company's (NYSE: PXP) financial statements are indicative of the company's strength. It has a proven plan for growth and an experienced management team who recognize the opportunities to build its portfolio.

Before December 18, 2002, PXP was a wholly owned subsidiary of Plains Resources Inc. (PLX). In May 2001, James C. Flores became PLX's Chairman of the Board and Chief Executive Officer (CEO). Later, he became the Chairman and CEO of PXP when it completed a tax-free spinoff from PLX.

PXP, the upstream Exploration & Production assets of PLX, began trading on the New York Stock Exchange in December 2002. The separation of PXP from the midstream business, PLX and its controlled entity, Plains All American Pipeline, L.P. (NYSE: PAA), allowed both companies to prosper under separate corporate and capital allocation strategies that reflected their individual businesses. Subsequently, PLX was acquired by Vulcan Energy Corporation in 2004.

When the companies were split, PLX operated in a different market environment.

Then the environment had low commodity prices, and PLX was heavily leveraged. Plains Resources was the primary shareholder of PAA, a crude oil midstream pipeline gathering and marketing master limited partnership. PLX owned forty-six percent of the general partner interest and twenty-five percent of the limited partner interest. In addition, the exploration and production business focused on mature oil assets located in the Los Angeles Basin, San Joaquin Valley, Illinois, and Florida.

The growth vehicle included the pipelines and gathering business of PAA, resulting in increased distributions to PLX. The incentive structures included in the general partnership, made the returns financially attractive, allowing PLX to grow the distribution of PAA, but at the expense of the exploration and production side.

Since the split, PXP's acumen in the oil and gas industry is reflected in its profit generation and management decisions in selecting viable paths and maintaining performance. PXP is an independent oil and gas company engaged in the upstream oil and natural gas business. The company acquires, develops, explores for, and produces oil and gas. Its properties are located in the United States where it owns oil and gas operations onshore and offshore in California, the Gulf Coast Region, which includes the Haynesville Shale and Eagle Ford Shale, the Gulf of Mexico, and the Rocky Mountains.

Assets in PXP's primary focus areas include mature properties with long-lived reserves and significant development opportunities, as well as newer properties with development and exploration potential. The company's balanced portfolio of assets and its ongoing risk management program position it for the current commodity price environment as well as providing for future potential upside as it develops its resource opportunities in California, Eagle Ford Shale, and the Gulf of Mexico.

PXP has experienced remarkable growth, delivering sound operational performance by establishing record production and reserve volumes. It produced approximately 9.3 million barrels of oil equivalent (BOE) and had proved net reserves of 253 million BOE by year-end 2002.

In May 2003, PXP completed 3-D seismic imaging of the deep sands of the prolific California Inglewood Field. That was the first documented use of 3-D seismic technology in the Los Angeles Basin and proved viable for deeper formations, positioning the company for development of multiple reservoirs below 3,500 feet. PXP began drilling in this region in 2004.

These advancements proved PXP's strength as a separate entity. Net income for 2003 totaled $59.4 million compared to $26.2 million the previous year. Oil and gas production of 12.3 million BOE was 32 percent higher than the 9.3 million BOE in 2002.

Ready to grow, PXP acquired 3TEC Energy Corporation for approximately $432 million in stock, cash, and assumed debt. The acquisition was completed in June 2003, dramatically increasing the company's exposure to the North American natural gas market and providing growth opportunities in several key gas-prone regions of the country. The merger increased the public float of PXP shares and doubled the company's size.

Another successful initiative was acquiring Nuevo Energy Company (NYSE: NEV) in

2004. The effort created significant synergies by consolidating California operations and enabling PXP to gain market share in a dominant oil resource position in California, resulting in a fifty-nine percent stock price appreciation. The venture positioned PXP as the fourth largest producer in California.

The Neuvo acquisition increased opportunities for growth in several key California resource basins. PXP became a leading participant in the domestic upstream business, resulting in upgrading the

Above: A worker checks data on a well in the Inglewood Field, which is a part of the Los Angeles Basin. Other PXP Los Angeles Basin properties include Las Cienegas, Montebello, Packard and San Vicente.

Below: PXP San Joaquin Basin properties are located primarily in Cymric, Midway Sunset, and South Belridge Fields in California. These are long-lived fields that have heavier oil and shallow wells.

Above: A worker retrieves data from a field in the San Joaquin Valley. PXP has approximately 16,000 acres in the San Joaquin Basin. In addition, PXP has the Arroyo Grande Field located in San Luis Obispo County, California.

Below: PXP's headquarters is located in Houston, Texas. Two workers review geological data for a field.

company's credit ratings by adding PXP to the Standard and Poor's (S&P) MidCap 400 Stock Index.

The company experienced a "breakout year"—one of tremendous growth and change—in 2004. Following the merger, PXP began restructuring Nuevo's debt, its unfavorable hedge positions and selling non-core assets. After divesting several properties in Illinois, South Texas, and New Mexico, PXP gained momentum by producing 22.9 million BOE in 2004, an increase of eighty-six percent over the previous year.

In early 2005, PXP expanded its California holdings by purchasing additional producing properties in the Los Angeles Basin and divesting some of its East Texas interests, in addition to a 16.7 percent interest in the offshore California Point Arguello unit. By the end of the year, PXP had drilled approximately 270 wells, nearly an eighty-three percent increase over 2004, with an overall success rate of ninety-seven percent.

Furthering expansion, PXP achieved success as an explorer with positions in two large deepwater oil discoveries, Big Foot and Caesar, drilled in 2005 and 2006 respectively. As a result of the extended development timeline driven by the major operators in 2006, PXP elected to sell its interest in the two deepwater Gulf of Mexico discoveries to Statoil ASA for $706 million.

In May 2007, PXP acquired certain properties in the Piceance Basin from a private company for $975 million in cash and one million shares of common stock valued at approximately $45 million. The properties included interests in oil and gas producing properties in the Mesaverde geologic section of the Piceance Basin in Colorado, plus associated midstream assets, including a twenty-five percent interest in Collbran Valley Gas Gathering, LLC.

In November 2007, PXP purchased Pogo Producing Company (NYSE: PPP) in Houston for approximately 40 million shares of common stock valued at approximately $2 billion and $1.5 billion in cash. Pogo was engaged in oil and gas exploration, development, acquisition, and production activities on its properties primarily located in the onshore United States, offshore Vietnam, and New Zealand.

Pogo had been on the market for a long time, had a good asset base, but was inactive for so long that momentum was lost. It took a lot of work and staff dedication to finalize the transaction. The synergies of combining Pogo and PXP resulted in significant annual cost savings.

Later in 2007, PXP announced divestitures for approximately $1.55 billion for half of its interests in the Piceance and Permian Basins to a subsidiary of Occidental Petroleum Corporation or Oxy. At the same time, PXP also announced the sale of the San Juan Basin in

New Mexico and Barnett Shale in Texas to XTO Energy Inc. for $200 million. In December 2008 the remaining half of PXP's interests in the Permian and Piceance Basins was sold, as well as interests in West Texas and New Mexico to Oxy for approximately $1.25 billion. PXP also exited the New Albany Basin in 2008.

PXP acquired from Chesapeake Energy Corporation a twenty percent interest in Chesapeake's Haynesville Shale properties in North Louisiana and East Texas in July 2008 for approximately $1.65 billion. Working closely with Chesapeake, PXP developed its expertise with horizontal drilling. The addition of Haynesville increased the growth and economics of PXP's gas portfolio. Three years later, PXP's daily sales volumes averaged approximately 180 million cubic feet per day.

Company officials keep everyone well-informed about particular projects or events before implementation. A comprehensive plan is developed before any transaction. PXP's executive management group has more than twenty years of experience in analyzing risk and managing it with a strong pulse on the industry and the economy.

PXP exploration investment in the Gulf of Mexico yielded numerous material discoveries, one of which was the Flatrock well drilled with McMoRan Exploration Co. (NYSE: MMR). The Flatrock discovery well found significant accumulations of gas/condensate pay in multiple intervals. Five productive wells were drilled in 2007 and early 2008 in the Flatrock area of South Marsh Island Block 212. Production from the Flatrock area began in January 2008.

The Flatrock development in the Gulf of Mexico and the Haynesville Shale Project were major contributors to a revenue increase in 2009. Full-year average daily sales volumes increased eight percent compared to those a year earlier, excluding the impact of its 2008 divestments. Proved reserves increased twenty-three percent.

In 2009, PXP was successful with the exploration effort in the new Davy Jones discovery with McMoRan in the ultra-deep formation in the Gulf of Mexico Shelf. PXP can trace its strong working relationship with McMoRan after signing an exploration agreement in November 2006 to participate

in several of its Miocene exploratory prospects in the Gulf of Mexico.

In late 2010, PXP sold all interests in its Gulf of Mexico leasehold located in less than 500 feet of water to McMoRan for approximately $86 million in cash and 51 million shares of McMoRan common stock. The sale maximized value for both PXP and McMoRan shareholders from the ultra-deep program's discoveries and exploration potential and PXP's ownership position.

In 2010, PXP entered the liquids rich Eagle Ford Shale in South Texas by acquiring 60,000 net acres for approximately $596 million. Eagle Ford production has steadily grown to the point where in December 2012, PXP averaged 42,191 BOE per day production—a nearly five-fold increase over 2011. The company attained

Above: A tank storage facility in the Eagle Ford Shale. Net average daily sales volumes during the fourth quarter of 2012 were 40.4 thousand BOE per day.

Below: A well is being drilled in the Eagle Ford Shale. Based on 80-to-130-acre well spacing, PXP anticipates over 500 potential well locations.

excellent production growth with efficiencies across all aspects of its activities.

Financial highlights for 2010 included average daily sales volumes of 88,500 BOE, a seven-percent increase year-over-year and proved reserves growth of sixteen percent compared to 2009.

PXP is dedicated to corporate growth and generating revenues, and embraces its corporate responsibilities to employees and the communities in which it operates. The company trains and empowers employees to perform activities in a safe manner and follows the best available environmental practices. It often provides donations to local charities and contributes to the United Way. For example, in the Inglewood Field, the company worked with local decision makers through a cooperative effort to develop an urban community park.

Management expects to continue growing reserves and production through long-term development of its existing project inventory in each of its primary operating areas, and by building future development projects through exploration primarily in the Gulf of Mexico, California and liquids rich resource plays such as the Eagle Ford Shale.

In October 2011, PXP secured $430.2 million net cash proceeds from EIG Global Energy Partners to finance deepwater Gulf of Mexico activities. The company's most visible Gulf project is the Lucius development, a sanctioned project with Anadarko, Exxon,

Apache, Eni and Petrobras as partners. Construction of the Lucius truss spar floating production facility to be located in Keathley Canyon is on-going. The Lucius spar will have the capacity to produce in excess of 80,000 barrels of oil per day and 450 million cubic feet of natural gas per day in 2014.

On November 30, 2012, PXP completed its biggest acquisition yet. PXP acquired all of British Petroleum's (BP) interest in Holstein, Horn Mountain, Marlin, Dorado, King, Ram Powell, Diana, and Hoover oilfields and all of Shell's interest in the Holstein oilfield in the deepwater Gulf of Mexico for $5.9 billion. BP sold these assets to offset its costs from the 2010 Deepwater Horizon rig incident.

This acquisition fits perfectly with PXP's strategic approach of growing its operated oil production with low-cost high margin barrels. The world-class, long-life assets have excellent redevelopment opportunities and have a large reserve base that can be multiplied many times over by using the same "hub and spoke" strategy that the majors implemented. The assets provide a substantial improvement in gross margin per barrel while adding 64 thousand barrels of oil equivalent per day production of which eighty-three percent is oil.

As previously shown, the company has a consistent record of strong financial performance. Total revenues for 2012 were $2.6 billion, a thirty-one percent increase from 2011. Proved reserves increased seven percent from

Left: The Marlin Hub is a tension leg platform located in water depth of approximately thirty-two hundred feet in the Gulf of Mexico. The Marlin Hub is a production facility for three fields: the Marlin Field, Dorado Field and King Field.

Right: The Horn Mountain platform is a truss spar in water depth of approximately fifty-four hundred feet in the Gulf of Mexico. The Horn Mountain Field is located in Mississippi Canyon blocks 82, 126, and 127.

2011 to 440.4 million BOE. As of December 31, 2012, PXP had working interests in 3,193 gross (3,061 net) active producing oil wells and 1,544 gross (209 net) active producing gas wells.

In reviewing corporate growth statistics, PXP produced approximately 9.3 million BOE in 2002 and had grown to a record 38.9 million BOE by year-end 2012. Originally, PXP had 354 full-time employees, of which 250 were field personnel involved in oil and gas-producing activities. As of January 31, 2013, PXP had 906 full-time employees, 335 of whom were field personnel. Upon full transition of the BP Gulf of Mexico platforms, PXP intends to add 138 full-time employees. PXP's culture emphasizes hiring good people, treating them well and helping them succeed.

PXP's crude oil hedging program is expected to protect up to ninety percent of oil sales volumes through 2015, locking in strong cash flows and protecting against downside price risk. The company has a portfolio of durable onshore and offshore assets capable of doubling oil production by 2020 while generating substantial cash flow provided by operating activities.

On December 5, 2012, PXP entered into an agreement and plan of merger with Freeport-McMoRan Copper & Gold Inc. (FCX), which will acquire PXP for approximately $6.9 billion. FCX also plans to acquire McMoRan Exploration Co. in a separate transaction. The merger of these three companies will create a premier U.S. based natural resource company with a growing production profile and an industry leading global portfolio of mineral assets and significant oil and gas resources.

The new oil and gas business division under FCX will include the combined assets of McMoRan and PXP. Jim Flores, who will become the vice chairman of FCX and CEO of FCX's oil and gas operations, will lead the new division. His leadership team will remain focused on increasing margins while targeting a significant organic oil growth rate and protecting the downside risk of commodity prices. The division sees its concentration in California, the Eagle Ford Shale, and the Gulf of Mexico as the catalyst that will drive its business for the future. The mission will remain the same: People building value together to find and produce energy resources safely, reliably, and efficiently.

The oil and gas division is headquartered in Houston, Texas.

Left: PXP operates four platforms: Harvest, Hermosa, Hidalgo (pictured) and Irene near the California coastline. Hidalgo is an eight-pile shelf platform in water depth of approximately 430 feet.

Below: The Holstein platform is a truss spar in water depth of approximately forty-three hundred feet in the Gulf of Mexico. The Holstein Field is located in Green Canyon blocks 644, 645, and 688.

JOHN FRANKS AND FRANKS PETROLEUM INC.

1925-2003

Above: During World War II young Bombardier John Franks is the second from the right standing.

Below: Young entrepreneurs from left to right, Dot Brammer, John Franks, Alta Franks and Bob Brammer.

While John Franks' rise to head a company of his own was relatively fast, it was not easy. His story began on a fifty-acre Haughton farm where young Johnny Franks grew up, the youngest child in a family of six children.

He was born April 21, 1925, in Haughton, Louisiana, one of the two sons of John M. Franks. His father was a driller for the old Carter Oil Co., the predecessor to the Standard Oil Co. of Louisiana. The farm was only a one-horse affair with the usual garden, truck crops, and cornfield being planted. The main source of income was his father's wages earned in the oilfield. He died when John was only sixteen.

Franks graduated from Haughton High School in 1942, and the same year, entered Louisiana State University (LSU) in Baton Rouge, enrolling in the school of journalism as a budding young reporter. But newspaper plans never bloomed as the call for young men in World War II reached Franks and he entered the service, becoming a bombardier, radar specialist, and full-fledged member of "the greatest generation."

In 1946, the war was over, and Franks went back to LSU. However, he canceled his journalism plans and enrolled in the school of geology. A little older, Franks said that he entered the field because of the job opportunities that were available at the time. "Then, when I got out I found that there wasn't nearly as much demand for geologists as there was when I enrolled." So, after graduation Franks went to Kansas and signed on with a construction company.

After some time, Franks was contacted by Midstates Oil, which was a small company in Shreveport with its main office in Tulsa. Midstates had contacted LSU for names of those who had graduated with a major in geology to interview for an opening in the Shreveport office. After the interview, Franks was hired by the Midstates vice president and went to work under the guidance of Jack Grigsby. Midstates was significant for a more important reason. Franks met his wife of fifty-one years, Alta Vascocu, there. They married in 1952 and she left Midstates for Caddo Oil Company later that year.

At Midstates, Franks was responsible for the area of interest in East Texas, North Louisiana, Southern Arkansas, and West Mississippi. He spent many days and nights "sitting on wells" as was the practice at the time. Grigsby was a good teacher for Franks in practical geology and was aware of Franks' value to the company.

Sometime around 1954, Grigsby left the company to be an independent and, at that time, recommended Franks for head of the geology department at Midstates. Later that year, with Midstates' permission Franks did some work for Ralph Gilster. Gilster was impressed with Franks and unsuccessfully tried to hire him.

About that time, Franks was contacted by C. H. Gee, who was an employee of States Oil Company, to go to Benton Harbor, Michigan, to interview for a job as a geologist. Franks flew to Michigan, interviewed, and was hired. He signed a contract that included a small participating interest after pay out and planned to leave Midstates. Franks was definitely motivated by an interest in the properties. Shortly after Franks was hired, but before actually moving, the owner of States Oil Company was tragically killed in a plane crash and Franks was released from the contract before it began.

About that same time, Franks was contacted by Gilster again. This time a deal was struck that allowed Franks to participate in the prospects they would create. So, Franks joined with Ralph Gilster and James E. Kemp as a geologist with Latex Oil and Gas. Gilster was the principal owner of the firm. Soon,

L. R. "Bob" Brammer, Jr., came on board to join them as engineer and a long term business relationship with Brammer began. Brammer later left to join Nemours Corporation.

In 1957, Latex was dissolved and, ready-or-not, Franks was on his own. With the financial backing of Gilster, he opened an

Young John Franks in 1964 now on his own.

Not one hundred percent work, left to right: Bob Brammer, Jackie Devall, John Franks, Bonnie Ackord and Arnold Chauviere at the East Ridge Country Club, Shreveport in 1969.

office as consulting geologist in the Johnson Building and engaged in buying leases, drilling wells, and operating them under his own name or Franks & Gilster. He continued to work for others, as well as his own interests. He did a lot of "well sitting" for various companies and maintained a good relationship with Gilster for many years. He moved his office to the Petroleum Building on Market Street and, then again, to the Petroleum Tower on Edwards Street.

The period from 1957 to 1969 was extremely productive for Franks. At some point during this period he began using the name Franks Petroleum. Also during this period, he built lifelong relationships with key folks like geologists Henry Goodrich and Gene Robinson, landman/attorney Gerry Huggs, engineer Bob Brammer and many others all joining John's business at one time or another. In 1958, Franks asked his brother Joe T. Franks, to come to Shreveport from his job with the Department of Conservation in Baton Rouge, and join him in business. Joe accepted the offer and worked for Franks until 1961 when Joe suffered a stroke. He returned in a limited capacity after recovering.

Franks recalled in an early interview that the most significant find of the company was the Holmes No. 1 well in Bethany-Longstreet Field in 1957. The well produced at a rate of 50 million cubic feet of gas per day with 80 barrels condensate per million. Operations expanded from this discovery and the firm became active in Louisiana, Mississippi, and South Arkansas.

Then, unexpectedly, Franks' friend and business partner Gilster died in 1964. Obviously, Gilster thought a lot of Franks, naming him co-executor of his estate. He worked closely with attorney Herschel Downs in the important matter of handling Gilster's estate. Herschel later became president of Franks Petroleum Inc. for a period of time.

Young Franks' ability as an oil finder was held in high regard by his colleagues. As one individual put it, "If Franks buys any acreage in an area then I want some of it, too." Somewhere during this period, Franks became totally involved in his own business interests.

Being in business for himself was always the ultimate goal. Quoting Franks in a newspaper article at the time, "It seems as if my father was always trying to go into business for himself—but he never quite made it. Most of his life he was a driller—but at one time he owned a sawmill and another, he was a drilling contractor. Both of these ventures were unfortunately doomed to failure. The sawmill was started during the heart of the depression and my father had plenty of good lumber, but no market. As a drilling contractor, he acquired some leases near Zwolle and went broke drilling dry offsets to producing wells."

Franks became one of the most respected, admired, and influential people in the North Louisiana oil and gas community. He possessed a very strong work ethic and was ever searching for, and exploring, new ideas. He found great success in the Hosston and Cotton Valley trends in North Louisiana, being one of the first to recognize the economic potential of the tighter gas sands in these plays. His company, then well-known as Franks Petroleum, had operations in Louisiana, Alabama, Mississippi, Florida, New Mexico, South Arkansas, and East Texas.

The business continued to grow and in 1963, Franks bought a building on 244 Montgomery Street north of downtown Shreveport. In January 1966, he formally incorporated his business as Franks Petroleum Inc. About this time, Brammer wanted to go into business for himself also. In 1968, he formed Brammer Engineering, Inc. with Franks as a significant shareholder. His initial office was in the building at 244 Montgomery Street with Franks Petroleum Inc. Later Franks transferred his interest to Brammer but they continued a lifelong business and personal relationship until Franks' death.

A lot of folks in Shreveport learned their craft at Franks Petroleum Inc. Many went on to be successful on their own. Many key employees stayed with Franks Petroleum for a long time including Executive Assistant Diane Marlowe, Geologist Edward Yarbrough and Vice President, Board member and Chief Engineer Fred H. Plitt. In the 1980s you would sometimes hear folks in the oil and gas business say that "everybody has worked at Franks" at one time or another.

Although Franks was a geologist, he found almost all business and investment opportunities interesting. The more challenging and difficult the opportunity the better, including thoroughbred horse racing. Franks entered the thoroughbred industry in the late 1970s with two broodmares and one race horse. He won his first race at Louisiana Downs on July 18, 1980.

John at this desk in his office on Montgomery Street in 1981 working away.

Special Insert In This Issue
UPDATED STATISTICS FOR
SIRES OF SALE YEARLINGS

$2

SEPTEMBER 10, 1983

THE BLOOD-HORSE

A WEEKLY MAGAZINE DEVOTED TO IMPROVING THOROUGHBRED BREEDING AND RACING

John Franks, At Hurricane Bluffs Training Center In Louisiana

Oilman John Franks, The Current Leading Owner
Use Of Swimming Therapy For Horses
Major Stakes Of Labor Day Weekend

John Franks on the cover of
The Blood-Horse *magazine in 1983.*

The Blood-Horse magazine, he said: "Nobody in this business has fed more horses and fed more people than we have. By having lots of horses, we've created lots of jobs, bought a lot of feed, bought a lot of tack, and bought a lot of fertilizer. And I'm proud of that."

By the late 1980s, Franks Petroleum Inc. had grown into one of the largest independents in the South, at one time operating 325 plus wells with interests in over 500 more. Franks really enjoyed the challenge of finding oil and gas. However, in June 1989, Franks sold most all his oil and gas properties to Sonat Exploration Co., a subsidiary of Birmingham, Alabama based Sonat, Inc. It was a big move by Sonat into North Louisiana as well as East Texas by purchasing ninety thousand net acres of producing properties from Franks.

Being sixty-eight years old at the time, it was Franks' attempt to "retire." His exit from the oil and gas business garnered much attention. Even with all his other business interests, he was an "oil man" in his own mind and to all who knew him well. Many were surprised.

Franks often said he "was born with a burr under this blanket." Retirement in the traditional sense did not really occur. Franks continued his business and investment interests and created several new companies after the big sale in 1989. He also continued his interest in real estate and his thoroughbred horse business.

Ultimately, his horseracing business grew to more than 1,000 thoroughbred horses. Franks was voted the Eclipse Award as North America's leading owner four times, in 1983, 1984, 1993, and 1994. Franks also won an Eclipse Award as the owner of homebred Answer Lively, who was the champion juvenile colt in 1998. Sometimes Franks was questioned for having too many horses in winning the awards. In a 1995 interview with

Over the years, Franks was honored many times. Shreveport Chamber of Commerce recognized Franks as "Business Leader of the Year" in 1988. In 1994, Franks was one of the first inductees into The North Louisiana Junior Achievement "Business Hall of Fame." He also served on the Board of the First National Bank of Shreveport and the Louisiana State University Board of Supervisors.

A longtime resident of Shreveport, Franks was a member of Trinity Heights Baptist Church, which was next door to his home. As a very strong southern Christian man, he stated many times, "Everything I have comes from God." He also credited the influence of a good home life as a child along with the love and support of Alta, his wife of fifty-one years.

Franks was instrumental in the creation of Live Oak Retirement Center (now a part of The Oaks of Louisiana owned by Willis Knighton Hospital System). During that effort, Franks' friends Hugh and Winona Ward gave him a plaque with a quote from George Sands that they thought described his philosophy of life. "Guard well within yourself that treasure, kindness. Know how to give without hesitation, how to lose without regret, how to acquire without meanness."

Franks died December 31, 2003. He is survived by his beloved wife, Alta V. Franks, and two daughters. He left a legacy of outstanding accomplishments, much kindness to his fellow man, love for his family, employees, and country; and was grateful for all of God's abundant blessings. His was a great life indeed!

Above: John Franks and two of his best friends, Archie and Abbie.

Left: John Franks not too long after the big oil and gas sale and "so-called" retirement.

DAN A. HUGHES COMPANY, L.P.

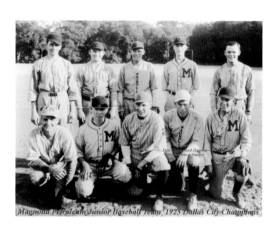

Magnolia Petroleum Junior Baseball Team, 1925 Dallas City Champions

Top, left: Dan, June, Dudley and Jane Hughes, c. 1935, Wichita Falls, Texas.

Top, right: Magnolia Petroleum junior baseball team, 1925 Dallas City champions. Dan Greenwood Hughes, father of Dan Allen Hughes, founder of Dan A. Hughes Company, L.P., is pictured second from right in the front row.

Below: Dan A. Hughes, Sr., founder of the Dan A. Hughes Company, L.P.

Bottom: Dan Allen Hughes, Jr., president of the Dan A. Hughes Company, L.P.

Dan Allen and Dudley Joe Hughes, identical twins, were born in Monroe, Louisiana, on August 14, 1929. The twins' father worked for Magnolia Oil Company and was in the relatively new business of laying natural gas pipelines from the Monroe Gas Field to various towns and markets in the southern area. The pipeline division of the company, in an early stage, was merged into United Gas Pipeline Company to which the twins' father was employed until his retirement. After living in several towns along the pipeline system during the children's early age, the Hughes family settled in Palestine, Texas, where his father worked as superintendent of the United Gas Pipeline Company in the East Texas area. The twins grew up in Palestine, calling Texas their home for many years. While in high school, young Dan worked summers on a roustabout maintenance crew on the hundreds of miles of United Gas' natural gas pipelines. Dan worked at an adult job even though he was a teenager because World War II had led to labor shortages.

In college, he spent his summer vacations working in the Oklahoma oilfields as a roustabout and did other field jobs for Magnolia Oil Company. He graduated from Texas A&M in 1951 with a bachelor's degree in geology and went to work for Union Producing Co. in Monroe, Louisiana. After a few months, he was called into the Army as an artillery officer, where he served in the Korean Conflict, receiving a Bronze Star for his actions.

After receiving his Army discharge, Dan again joined Union Producing Company (now Devon), and went to work in New Orleans as a geological scout, which was the company training program for geologists. Oil exploration in South Louisiana was booming at that time

and there were many oil and gas discoveries following the dormant period of World War II. It was a great time to live in New Orleans and share the excitement of the people involved.

Later Dan was transferred to Beeville, Texas, and continued geological scouting. This period of scouting enabled him to travel throughout South Texas where he met many of the independent oil and drilling contractors and ranchers, thus becoming familiar with the South Texas oilfields. Following this training period, he spent several years mapping all of the Cretaceous, Wilcox and Frio Trends of South Texas, and doing evaluations on many wells consisting of coring, testing, and logging. Union Producing Company leased thousands of acres and drilled many wells on his prospects. This was an invaluable experience that helped him later in becoming a success in the oil industry and developing numerous oil and gas fields.

In 1961, Dan resigned from Union Producing Company to become an independent geologist and accepted a retainer from Caddo Oil Company of Shreveport, Louisiana, to do consulting work in South Texas. He realized there were several "old" shallow oilfields in the San Antonio area that had only been partially developed. The new procedure of sand fracking made these marginal shallow wells commercial. Caddo purchased leases around the possible extensions to these old fields. Operating from Beeville, a massive field extension drilling program was conducted in the Bear Creek, Von Army, Leming, Somerset, and Taylor Ina Fields in Bexar, Medina, Frio, and Atascosa Counties, Texas. Approximately 450 shallow wells were drilled and completed

as oil wells based on his geology. Dan received an overriding royalty for this work, which provided the funds needed to expand the company into larger projects.

In 1965, Dan formed the Hughes & Hughes Oil and Gas Partnership with his twin brother. Dudley lived in Jackson, Mississippi, and worked primarily in the Mississippi and Alabama areas, whereas Dan lived in South Texas and worked the South Texas areas. They combined their resources and began drilling deeper wells, earning a larger share of the working interest because of it.

The first significant South Texas strike for the company came in 1967 with the drilling of the Hughes & Hughes No. 1 Beasley-Connevey in Webb County, Texas. The well, located in a remote area north of Laredo, was the discovery well for the Las Tiendas Gas Field. This shallow field has several gas sands in the interval 2,800 to 3,600 feet and initially resulted in twenty-two producing Wilcox wells. Later, a deeper development in the seven-thousand-foot level resulted in many Olmos wells over the same acreage. This 11,000-acre field was large enough to entice Houston Natural Gas Company to build a 114 mile pipeline to connect its Houston area gas system to this Las Tiendas Field in Webb County, Texas.

The Hughes & Hughes Partnership discovered a number of oil and gas fields in the Mississippi and Texas area. In 1972 the partnership was approached by Edwards Bates & Co., an English banking company, to purchase all of its production in Mississippi and South Texas. After an evaluation of all of the wells, the English company decided that it preferred the deeper Mississippi oil wells rather than the shallow wells in South Texas. The offer to buy was too low in South Texas, but the Mississippi production was sold.

Following the sale of its Mississippi Hughes & Hughes operations to the English

company, Dudley joined Chesley Pruet to form a company operating under the name of Pruet & Hughes. Chesley Pruet would have half-interest in the company, and the Hughes & Hughes Partnership would jointly have the other half interest. The company was very successful in finding some Smackover oilfields and various other fields in Mississippi and Alabama. The original purpose of the company was to build a corporation which would go public when a certain amount of

❧

Top, left: Dan A. Hughes, Sr., Sydney Harbor, Australia, 2001.

Top, right: Dan A. Hughes, Sr., termite mounds in the Canning Basin, 150 miles inland from Broome, Australia, 2001.

Left: Discovery well #1, Woodada, Woodada Gas Field, 175 miles north of Perth, Australia, flowing thirty million mcf/day, 1979.

Below: Left to right, Dan A. Hughes, Dan Allen Hughes, Jr., and Dudley J. Hughes, All American Wildcatter Convention, 2003.

Top, left: Dan A. Hughes Company, L.P.—
HSU 26 #1 state well, Pedregosa Basin,
Hidalgo County, New Mexico, (most
southwest corner of New Mexico) 2009.

Top, right: HUPECOL (Hughes Petroleum
Colombia) Jaguar #T 5 development well,
Caracara Oilfield, Llanos Basin,
Colombia, 2005.

Below: Dan A. Hughes Company, L.P.—
Claude Ballard #1 discovery well,
West Barton Wilcox Gas Field, Bee County,
Texas, December 2006.

production was developed. However, in 1975, an offer was made to purchase its production and leases by the French Oil Company, Elf Acquataine. It was decided to take the deal.

In considering whether to continue operation in Beeville or leave for a larger town, the company bought its first airplane in 1972. The company found it could operate from this smaller town and fly its personnel anywhere in the Gulf Coast—Texas, Mississippi, or Louisiana—and be back the same day, which allowed it to continue its large operation in Beeville. The company has since owned a series of planes that helped contribute to its growth. Another consideration for remaining in Beeville was that the South Texas quail hunting was the best in the United States.

Along with its South Texas operations, Dan participated in many Louisiana operations, some as operator and some as non-operator. These included the Cotton Valley Dome, Kings Bayou, Black Bay, Lake Hatch, Lapeyrouse, Gueydan, and others. Dudley, operating from Jackson, Mississippi, also had some partnership operations in Louisiana that were operated from the Jackson office.

In 1970 the company participated in a series of wildcat wells in western Canada with Anderson Exploration Company that resulted in several discoveries of relatively shallow oil and gas fields. The most significant of these was the Dunvegan Field, which turned out to be a 1.6-trillion-cubic-foot reserve. Dan was fortunate

to get into this program through his friend, Bob Gowdy, who had transferred in the mid-1960s from San Antonio to Calgary, Alberta, by the Midwest Oil Corp.

With the success in Canada, Dan started looking at the possibilities in other foreign countries and took a deal on a prospect in Western Australia in 1978. After doing some seismic work and drilling a well, Dan discovered the Woodada Gas Field located about 175 miles north of Perth. Even though it was not a large field by international standards, it was at the right place at the right time, and Dan was able to sell gas to Perth and the project turned out to be a very lucrative venture.

In 1980, Dan Allen Hughes, Jr., graduated from Texas A&M University and joined the company, spending his first year in Australia developing the Woodada Gas Field. The operation became much more efficient after some adjustments were made on his recommendations. In 1982, in order to get each partners' grown children involved in the business, it was decided to dissolve the Hughes & Hughes Partnership. From that date on, each party operated individually. At times, the twins participated in each other's prospects, but there was no joint interests created automatically as in the partnership.

Searching for more foreign venture and new areas, in 1996 Dan A. Hughes Company, L.P. began looking at South America. After investigating Bolivia, Peru, and Colombia, the company settled on Colombia as areas with significant potential. Operating as HUPECOL (Hughes Petroleos De Colombia), a partnership was formed between Dan, Sr., Dan, Jr., and John Saunders, Jr. Several concessions were acquired and a discovery on one of these by the name of Caracara, was developed to the point of producing 26,000 barrels of oil per day. A thirty-mile pipeline was built to deliver the oil to a major pipeline. After being developed and produced for a period of time, this field was sold to the Spanish oil company CEPSA. Three other concessions have been developed and sold to various companies. HUPECOL is continuing exploration in Colombia, and has several concessions with very favorable seismic that it plans to drill in the near future. The company has drilled 126 wells in Colombia at the present time.

Dan A. Hughes Company, L.P. became heavily involved in the horizontal shale plays. It was fortunate to get in on the early stages of the Barnett Shale Field in the Fort Worth-Denton area of North Texas. It initially purchased some federal leases that were up for bid in the area and followed by buying several thousand acres around and south of the city of Denton. The company then began drilling

Barnett Shale wells and got its first experience in horizontal drilling. Approximately twenty wells were drilled, some of which were very good, particularly the horizontal ones. One of its best wells was a horizontal well drilled under the City of Denton airport. After several months of production, it was decided to sell the properties since the operations were very difficult in this highly populated area. The production and leases was listed for sale and was eventually sold to Dunes Petroleum Company.

Above: Dan A. Hughes Company, L.P.— geological staff at the main office in Beeville, Texas, 2008.

Below: Dan A. Hughes Company, L.P.— staff photograph at the main office in Beeville, Texas, 2008.

Following the success in the Barnett Shale, the company began working other areas with the idea of finding other formations that might be a source bed for horizontal drilling as the Barnett Shale had been. In the Arkhoma Basin in Arkansas, there was an indication of some activity on a formation called the Fayetteville Shale, which was the same age geologically as the Barnett Shale production. Several companies were leasing in the area and horizontal wells were being drilled on this play. Dan A. Hughes Company, L.P. began working in Arkansas, about forty miles ahead of the area that was being active and leased approximately five thousand acres. Preparations were made to drill this acreage block when Chesapeake Production approached the company to buy its leases. The offer from Chesapeake was so strong that it was decided that this was the best course to take and a great return was made on the investment.

Another shale play, the Eagle Ford formation, was developing in South Texas in the company's main operating area. The company had drilled an old well in Karnes County, Texas, years earlier and tested some oil from the Eagle Ford formation. This looked like an ideal place to begin

Above: Left to right, Dan Allen, Jr., and Dan, Sr., after a successful duck hunt at Jim Flores Duck Camp at Little Pecan Island, Louisiana, 2012.

Below: This 2010 painting is titled Heart of the Eagle Ford Shale. *Eagle Ford Shale is located in Karnes County, Texas.*

purchasing leases. Dan A. Hughes Company, L.P. purchased about fifteen thousand acres around the well and began competing with EOG who was in the area also. A deal was made with EOG to jointly merge Hughes' acreage and together they formed a thirty-thousand-acre drilling unit. Also, the Hughes Company continued acquiring leases on each end of the play outside of this unit and eventually had an interest in a gross of sixty thousand acres. The first well was drilled on this unit in 2009 by Dan A. Hughes Company, L.P. Eighteen wells were drilled and completed jointly with EOG.

Plains Exploration and Production Company made Hughes an offer to buy all of its Eagle Ford wells and leases. Hughes accepted this purchase.

Dan A. Hughes Company, L.P. is working many new areas. It is drilling a series of new horizontal wells being completed in the Buda Lime in the western area of the Eagle Ford trend. The same area appears to have a great potential in the Pearsall Shale. At the present time, the company is testing a Brown Dense (Smackover) horizontal well in the Monroe Gas Field area on a twenty-five-thousand-acre lease from Plum Creek Southern Timber Company. The company acquired a two-hundred-thousand-acre lease block in southern Florida on which a Sunnyland Lime well is being drilled. In foreign operations, the company has completed a seismic program in Belize and is preparing to drill a wildcat well in the near future. Also, negotiations are under way to acquire a series of concessions in Italy and Sicilia.

Dan A. Hughes Company, L.P. now has approximately seventy-five employees with offices in Beeville, San Antonio, and Houston, Texas.

Both Dan, Sr., and Dan, Jr., who is now president of the company, plan to continue exploring and wildcatting for hydrocarbons in the Gulf Coast and worldwide. A long history of good partners, timing, excellent and loyal employees, and some luck has led to their continued success.

Above: Left to right, Dan Allen Hughes, Jr., Dan A. Hughes, III (D.A.) and Dan A. Hughes, Sr.

Below: Three generations of the Dan A. Hughes Company, L.P., left to right, Dan A. Hughes, Sr., Dan Allen Hughes, Jr., and Dan A. Hughes, III (D.A.), 2013.

PETROQUEST

PetroQuest was formed in 1985 as a Gulf Coast exploration company to take advantage of a vibrant market for exploration/exploitation and development projects. Crude prices were approximately $25 per barrel; and within six months, both crude and natural gas prices would begin to tumble. Six months later, crude prices were down sixty percent to $11 per barrel. U.S. rig utilization bottomed in the third quarter of 1986 at approximately 660 active rigs, dropping from a high of 4,500 rigs in 1981. Through all of the industry change PetroQuest survived while many other companies did not. Unfortunately, that would not be the last time the market for oil and gas would collapse and the industry would suffer.

The company's founders were Charles Goodson (landman), John C. Duncan (geologist), Alfred Thomas II (petroleum engineer), Ralph Daigle (geophysicist), and Forrest Germany (landman). The company's first employee was Patrick Landry (geologist) who remains with the company today and who has found millions of barrels of oil along with an equivalent amount of natural gas.

Early relationships that contributed greatly to the growth of the company, (forged long before it went public) were with Jim Flores and Billy Rucks who, along with their team at Flores and Rucks, (Gus Zepernick, Bryan Hanks, Patrick Regan, and Dave Morgan, to name a few) helped to generate and assemble a multitude of projects throughout South Louisiana and the Gulf of Mexico esulting in numerous discoveries. Many of those discoveries are still producing today. Also it should be mentioned that all of the

above have continued on to tremendously successful careers in the energy industry and remain friends of the company today.

Another important relationship for a company operating in Louisiana in the early days was the strong partnerships forged with state and local governments. The bonds and trust that were formed lasted far beyond elected officials' terms in office or civil servants' retirements. The energy industry is engrained into the fabric of Louisiana, and unlike other parts of the country, the majority of its citizens understand how important the industry is to the state and to the nation. By far, one of the most important relationships which helped to bridge almost every aspect of PetroQuest's business with the state and federal government officials and agencies is with Don Briggs, president of the Louisiana Oil and Gas Association (LOGA), an organization, which Goodson, Dan Fournerat, general counsel of PetroQuest, along with many others helped form. Goodson states "Don is a man that personifies the energy industry not only in Louisiana but in the nation."

LOGA is a key ingredient as to how the weakened energy industry survived a continuing assault by a predatory environment that saw oil and gas revenues and reserves as a choice revenue stream to attack. The majors were the preferred target, but as they all but abandoned Louisiana, the independents were an acceptable second choice. LOGA was clearly the catalyst to survival and Don Briggs and CeCe Richter were the heart and soul. "We will never be able to thank them enough," states Goodson.

After leaving Callon Petroleum in order to partner with a great team to start PetroQuest, Goodson, currently serving as chief executive officer, lived in Natchez for about a year prior to moving his family to Lafayette, Louisiana. The other founders except Forrest were long term south Louisiana residents. At that time, Goodson owned a house, a car, and had a nice nest egg in savings. A year later, having paid drilling and completion costs on several wells, the nest egg was gone. He was desperate to consolidate the team, so he virtually gave away the house, losing all of the equity, and rented a drab house in Lafayette. "My wife and young daughter named it 'The Brown House', everything was brown! The real estate market in Lafayette along with the

PetroQuest's corporate headquarters, Lafayette, Louisiana.

 *(marker)*

Cactus 133 in Pittsburgh County, Oklahoma, drilling in Woodford Shale.

energy industry was in shambles" he says, thinking back. But, he still owned his car. That is, until another turn-of-events occurred. It was a cold and rainy morning before daylight in late December 1986. The industry was in full-fledged recession with commodity prices collapsing. He was driving to the Lafayette airport to meet J. C. Duncan for a three-city sales trip. He was thinking that he wanted to get the trip over with and get back to Lafayette and enjoy Christmas. En route to the airport in the pouring rain, a detour directed him behind a group of warehouses and across some unmarked railroad tracks. As he crossed the tracks, his car was literally thrown into the air by a train. Strike three! Now house, savings and car were gone. He says he thanked God that he was only bruised and had the wind knocked out of him and not injured more seriously. A few minutes later, as the conductor ran up to his car after having stopped the train, he saw Goodson standing between the train and his obviously "totaled" car that was standing vertical having been thrown into a ditch. When the conductor looked into the car and seeing no one he asked, "Where is he?" Goodson replied, "I am the driver" The excited trainman shot back, "I have never seen one survive before." "That was truly the bottom. I felt worthless. I had a young wife, a one year old child and things were not looking good. That's when you realize how important family, friends and partners truly are," states Goodson.

In these early days, PetroQuest sold its projects to companies located primarily in Houston and Dallas; but, by the late 1980s, many technical staffs in these companies were simply screening deals to appear busy. Each brochure in those days was meticulously assembled with hand-colored maps, folded and placed in a very specific order. It was not unusual to show a prospect a hundred times in a matter of weeks. Goodson spent several weeks on the phone all day long, calling company after company, carefully describing the project and economics, hoping they would simply schedule a meeting to let PetroQuest attempt to sell them on the idea.

In 1988, Goodson recalls when he and Duncan were in Houston having shown a deal more than forty times that week. As they were finishing, Duncan went through his ritual of folding up the maps and putting the brochure back in its logical order. Goodson began closing the meeting as he always did with pleasantries and going over wells and recent discoveries along with news on industry friends who were constantly changing jobs. He finished by asking the all-important question, "Do you think you have an interest in the prospect?" [This was a good low-risk project that, when eventually drilled, was a discovery and tested seven million cubic feet per day of gas and 500 barrels of oil and has accumulated over 1.25 million barrels of oil equivalent.] The response was "Charlie we really are just tire kickers and haven't taken a deal in six months and probably won't take anything for the rest of the year." Goodson walked out of that meeting and said to Duncan, "I did not think I would ever say this, but, I give up J. C." However, remaining persistent and persevering, they took a different route and called every individual they had dealt with in the past and eventually assembled a group of private partners, many of which still invest in deals with PetroQuest today and they never looked back.

The drill was the same, time after time: generate the project, assemble the leases, draft up the brochures and sell, sell, sell, until it was sold, sold, sold! While Goodson is a tremendous fan of former President Reagan, he refers to one of Reagan's early pieces of legislation that virtually shut down the industry. Before Reagan took office, federal income tax rates had escalated to a maximum of seventy percent. After taking office, legislation was passed reducing the maximum rate to thirty-eight and half percent. In conjunction with the lower tax rates, many of the favorable tax treatments were eliminated. The first things to go were high risk investments. At the top of the list were South Louisiana exploration projects. Those investments and projects, along with the collapse of commodity prices, pretty much nailed the coffin shut. Without the benefit of tax exemptions, several dry holes in a row were all it took to alienate even the most die-hard investor. During this time, relationships with partners and investors were vital to survival. Partners were the life blood of the industry. PetroQuest officials hunted, fished, socialized, and vacationed with them. We respected their money as if it were our own. Years later, someone said they never saw a more impressive string of prospects. "You guys were beyond loyal to us."

PetroQuest's success rate for a number of years after that averaged over seventy percent, which, in those days before 3-D and shale plays, was unheard of. The relationship with Flores, Rucks and Morgan was key to that success. The company focused more on making money for all the partners involved as opposed to generating prospects that would excite the larger companies in Houston. They were successful in acquiring a producing property from Mobil (now EXXON Mobil), called Kent Bayou Field for $75,000. After working over one well in the Continental Sand, the property generated over $50,000 per month in revenues. Shortly thereafter, Flores and Rucks were successful in helping to acquire a farm-out on an adjoining five thousand-acre lease through Jim Perkins at Shell located at Turtle Bayou Field. The farm-out required the group to drill a fifteen-thousand-foot Hollywood sand test within three months. The results of that well changed things forever. The well, known as the Germany (now PetroQuest) CL& F #1 logged over two hundred feet of pay and established PetroQuest and its partners as a success in South Louisiana. The Turtle Bayou/Kent Bayou Field complex is still active today having produced over 400 Bcfe since 1990.

Reflecting on the past, Goodson says that the early days were all about developing relationships with "salt of the earth" great people. Goodson adds that the team sometimes met polar opposites. One of many interesting trips was one of many lighter experiences Jeanne (his wife) and he spent with Forrest and his wife in Dallas. Forrest (Germany) had an endless expanse of interesting and great friends. His family was well-known in Texas, was very gracious as a PetroQuest partner, and opened many doors. While Goodson felt financially betrayed by President Reagan, he also realized the President and Vice President George H. W. Bush truly cherished century old relationships; this particular weekend was as a result of the nation's leaders' patriotism and relationship with Britain. The son of the first female prime minister of England and his Texan wife rounded out PetroQuest's group of six. According to Goodson, "We had a great weekend. With the weekend about over, and this gentleman from England about to leave, Germany said to our friend, 'You need to look at some of our oil and gas projects in South Louisiana. We have been very successful.' The guest, in a very British accent, replies, 'Oh, very well, if I must. You know we have the North Sea.'

"Not knowing how serious to take all of the back-and-forth bantering, I went upstairs, grabbed a brochure and made a full presentation. When I finished the presentation, he asked 'how does this work?'

"I replied, 'we drill and hopefully, complete the well. Once production begins, we should see payout in a little over a year. At that point our guest stopped and asked 'what is payout?' I explained that is when you get all of your money back. He replied, 'Oh, I have my money, why on earth would I want to get it back?' With that I folded up the brochure and enjoyed the rest of the weekend," laughs Goodson in retrospect.

Near the end of the 1980s, PetroQuest and its partners were pooling their ideas and using a successful team effort forged with a great group of partners. They jointly drilled a long string of very successful projects that guaranteed the company had a bright future. "Bottom line, we all had fun and made money," says Goodson.

Combining friendship with business was always rewarding. One of those relationships began in 1988 when Goodson received a call from Bill Leuschner whom he did not know at the time, and who literally bought a twenty-five percent interest in several deals over the phone. In all fairness he had already checked out the company through John Strong, a friend who had invested alongside Goodson for over a decade. That phone call eventually resulted in the combination of American Explorer and Optima, which eventually led to the modern day NYSE listed PetroQuest Energy (PQ). Leuschner and Bob Hodgkinson served on the PetroQuest Board for a number of years. While Leuschner has passed on, Hodgkinson remains a close friend, shareholder, and is currently very active in the oil and gas business.

During the mid-1990s things coalesced into a real company. PetroQuest continued to develop

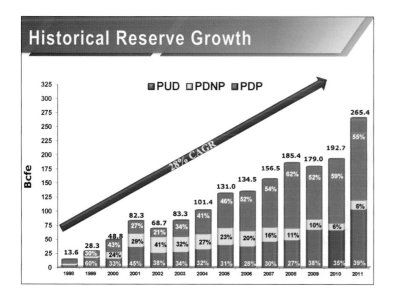

Historical Reserve Growth

Turtle Bayou, along with buying a number of fields across southern Louisiana including Bully Camp and Valentine in Lafourche Parish. It also designed and shot a number of 3-D surveys and was an early mover in using the data to redevelop fields in South Louisiana, which continues to this day. With 3-D the company was not only able to see with clarity what was left, but also how money was wasted, missing objectives with the older 2-D technology. At this time, the company began to transition into the shallow waters of the GOM. That proved to be rewarding, as PetroQuest qualified as an offshore operator, and began participating in offshore lease sales.

In 1998, the company, aided by some very talented lawyers and investment bankers, successfully merged American Explorer and Optima. Dan Fournerat along with Rob Reedy and his skilled team at Porter and Hedges took two very complex companies, one public in Canada, and one private in the United States, and transferred the corporate domicile from British Columbia to Delaware and with that, PetroQuest was born. One of Goodson's proudest days was in 2005 when he was standing with other PetroQuest executives, board members and Pat Landry as he witnessed his daughters, Fallon and Caroline Goodson, ring the opening bell on the New York Stock Exchange (NYSE) having recently moved the company from the NASDAQ.

After going public in 1998, many would assume things would settle down and simply move forward. The PetroQuest that emerged from the merger was essentially a look-alike against many previous success stories that focused on southern Louisiana's Gulf Coast and GOM as a business model. After four years in the public arena, PetroQuest found itself at the proverbial "fork in the road." The stock was up approximately 1,025 percent since the merger. However, after slightly missing production guidance one quarter, the stock drifted down eighty-three percent. It was an epiphany, as the resource plays, beginning with the Barnett Shale, were on every analyst's radar screen. The company, up until that time, had ignored the relevance of the soon-to-evolve resource play revolution. In some ways the disastrous quarter caused a total refocus of the company; and, as a result, today ninety percent of its reserves and seventy-five percent of its production are located in a number of resource basins around the country. "Sometimes you have to fail to succeed," quotes Goodson.

As important as the growth of reserves and production were in the early years, developing and maturing partner relationships was equally important. Flores and Rucks moved on to tremendous success at Ocean Energy. However, Rucks came around full circle in late 1998 after retiring from the public arena when he joined the PetroQuest board of directors, and is one of the longest standing board members along with Wayne Nordberg who also joined the board at that time. Mike Finch, Tony Gordon and Dr. Charles Mitchell joined in later years. Flores continued to build public companies all of which have been successful. One of the benefits of the public market is the ability to follow industry friends by investing alongside their success, which PetroQuest has endeavored to do.

While Duncan has passed on, Thomas, Daigle and Germany are all currently very active in the business. Key long term investors were the Strong family, Alex Theriot, Jim Sowell, Tom Muse, Tom Price, and Dick Bonnecastle along with many other friends and family members.

During 2003 the company began implementing a strategic goal of diversifying its reserves and production into longer life and lower risk onshore basins. As part of the strategic shift to reduce the average working interest in higher risk projects, it shifted capital to high probability of success onshore wells. That reduced the risk associated with drilling individual wells by expanding its drilling program across multiple basins.

In retrospect the pullback in the stock in 2003 prompted the company to redefine a long-term business plan, along with filling in an organizational chart with a talented group of individuals. PetroQuest's senior staff consists of W. Todd Zehnder, chief operating officer who is a certified public accountant; Daniel G. Fournerat, who joined the company in 2001 as vice president, general counsel, chief administrative officer and secretary. J. Bond Clement is an eight-year company veteran and executive vice president, chief financial officer and treasurer. Art M. Mixon, with twelve years seniority is executive vice president of operations and production. Tracy Price recently joined the company in 2012 as executive vice president of land and business development. Stephen H. Green, who joined the company in 1999, is senior vice president of exploration. Edgar A. Anderson, with more than

thirty years in the industry is vice president of the ArkLaTex region; and Mark K. Castell is vice president of Oklahoma assets in Tulsa. In reviewing the company's depth chart all the way to the most important spokesperson for the company, Deryl Patin, our receptionist, you could not find a more dedicated group that has weathered the test of time and a commodity market that continues to test the industry's resolve.

PetroQuest's successful onshore ventures include: Acquiring proved reserves and acreage in the Southeast Carthage Field in East Texas in 2003; and entering the Arkoma Basin in Oklahoma in 2004. It continues today to explore its mid-continent assets and opened a very successful Tulsa office. In 2007, PetroQuest acquired a position in the Fayetteville Shale trend in Arkansas and accelerated the development of the Woodford Shale play in Oklahoma. To date, the company's Arkoma Basin has drilled hundreds of wells and operates a growing production base in excess of 150 Mmcf per day.

In the summer of 2011, the company made the single largest discovery in its twenty-eight year history at its La Cantera project in Vermillion Parish, Louisiana. The discovery well, Thibodeaux #1 was drilled to a depth of 18,500 feet and logged 248 net feet of pay. A subsequent well, the Broussard Estates #2, was drilled approximately one-half mile from the Thibodeaux #1, and logged 310 net feet of pay. The current total daily production from this three well field is approximately 120 Mmcfd.

Since it began its diversification efforts in 2003, the company has grown proved reserves 220 percent and production by 250 percent. Today the company's footprint expands from the Gulf Coast Basin through East Texas and into Oklahoma and the mid-continent. The company's strategy of using cash flow from the Gulf Coast Basin to fund its expansion into the lower risk resource plays is something that is monitored by others in the industry. With a solid foundation of great experienced employees and high quality assets the company is well positioned for the next era in its history.

There are two events that obviously affected a much larger group than simply PetroQuest and the energy industry. These events were far too important to not be singled out and have been used as a way to illustrate how PetroQuest

Woodford Rig—Tom Bell Memorial Well.

is connected to this great country and its economy—the tragic events of Tuesday, September 11, 2001, and the Financial Crisis.

"PetroQuest was a presenting company at the Morgan-Keegan Energy conference in New York City the week of 9/11. Mike Aldridge and Bob Brooksher then CFO and VP Investor Relations were with me at the conference. We had a full day of one-on-one meetings planned that Tuesday. First up was Gagnon Securities beginning at 7:00 am and followed by a meeting with the American Stock Exchange who was then located adjacent to the World Trade Center in the Financial District. Our first meeting was running long, when one of the Gagnon security traders stepped into the conference room and informed us a plane had flown into the WTC. Neil Gagnon who was a lifelong friend of Wayne Nordberg, who was also at that time already a PetroQuest board member, immediately reacted as Wayne's office was on the eighty-ninth floor of WTC Tower II. Obviously we never made it to the second meeting as we were trying to reach Wayne and his assistant, Lillian Preziosi. The Gagnon offices were a block off Central Park and we simply shut down the meeting and began watching the events unfold on a large monitor in Neil's conference room. Out of nowhere the second plane flew across the screen and struck Tower II and the world changed forever. The next four days created volumes of stories for us which were quite similar to many others in the Greater NYC area. Eddie Rosenthal of CRM who controlled a large block of PQ stock tracked us down and insisted we move out of the city and into his house forty miles north. Eddie and his wife, Zita, will never be forgotten for their kindness and generosity. Wayne was on his way up the East side expressway as the first plane hit. He quickly turned around and ended up with his family at their farm in New Jersey. However, his assistant Lillian was at her desk, which faced south toward the Statue of Liberty and actually saw the remnants of the first plane exit the building. Her story is riveting and her actions were heroic as she circled the floor telling all who would listen to clear out. Those that listened did not pause and fought with Lillian through the chaos, barely making it out. Many others at KBW unfortunately did not," recalls Goodson.

On June 23, 2008, PetroQuest closed at $27.49, an all-time high up over 1,200 percent after going public ten years prior. For the year it was up 234 percent based on the growth of the reserves and production and the success being realized from the Woodford shale in Oklahoma as natural gas peaked at over $10 per MCF. Less than nine months later as the Financial Crisis enveloped the energy industry, with the energy commodities being the last to succumb to the crisis, PetroQuest would close at $0.96 in early March 2009. The world had given up on the stock market and North America was in full belief the shale plays were real and contained a healthy hundred-year supply of natural gas. Fortunately, PetroQuest was reaping the benefits of having hedged seventy percent of its production and had released all of the drilling rigs previously under contract. During 2009, PetroQuest paid off all debt under its $130-million revolver lead by JPMorgan and did not drill a single well as a prudent hedge against a rapidly declining natural gas price. Most importantly with the board of directors support, the company did not lay off any employees as there was a lot of work to do to understand the great assets we had assembled. One year later having clearly proven the Woodford was a tier one shale play, PetroQuest entered into the single most important transaction of the company's history; a $234 million joint venture with NextEra, the unregulated arm of Florida Power and Light.

In summary what is described above are personal and professional vignettes that are part of the history of a great company—one that has ridden the waves up and survived the troughs of a volatile industry and economy as a private and now public company. However the most important reasons lay not in its growing reserves or cash flow but because of the great group of employees that have worked tirelessly as a team and the unwavering support of a fully engaged and invested board of directors that combined to create and grow PetroQuest Energy.

Broussard Estates #2 well at the La Cantera Field, Vermilion Parish, Louisiana.

DENBURY RESOURCES INC.

One of the unique success stories associated with energy production in the United States, and certainly Louisiana has to be Denbury Resources Inc. Denbury's story did not start out all that different from other successful small independents, but it did take a fork in the road that has allowed Denbury to successfully utilize carbon dioxide ("CO_2") injection to recover oil from otherwise depleted fields. Denbury's unique business model has created an oil and gas company with the proven ability to improve local economies, reduce our country's dependence on imported oil, and permanently store man-made CO_2 that would otherwise be released into the atmosphere.

Denbury began as a very small independent in 1990, as the brainchild of an English born, Oxford-educated geologist, Gareth Roberts. Gareth left Texaco for a small independent that was exploiting production opportunities in Mississippi and Louisiana. Upon deciding he could do it himself, and better than the way he thought everyone else was doing it,

he formed Denbury with the backing of various domestic and international investors. Denbury, interestingly enough, was named after the street Gareth lived on in London. Gareth's initial business strategy was to acquire older, mature and depleting oilfields from the majors, work them harder, smarter and more economically and scratch out the last remaining reserves; for a profit, of course.

In the early days, this strategy served Denbury well, allowing the company to grow quickly and steadily. In Louisiana, Lirette, Bayou Des Allemends, Chavin, Bayou Rambio, Bay Baptiste, DeLarge, Gibson/ Humphries, Lake Chicot, and Lapeyrouse Fields were among the initial fields purchased in the Gulf Coast Region. In Mississippi, Denbury added Eucutta, Yellow Creek, East and West Heidelberg, King Bee, McComb, Laurel and Little Creek Fields. Along the way, Denbury also added offshore Louisiana production from blocks in West Delta, East Cameron, West Cameron, High Island and Main Pass.

Above: Jackson Dome in Mississippi.

Below: Riley Ridge in the Rocky Mountains.

In the mid-1990s, most companies were moving away from oil production and into gas production. Denbury, however, believed that oil production was quickly approaching "peak oil" on a global production basis and therefore would experience a sustained increase in price. In order to effectively capture the upside Denbury foresaw in oil price, Denbury seized an opportunity to position itself for the future and capture a mostly untapped reserve base in tertiary oil production.

This "fork" in the road came both quietly and decisively in the form of an obscure report found in the field files from an acquisition of properties from Amerada Hess, which indicated that large amounts of oil reserves could be economically recovered through the use of CO_2 injection. Although this method of tertiary production was being widely used in many West Texas fields, CO_2 had not been produced or commercially injected into fields in Mississippi or Louisiana on any sustained basis. The next piece fell into place for Denbury after studying an abandoned Shell CO_2 Project. The Shell Project began with the discovery of large CO_2 reserves located in an area known as Jackson Dome, just north of Jackson, Mississippi. Shell's plan was to build a pipeline from the Jackson Dome CO_2 source through Mississippi and down to Weeks Island on the Gulf Coast of Louisiana. Once implemented, the plan would allow Shell to capture otherwise stranded oil reserves all along the pipeline route. Injection began in the early 1980s in Little Creek Field in Mississippi, and at the terminus of the pipeline in Weeks Island, Louisiana.

Then, in 1986, with the collapse of oil prices, the project had become uneconomic

and Shell elected to stop investing in its development plan. The portion of the line from Donaldsville, Louisiana, to Weeks Island was abandoned and the only remaining field under CO_2 injection was Little Creek Field in Mississippi. The remaining CO_2 reserves being produced were sold to industrial customers for such various uses including carbonating soft drinks, making dry ice, and in fire extinguishers.

In 1999, Denbury acquired Little Creek Field and one year later, the CO_2 reserves at Jackson Dome. Denbury has been exploiting this tertiary niche ever since.

Under the direction of Gareth until his retirement and move to the board of directors in 2009 and then Phil Rykhoek, who was part of the original Denbury executive team, Denbury has steadily increased its Gulf Coast CO_2 footprint with the acquisition of CO_2 fields in Mississippi, Louisiana, and Texas. These combined acquisitions along with development of Jackson Dome CO_2 reserves and the development of over 1,000 miles of CO_2 pipelines have allowed Denbury to become the leading CO_2 enhanced oil recovery (EOR) developer in the Gulf Coast Region and one of the largest in the nation. Denbury accepts the responsibility that comes with efforts to expand America's CO_2 pipeline network and EOR production capability. The company has grown considerably during recent years, adding key professionals who

Left: Aerial view of the Green Pipeline in the Gulf Coast Region.

Right: The Greencore Pipeline in the Rocky Mountain Region.

Above: The CO$_2$ fields in Heidelberg, Mississippi.

Below: The CO$_2$ fields at Lockhart Crossing in Louisiana.

are experienced in guiding the expansion with great skill, efficiency and adherence to environmental health and safety regulations.

Denbury's experience in CO$_2$ pipeline development extends to over one thousand miles of pipelines, the vast majority of which was built specifically to transport CO$_2$. In 2010, Denbury commissioned the 325-mile Green Pipeline, a 24-inch CO$_2$ pipeline extending its existing Mississippi system across Louisiana and into Texas. The Green Pipeline, was initially designed to transport over 800 million cubic feet per day (MMcf/d) of CO$_2$, and can be upgraded to transport additional volumes

when needed. In the construction of the pipeline, Denbury employed only the highest standards for compliance with wetland delineation, sensitive habitat, and cultural resource requirements. A key driver in the design and implementation of the Green Pipeline is the ability to capture man-made CO$_2$ from industrial sources from the many refineries and power plants along its route. Denbury is in a position to accept large volumes of man-made (anthropogenic) CO$_2$ that, in turn, can be permanently stored in the Gulf Coast region to produce large quantities of otherwise stranded oil from existing oilfields.

The Green Pipeline is currently transporting CO_2 from its natural source at Jackson Dome to Lockhart Crossing Field in Louisiana and to Oyster Bayou and Hastings Fields both located in Texas. The company plans to expand the line within the next few years to accommodate its most recent Gulf Coast acquisitions of Conroe Field and Thompson Field. Additionally, Denbury expects to ship its first man-made anthropogenic CO_2 on the line in 2013.

All successful companies need to continue to add reserves in order to maintain growth. With the development of CO_2 in mind, Denbury was attracted to and subsequently acquired Encore Acquisition Company based on its significant potential of flooding its large legacy oilfields in the Rocky Mountain region with CO_2. This expanded Denbury's foothold in the area, and created a second CO_2 enhanced oil recovery core area to complement its leading position in the Gulf Coast Region. The acquisition nearly doubled Denbury's proved reserves and production, as well as providing Denbury with three additional growth areas, which included the future CO_2 EOR assets of Bell Creek and Cedar Creek Anticline (CCA), and a significant position in the Bakken Shale play.

Denbury's business model obviously requires significant volumes of CO_2 and Denbury continues to focus on expanding its sources. In 2010 it acquired 100 percent of the working interest in the Riley Ridge Federal Unit, located in southwestern Wyoming and also one hundred percent of the CO_2 rights in adjacent to Riley Ridge in the Rands Butte Field. Riley Ridge, and Rands Butte are naturally occurring resources that contains natural gas, helium and CO_2. The natural gas and helium are separated and sold, and the remaining CO_2 will be injected into the reservoirs of future Rocky Mountain Fields. The Riley Ridge and Rands Butte Fields also contain a significant resource of potential CO_2 reserves. The potential for field expansion could ultimately become Denbury's primary source of CO_2 for its Rocky Mountain EOR operations; along with several contracts Denbury has entered into for the CO_2 production rights from various anthropogenic sources in the Rocky Mountain Region.

As with its Gulf Coast CO_2 model, a pipeline is required to efficiently move CO_2 from source to field in the Rocky Mountain Region. Denbury expects to complete the first phase its Greencore Pipeline around the end of 2012, which will, ultimately, carry the majority of CO_2 required for the identified EOR opportunity in the Rocky Mountain Region.

Denbury has been fortunate over time to carve out a niche that not only secures a vast reserve base well into the future, but also provides options for our nation to permanently store anthropogenic CO_2 as part of creating an environmentally stable future. Denbury's commitment to act in a professionally responsible manner, protect the environment and secure the health and safety of its employees and the communities in which it operates has always been its primary responsibility.

With a growing reserve and production base, opportunities to continue to add reserves for the next fifty years and a commitment to be both environmentally and corporately responsible help define Denbury as one of the oil and gas industry's major success stories. From humble beginnings in Louisiana and Mississippi to an ever expanding footprint, Denbury looks to a future where its employees' grandchildren will still recover increasing quantities of domestic oil from fields other companies had written off for dead.

Above: Phil Rykhoek.

Below: The Plano Campus.

BADGER OIL CORPORATION

Paul Hilliard could be called a dreamer of big dreams, an entrepreneur, and a modern-day Horatio Alger. He is also a believer in setting goals and working hard to achieve them. He has been doing both quite successfully for more than eighty-seven years!

Clayton Paul Hilliard was born in 1925 in Sandburr Coulee, Wisconsin, where he helped his mother and two brothers tend to the family's small farm and dairy because his father was in poor health. "It was a daunting experience," he recalls. The years of the Great Depression, coupled with severe drought made the family's life even more difficult. There was no electricity or indoor plumbing, and no car to drive the twelve miles into town. "We were frugal, using, reusing, and refitting everything we could to avoid spending money on new things," he adds today from his office on Ambassador Caffery Parkway in Lafayette, Louisiana. "My brothers and I often cross-country skied to attend a one-room school." He attributes his early learning experiences as the basis for his quality education.

Today, the ebullient president of Badger Oil Corporation has vivid memories of his early days growing up in Wisconsin—The Badger State—for which his company is named. He recalls a younger brother who accidentally started a fire, destroying the family's hay supply. "We were forced to sell all livestock but the cows when we rented a house in town. We boarded the cows in a nearby barn so we would have income from the small dairy. As a youth, I delivered milk and cream and made cottage cheese; and I even supplemented the family's income with a newspaper route."

While delivering newspapers, he often stopped to read them. He was intrigued with the information he read. The stories opened the world to him about events and places, stimulating a keen interest in geography and history.

He was fourteen when his father died and his mother remarried. He wanted to complete his education at the same school, so instead of moving with his mother, stepfather and siblings, he chose to live with an aunt and grandmother.

At seventeen in 1943, with WWII already underway, Hilliard did what many young men his age did. He joined the military by enlisting in the Marines where he flew more than fifty missions as a radioman/gunner in "Dauntless" dive bombers over the Solomon Island and Philippines. Following the war, the GI Bill was enacted, and he had just married. Because he wanted a better life for his family than he had growing up, he used the newly created bill to finance his undergraduate education at Wisconsin University and Triple Cities College, which eventually became part of the New York State University system. It was while attending the latter school that he learned about the University of Texas in Austin admitting students to its law school if they had at least a B average at the end of their junior year. Hilliard's grades met the requirement; so, in 1951, he graduated from the University of Texas School of Law.

"The most an attorney made in those days was about $260 per month," he says. "By then, with two young daughters and a wife to

Above and below: Paul Hilliard.

support, I knew I needed to earn more." That is when a California company recruiter (now Chevron) offered him $100 more per month to join their firm as a landman. He was glad to get the job.

The oil business was new to him, having only seen them [oil wells] from a distance; yet, he knew he wanted to provide the best he could for his family. In July, he arrived in New Orleans where he worked in that capacity for three years. In 1954 he went to work for H. L. Hunt as a South Louisiana district landman—the only employee there. The work was fast paced and the situation somewhat disorganized, so with just four years' experience under his belt, he decided to form his own company, naming it Badger Oil Corporation.

Since then he has logged a fifty-seven-year love affair with the oil industry. Some call him a "typical" independent, which he calls an oxymoron. "You cannot be typical and be independent," he laughs. "Actually," he adds, "in the early days, we were 'dependents' because we relied on others for investment capital and technological experience. Therefore, I am humbled and ever grateful for the advice and assistance, and sometimes fatherly guidance and correction, received from those who have gone on to the 'silent city'."

Like his oil industry competitors, he has experienced the ups and downs of the oil business with fluctuating gas and oil prices. "Lower-price oil usually means lower-priced natural gas because a lot of our market is switchable, particularly in the industrial and utility sectors," he says. "While we [the independents] are adept at conducting oil and gas exploration ventures, we're not known as prudent economists."

He admits to witnessing good days and bad days in the business; but it is the good days that

he savors. They are the ones that manage to help him survive the roller coaster ride of the oil industry.

Hilliard views the oilfield service and supply companies as invaluable and indispensable to the industry. "I have never been involved with another business or industry that has comparable contractors. Perhaps, it is because the upstream industry is a 24/7/365 operation."

Some might even say he loves the oil business so much that he has oil running through his veins. Oil is his life—what he enjoys doing. "If I woke up in the morning and was not facing a day when I wouldn't be associated with the search for oil and gas, it would be an awfully dull day," he adds.

He could talk for days about his life in the Louisiana oil patch, though often, he says, the business is handicapped by Mother Nature. "She is perverse and extremely unpredictable. We saw the damage she inflicted on the area and the industry when Hurricane Katrina hit. Still, we're guilty of being overconfident. I have never been involved in drilling a well without feeling that it was going to produce. I've never bought a lease without thinking that it was going to be a productive one. Yet, I realize that, statistically, the hole is probably

an exercise in futility and the lease is probably worthless. I don't know if it's true optimism, or bullheaded determination that things will get better."

He defines the oil industry as having four legs—geological, mechanical, economical and political. "Until 2008, we had a stable leg." The company remains small with twenty-five employees in its Lafayette headquarters and satellite office in Houma, Louisiana. "I've had the good fortune to have some of the smartest, most competent people I know working for Badger," he says.

Hilliard has taken a leadership role in the oil and gas industry, and in his adopted hometown of Lafayette. He was instrumental in starting the Louisiana Oil and Gas Association, the trade group that represents not just independent producers, but service companies as well. He has also served as chairman of the Independent Petroleum Association of America (IPAA), the national trade group for independent producers. He sees the IPAA's role as one of educating Congressmen, their staffs, and the committees that deal with energy matters. "We've worked hard, but we haven't achieved enough, primarily because many of those in politics don't

understand our industry well enough to know the difference between upstream revenues and downstream profits."

Over its fifty-plus-year history, Badger has transitioned from solely a prospect generator to generator and operator, with its exploration effort focused on south Louisiana and the shallow shelf of the Gulf of Mexico. It concentrates efforts within specific areas of focus, specifically in-and-around existing oil and gas fields. A typical large field has existing three-dimensional (3-D) seismic data, extensive well control, and existing infrastructure. Because of these qualities, Badger believes significant profitable opportunities remain in these areas. The company's expertise lays in the exploitation of existing productive state water and Gulf of Mexico fields via integrated, geophysical, geological, and engineering evaluations.

Badger has attracted high-level energy experts to facilitate the transition from generator to being an operator. Badger remains small and nimble, but it can match the technical capabilities of much larger companies.

In 2009, Badger Oil Corporation celebrated the fiftieth anniversary of its founding. That milestone coincided with the 150th anniversary of the birth of the domestic oil industry, with the first commercial oil production of the Drake well in Pennsylvania. Throughout those fifty years, Badger has survived numerous oil booms and busts, but all the while its roots were firmly planted in Acadiana.

In addition to his business, Hilliard supports numerous philanthropic and community initiatives, including contributions to the National World War II Museum, where he serves on the board of trustees, and the Paul and Lulu Hilliard University Art Museum at the University of Louisiana in Lafayette, (he and his late wife, Lulu, were the lead donors). Hilliard is also a founding director of MidSouth National Bank. Hilliard has always valued his conservative upbringing, which is why he treasures one of the biggest honors to be bestowed upon him—the Horatio Alger Award. "When I was a boy, I often read books by Horatio Alger, Jr. I never imagined that one day I would be inducted into an organization

that would recognize me for accomplishments. The national award acknowledges individuals who have achieved success despite humble beginnings. I am humbled. It is one of my most treasured accolades.

"In thinking of the last sixty years, it occurs to me that this industry affords an element we all need to learn and that's humility. There are few better teachers of humility than the 'dry hole'. Yet, it's those dry holes that are essential to success in exploration because you don't find better or more essential geological leads than those monuments to stupidity. Knowing where it is not seems to be a required stop in determining where it is, or as it states in Proverbs: …before honor is humility."

JACK T. EVERETT

Above: Jack T. Everett, a Navy aviation machinist mate.

Below: Jack T. Everett with his daughters. Left to right, Sharon, Jack and Terri, 1964.

For nearly half a century, Jack T. Everett, an independent oilman, embodied the wildcatter spirit in North Louisiana.

"Keep the bit in the ground," he would say, summarizing his approach to the oil and gas business. In a radio interview in 2010, two years before he died at eighty-three, Everett estimated that he and his many partners had drilled more than a thousand oil and gas wells in his long career. "I love wildcatting," he said. And many of those partnerships, amazingly enough, were sealed with a handshake. Many of those wells, in other words, represented a gentlemen's agreement. "A handshake always meant more to me than anything in writing," Everett said. "I take people at their word, and I've been fortunate in meeting the right people."

Born in 1929, Everett grew up during the Great Depression in the Trinity Heights neighborhood of Dallas, which he jokingly described as "Hungry Heights." Hard times honed his survival and deal-making skills. As a youngster, he shined shoes, worked in a used car lot and generally hustled for every quarter he made.

In those days, Sun Oil sponsored a basketball team, and that made the company an alluringly good fit for a certain 6 foot, 3 center who was graduating from Adamson High

School. Starting in the mailroom and perhaps on the basketball court, Everett worked at Sun Oil briefly before joining the Navy, where he was stationed on an aircraft carrier.

After the Korean War, he returned to Sun Oil and worked there just long enough to receive some valuable advice: If he was going to be successful, a high-ranking executive once told him, if he was going to rise in the ranks at this oil company, or any large company, he had to acquire a college degree.

That advice, along with an especially profitable poker game, sent him to North Texas State College, which is now the University of North Texas. Going to college on the GI Bill, he graduated in 1956 with a degree in business.

And so with his degree in hand and wife, Win, at his side, Everett returned to Sun Oil a month or so later to work in the land department—and play basketball, of course. For the next seven years, he worked as a land scout in the Permian Basin. It seemed to him, he would say years later, that he drove up and down every dirt road in West Texas looking for prospects and possibilities.

Independent by nature and never averse to taking a reasonable risk in exchange for the possibility of a lucrative reward, Everett was born to be a wildcatter, or so it seemed. And even though he would always fondly recall his years at Sun Oil, the time to move on and step out on his own arrived inevitably in the mid-1960s, after he and his second wife, Marcy, moved to Shreveport, Louisiana.

There, Jack entered into many of the partnerships and friendships that lasted a lifetime and were, he would always say, essential to any success he had. Early in his career, Everett partnered with Leo Recknagel, for example, and, much later, with Hood Goldsberry, experienced and astute businessmen. Those partnerships were golden and, Everett would always say, lucky.

"It's a risky business," Everett said, referring to the oil and gas business during that 2010 radio interview. "No matter how smart you are, you have to be lucky...I've been the luckiest person in the world."

Looking for possibilities, Everett drove the rural roads of North Louisiana, a portable typewriter and a stack of lease forms in the

backseat of his long Cadillac and a large bankroll in his pocket, just in case there was a deal that required a cash sealant. More than a few times, he took his young daughters, Terri and Sharon, along, pacifying them with cupcakes or snow cones while he ran the courthouse records. Everett once told a story about negotiating a lease with an especially stubborn farmer—or maybe the farmer was just excessively proud of a local product, for he would not agree to anything until the tall Texan drank some homemade moonshine. The tall Texan, as it turned out, was sick for days.

Everett worked jointly with a number of independent oilmen, particularly geologist Perry Holloway, fellow landman Charlie Meadows, and petroleum engineer Robert Adair, taking leases and selling oil prospects to investors. Often they put together deals that they then would broker to larger oil companies. They also bought royalty and minerals whenever they could. As they brokered their deals, they kept overrides and designated areas of mutual interest for future development. Tenneco Oil Company, and later J-W Operating were major clients and long-time partners in Desoto Parish's Caspiana Field, an area that proved rich in natural gas. At the time of Everett's death, he had over five hundred interests—working, royalty, and overriding—in that field alone.

Although he focused on North Louisiana, Everett and his partners also drilled wells in Texas, Oklahoma, Alabama, Mississippi, and even Ohio. He was very active in Arkansas, where he partnered with Adair, Smackover Oil and Gas and Wilson Sewell, and later, Robert Reynolds, of Shuler Drilling.

In 1976, Everett and Holloway teamed up to lease a block of Exxon's fee minerals near New London Field in Union County, Arkansas. Over the course of the next ten years, he and Holloway developed the LaPile Field with Shuler Drilling ending up with twenty-five successful wells and nineteen dry holes.

Everett's other big finds were in Leatherman Creek Field in Claiborne Parish and Converse Field in Sabine Parish. Holloway, who would later become president of Holloway Energy, also did the geology on the Converse Field.

Above: Everett Farms with a Haynesville shale gas well being drilled in the background.

Below: Marcy and Jack Everett, 1990s.

formed in 1980, along with Everett's Granja Corporation, operated eleven Whitney wells in the Converse Field.

For many years, Everett was a fixture in the card room at the Petroleum Club in Shreveport, where he enjoyed a good game of gin rummy, and in the dining room, where he met with the same lunch crowd for over forty years. He jokingly referred to the Club as his office and loved the camaraderie of the gang that referred to themselves as "Oilfield Trash."

The 1970s and 1980s were a heady time in the oil and gas industry and Everett was masterful at mixing business with pleasure. The Everetts made annual trips to Acapulco where investors, friends and family all converged to make memories that would last for years. Friendships were cemented, as well as deals. Hot summer weekends were spent cruising Lake Bisteneau on the "Bisteneau Bulldozer," at least until the boat burned to the pontoons, forcing the Everetts and fellow oilman Bob McIntyre to abandon ship.

Top: Left to right, Jack T. and Marcy Everett, and Margie and Leo Recknagel.

Above: Left to right, Hood and Linda Goldsberry, and Marcy and Jack T. Everett.

"We were both hungry in those days," Holloway recalled, explaining their success. "And when you're hungry you work harder and you put more into the business."

Holloway remembered flying with Everett up to Cincinnati to meet with representatives of the Whitney Corporation, which owned considerable acreage in Sabine Parish. And that led, of course, to more deals and partnerships, particularly with Rob Kreidler of the Whitney Corp. At one time, Everett Oil,

Always on the lookout for an opportunity, Everett tried his hand at many new ventures during this time, including Plum Orchard Marina on Lake Bisteneau with good friend Ed Wallbaum, and The Millcroft Inn, a restaurant near Cincinnati. Partial ownership in Bailey Drilling with buddy Jerry Bailey came and went, as did the "311 Edwards Street Pub," a popular bar in downtown Shreveport. Everett also bought the AutoPark Garage and Parking Lot in downtown Shreveport, an enterprise that his family still owns and operates.

For Everett, owning racehorses had been a lifelong dream, and the opening of Louisiana Downs sparked his passion for sport and thoroughbreds. He was among the leading owners at the Bossier City Racetrack during its early years, in the 1970s and 1980s. He also bred many of his racehorses, and Everett Farms in Desoto Parish became his favorite retreat. One of his horses, Granja Suerte, won eleven races in her career, including three stakes races. Everett thought so much of the mare that he named his operating company after her. In 1985, he and some partners purchased and imported a horse name Charming Duke from France. In his first start in America, Charming Duke won a division of the famed Hollywood Derby. Horses such as Moving Miles, Hail Tudor, Papa Mac, and Mogumbo Cat kept the Everetts in the winner's circle.

Everett loved everything about the oil and gas industry, especially its people. He understood the essential deal at the center of the industry: accepting risk in exchange for the intriguing and tantalizing possibility, however tenuous it might be, of discovery. Only health issues could have slowed him down, and they slowed him only a little. The turn of the century found him investing in others' prospects more than developing his own. He particularly enjoyed working with Joel Chevalier and Petro-Chem Operating Co., as well as trusted partner and long-time friend Goldsberry. Hood included Everett on one land deal simply because the tall Texan was the luckiest man he knew. If Everett's in the deal, Goldsberry said, they would be sure to make money. Whether or not luck had anything to do with it remains a matter for discussion, but the acreage sat atop one of

the early Haynesville shale plays in Caddo Parish and so, along with other carefully studied assets, proved to be rewarding for the entire group.

After nearly a half-century of "keeping the bit in the ground," Everett became a part of North Louisiana's history: He became a leading representative of an enduring character in the narrative of the oil industry, the wildcatter. He died in July 2012. He is survived by his wife and partner of almost fifty years, Marcy, his two daughters, five grandchildren, a great grandson, and, of course, Everett Oil.

Above: Jack and Marcy Everett in Acapulco.

Below: Mogumbo Cat *takes first, Louisiana Downs, 2010.*

ANDERSON OIL & GAS CO., INC.

Only twenty-three years old in 1914, W. C. Feazel could have been called a futurist. He moved from his birthplace in Point, Louisiana, to Monroe, Louisiana, to join the infancy of the gas and oil industry. His efforts are recognized as laying the groundwork for what is known today as Anderson Oil & Gas Co., Inc.

Feazel entered the oil business as a lease-broker in the Monroe Gas Field; and, within two years had saved enough money to acquire some leases and started the drilling of his own wells in the Monroe Gas Field. He began expanding his business in the early 1920s, and began operations in the Haynesfield Field in Richland Parish, Louisiana. During the 1920s, he had expanded his operations, beginning new ones in the Haynesville Field, the old Jackson Gas Field in Jackson, Mississippi. In the late 1920s, he began operations in the Richland Field in Richland Parish, Louisiana.

His reputation as an astute oilman had positioned him well when he decided to enter politics. He was elected to the Louisiana House of Representatives from the Ouachita Parish, serving from 1932-36.

In 1938, Feazel, along with N. V. Kinsey, put together eight thousand acres in what is now the Carthage Gas Field. After that discovery well, the two put together more than thirty-eight thousand acres that were developed into one of the largest gas fields in the United States. Together, they drilled the Jordan Number One in a cornfield on the Carl Jordan farm, a short distance east of the city of Carthage. The third and last well, which can be termed discovery, was drilled in 1943 on the Jordan farm. The field was developed when equipment and other material became available after WWII. Feazel had production going in all the North Louisiana Parish, and many in South Louisiana.

A year later, Feazel sold all his interest above the top of the Travis Peak to the Chicago Corporation, moving all his oil and gas business to Shreveport. The company was known as The Feazel Interest. It consisted of W. C. Feazel, Lallage Feazel, G. M. (Jake) Anderson, and Gertrude Feazel Anderson.

On May 18, 1948, Governor Earl K. Long appointed him to the United States Senate to fill the vacancy upon Senator John H. Overton's death. He did not seek reelection and, instead, resumed his oil and gas business in Monroe and Shreveport. His Senate seat was filled with the election of Russell B. Long, son of Huey P. Long, Jr.

In the early 1950s, The Feazel Interest was involved with the discovery of the Hico-Knowles, Dubach and Lisbon Field in North Louisiana. With the increased petroleum production, The Feazel Interest and Southwest Gas built the Dubach Gas Plant in Lincoln Parish.

In 1959, The Feazel Interest discovered the Jonesboro's field in Jackson Parish, Louisiana; and, that same year, The Feazel Interest built the Blackburn Gasoline Plant north of Minden, Louisiana. Today, The Feazel Interest is involved in production in North and South Louisiana, South Arkansas, Texas, Mississippi, and Alabama.

Feazel, a long-time member of West Monroe Baptist Church, passed away in 1965. He is interred at Hasley Cemetery in West Monroe. Partner, Jake Anderson died two years later. Feazel's grandsons, Hank and Bill Anderson, took over the operations of The Feazel Interest. When the two assumed the company's leadership role, the name was changed to Anderson Oil and Gas, Inc.

While Hank, president, says the company has a rich history in the oil industry, it was Glassell and Glassell who drilled what is known as the first well in the Carthage Gas Field in 1936. "Prior to that, there was no concerted effort to drill other wells because there was no market for natural gas."

With the drilling of the Cotton Valley Well in Carthage in 1977, The Feazel Interest returned to Carthage Gas Field where over four hundred Cotton Valley wells have been drilled. Since the founders' deaths, the company has made many discoveries. One of the larger discoveries was the Grayson Oilfield in 1993 in South Arkansas.

The Carthage Gas Field Petit production, today, is approximately 1.5 trillion cubic feet (TCF), and the Cotton Valley is 2.0 TCF. Drilling in the Haynesville Shale is underway, with approximately ten wells having been drilled. "The production is very good," says Hank. "The Anderson-Feazel group of companies produces 11,000 MCFPD (one thousand cubic feet of gas per day) and 1,200 barrels of oil equivalent."

The company has undergone reorganization, and is now known as Anderson-Feazel Investments, which includes interests in Hampton Inns and Homewood Suites. There is also a holding in the timberland throughout North Louisiana and other states.

The Anderson and Feazel families believe in being active community citizens; and, are known for their philanthropy to Centenary College of Louisiana.

Prosperity came to Monroe, Louisiana, with the discovery of their great gas fields. One product of this prosperity was the G. B. Cooley house, originally constructed in 1910 in the Prairie Style reminiscent of Frank Lloyd Wright. The actual architect of the house was Walter Burley Griffin. Beautiful interior details tie furnishings to the exterior of the building.

The hazards of the early oil industry were great.

PHOTOGRAPH COURTESY OF THE
LOUISIANA STATE MUSEUM.

ABOVE: PHOTOGRAPH COURTESY OF THE MINERALS
MANAGEMENT SERVICE, VOLUME VI, AND JACK McCULLY.

LEFT: PHOTOGRAPH COURTESY OF THE MINERALS
MANAGEMENT SERVICE, VOLUME VI, AND JERRY SHEA.

EXPLORATION & PRODUCTION

JUSTISS OIL COMPANY, INC.

The name "Jick" Justiss is well known in the oil industry of the Gulf South. Although James Fowler Justiss, Sr., is now deceased, it was he, along with Calvin G. "Cal" Mears, who founded what is known today as Justiss Oil Company.

Left: Jick Justiss (left) and James Justiss, Jr., (center) age 14.

Top, right: A blowout in Olla Field, Louisiana, July 3, 1940.

Bottom, right: Left to right: H. L. Hunt and Jick Justiss, 1941.

Born in 1896 in the South Arkansas community of Cairo, Jick was the son of college educated parents, notable for the day. He had three brothers and five sisters, but when his father died of pneumonia, it was fourteen year old Jick who was able to care for the family, run the farm, and only occasionally attend school.

In January 1921, "black gold fever" spread throughout Southern Arkansas when the discovery well of the El Dorado Field blew in, soaking trees and countryside. Jick began working as a muleskinner in the oilfields, moving drilling rigs and oilfield equipment. It was not long before he owned his own team, and then bought six additional mule teams with wagons. With this greater moving capacity, he became a regular contractor for several big operators around Smackover, an area rich in petroleum.

While operating his mule team contractor business, Jick met legendary oilman H. L. Hunt during the boom days. Hunt realized that Jick was hard working and conscientious, and Jick became Hunt's preferred moving contractor. When the boom at Smackover began to cool in 1926, Jick sold most of the mules. With little-to-no income, he could not afford to feed the animals. A year later, when Hunt returned to inspect his properties, he learned that Jick was experiencing tough times. He encouraged Jick to sell the remaining mules and offered him a job as a roustabout in Tullos, Louisiana.

Jick sold his business, moved to LaSalle Parish, and began working for Hunt. Later, he was promoted to oil treater and pumper on the Urania "A" lease in the Tullos-Urania Field. Jick was a fast learner, and shortly thereafter, was promoted to assistant production superintendent under Tom Carter. Upon Carter's untimely death, Jick became superintendent, in charge of overseeing Tullos-Urania operations for Hunt Oil Co. In 1928, he proved himself to his employer by reducing costs on equipment, manpower and work-overs. Hunt was shipping some 500 railroad tank cars of oil per month from the Tullos area, and he was quite pleased when Jick also slashed the shipping budget. Jick, despite his limited experience in the business, was charged with the recompletion of previously abandoned wells. He performed his tasks successfully and gained the confidence of his boss and the respect of his peers.

In 1929, Jick married Wilma "Mac" Morphis. In 1930 oil was discovered in East Texas. Hunt finished negotiations with lease owner, Dan Joiner, promoted Jick to general superintendent, and transferred him to attend the newly discovered field. Many others followed Hunt to Texas, where they lived in provided lodging, much like mill villages, enjoying camaraderie, baseball, and retail and professional services provided by migrant vendors. Jick managed Hunt's entire field operations there, including the supervision of a dozen drilling rigs and the first pipeline gathering system to serve the East Texas Field. From then on, Jick was in charge of all of Hunt Oil Company's varied field operations, but his primary interest was in drilling. His devotion to this phase of the business paid dividends and he gained fame throughout the region as a "can do" operations manager. Jick supervised the drilling of discovery wells in several states to include Arkansas, Louisiana, and Texas. Some of those fields bear such well-known names as Magnolia, Bear Creek, Cotton Valley, Olla, Nebo, North Carterville, and Chapel Hill.

While living in East Texas, the Justiss' had two children, James, Jr., and Paula. In 1937 the family moved back to Louisiana to develop Hunt's drilling operations in the Cotton

Valley Field in Webster Parish. It was there that Hunt encountered a pay-sand, which he named the "Justiss" after his superintendent. (Today, Justiss Oil Company geologists still encounter this Justiss sand and smile at the physical reminder of the man they never knew, but whose relevance to Justiss Oil and the industry is perpetual.)

World War II placed petroleum in high demand, threatening the supply of oil, and the post-war economic boom continued to provide a strong demand for petroleum. Jick was confident that he could make a better living by starting his own business. On April 16, 1946, he partnered with Cal Mears to form Justiss-Mears Oil Company. Mears, a well-known entrepreneur and investor, had the

James F. Justiss, Jr.

contract drilling, exploration, and well and lease services across the Southern Gulf Coast from Texas to Alabama. The company remains a privately owned, family-operated business with six drilling rigs with depth ranges up to 16,000 feet and 14 work-over units. Also under the Justiss umbrella are two manufacturing divisions operating in the domestic and international markets. Baker Tank Company specializes in the design, fabrication and field erection of petroleum storage tanks, production equipment and API code vessels for onshore and offshore applications; and Altech is an aluminum technology division, which designs, manufactures and installs internal and external floating roofs.

Justiss Oil Company, Inc. continues to be a leader in the industry, expanding areas of interest and service regarding exploration, technology, safety, and environmental and governmental issues. A new generation is leading the way as W. B. "Bo" McCartney, Jr., executive vice president and J. F. "Jim" Justiss, III, vice president of operations continue the tradition of growth and change to meet the demands of today's market. We also continue our commitments of fairness and concern for our employees and of support to our community. We would like to dedicate these pages of our heritage to our past and present employees. Their service has played an integral part in the longevity and success of Justiss Oil Company.

Above: Justiss Oil Company Rig 60.

ability to arrange financing for the venture. Both Mears and Justiss had invested $25,000 in working capital to form the company. Justiss' character, along with his reputation of having extensive knowledge of and success in the oil industry helped cinch the loan for $50,000.

The Justiss' were blessed with a third child in 1948, Eddie Justiss, but were devastated only fourteen years later to lose him in a tragic accident.

Since the partners purchased the first abandoned well, re-worked it and placed it back on production, the company has grown to be one of the oldest, most experienced independent drilling contractors in the nation under the management of James F. Justiss, Jr. Now Justiss Oil Company, Inc. provides

Natural gas exploration and development of the Wilcox Formation in Central Louisiana is closely linked to efforts of brothers Harry and Frank Spooner. In 1966 there was a single well producing gas from the Wilcox in Caldwell Parish. Gas sold for 15 cents/mcf, Louisiana severance tax took 2.3 cents/mcf and compression expenses devoured another 2 cents/mcf.

The Spooners drilled two step out wells and extended the productive area of Sardis Church Field.

Were there other areas in Caldwell Parish prospective for gas? Well control was very sparse, gas prices bad, but production rates were good and drilling costs, low. With three interstate and one intrastate pipeline crossing the Parish any gas found would not be stranded. The Spooners made the decision to do some serious wildcatting.

Five prospects were identified and leased in 1966. In 1967 drilling began and on five successive weekends, a Wilcox discovery was made on each prospect.

Other operators soon joined the play. An active drilling program in 1968, 1969, and 1970 by Spooner and others yielded three or four discoveries, but many dry holes. The play faltered.

Harry decided to pursue "greener pastures" in Mississippi. Frank remained in Louisiana to operate the production they had found. In late 1971 gas prices began to improve and Frank drilled the discovery well for Banks Springs Field. During the decade he drilled four or five wildcats a year with a discovery each year. In the Wilcox play the Spooners had a total of thirteen new discoveries and production in seven fields found by other operators.

In 1980, Frank formed Spirit Petroleum Company. Harry had pre-empted the name Spooner Petroleum Company for his operations in Mississippi. With declining gas prices in 1983, Spirit focused on oil exploration in Arkansas and was moderately successful.

The late 1980s brought plummeting oil prices and Spirit suffered through a long string of dry holes. Finally, in 1997, in an attempt to change his luck, Frank renamed the company Mark V Petroleum. The tactic worked and the company drilled a number of successful development gas wells in subsequent years.

Mark V Petroleum and Spooner Petroleum assembled a fifteen-thousand-acre block of leases in Caldwell Parish in 2001 for a coalbed methane project. With the help of industry partners Sklar Exploration, Pruet Production Company, and Hughes Oil, coalbed methane gas production was established and the field was named Riverton. In 2005 the Office of Conservation approved the first production units for coalbed methane in the state for the Riverton Field. In 2005, Southwestern Energy purchased the majority of the working interest in the field and drilled an additional thirty wells.

Mark V Petroleum has continued to explore the Wilcox Formation for oil and gas in North Central Louisiana.

MARK V PETROLEUM COMPANY

Left: A Wilcox production well, Caldwell Parish, Louisiana.

Below: Fracking a Mark V Petroleum Company coalbed methane well, Riverton Field, Caldwell Parish, Louisiana.

McGowan Working Partners, Inc.

John W. McGowan gave meaning to the word "re-engineering" long before it became a business buzzword in the 1990s.

Following graduation from Louisiana State University (LSU) with a degree in geology and two years in the Army, he went to work on a seismic crew in New Mexico. He worked there during the day and analyzed cores for Core Laboratory at night. It was then, after gaining a few years' experience in the oil industry, that the young father of three thought it possible to re-work older oil wells that had become non-productive.

He was so motivated by the idea that, in 1961, he moved his family back to Mississippi and bought the Dixon No.1, his first oil well in Pickens Field. This well, and several others had been quite productive in the 1940s; but, over the years declining production rendered these wells uneconomic. However, John discovered that if you moved a lot of fluid, while the oil cut would go down significantly, the decline in the oil production shallowed up significantly. If he could devise a way to make a low oil cut, high volume fluid well economic he may have a long lived asset. That was true, but he encountered a problem: What was he to do with all the produced fluid once the oil was skimmed off? Because he was only getting about $2.70 per barrel of oil, he needed to find a way to economically dispose of the excess produced fluid and increase his revenue simultaneously. That prompted him to begin to find a way to dispose of produced saltwater (waste when separated from the oil) without using mechanical pumps.

He found that the cost of setting up a pumping and disposal facility that could produce two thousand barrels of fluid a day for a one percent oil cut, and disposition of the remaining 1980 barrels of produced fluid was

not (and still is not) an inexpensive undertaking. It was difficult finding people who were interested in investing in a young geologist's idea that would make profit by producing a mature oilfield making a one percent cut, moving large volumes of fluid with a huge upfront capital cost. "In fact, there were none," John McGowan remembers today.

The early days provided a great learning experience. McGowan found that if he produced fluid while the oil cut is reduced, he could produce enough oil to make a profit when operating expenses were kept under control. This is where the saltwater disposal system becomes vital to the economics of the business. Times were hard; yet, he persevered. There were weeks when McGowan collected a load of junk pipe and took it to the scrap dealer on Thursday to make payroll on Friday. He felt he had a good month if he made $500 profit.

In the early years of his business, McGowan bought wells randomly, and eventually purchased the operating working interest in Holly Ridge Field, Tensas Parish, Louisiana, in 1975. This field was a large, mature Wilcox oilfield discovered in the 1930s, but was no longer economically feasible for the current producers. There, he went to work drilling 100 wells, completing about 45 as oil producers, and turning about 30 into disposal wells.

When McGowan finished Holly Ridge in 1978, that field was producing about 800 barrels of oil per day, 100,000 barrels of waste per day, and enough casing head gas to run an Ajax Motor for each of the pumping units. With that system, every well he completed went to about one percent oil after the first week. Every barrel of the saltwater went into the thirty disposal wells, which were all interconnected without use of a pump.

Today, the Holly Ridge Field produces 350 barrels of oil per day, along with 110,000 barrels of saltwater, with a 3/10 percent oil cut. He has realized six million barrels of oil from Holly Ridge at oil cuts never exceeding one percent. The geological formation from both a producing standpoint and a disposal standpoint must have certain characteristics in order to install a production system such as that used by McGowan Working Partners. One of the bigger hurdles was educating the regulatory agencies in the states where McGowan used its distinctive method of saltwater disposal. This was and continues to be a challenge today.

McGowan Working Partner's growth was evident after John completed and paid for Holly Ridge. In the mid-1980s, it expanded operations into the Gulf Coast Regions of Texas and Alabama, as well as spreading further outward in Louisiana. It sought property that was affordable that required a lot of re-working and re-equipping. At this time of expansion, John began allowing his employees to participate in the working interest in the oilfield he acquired. Thus was formed McGowan Working Partners. These

employees/partners derived a large part of their income from this ownership. John found out that not only does this ownership instill loyalty to the company, but a lot of the solutions to the problems we encountered in re-working these old fields emanate from these employees/partners.

Developing the system of saltwater waste by utilizing older wells and not having to rely on mechanical pumps was the solution he sought to achieve when he bought his first well. Now, in 2012, that remains his mission: To re-work and re-engineer mature oil fields so that hydrocarbons can be produced economically for many years after traditional methods of production have rendered the production uneconomical.

While John McGowan, at seventy-eight, is still active in the company's daily operations, there are several longtime employees who handle the day-to-day operations. David Russell, a former contract landman who began working with McGowan in 1980, joined the company fulltime two years later. He has risen up the ranks, and now serves as president of McGowan Working Partners. Like McGowan, he holds a degree in geology, which he uses in regulatory capacities. Mart Lamar, Joe Haney and Cardy Miller, degreed engineers, along with Charles Johnson, geologist, are responsible for evaluating the oilfields and implementing the work in the field. All of these people are hands on which means they roll up their sleeves and get directly involved with the work over and field work. Russell says that knowing John McGowan for thirty years has been a blessing. "I learn something from him every day. The lessons could be about geology, engineering, or down hole problems on wells. Or, they could be about dealing with people and situations...or patience...how to live life in an honorable way...how to focus on what is important; and even forgiveness."

McGowan Working Partners' home office is located in Jackson, Mississippi, where John was born and reared. (His ancestors came to Mississippi when his great-grandfather was given 640 acres of land in Jones County. It was payment for fighting alongside General Andrew Jackson at Chalmette, Louisiana in the War of 1812.)

McGowan Working Partners, Inc., has approximately 110 employees with about eighty percent located in the fields in which they work. Many of the employees are second and third generation people—sons and daughters of those who worked for the company in earlier days. McGowan has oilfield operations in Texas, Mississippi, Louisiana, New Mexico and Arkansas. All operations are land-based with operations in over 60 oilfields and 900 total wells.

Bottom, right: John W. McGowan.

William (Bill) Lane Douglas aspired to becoming a skilled explorationist. Following graduation from New Mexico Military Institute in 1947, then Oklahoma University and Oklahoma State in undergraduate programs, he graduated from Oklahoma City University Law School in 1955, passed the bar and was admitted to the Oklahoma Bar that year.

It was expected that he would practice law. Instead, he joined Sohio's Land Training Program and worked for Atlantic Refining (ARCO) until 1960. He became district landman for Southwest Gas until 1966, when he founded Prospects Brokerage, Inc. His focus now being exploration, he began acquiring drilling prospect concepts from independent geologists, acquiring the acreage himself, and selling the prospect to drilling operators.

He was co-founder of Damson Oil Corp. (AMEX) in 1967, and was exploration agent for Washington Gas Light Company, serving the Washington-Virginia-Maryland area in 1974-1975. From his love of exploration, he was involved in drilling over 500 wells in south Louisiana, purchasing over 10,000 leases with initial assembly responsibility for almost 200 drilling prospects.

He has plugged and restored about three hundred wells that were either dry holes or depleted producing wells. This included supervising cleanup, preparing final releases with signatures. In curing titles, he has prepared many hundreds of possession affidavits and cured hundreds of title opinions. Before 1960, he even obtained affidavits of bastardy.

With his legal background, he has done contract evaluation as part of due diligence, working with industry contracts, joint operating agreements, farmouts, purchase agreements, and proposals. In areas frequently requiring new contracts for production needs, he has prepared the contract for submittal to the attorney in charge, saving serious money for the client operator. He has prepared hundreds of title certificates, abstracts from severance, etc.

His strongest skills beyond exploration are remarkable trades. In 2009, he purchased 2,100 acres of leases, not options, for $7.50 per acre and a 3/16 royalty from 11 families. One family's last lease was $200 per acre and a 25 percent royalty. His negotiation skills have enabled him to bring difficult parties to agreement.

W. L. DOUGLAS

William "Bill" Lane Douglas.

His greatest single leasing work in an early prospect for Damson Oil was a fully developed subdivision of twelve hundred lots, all with homes over the prospect with deviated drilling. With the Civic Association's president, Bill hosted a public meeting with refreshments at a local restaurant meeting hall. The Civic Association agreed to host "coffee signing parties" to lease each lot for $2/lot, 1/8 royalty, and 1/24 ORR for the Civic Association. The Civic Association received $1, half of the $2/lot. The total cost was $2/lot, the meeting refreshments and a total royalty burden of one-sixth. The Civic Association has received $100,000 in only the early years of its production.

Bill is a member of the American Association of Petroleum Landmen, Lafayette Association of Petroleum Landmen, and served on both the board and the Speaker's Bureau for Independent Petroleum of America and the Louisiana Oil and Gas Association.

TOCE OIL CO., INC., AND
TOCE ENERGY, L.L.C.

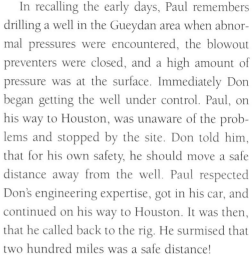

Above: Paul Toce and Don Chamblin, 1977.

Below: Left to right, Ricky Dupuis,
Earl Marquardt and Victor Toce, Port Barre
Field, St. Landry Parish, Louisiana.

Paul M. Toce knows the oil business. He worked for eight years in South Louisiana as a geologist with Shell Oil and two independent oil companies. In 1962 he ventured out and founded his own business, drilling and operating wells as Paul M. Toce. On June 25, 1976, he formed Toce Oil Co., Inc.

Over the years he hired highly skilled geologists Gary Reagan, Lew Nelson, Jack Traver, Andy Gambill and John Harris, who all contributed to Toce Oil's early success. In 1977, Tom Schiller was hired as executive vice president and was instrumental in the day-to-day operations of Toce until his retirement in 1998. In keeping with the practice of hiring the best, Don Chamblin worked as an engineer for Toce for more than twenty years, drilling, completing, and producing everything from a 6,000-foot development well to a 17,000-foot exploration well until his retirement.

In recalling the early days, Paul remembers drilling a well in the Gueydan area when abnormal pressures were encountered, the blowout preventers were closed, and a high amount of pressure was at the surface. Immediately Don began getting the well under control. Paul, on his way to Houston, was unaware of the problems and stopped by the site. Don told him, that for his own safety, he should move a safe distance away from the well. Paul respected Don's engineering expertise, got in his car, and continued on his way to Houston. It was then, that he called back to the rig. He surmised that two hundred miles was a safe distance!

Following in his father's footsteps Paul's son, Victor, worked as a geologist for Tenneco Oil Company in its Gulf of Mexico exploration and production departments from 1980-1988. When Chevron acquired Tenneco, Victor joined his father in the family business. After several "character-building years," Victor became more involved with prospect generation and managing the operations of Toce Oil, overseeing all phases of the business. His father's favorite expression is, "While Tenneco may have taught Victor how to run, it was Toce that taught him how to race!" In 1997, Toce Energy, L.L.C. was formed by Victor and Paul to expand, develop, and refine the large number of prospects generated through the years.

Early field discoveries and field extensions that launched the success of Toce Oil are: Crowley, Lottie, Duson, Lawson, East Rayne, West Rayne, Bayou Fer Blanc, West Gueydan, and Gueydan Dome Fields. Later successes for Toce Oil and Toce Energy include Gillis English Bayou, Bayou Des Glaises, Leeville, Bay St. Elaine, Mulvey, Cecelia, Port Barre, Beacons Gully, and Gueydan Canal Fields.

Today, Toce Energy is engaged in exploration, development, and acquisition of oil and gas properties. The company has purposefully limited its activities to its area of expertise, South Louisiana. Toce originates and markets almost all of the oil and gas prospects in which it has been involved. It sells fractional working interests in its oil and gas prospects to public corporations, independent energy firms, and individuals. Toce is responsible for the drilling, completion, and operation of most of the prospects generated.

It has operations onshore and in state waters along the Gulf Coast. It has served as operator for major oil companies such as Texaco, Exxon, and Shell, and large independents such as Hunt Oil, Bass Enterprises, Apache, and Oryx. Toce Oil, Toce Energy, Paul Toce, and/or Victor Toce have always retained an at-risk working interest in the prospects originated and operated by the companies. This gives full credence to the Toces' commitment to generate and sell only prospects that are economically viable for their investors.

Toce has drilled over 200 conventional wells in South Louisiana with an overall success ratio of 72 percent. With the incorporation of 3D seismic into the detailed subsurface mapping, the success ratio has steadily increased over the years to a current ratio of eighty-eight percent over the past five years.

"Toce Oil and Toce Energy are dedicated to its mission statement of providing maximum return on investment to its investors through oil and gas exploration, production, and acquisition opportunities in its primary focus area of South Louisiana," says Victor.

Currently, Toce Energy has internal geological, geophysical, land, production, and accounting departments. It is staffed to handle all phases of the exploration and production business. There are six fulltime employees, some who serve in similar capacities at both Toce companies. At Toce Energy, Victor is managing member and president. At Toce Oil,

Paul is founder and president and Victor is executive vice president. At both companies, Ricky Dupuis is vice president–land; Carole Credeur is accountant; Virginia "Ginny" Peck is land assistant; and Jennifer Robert is production analyst. Earl Marquardt supervises all of the drilling and production operations for both companies. Toce also employs hundreds of local consultants to cover all phases of the oil and gas business.

The Toce companies are located in the wholly owned Toce Building, 969 Coolidge Street, in the Oil Center of Lafayette, Louisiana and at www.toceenergy.com.

Above: Paul Toce with son, Victor, 2012.

Below: Production facilities, Leeville Field, LaFourche Parish, Louisiana.

HOUSTON ENERGY, L. P.

Colleagues and long-time friends Ronald E. (Ron) Neal and Frank W. (Billy) Harrison, III relinquished their positions with Amoco Production Company in search of the American Dream. As geologists, they wanted to use their past experiences in the oil industry to start their own business.

Previously, Billy served as division and operations geologist at Quintana Petroleum Corporation, and Ron was exploration manager for West Texas and the Texas Gulf at Davis Oil. Then, in 1988, they co-founded Houston Energy, L. P (HE).

In 1994 they initiated the company's Shelf Exploration program followed by the Deepwater Exploration program in 2004. Now, some twenty-five years after founding the venture, their privately held, independent oil and gas company is engaged in active exploration programs offshore of the Gulf of Mexico, South Louisiana, the Texas Gulf Coast, West Texas, and Southeastern New Mexico. The company is dedicated to economically finding and developing oil and gas reserves for its partners.

In recent years, Houston Energy has placed major exploration emphasis on the offshore Gulf of Mexico. This area offers an independent company such as theirs various options and opportunities due to the availability of large, affordable volumes of 3-D seismic data and existing infrastructure with known royalty scales. Houston Energy has over 80,000 square miles of licensed 3-D seismic data and a staff of 40 employees, 22 of whom are degreed geoscientists.

The company goal is to create and assemble quality drilling opportunities based on thorough integration and refinement of all available data. Complete integration of the geology and geophysics is necessary to help diminish risk. This is accomplished by acquiring 3-D seismic data reprocessing when necessary, and applying other geophysical techniques such as those mentioned above. Prior to actual drilling, the seismic data is interpreted within the proper structural and depositional geologic framework.

In keeping with its overall exploration philosophy, Houston Energy keeps a balance between the high-risk/high-return deep prospects with shallower lower-risk/lower-return prospects. Its diversified exploration program includes shallow salt dome plays, field infill and step-outs, and seismic "Bright Spot" prospects, as well as shelf and deepwater prospects using some of the industry's most advanced geophysical processing such as RTM and TTI.

Currently, Houston Energy holds license to over twenty-eight thousand square miles of 3-D data in the Onshore Gulf Coast.

In 1961, Frank Harrison, Jr., entered into a successful partnership with long-time friend, Jack Martin. Known as Martin & Harrison, the business lasted until 1978 when the two amicably dissolved the partnership and Harrison went into business for himself.

The oil and gas industry was at its peak, so Frank felt the timing was right to begin a venture on his own. At that time, he launched several companies, but the one that survived and continues to thrive is Optimistic Energy, LLC, an exploration company formed in 1981 that develops prospects, raises funding, and drills wells. He also owns Harrison & Associates, which does geological consulting for a number of independent and major operators in the oil and gas industry.

Believing that bigger is not necessarily better, Harrison is not interested in building a large-structured organization. "We're small, and that's the way I want to keep it," he says. "What we've done is operate with very low overhead and just a few key competent, solid individuals who are well experienced. We have employees like Holmes Smart, Gary Parrish, Bill Pyle, and David Sturlese who are level-headed and experienced in their areas of discipline. That's the key to our success."

With Optimistic Energy's experience in South Louisiana, Harrison believes the area is probably still the best province in the United States in which to find good, substantial reserves of oil and gas. He says the company has ventured into what appeared to be greener pastures; but, "When it comes down to it, South Louisiana offers the best opportunity per foot drilled to find the best reserves of oil and gas." For the past ten years, Optimistic Energy has invested in 3-D technology, resulting in outstanding discoveries of oil and gas reserves in South Louisiana.

Throughout Harrison's successful career as a practicing geologist, he has continually

been involved with professional societies and worthwhile organizations for which he has assumed various leadership positions. The culmination of these honors was his election to the presidency of the American Association of Petroleum Geologists in 1981-1982, and "LAGCOE Looey" in 2009.

Frank Harrison, Jr.

Harrison received an honorary Ph.D. degree from Louisiana State University in 2010, and has received the Legendary Oilman award from the Drake Foundation. He is an honorary member of the Lafayette Geological Society, American Association of Petroleum Geologists, the Society of Independent Earth Scientists, and the Gulf Coast Association of Petroleum Geologists.

Optimistic Energy, LLC is headquartered at 200 North Audubon Boulevard in Lafayette, Louisiana 70503 and has a satellite office at 1415 Louisiana Avenue, Suite 2400 in Houston, Texas 77002.

OPTIMISTIC ENERGY, LLC

HOGAN DRILLING AND HOGAN EXPLORATION

As with most business ventures, the beginnings of contract driller Hogan Drilling Company, Inc., and later, its oil and gas production affiliate Hogan Exploration, Inc., were humble. In 1976 in a cow pasture on the family farm in Caldwell Parish near Columbia Louisiana, known as Hogan Plantation, a wildcat driller, lured by the promise of a free lease in return for a commitment to drill, discovered natural gas in the shallow Wilcox formation. Declaring, "That was too easy," the plantation's owner who had encouraged the venture, former Louisiana Governor John J. McKeithen (1964-1972), decided to get into the oil business himself. That proved to be a very worthwhile idea.

Never short on self-confidence Governor McKeithen founded Hogan Drilling in 1977. But after a year or so of experiencing the fact that the oil business was not so easy after all, evidenced by a costly blowout and a collapsed derrick, he summoned his nephew Bob Meredith. A petroleum engineer and native of Columbia, Bob had lived with his uncle in the Governor's Mansion a few years earlier while attending LSU. He had worked for Chevron in New Orleans and was employed with a small independent firm in Tulsa, Oklahoma, when he got the call from his Uncle John. "Bob, I've got to get in this right, or get out of it." Elated at the opportunity to return home, Bob cautioned his uncle that going into the oil business required a lot of capital that neither of them had. His uncle's reply? "I have excellent credit." Bob moved home May 1, 1978.

The governor was fascinated with drilling operations. He loved the banging and clanging and the roar of engines and was interested in duplicating wildcatter Frank Spooner's shallow Wilcox success in his cow pasture. After selling his initial ill-fated venture, he set out to construct a brand new trailer-mounted drilling rig in his farm shop, designed to drill to about forty-five hundred feet, just right for Caldwell Parish and surrounds. He brought in noted Monroe Gas Field veteran Sonny Brodnax, a recognized shallow rig expert, as his rig-building guru. The governor was a popular political figure and a highly-respected country lawyer. Neither was an oil and gas business executive. That led to Uncle John calling nephew Bob. They would become great partners.

Bob was more interested in geology, downhole engineering, and discovering oil and gas rather than drilling services, and redirected the focus of the company to exploration, where he thought the money was bigger. But owning a highly efficient drilling rig was a huge advantage and the company would become its own best customer. He formed Hogan Exploration and hired geologist Richard Keller to generate drilling prospects. Concentrating on Caldwell, Winn, and LaSalle Parishes, success came quickly with the 1978 discovery of the Pistol Thicket Field, the first of many early wildcat gas discoveries. Bob gave major responsibilities to his brothers, Dick and Scott, and negotiated a 1982 exploration agreement covering over 250,000 acres that fueled a frenzied drilling program. Drilling three wells per week to three

thousand feet delighted Governor McKeithen who would escort the frequent rig moves in his farm jeep with a yellow flashing light on top. For years the rig rarely stacked, but company policy was to shut down on Christmas, Easter, and the first day of deer season. It really was an extraordinary operation in efficiency.

Employment grew rapidly and Hogan became a "big fish in a small pond." An article in the *Los Angeles Times* cited Hogan as being the fourth leading driller of wildcat wells in the nation in 1985 behind Shell, Exxon, and Mobil and ahead of Sun and Texaco. During the oil price collapse in 1986, gas producer Hogan moved to balance its production with more oil and bought a number of old fields in LaSalle Parish from the Hunt Companies that it aggressively redrilled. In 1988, Hogan built ten miles of eight inch pipeline across Caldwell Parish opening up the gas market. In 1989, *Petroleum Information* named Hogan as "top operator in the North Louisiana/South Arkansas region both in terms of total completions and new field wildcats." In the early 1990s, Hogan expanded, buying several producing properties in multiple deals, including two big fields from Exxon in Mississippi. But in the late 1990s, with oil prices plummeting, twenty year employee "Babe" Crooks, the ultimate "Hogan hand," stood on the steps of the State Capitol and delivered an address that drew attention to the plight of the oilfield and its employees.

Under Bob's direction, Hogan grew wildly with the drill bit, survived numerous oil price busts, and reached some national acclaim. For most of twenty years it prospered and employed many people in a rural parish with oil prices at about $18/bbl. It was the biggest and most eye-catching oil and gas enterprise that Caldwell Parish would likely ever see. But in 1999, with oil prices below $10/bbl and the "boom and bust" industry mired in

yet another historic bust, Hogan also went bust. Uncle John died that year, Hogan went out of business shortly after, and Bob moved on to other oilfield pursuits. All in all, they had a pretty good run.

KINSEY & KINSEY

Norman Victor Kinsey, Sr., was born in Anderson, Indiana, in 1894. While serving in France during World War I, he became friends with a fellow serviceman from Tulsa, Oklahoma, who offered him a job in the oil business when they completed their military obligation. Not knowing a thing about the fledgling industry, Kinsey threw his hat in the ring and never looked back.

After a brief orientation, Kinsey was dispatched to Homer, Louisiana, to sort out some lease problems during the 1920 oil boom. He thrived in the chaos and developed a knack for getting things done. Drilling for oil offered mystique and money and Norman was soon ready to strike out on his own.

Since he did not have any formal geological training, he decided to try his hand as a drilling contractor. In those days the wooden derricks were built on location so once he

Norman V. Kinsey, Jr., standing at one of his father's drilling rigs in South Louisiana, c. 1930s.

acquired a one-lung steam engine and a second-hand draw works, he was in business. He managed to get by with some success until the late 1920s when he sold his drilling rig and signed on as one of the first agents for the newly formed minerals division of Louisiana's Department of Conservation. In this new position, Kinsey was able to travel the state as he dealt with independents and majors and continued to build his knowledge of the industry. By the late 1930s he was ready to try his luck as a wildcatter. He began by brokering leases and assembling prospects in southern Louisiana but soon turned his attention to the East Texas oil and gas boom.

Norman's son, Norman V. Kinsey, Jr., was serving in the Army Air Corps in North Africa during WWII when he received a letter from his mother stating that his father and his partner, W. C. Feazel, had drilled a "nice" gas well in Carthage, Texas. It was to be a prophetic and life changing event. After the war, Norman, Jr., returned home and attained a law degree from LSU before joining his father in the oil business.

Kinsey, Sr., had a hunch that Panola County was sitting on a huge uplift containing hydrocarbons and the first Feazel and Kinsey wells came in producing over two hundred million cubic feet per day of gas from the Upper and Lower Pettit formations. The original lease block was only 7,000 acres and had been bought for a $1-per-acre bonus. With the limits of the field still undefined, it soon became obvious that they needed to continue expanding their block. All of this required capital, and the partners needed to sell off some of their working interest to raise funds. Norman, Sr., set up an office in the small town of Carthage, where he was one of the first persons to have a telephone. Years later, he fondly remembered his entire phone number was simply "22."

When later asked how a tiny independent was able to stay ahead of the majors, Norman, Sr., simply explained that during the war, company men only worked Monday until Thursday, as Friday was reserved for gathering items from the local farmers that were restricted by war rationing like butter, eggs, and milk. He worked six days a week and then bought royalty after church on Sunday.

With Kinsey buying the leases and Feazel providing the money, they were ultimately able to assemble a lease block exceeding thirty thousand acres on the crest of the massive structure. The pace of drilling increased with the infusion of fresh capital and the production grew to the point where the majors could no longer ignore the discovery. Over time, the productive area grew to encompass virtually all of Panola County, which covered over two hundred thousand acres. Since 1943 the field has produced over 11 trillion cubic feet of gas and 200 million barrels of oil from over 5,000 wells. Now that the Haynesville formation has proved itself commercial, the odds are the field will be producing well beyond its hundredth birthday.

Getting all this gas to market was the next major obstacle for the Kinsey duo. There was not enough transmission capacity and a solution was desperately needed. In 1946 the Federal government declared the "Big Inch" and "Little Inch" pipelines that had been previously used to transport oil from the East Texas oilfield to the refineries in the northeast during WWII as surplus and they were to be auctioned off to the highest bidder. Kinsey & Kinsey joined a group of venture capitalists to bid on the pipelines but were outbid by a

group that ultimately became Texas Eastern Pipeline. When the investor group received the news that their bid had come up short, they decided to build an entirely new pipeline from scratch and together, with four other businessmen, formed Trans-Continental Gas Pipeline (Transco). Their first order of business was to place the largest order for steel pipe in United States history and commence building a new pipeline stretching over two thousand miles from the Rio Grande to New York City. Kinsey, Sr., was a founding director of the new company and served until his death in 1960. Following him, Norman, Jr., served on the Transco board for the next thirty-one years.

Shortly after completing the Transco line, Kinsey & Kinsey helped to found other natural gas transmission lines such as Pacific-Northwest Pipeline Corp. (now El Paso), Texas-Illinois Natural Gas Pipe Line Corp. (Mid-Con), and Piedmont Natural Gas Company.

Left: Norman V. Kinsey, Sr.

Right: Norman V. Kinsey, Jr.

Norman, Jr., successfully guided and grew his family's business for fifty-one years until his death in 2011 at the age of ninety.

Today, the third generation of the Kinsey family continues the legacy in Carthage and remains active in the Louisiana oil and gas business.

SKLAR
EXPLORATION
COMPANY, LLC

Like his father and grandfather, Howard F. Sklar knows oil exploration. Howard is the chief executive officer (CEO), owner and operator of Sklarco, LLC, and its affiliated operating company, Sklar Exploration Company, LLC, independent exploration and production companies in Shreveport.

Sam Sklar, the patriarch, was fondly known in the oil industry as "Mr. Sam." He was born in Wolochisker, Russia, and immigrated with his parents to the United States (and Shreveport) in 1890. It was he who started the business, eventually passing it onto his son, Albert, Howard's father.

As a young man, Sam began buying, selling and trading scrap metal to make a living during post-depression years. His entrepreneurism in selling oilfield pipe to oil and gas operators, and participating in oil and gas prospecting as an owner, was the basis of the business today as three generations have come to know. His big break came in 1931 when he became one of the original shareholders of Delta Drilling Company.

For more than eighty years under the leadership of three generations, the Sklar family has prospered in the oil and gas industry. Sklar owns interests in oil and gas wells located throughout the United States. The company's exploration and production activities center on the hydrocarbon-rich Lower Gulf Coast basins, primarily in South Texas, and in the Interior Gulf Coast basins of East Texas, North Louisiana, South Arkansas, South Mississippi, and South Alabama.

Top, left: Albert Sklar.

Top, right: Founder Sam Sklar.

Below: The conference room.

According to Howard, "It is an honor and a privilege to follow in the footsteps of my father, Albert, and grandfather, Sam, and to lead this generation of the family's exploration and production activities. In many ways, our current activities are similar to those of the past. We are active in many of the same basins, and have maintained business relationships with some of the same employees, investors, and vendors. We have even experienced a proliferation of activities in the old fields, which have been core properties for the Sklar family for decades."

He adds that the oil and gas business is different today than it was years ago. "The maturity of onshore oil and gas exploration has prompted us to drill to deeper depths and explore in basins we previously ignored." He cites those as South Texas Gulf Coast and South Alabama. "Higher natural gas and crude oil prices have caused us to redefine our understanding of a 'good well' and seek hydrocarbons in rock, such as coal and shale. At one time, we considered them to be insufficiently porous and permeable to produce. The scarcity of experienced personnel and good equipment makes our relationship with employees and vendors more important than ever."

Sklar Exploration is an "independent" in the best sense of the word. It does not try to please shareholders and banks, and is free to make the best long-term decisions regarding

drilling and completing wells—regardless of the short-term consequences. At the same time, the company is innovative in adapting to new techniques.

Howard says he understands that failure is a part of any exploration business and all employees learn from experiences, regardless of their success or failure. "We are not always looking to sell assets, and believe instead, that good assets are hard to find. When discovered, they should be aggressively developed," he adds.

Sklar Exploration currently owns interests in nearly 1,000 wells; and operates approximately 50 of those. Its significant property interests over the years have been in Willow Springs, Elm Grove, Rodessa, Lisbon, Magnolia, Fairway, and Bryan College Station Fields.

When Howard joined the family business in the early 1990s, he participated in several significant oil and gas investments. Among them were Oletha Field, Large Royalty Packages, Harper, and Bowman Creek Fields.

Among the more recent exploration and exploitation activities are: Little Cedar Creek, West Arcadia, Laney Road, Riverton Coalseam Natural Gas, Kings Dome and South Kings Dome, Bovina, Steel Creek (Cotton Valley) and South Thornton (Rodessa), Cedar Grove, Latham, and Alabama Ferry West (Glen Rose) Fields.

Through the development of legacy assets and the acquisition of new assets, Sklar has participated as a royalty owner, an overriding royalty owner and/or a working interest owner in the development of numerous shale trends throughout the country, including the Bakken Shale in North Dakota, the Haynesville and Bossier Shales in Northwest Louisiana and East Texas, and more recently, the Eagle Ford Shale in South Texas. Sklar is committed to building and growing a highly educated and certified team of experts who are specialists in the oil and gas industry.

Howard's father and mother, Miriam, believed that because of their successes,

they should be supportive of the community and endeavors that helped them become successful. They established the Albert and Miriam Sklar Foundation, which contributes financially to eleemosynary organizations such as the B'Nai Zion congregation, Baylor School of Medicine, Boy Scouts, Junior Achievement, Massachusetts Institute of Technology, North Louisiana Jewish Federation, Sci-Port Discovery Center, Shreveport Opera, Shreveport Symphony, and United Way of America, among others.

Sklar Exploration Company, LLC's main office is in downtown Shreveport, with field offices in Arcadia, Louisiana, and Conecuh County, Alabama.

Above: Howard F. Sklar, the chief executive officer, owner and operator of Sklarco, LLC.

Below: Sklar executives.

HPS Oil & Gas Properties, Inc.

In January 1979, three friends in Lafayette sought to turn a negative situation into a positive venture. It was slow going at first with only Sabine Royalty, Dynamic Exploration, Conoco and Getty, as clients. Still, they became successful.

The industry deregulation had created a shortage of qualified field landmen. Seizing the opportunity, Pit Hesterly, Mike Patton and Gary Salmon formed HPS Oil and Gas Properties, Inc., a full-service land company. The name of the company—HPS—incorporated the initials of the partners' last names.

The first years of operations were dominated by demand for services; however, the next eight to ten year period was a constant struggle with extreme competitive forces and constantly changing work areas. As a result, HPS sought work out-of-state, concentrating primarily on lease acquisitions, due diligence and title research. During that time, the company performed land services for numerous small independents such as Mayne & Mertz, as well as major operators such as Mobil and Shell Oil, working wherever the project took the staff. This allowed HPS to vastly improve a wide range of service areas.

By the end of 1987, Salmon had bought out the other partners and was committed to his vision of growth for the company into the future. The 1990s ushered in new technology

for onshore exploration, as well as office management. The computer age provided the company with land management database systems to generate leases, drafts, purchase reports, title reports, and summary schedules that could be handled more efficiently, replacing long-used typewriters and carbon copies.

By the mid-1990s, HPS was involved in a highly successful exploration effort in Southwest Louisiana. This project began with a hundred square mile 3-dimensional (3-D) program where HPS handled all of the land-related duties, including permits, options, leases and damage negotiations, and subsequently expanding into approximately a thousand square miles, building the foundation leading to a successful drilling program lasting for more than fifteen years.

Today, the company is engaged in all phases of mineral acquisitions, curative, 3-D seismic projects, due diligence, and related tasks. Computerization has greatly improved the efficiency of HPS. Over the years, the company has worked with software engineers in order to develop industry-specific computer programs and land management database systems. Additionally, HPS has made great strides in their mapping abilities through their utilization of the ArcView Mapping System.

The 3-D seismic programs increased the need for additional field landmen; and, as HPS focused on that area, the company began to flourish. HPS handled the lease administration, including rental payments, damage settlements, Right-of-Way acquisition, abstracting and curative.

In addition HPS is involved in research of title/courthouse, production mineral history, negotiation, contract preparation and administration, abstracting for title examination, and mapping.

Key, loyal employees moved into management roles, allowing the company to properly manage large projects. HPS' core group of managers and coordinators have been with Salmon for over twenty years. The company stresses continuing education, and each project coordinator has passed the CPL or RPL test requirements provided by the AAPL. Office manager Ann Peltier, has 28

years of employment; Gerald Broussard, senior project coordinator, 27 years; Jay Bivins, senior project coordinator, 26 years; and Mark Hemphill, senior project coordinator, 20 years. Salmon says, "It was great to be able to elevate them into management roles and see the company thrive because of their efforts."

The company's mission is to provide the highest standard of petroleum land services. "HPS corporate philosophy," says Salmon, "is to provide a strong work ethic as its foundation; demanding open communication, trustworthiness, and technical ability from its employees. This allows us to excel in the petroleum land service field. Employees at HPS have a strong commitment to these values, and their efforts enable us to continually improve the organization and what we do."

Since the Millennium, HPS has benefited from advances in horizontal drilling, reservoir plays (shale), Large Trend Leasing efforts which has created a strong demand for additional manpower.

Based on past success, HPS Oil and Gas Properties hopes to expand its work to include the entire nation, and provide the highest standards of petroleum land service anywhere.

HPS Oil and Gas Properties is located in Lafayette, Louisiana and on the Internet at www.hps-og.com.

MERLIN OIL & GAS, INC.

Early in the nineteenth century, Louisiana was thought to be ripe for oil and gas production, and Lafayette emerged as a base for oil and gas.

Above: Standing, left to right, Melissa McGill, Shelly Maturin and Darlene Touchet, seated is Mark Miller.

Below: Washington Field 3-D extension.

Since then, the oil industry has faced many challenges with its share of ups and downs. By 1986 the dip in the oil and gas economy prompted Mark Miller to found Merlin Oil & Gas, Inc., for producing property acquisitions and leases. Merlin's plans were to purchase interest in oil and gas deals while providing a platform to create and exploit properties with three-dimensional (3-D) seismic shoots.

Founding members of Merlin Oil & Gas, along with Miller, were Lana Romero and Dirk Kellogg. Together, they began a successful pattern of nominating and bidding on Louisiana State Oil and Gas leases as a silent entity for several oil companies, including Anadarko Petroleum Corp., Diamond Shamrock Company, Apache Corporation, and Pennzoil Corporation.

In the late 1980s and early 1990s, bidding for these leases required a high degree of research and planning to counter competition. Moving forward, Merlin assembled a large wildcat prospect, twenty-one thousand feet (Tiger Pass) in Plaquemines Parish with Bruce Wallis; and won bids from the State of Louisiana, Plaquemines Parish Government and Plaquemines Parish School Board on a sixteenth section—all, on the same day!

In 1997, Merlin was engaged to work with Pennzoil and Geco-Prakla (now Schlumberger) for the required land permitting in 3-D shoots. As is sometimes typical for small companies, working for Schlumberger necessitated rapid growth. The newer technology and rapid growth almost sent Merlin into receivership. Fortunately, Merlin was in a position to avoid financial failure and moved forward. Merlin helped assemble twelve major seismic shoots in South Louisiana. The effort was under the guise of Edwin J. Kyle, a pivotal force in securing 3-D seismic permits from the U.S. Army Corps of Engineers. This endeavor has provided positive growth for Merlin. In fact, the experience and opportunity led to the eventual 3-D projects created by Merlin and some of its working interest partners.

The Meredith Project (Avondale 3-D) was formulated by James Crane, Sammy Pyle and Merlin Oil & Gas, along with the help of Johnny and DeMerris Abaldo.

In 2001, Merlin, along with William "Bill" Douglas, and the help of attorney Newman Trowbridge, Jr., successfully assembled and began the Washington Field seismic shoot on the Thistlewaite Wildlife Management Area. Merlin's continued friendship with the Thistlewaite family is treasured and has proven a viable business venture for both parties.

Subsequently, Merlin and partners such as NorthCoast Oil and Mack Energy successfully assembled the YellowDog 3-D shoot. This union of explorationists resulted in the GoodHope 3-D Survey completion in 2008, covering an area of 110 square miles in St. Charles Parish and including the Bonne Carrie Spillway, Waterford Nuclear plant, and multiple refineries that had never been shot before with 3-D seismic.

In 2007, Merlin began working with Bruce Smith and Denbury Resources, Inc., for the right-of-way (ROW) acquisition, planning and execution of the Green Pipeline from Napoleonville, Louisiana, to Hastings Field, Texas. The 320 mile carbon dioxide (CO_2) pipeline became the longest project of its type in North America. For five years, Merlin was involved with the project directed by Lee Sonnier and managed by David Collins.

Current members of Merlin's management group includes Angela Miller, Melissa McGill, Darlene Touchet, Staci Pitre, Shelly Maturin, and Ray Ayala.

Merlin's business is based on a mutual respect between the landowner and the company. "Our goal is to perform pipeline ROW acquisition or energy exploration as a guest within the great state of Louisiana and its communities. We intend to leave the smallest footprint possible in the course of our exploration activities; and pledge to operate in an environmentally responsible manner. Our future requires that we are welcome in our energy exploits under the aegis of state government in any community, anywhere in the country," says Miller, president.

He adds that Merlin has experienced landmen working with us in all our offices. We provide mapping and map driven databases for clients; and, utilize the land management services data and mapping system developed by Bluetick Software.

Miller acquired his CPL in 1989; and, obtained his Environmental Site Assessor's (ESA) certification in 1991. He co-authored the field manual for the ESA course for the American Association of Petroleum Landmen (AAPL); and co-wrote the *Louisiana Courthouse Directory*. He has served as president of the Lafayette Association of Petroleum Landmen (LAPL) and has served on various committees with the American Association of Professional Landmen. In addition, he currently serves on the College of Business Dean's Advisory Council at the University of Louisiana—Lafayette. He has worked with the Professional Land Resource Management Program (PLRM) since its inception in 1983. Miller has served on the board of directors of I.P.A.A. from 2008 to 2012 and is currently serving as a ULL Foundation Board Member.

Above: Left to right, Lewis Bernard, Lawrence Thistlewaite, Ric Thistlewaite, Patrick Thistlewaite, Bill Douglas, Ann Thistlewaite, Mark Miller, and Bill Guidry.

Below: Left to right, Angie and Mark Miller, Congresswoman Virginia Foxx, Cole, McKenna, and Meredith Miller, Washington, D.C.

MIDSTATES PETROLEUM COMPANY, LLC

Steve McDaniel introduced his father, Robert "Bob" McDaniel to Ray "Butch" Royer, thinking they had the potential of becoming successful business partners. Steve was also convinced that the McDaniel and Royer families, residents of central and south Louisiana, were ideally positioned to initiate modern re-development of a latent geologic trend in their home state. He was right on both points.

They formed Midstates Petroleum in 1993 as a closely held, family-controlled business venture, with its first corporate office located in the loft of Butch's barn. They focused on reactivating oil and gas activity in dormant fields, near the towns of Pine Prairie and DeQuincy, the life-long homes of the founders. For the twenty years the company has been in existence, its mission and business model have remained the same. Midstates focuses on finding new reserves using new technologies in old and 'overlooked' areas.

Butch's early experience was in oil drilling and drilling risk management, and during a subsequent industry downturn, he established an oilfield construction and environmental remediation business near DeQuincy. Bob began his career in the Pine Prairie oilfield during the "boom" days of the 1940s and has remained actively involved in that oilfield since that time. He raised three sons, all petroleum engineers degreed from Louisiana universities, all of whom "volunteered" their efforts to the company in the early years of Midstates.

Steve conceived the business plan of reactivating this historic oil trend in central Louisiana where the McDaniels and the Royers lived. The idea had merit because oil prices were low, activity and investment by other companies in these areas was virtually nonexistent, and Midstates' formation came at a time when community unemployment was relatively high. The company benefitted from little competition for prospects, and local residents benefitted from access to new jobs as well as improved land and mineral value. With the long term growth and benefit of the company in mind, the founders drew no salaries or other distributions for fifteen years; all cash flow generated by Midstates was reinvested in the company's operations.

The mission statement, according to Steve, "Is to apply commercially viable modern theories and techniques to explore for and produce new oil and gas reserves in a safe and environmentally responsible manner for the purpose of providing economic benefit, improving the lives of employees, partners, stakeholders, and communities in which it operates, while contributing to the nation's domestic energy needs."

Midstates' activity in Pine Prairie field, a cornerstone field for the company and fourth generation home of the McDaniel family, typifies Midstates' strategy of discovering new reserves previously bypassed or overlooked by others. Midstates successfully sought geologic targets and concepts that had not been recognized throughout the field's hundred-year history. By understanding and appreciating history and challenging conventional wisdom, Midstates continues to identify and produce resources that have long remained unrecognized by previous operators.

In the DeQuincy area, Midstates typically pursues deeper, more challenging targets. "We have applied new technologies to our exploration, drilling, completions, and surface facility installation efforts. In most cases, we have been encouraged at the invitation of landowners to explore for oil and gas on their property. Many of our successes can be traced to local knowledge of historical activities that had ceased during periods of contraction in the industry," adds John Crum, the company's current chief executive officer.

The company's operations began in 1993 with the founders' initial investment of $300,000 and activity directed near DeQuincy. In 1999, when oil prices fell to approximately $10 per barrel, Midstates purchased its initial interest in Pine Prairie Field and immediately began reducing costs to restore economic viability to the field.

In 2004, Steve walked away from a successful career in investment banking to devote his full-time efforts to building Midstates. He then began to recruit a core group of employee/partners with skills in geology, engineering, land, finance, and accounting. Two years later, the company established its first credit facility with Wells Fargo Bank. In 2008, Midstates partnered with First Reserve Corporation to access growth capital and build a business of greater scale.

In 2012, Midstates went public and listed its shares on the New York Stock Exchange and expanded its business into Central Oklahoma and Kansas. In 2013, Midstates further expanded its business into Western Oklahoma and the Texas Panhandle. Latest production records show Midstates' production of approximately twenty-five thousand barrels of oil equivalent per day.

The founders have always believed in aligning the interests of employees and owners of Midstates in order for the company and the individual to prosper. Because of this forward thinking, all employees were invited to purchase ownership in the company. All employees also become partners by virtue of their stock ownership in Midstates.

In addition to enriching the lives of direct stockholders, Midstates has invested approximately $1 billion to date, in Louisiana alone, creating jobs and supporting local businesses. The economic benefit resulting from Midstates' activities has been responsible for building four local churches of different denominations, and one church affiliated family center. The founders believe strongly in supporting community efforts as the community has supported them.

Midstates Petroleum Company is headquartered in Houston with offices in Tulsa, Pine Prairie and DeQuincy, Louisiana.

OWEN DRILLING CO.

Above: James Owen poses in front of a "Christmas Tree" atop a 19,500-foot gas well drilled by his company, 1974.

Below: Corita and James Owen.

James Porter Owen was a risk-taker and resourceful entrepreneur in the oil industry in the days when others lacked the initiative or funds to become successful. As economists would say today, "Pappy" Owen never saw a "lost opportunity." He had learned enough about the oilfields to know that was where he wanted to be.

Owen Drilling was founded prior to today's business models where there are formal business plans. Owen was the entrepreneur venturer/wildcatter who analyzed the area's geology and previous drilling successes and failures and, then, with savvy guts and intuition, made drilling decisions.

Born March 28, 1898, in Waco, Texas, he was the second youngest of five children. He learned at an early age that life could be hard. At age two, he lost his mother, and three years later, his father. As families did, then, an aunt and uncle (brother and sister), took the orphaned children to rear.

After finishing public school, he became a bricklayer, earning his tuition to Southern Methodist University (SMU), among the first class the year the college was founded.

In 1917, he enlisted in the Army Signal Corps and became a pilot with only four hours and forty-three minutes of instruction, soloing in the famous Curtis "Flying Jenny." After crash-landing two airplanes in one day, he successfully soloed on the third attempt. His instructor was quoted as asking, "Did you realize that you have torn up two airplanes and they cost the government $4,000 each?"

He held a lot of different jobs upon discharge. He sold cotton seed in west Texas, traded mules in Louisiana, was a claims adjuster, owned an automotive company, owned and operated a bus line that transported soldiers between camps, and worked in the oilfields of Mexico and west Texas. Perhaps it was that "try-and-try again" attitude that prompted him to pursue a career in the oilfields.

He married Corita Crist, another SMU graduate February 17, 1922. Son James, Jr., was born December 3, 1922, and later became manager of his father's company. James, Jr., died in 1992. A daughter, Corita Jean Owen was born February 24, 1936. She married James R. Smith who became comptroller in 1962. Corita says of her father, "With the gambling gene, he was a natural risk taker. With risk came not only gains, but also losses. These, too, were part of his career."

In 1945, along with three other partners, he bought a refinery renaming it Owen Refining Co. He sold it a year and a half later when it was no longer profitable.

Later, he formed Owen and Lamb Drilling Co. with Ed Lamb and son, W. C. Lamb, a tool-pusher. The company was a loose organization and the partners understood that they could take deals and drill on their own.

When Owen's independent venture in the Maxie Field in Acadia Parish, Louisiana, in 1948 was successful, he bought out his partners and founded Owen Drilling Company. New partners H. L. Hunt and the Hassie Hunt Trust wanted to plug the well; but Owen persisted, and struck oil at 10,576 feet. After that hit, he was quite successful from 1948-1962.

In 1966, Owen drilled the Leo Fontenot, the deepest well along the Gulf Coast and in Louisiana. The record well, drilled to a depth of 23,157 feet was located on the outskirts of Kaplan, Louisiana. That record held for many years. Owen Drilling ceased operations in 1972 when he declared bankruptcy; however, he made a comeback as an independent operator.

Considered a "Wildcatter," Owen became actively involved in the oil industry during WWII. He was a founding member of the All American Wildcatters' Association, an organization of one hundred members. A definition of members was, "One who contributes to and causes wildcat wells to be drilled. He may be one who raises risk capital, one who works up drilling prospects, a major oil company representative who encourages wildcatting by independents by providing incentives and other information, or one who, in lieu of being a wildcatter, has made significant contribution to the wildcatting profession." The organization creed was: "My word is my bond." He was a founding member in 1968.

Reminiscing about his experience in the oil industry for a memoir published in 1989, he said, "The fourteen year period from 1948-62, when I made my big sale to General American were years of rapid growth. The industry and I were growing at the same time; and I was taking advantage of every opportunity I could. It was easier to wheel-and-deal then, than it is now with the legal entanglements that accompany any modern-day ventures." As an independent contractor, he found it necessary to sell his production occasionally to finance other ventures. Still drilling in his eighties, he remarked, "I can't understand why people aren't interested in going in with me on some of these deals."

In 1987, at age eighty-nine, Owen was honored by his fellow All American Wildcatters with the BFU—Big Foul Up—Award, not for his failures in the oil business (which included two bankruptcies), but for his decision to stop drilling and write a book. Owen passed away in 1991 at ninety-three.

Above: Auson Well, 1979.

CHET MORRISON CONTRACTORS, LLC

Above: Flagship dive support vessel Joanne Morrison.

Below: The 7,700 LT floating drydock in Alvarado, Mexico, bears Morrison's father's name.

A third generation member to the family lumber and hardware business, Chet Morrison understood the dedication and commitment a business required. With a 1982 mechanical engineering degree from Louisiana State University, Chester F. Morrison, Jr., began his entrepreneurship and still remains energized by the challenges and fulfillment it brings.

Creating the original Chet Morrison General Contractors, Inc. as a residential construction company in 1983, it was not long until Morrison's ambition propelled him into industrial and oilfield-related work, landing one of his first projects for Chevron pouring concrete foundations near Port Fourchon. Morrison fostered the growth of the multiservice and multi-country entity through internal development, selected acquisitions and project diversification, composing a creative, sure-footed plan and a hardworking, dedicated staff. Today, as a part of Morrison Energy Group, which includes Chet Morrison Contractors, Trinidad Offshore Fabricators and Cochon Properties, LLC, the Houma-headquartered company has grown to include offices in Louisiana, Texas, Mexico, and the Caribbean island of Trinidad and Tobago.

Chet Morrison Contractors (CMC) is known for its solution-based contributions to the oil and gas industry performing services ranging from marine and land-based construction to the plugging and abandonment of oil and gas properties. With more than six hundred employees, the company provides services to a broad base of customers, including major and independent oil and natural gas producers and pipeline transmission companies.

While the 1980s experienced declining oil prices eventually leading to an oilfield depression, the 1990s brought a more attractive stage for oilfield growth. This was the time when Inland Marine Operations were launched and Offshore Operation shortly followed. In 1997, CMC opened a Harvey fabrication facility on the Harvey Canal Waterway. Business growth was steady but the cyclical ups and downs of the business pushed for more security with additional expertise and value-added services.

Recovery from the oil price dip of 1998 slowed the market in 1999 and 2000 but demand for offshore pipelines resumed a long-term growth trend[1]. This gave incentive to the increasingly strengthened leadership to take its next step, emerging into the pipeline construction market with two retrofitted pipelay barges. The trend continued and the Pipeline Construction business unit grew to become CMC's Subsea Operations with the addition of experienced diving management and diving personnel to operate a custom-fitted Diving Support Vessel (DSV).

In 2001 the employment and partnership with an international businessman presented additional diversification with the opening of a Veracruz office and purchase of a facility in Alvarado, Mexico. With strategic access to the Gulf of Mexico (GOM), the facility and personnel were poised for the construction and installation of its own floating drydock. Completing the project incident free, with a native workforce, the construction of the drydock became a testament to the company's ability to develop a large-scale project from conception to completion.

While Mexico operations were being groomed for growth, a 2004 partnership in LaBrea, Trinidad, was formed, birthing Trinidad Offshore Fabricators (TOFCO). Trinidad & Tobago (TT) had a strong market for fabrication, but the local work force had little training in this arena. With its U.S. expertise, CMC staffed TOFCO with expats on a one-to-one ratio to mentor the locals in each skill classification. This appeased the TT Energy Ministry looking for domestic growth and proved to be a successful business plan, as TOFCO today is self-reliant on its local labor force. From humble beginnings, it pressed time for safe scheduled completion of major decks, jackets and components for BHP, bpTT, BG, and EOG.

Domestically, strong leadership was in place, allowing for the opportunity to expand into the diving market with the purchase of three additional DSV's, one of which was retrofitted into one of the largest four-point DSVs in the GOM. This flagship vessel, which fittingly bears Morrison's mother's name, *Joanne*, mobilized to its first project location immediately following its christening ceremony in 2008.

That same year, CMC began offering plug and abandonment services, greatly enhancing the company's ability to service an energy production field from sunrise to sunset. CMC's well services division is currently one of the largest providers of rigless P&A in the GOM and has successfully plugged wells for more than fifty operators, including many of the largest GOM operators.

Following the expansion into five energy industry sectors and opening eight locations, including three international facilities, Morrison Energy Group, LLC was formed as a parent company in 2010. It continues to serve as a catalyst for future endeavors on the horizon.

At this time the shale plays were flourishing. Utilizing the existing skill sets of CMC's team and long-standing relationships with customers in the offshore sector who were refocusing efforts onshore, CMC progressed into facility installation and maintenance operations. With success at performing heavy civil construction projects and pipeline maintenance projects onshore, CMC plans to place much emphasis on developing this area of its business.

The wide breadth of Chet Morrison Contractors' resources and capabilities form a network of innovation that continues to drive the company's success. Morrison continues to focus on this formula and relies heavily on the dedication of his numerous employees and loyal customers.

[1]*World Offshore Pipelines & Umbilicals Report.*

Above: CMC pipelay barge working in the shallow waters of the Gulf of Mexico.

Below: Diver installs tensioners on an x-brace to remediate damage at VR376.

STOKES & SPIEHLER USA, INC.

Above: Left to right, founders George Stokes and J. R. (Jess) Spiehler.

STOKES
S&S
1973   2013
SPIEHLER
40th Anniversary

Just out of college in the 1960s, George Stokes and J. R. (Jess) Spiehler met, gaining respect for the other's expertise in the oil industry. That relationship would later prompt them to jointly enter into several business ventures. Known as Stokes & Spiehler, the business is now in its fortieth year.

George started George W. Stokes, Inc., in 1973 and, it was not long before Jess joined him as a partner. While the two shared office space, they worked almost exclusively in the field. Realizing they needed someone to oversee the day-to-day operations in the office while they were on site, they hired Jacqueline Broussard, who is still with the company today.

Through the years, the company expanded operations into most all major energy producing areas of the world; and experienced several name changes as well as company additions. Currently, the companies under the Stokes & Spiehler umbrella are Stokes & Spiehler, Inc., (name changed from George W. Stokes, September 1, 1974); Stokes & Spiehler International, Inc., July 1980; Stokes & Spiehler Offshore, Inc., April 1995; Stokes & Spiehler USA, Inc., January 1998; Drilling Partners, LLC, June 2002; Stokes & Spiehler Properties, Inc., March 2005; Stokes & Spiehler Onshore, Inc., January 2006; and Stokes & Spiehler Regulatory Services, L.L.C., December 2011.

International, Offshore, USA and Onshore are various companies performing operational and administrative services with some general ties to each company's name, i.e. International, Inc., is for international operations, Offshore, Inc., is for offshore operations and Onshore, Inc., is for onshore operations. Drilling Partners, LLC is a turnkey drilling

company primarily servicing the Inland Water and Shelf market. Properties, Inc., is for the company's non-operated oil and gas working interest. Regulatory Services, L.L.C., the newest company, purchased a company named Regulatory Services, Inc., (formed by J. V. Delcambre in 1996), merging it with some in-house personnel. The combined company provides government permitting and regulatory compliance services.

"Stokes & Spiehler's Health, Safety & Environmental programs are second-to-none in the consulting industry," says Bruce Jordan, president. "These programs are audited and approved by virtually all operators in the Exploration & Production (E&P) industry, and we continue to receive accolades for safety operations and effective regulatory compliance."

Built on hard work and longevity, the rest, they say is "history." Today, Stokes & Spiehler provides a wide range of engineering and operational consulting primarily in Louisiana, Texas, Mississippi, Oklahoma, Alabama, and the entire Gulf Coast offshore as well as the Marcellus and Bakken shale developments and international outposts. Since 1973 the firm has provided these services on a continuing basis to individuals, and independent and major oil companies.

Stokes & Spiehler engineers supervise the drilling of an average of 200 wells annually. Wells are drilled as turnkey, daywork, or managed projects. The Stokes & Spiehler team includes more than 250 highly experienced contract personnel with expertise in drilling, completion, workover, concentric, and production operations. This industry-trained group is augmented and supported by a staff of degreed engineers whose efforts are directed by management professionals with backgrounds with one or more major oil and gas companies. Their combined expertise provides insight into a client's needs with multifaceted operations.

Stokes & Spiehler's history of working with large and small operators in many of the major oil and gas producing areas, both domestic and international, allows them to tailor a project to the client and locale. The company has grown exponentially since its founding and now has approximately forty employees in addition to the 250 contract field personnel.

The company knows the value of a detailed plan, realizing that it is critical to understand the big picture. Extensive research, evaluation of all offset well data, and close attention to detail are all critical to the development of a well plan that provides the flexibility necessary to be updated as conditions warrant.

With professional attention to day-to-day business, Stokes & Spiehler continues to thrive. It offers general consulting services pertaining to drilling, production and completion. It is heavily involved in permitting, location preparation, AFE and well programs, supervised drilling, completion, workover, construction and production operations, procurement of materials and services, including turnkey, project management, or daywork drilling contracts.

Key personnel, in addition to the two founders during the early days, were Lynette Clarke, Gene Carpenter, Freddie Ledet, Steve Boudreaux, Bill Flores, Jr., and Greg Lewis. Employee/shareholders who continue to play key roles are Bruce Jordan, Jacqueline Broussard, John Long, Holli Cramm, Keith Stokes, Tony Shell, David Gautreaux, Mark Stringer, Don Long, Tracy Judice, Sid Cox, Gene Guidry, Russ Bellard, Blair Leblanc, Chris Allen, Donnie Busscher, Patrick Finney, Larry Fowler, Mike Nance, Reed Lormand, and Allen Gros.

The mission is to provide superior quality field personnel and office engineering personnel to the oil and gas drilling, production and exploitation operation efforts of numerous exploration and production companies domestically and internationally.

The business plan is to strive for excellence, while remaining well founded in the core business of well site consulting and office engineering. Client satisfaction is the company's ultimate goal.

Stokes & Spiehler has offices at 110 Rue Jean Lafitte in Lafayette, Louisiana, and 9720 Cypresswood Drive in Houston, Texas.

TMR Exploration, Inc.

When John S. Turner, Jr., and his two original TMR partners began their search for liquid gold in the Louisiana oilfields in the 1980s, the last place they thought they would find oil was in a shallow oilfield underneath an eight-hundred-acre lake. Yet, they had a "hunch" they had to pursue.

The three men founded TMR Exploration, Inc., in 1984. Two years later, in 1986, they struck oil under the eight-foot deep lake located near Springhill, Louisiana. While they had successfully drilled several Cotton Valley producers in other areas earlier, "We hit a home run on that one," says Raymond (Ray) Lasseigne who, with Turner bought out the other men in 1989-90. Lasseigne is president and CEO of the company, today, while Turner is chairman of the board.

As an independent oil and gas producer and operator, TMR Exploration first had to drill the initial well, constructing a dirt ramp about a quarter-mile into the eight-foot lake. This well actually proved to be the field discovery. Immediately, a confirmation well was drilled by again ramping out into the lake. The lake had served as the fresh water source for a paper mill owned by International Paper Company.

TMR's management team successfully negotiated rights to drain the lake; and, approximately ninety wells were eventually drilled with many located directly in the drained lake bed.

During the mid-to-late 1980s, during the oil industry downturn, the Louisiana legislature created a tax incentive through severance tax exemptions to encourage drilling activity. TMR turned to the Severance Tax Exemption Program (STEP) to assist with funding for its drilling efforts during the time period provided by lawmakers to develop the majority of that field. "It was our 'bread-and-butter' for a number of years," adds Lasseigne, "with peak production over two thousand barrels of oil per day (BOPD)."

As wells eventually became stripper, the company turned its attention to reducing operating expenses. Electricity was a big part of the company's lifting cost, so that problem was addressed first. While studying the feasibility of generating electricity with synchronous units, an article about induction electric generators was written by a consultant in Tulsa, and published in *World Oil*. During a discussion with the article's author, ironically, it was discovered that the induction electric generator was manufactured within a mile of the TMR office. TMR eventually purchased and installed five induction generators, which provided 100 percent of the electricity needs of the field, thereby reducing its electricity cost by about 70 percent. Produced casinghead gas was used as fuel for the generators.

TMR next turned its attention to high downhole costs. Tubing and rod wear was becoming increasingly expensive. A device was developed that allowed a pumping unit speed to be slowed down to as low as one stroke per minute. With this device, TMR engineers could run the pumping unit at the speed necessary to match reservoir inflow performance. Average well pulling frequency was improved from twelve months to forty months. This resulted again in high operating efficiencies and greater cost reductions.

TMR has drilled and produced vertical and horizontal oil and gas wells ranging in depths from 3,200 feet to 13,000 feet, and established production in four states.

Among the zones in which TMR has established production in Louisiana are the Tokio, Buckrange, Rodessa, Pettet, Hosston, Cotton Valley D, Bodcaw, Taylor, Justiss, McFerrin, and the Smackover, to name a few. In South Arkansas, TMR has established production in the Glen Rose, Paluxy, Rodessa Hill, Rodessa Kilpatrick and Smackover zones. In Mississippi, the company has drilled and produced wells in the Paluxy, Tuscaloosa, Rodessa, Hosston, and Cotton Valley zones. In Texas, TMR has produced from the Pettet, Cotton Valley, and the Jurassic.

With the expertise of its executive team, TMR has been a successful player in the acquisition arena with the purchase of individual wells, fields, and a significant oil and gas-producing company. Acquisitions range in value from $1 million to $100 million.

TMR's most recent exploration success came in 2006 with the discovery of the oil-bearing Cockfield zone on a twenty-sixthousand-acre block in south Louisiana. Lasseigne says the company had a significant learning curve because it was one of the first companies to successfully apply horizontal drilling and hydraulic fracturing stimulation in south Louisiana. The horizontal drilling technology resulted in considerable production improvement compared to vertical wells. The best well flowed over 700 BOPD, with a flowing tubing pressure in excess of 2,000 psi.

With approximately 22 employees and 200 wells in Louisiana, Texas, Arkansas, and Mississippi, the company focuses heavily on growing the company through exploration, exploitation, acquisitions, secondary recovery, and enhanced oil recovery.

Turner owns eighty percent of TMR, while Lasseigne owns twenty percent. Turner's experience can be traced to 1962 when he owned or worked for other oil companies and oversaw crude oil purchasing, transportation and pipeline construction. He was also the founder of a successful lignite exploration company, which discovered Dolet Hills, the largest lignite deposit in Louisiana. He has other holdings in real estate, warehouses, apartments, shopping centers, timber, entertainment, healthcare, farming, and horses.

Lasseigne is a petroleum engineer with over forty years of varied oilfield experience. He has experience in reservoir, drilling, and production engineering, prospect generation, acquisitions, and management. He has served the oil and gas industry through his activities in numerous industry organizations, including serving as chairman of the Louisiana Oil and Gas Association for three years. He currently is serving a six-year term on the LSU Board of Supervisors.

Headquarters for TMR Exploration, Inc. are located in Bossier City, Louisiana.

CENTRAL CRUDE, INC. & LOUISIANA TANK, INC.

It has often said, "When one door closes, another opens." That is exactly what happened for George Jordan, owner of a drilling company in Kilgore, Texas. When oil prices collapsed in the early 1970s, he moved his family to Lake Charles, Louisiana. It was there, that his mantra of "Oil wells are like people, it's hard to hold a good one back," prompted him to establish Central Crude Oil in 1974. A true visionary, his initial goal was to transport fuel oil to paper mills in Central Louisiana.

He believed that exploration and production (E&P) area companies operating wells needed a way to dispose of the saltwater by-product. That is when he founded Louisiana Tank, Inc. (LA Tank) in 1976; and, on the advice of his son Steve, opened the first saltwater waste disposal (SWD) that remains in operation today.

Steve became chief executive officer in 1981 upon the death of his father, representing the second generation in the family-owned business. At that point, he encouraged the company to build a barge terminal for a third-party company. "The turning point in the organization's focus came during 1980-81, when paper mills switched their fuel sources to natural gas, and eventually ceased operation. That, obviously, eliminated Central Crude's customer base. That resulted in the third-party company entering Chapter 11, leaving a barge terminal without a tenant, and multiple trucks with nothing to haul. We knew we had to look for alternatives," he says.

Central Crude is best defined as a midstream crude transportation and marketing company that purchases crude oil at the lease and uses its trucks to transport the oil back to its 150,000 barrels of oil (Bbl) barge terminal. The oil is sold and barged out to downstream refiners. The company also owns and operates crude oil pipelines throughout South Louisiana.

Steve developed what eventually became Central Crude's core business. Utilizing company assets, he realized a logical "fit" would be to purchase, transport, and provide storage for crude oil through the existing terminal, and barge the crude to the end user. "When I first took over the company at twenty-seven, people said we wouldn't last six months with me at the helm," adds Steve. "Now, thirty years later, I guess I proved them wrong!"

Under Steve's leadership, the two companies have expanded with Central Crude acquiring additional crude oil pipelines and gathering systems in South Louisiana, as well as securing other terminals in Southeast Louisiana. The company has satellite offices in Houston to handle marketing functions.

By integrating resources and expertise, Central Crude today has become quite versatile, providing a full-range of services in all aspects of moving crude from the wellhead and later selling to major refiners.

Central Crude continues to grow in the natural gas marketing, supply, field services, gas transportation and storage business. It has realized success by focusing on consistent, quality service to the producer while continually pursing end-user markets through transportation, supply flexibility and diversification. While many traditional natural gas market participants have vacated the business development segment of the natural gas marketplace, Central Crude's business development skills have led to significant growth in building gas-gathering systems and processing facilities that better meet customers' current needs as the industry changes.

LA Tank owns and operates a state-of-the-art saltwater disposal system in Lake Charles. Utilizing two injection wells, the system can safely and economically dispose of up to twelve thousand barrels of saltwater per day. In addition, its drivers extract fluids from pits, tanks and other storage facilities, transport brine and other non-hazardous drilling fluids to and from well locations, transport produced saltwater to disposal wells, and haul equipment to and from the well site accurately, safely, and efficiently. The company is fast-growing and service-oriented, promoting it to the "service company of choice" since 1976. It is committed to providing exceptional work with quality personal service that customers have come to know and trust. These ideals and hard work have enabled LA Tank to be recognized as the region's largest and most reputable oilfield service company specializing in non-hazardous

saltwater disposal. It continues to grow while opening a field office in Mire, Louisiana, and another commercial SWD facility in the permitting stage. Currently, the companies serve everyone from small independent producers to major oil and gas companies.

Central Crude and LA Tank strive to be the safest, most dependable and hassle-free oilfield service companies in the industry. "Our goals have never been to be the biggest; but, to provide key services to customers and treat each like our own," says the CEO. He adds, "With the same energy that drives our customer-focused activities, we place emphasis on sustaining the environment and safety of the communities in which we operate. We comply with all parish, state, and federal waste disposal requirements. That's important to us." The third generation of Jordans is now involved with the businesses, and family members/owners are looking forward to serving Louisiana's energy producers' needs for the years to come.

Combined, the companies employ about 150 individuals throughout Louisiana and Texas. For additional information on Central Crude, visit www.centralcrude.com.

Above: Chief Executive Officer, Steve Jordan.

LONG PETROLEUM, LLC

Long Petroleum, LLC, a third generation oil and gas exploration company located in Shreveport, Louisiana, was formed July 1, 1998, following the roll-up of certain assets contributed by Denman M. (Denny) Long, the Long family, and other working interest partners.

Denny, a Wyoming native (b. 1924) and graduate of the U.S. Military Academy, arrived in North Louisiana in 1952 as an Air Force captain stationed at Barksdale Air Force Base. The following year, he retired from the Air Force, married his wife of fifty-nine years, Mary O'Brien, and started his career in the oil and gas business. Like many family-owned oil and gas companies in North Louisiana, Long Petroleum really started with the discovery of the legendary East Texas Oilfield during the Great Depression, and represents the lasting legacy of five forward-thinking brothers unafraid to take a risk.

The brothers—Charles, Paul, Ray, Bill, and Harold O'Brien—had moved to Shreveport from Illinois in the late 1920s knowing the area's nascent oil and gas industry offered unlimited opportunity at a time when opportunities were scarce. In 1931, when the enormity of the East Texas Field was still not known, they pooled resources to acquire leases in Gregg County, Texas, betting everything on the play's potential.

brothers, Jones signed on for a fifty percent interest in the Gregg County leases. The new partners formed Jones-O'Brien, Incorporated, with the O'Brien brothers providing the management and Jones providing the operating capital.

Over the next half-century, Jones-O'Brien enjoyed tremendous success. In addition to the long-term development of the lucrative East Texas properties, Jones-O'Brien discovered and developed Tinsley Field, Bethany Longstreet and West Tyler, among others. The company's impressive run culminated in 1979 with the discovery of the extensive South Lake Arthur Field—one of the largest onshore natural gas fields in the United States.

Denny was a key member of the Jones-O'Brien team for many years before going out on his own, and it was there he learned many of the skills that have served him well. But Denny's great love and keen talent for his chosen profession were obvious to him even in his first job as a roughneck in 1953. Within twelve months, he was working for Arkansas Fuel as a landman scouting South Louisiana. Here, he was able to use his other real talent…dealing with people.

Right: Mary and Denny Long.

Below: Denny Long on location.

Broke, but determined to drill, they turned to Oklahoma businessman B. B. Jones, an investor in Ray's previous business venture, the Rotary Lift Company. Believing in the

In 1960, Denny partnered with two fellow oilmen in an ambitious drilling program—an adventure that came to a timely end after thirty-five dry holes. Wiser for the experience, Denny utilized his military engineering training to establish himself as an expert in designing and installing field compressors for natural gas. It was in this capacity that he was hired by Jones-O'Brien in 1964.

Denny spent the next several years overseeing a full-range of engineering projects, ultimately becoming exploration manager and joining the board of directors. In all, Denny worked almost two decades as a dedicated member of the Jones-O'Brien team.

In 1982, due to the inherent complications in ownership and management of a company in its second and third generation, the Jones-O'Brien stockholders elected to liquidate the company and distribute the assets to the owners. The liquidation created a diverse group of working interest owners, so a new entity, JO'B Operating Company, was created to manage ongoing operations.

Denny accepted new challenges, knowing the timing was ominous. The early 1980s saw the worldwide collapse of oil and gas prices, which devastated the industry, particularly independents. However, the Jones-O'Brien liquidation event in 1982 provided the reason and resources for formation that year of Long Petroleum, Inc., the original iteration of the current company, with Denny and Mary Long as its owners and shareholders.

Through his new company, Denny remained active drilling wells in East Texas, North Dakota, and South Louisiana while developing many former Jones-O'Brien properties, including the South Lake Arthur Field that Denny was so instrumental in developing while head of exploration at the company.

In 1988, with low prices still handicapping the industry, Denny recognized the opportunity to acquire oil and gas leases at reasonable costs and assembled a team to explore the Ark-La-Tex region, particularly the Smackover Trend of East Texas and South Arkansas. The move proved prescient with a number of significant discoveries in the area, including Big R and Trooper, West Fouke, McFarland Lake and West Texarkana.

As a result of these and other successes, Denny decided in 1998, to create Long Petroleum, LLC, a new entity with a more diversified asset base to allow the company to participate in ever-larger projects with minimal individual risk. Long Petroleum, LLC, continues to seek out high quality exploration prospects and opportunities to exploit emerging technologies. This strategy has proven successful in the horizontal James Lime, the Hosston and Cotton Valley and the Haynesville Shale plays of North Louisiana.

Denny Long.

Leading a management team that includes Dave Benscoter, Scott Lowe, Baker Barr, Barbara Hurst, and Kevin Long, Denny has adhered to the highest of standards, both business and personal, which he attributes to his family, Wyoming upbringing, West Point education, and Catholic faith. These upstanding values have helped make Long Petroleum, LLC, a respected member of North Louisiana's oil and gas community, and have guided Denny and his team in creating outstanding value for the owners and partners of the company.

SARATOGA RESOURCES, INC.

In the summer of 2008, Saratoga Resources, Inc., purchased a private company which owned and operated a number of oil and gas fields located in the transitional coastline and protected in-bay environment on parish and state leases of Southern Louisiana.

Right: Left to right, Chairman and CEO
Thomas Cooke and President Andy Clifford.

Saratoga paid $106 million in cash plus 4.9 million shares of common stock, a price equating to roughly $2 per thousand cubic feet of gas equivalent (MCFE), an excellent price considering the record high commodity prices in the market at the time. Saratoga recognized development and upside potential in the Harvest assets and immediately began licensing 3D seismic data and undertaking full field studies on the properties, spending close to $4 million on 3D seismic and field studies over the course of the next few years.

Today, Saratoga is an independent exploration and production company with offices in Houston, Texas, and Covington, Louisiana. Principal holdings cover 32,027 gross/net acres, with approximately ninety-three percent held by production (HBP). The company operates in twelve fields, with its largest positions being in Grand Bay and Vermilion 16 Fields. Saratoga has a deep inventory of high quality development prospects as well as shallow and deep gas potential that is not reflected in its reserves. Current production is weighted sixty percent towards oil, and the company receives premium LLS/HLS pricing on oil and uplift to Henry Hub on gas.

Grand Bay, discovered by Gulf Oil in 1938, is located in Plaquemines Parish in a marsh area east of the Mississippi River. With water depths range from 0-5-feet, Grand Bay has produced over 250 million barrels of oil equivalent (MMBOE) from 65 individual reservoir sands. Saratoga holds a 100-percent working interest (WI) for all rights at all depths in 17,000 acres of HBP leases. In addition, Saratoga owns a high quality, proprietary ninety square mile 3D seismic survey covering the field and its environs. The company has a large inventory of proposed development wells in the field.

Saratoga has mapped several deep and ultra-deep gas/condensate prospects with 5.8 trillion cubic feet of gas (TCFG) plus 600 million barrels of oil (MMBO) potential. One of these prospects, Zeus, is a 5,000-acre "turtle" structure in the Big Hum sands between 18,000-20,000 feet with bailout potential in the overlying Cib Carst and Tex W Sands, which reduces the commercial risk. In addition, 50 billion cubic feet of gas (BCFG) of shallow gas potential has been identified and mapped at depths above 5,000 feet.

The Vermilion 16 Field is located in state waters, offshore Vermilion Parish with water depths of approximately twelve feet. The company holds a 100 percent WI in several leases with 4,095 gross/net acres, mostly HBP, with all rights for all depths. This field was discovered in 1962, and has produced less than 400 BFCG from more than 30 individual reservoir sands.

Saratoga has identified and permitted several proposed development wells utilizing its nonproprietary twenty-five square mile 3D seismic survey.

The company has mapped a large ultra-deep gas prospect called Long John Silver with Wilcox, Tuscaloosa and Lower Cretaceous objectives at depths of 23,000 to 30,000 feet. The prospect sits in the main Lower Wilcox sand fairway between McMoRan's Davy Jones discovery to the southeast, and the Lineham Creek deep test, currently being drilled by Chevron and McMoRan to the northwest. Saratoga intends to seek one or more partners with the purpose of exploring the ultra-deep potential.

In addition, Saratoga owns and operates approximately 10,564 gross/net acres in several producing fields, offshore Plaquemines and St. Bernard Parishes, Louisiana. Saratoga holds a 100 percent WI in all wells and has licensed approximately 400 square miles of high quality 3D seismic data over the Main Pass and Breton Sound areas. The company also holds a 100 percent WI in 256 gross/net acres in Little Bay Field in St. Mary Parish, Louisiana.

As a result of the unprecedented collapse in global financial markets and the accompanying collapse in commodity markets in late 2008 and early 2009, following on the heels of two large hurricanes (Gustav and Ike) that temporarily curtailed production, Saratoga experience declines in revenues and profitability and a hostile overture from its senior lender. While the company never failed to make interest payments, it elected to seek protection from a hostile lender through Chapter 11 bankruptcy. The company emerged from bankruptcy just over a year later, in May 2010, having retained approximately 100 percent of its equity, and having paid all vendors, both secured and unsecured, 100 percent plus interest and legal expenses. During bankruptcy, Saratoga accumulated around $24 million in cash, paid approximately $12 million in expenses and spent maintenance capital of $6-7 million to maintain production at existing levels.

Since emerging from bankruptcy, Saratoga has successfully:

- Resumed full operations and grown production substantially from 2,300 boe/day to over 4,000 boe/day.
- Grown its market capitalization.
- Issued a combination of new equity and high-yield debt to completely pay back the original lender and accelerate development.
- Moved the stock to the NYSE MKT where it trades under the symbol "SARA."
- Hired additional staff at both corporate headquarters in Houston and operations staff in Covington.

Saratoga's goal is to execute on an aggressive development drilling program and the use of 3D seismic to substantially grow production, a model successfully deployed by Swift Energy in South Louisiana in the early 2000s when Swift acquired the Lake Washington Field in 2001 and took production from 1,000 barrels of oil equivalent production per day (BOEPD) to over 23,000 BOEPD in just six years to became the largest oil producer in Louisiana. Saratoga supplements its conventional development opportunities in established fields with exposure to ultra-deep gas plays, a model similar to Energy XXI.

Southern #3

Photo by Barnett

Crowley La.

EQUIPMENT SERVICES

OFFSHORE LIFTBOATS, LLC

The boat industry has always been a part of the Melancon family heritage, and the story begins with Johnny Melancon. Johnny first got into the boat industry as a commercial fisherman. His knowledge of boating came from his experiences out on the water fishing.

Liftbarges Inc.'s first 145-foot vessel the L/B Atlas.

In the 1960s, Johnny left the commercial fishing business and ventured for a time into the marine industry. Together, Johnny, and his brother James Melancon, founded a company called Melancon Boat Rentals. This was the original marine business to be owned by the Melancon family. Melancon Boat Rentals specialized in inshore crew boats and tugs. Although the company continued to flourish and grow, an accident prompted a quick end to Melancon Boat Rentals.

In 1969, James was working aboard one of his vessels on the Atchafalaya River. A dense fog caused James to park the vessel along the river bank one night. In the meantime another vessel was traveling towards them, following the tree line of the river. While James and his deckhand were fast asleep aboard a Melancon Boat Rentals vessel, the oncoming vessel struck them. James and his deckhand drowned in the river.

After the shocking death of his brother, Johnny could not bring himself to continue with Melancon Boat Rentals. Johnny stepped away from the marine industry for a few years and dabbled into the restaurant and bar businesses; however, Johnny's heart remained in the marine industry, and he decided to re-enter it in the early 1970s when he founded Galliano Towing.

He took his sons—John, Mike, and Reggie—along with him on the journey of building special boats for use in the oil and gas (O&G) industry. When they were youngsters in grade school, he took them aboard the company's vessels and began showing them the ins and outs of the boat industry.

It has often been said, "Like father, like son." That especially holds true of the Melancon family of Cut Off, Louisiana, and their string of family-owned and family-operated businesses.

Today, Offshore Liftboats LLC is owned and operated by son Mike and his wife Annie. The road to success has been a long one for the couple and their story begins and ends with one key element—family.

Galliano Towing was propositioned by Chevron to sign a three year contract. The contract was to build two liftboats. This contract began a chain of firsts for the Melancon family and the community of Lafourche. With a signed contract to build two liftboats Johnny sought out a business partner in Jude St. Romaine; and together in 1976, they founded Liftbarges, Inc. This was the first liftboat company owned by the Melancon family.

Bollinger Shipyard won the bid to construct Liftbarges' vessels, and they quickly began construction. Johnny and Jude's first vessel was a class 75-foot liftboat called the *L/B Eagle*; and, this was the first liftboat ever built by Bollinger Shipyard. This vessel was paid for by one of the first marine loans Community Bank of Lafourche had ever secured. After completing the first vessel, Johnny and Jude laid the keel for their second, which was a class 105-foot vessel called the *L/B Falcon*.

In 1978, Johnny began designing and building liftboats at his own shipyard, Rae Shipyard in Larose, Louisiana. It was during that time that his adult sons—John, Mike, and Reggie—became involved with the designing and building of Liftbarges Inc.'s first 145-foot-class vessel, the *L/B Atlas*.

Above: *Offshore Liftboats, LLC's Cameron.*

Left: *Offshore Liftboats, LLC's Kylie.*

Above: One of the first vessels ever purchased by Offshore Liftboats, LLC's L/B Maggie.

Below: One of the first vessels ever purchased by Offshore Liftboats, LLC's L/B Lauren.

With his interest in the business whetted, Mike attended the Maritime Training Academy in 1980, earning his Master's License and Tankerman's License. Mike still holds these licenses today (Master of Steam or Motor Vessels of not more than 1,600 GRT (Gross Registered Tonnage—Domestic Tonnage), 3,000 Gross Tons (ITC) Upon Near Coastal Waters; Master of Towing Vessels upon Great Lakes, Inland Waters and Western Rivers. He then began working aboard his father's tugboats as a captain. Mike had no desire to run liftboats at that time, so Johnny built a tug boat called *Dixie*, so that Mike could be a part of the business. Mike remained a captain aboard the *Dixie* until the growth of Liftbarges, Inc., prompted him to begin running liftboats instead of tugs.

In the late 1980s, Johnny and Jude dissolved their business partnership and sold the vessels belonging to Liftbarges, Inc. Johnny kept the *L/B Falcon* and began Falcon Operators, Inc. offering Mike the position of operations manager of the new company. However, to fulfill his duties in that capacity, Mike had to stop working offshore so that he and his wife could devote all of their time to run Falcon Operators, Inc. For the first few years, the company was operated out of Mike and Annie's home.

When Falcon Operators purchased an additional vessel, the 105-foot-class *L/B Lauren*, they realized they needed to expand the staff and offered the secretarial position to Annie's mother, Errol Valance. Eventually, though, Falcon Operators outgrew the couple's small home office, and they decided to construct an office building in Cut Off. When the new office building was complete, Reggie decided to rejoin the family's business ventures.

While Mike and Reggie helped Johnny operate Falcon Operators, their brother, John, ran Rae Shipyard. Rae Shipyard expanded throughout the years and is currently located in Leeville, Louisiana. Today, the shipyard is owned by John, Jr., and with the help of Johnny's daughter JoAnn Melancon, the brother and sister operate the shipyard together.

In 1992, Mike hired Gary Callais, also a licensed Master and experienced liftboat captain, to work aboard the company's vessels. Within four years, Gary was promoted to the office where he spent the next four years assisting Mike with company operations. Because both were experienced liftboat captains, Mike and Gary maintained unique relationships with vessel crews and customers, as well.

In 1995, when Hurricane Opal threatened the Gulf of Mexico and forced an evacuation of the Gulf, the *L/B Falcon* was on a job and unable to make it in to safe harbor. The crew evacuated the vessel and rode out the storm on land. Sadly, when the crew returned to work and set out to board the vessel, the *L/B Falcon* was gone. To this day the *L/B Falcon* has never been recovered from the Gulf of Mexico. Johnny, Mike, and Reggie however, were determined to not let the devastating loss impede the success of Falcon Operators. The vessel was replaced quickly and Falcon Operators continued to flourish.

After more than forty years in the marine industry, Johnny decided to retire from the business, and Mike and Annie purchased the two vessels belonging to Falcon Operators. At that time, Mike and Annie decided it was time for a name change—one that would help to brand their product and build a positive image within the industry. In August 2000, Offshore Liftboats, LLC was created. Utilizing liftboats, which are self-propelled, self-elevating deck barges, the company provides a stable platform by which its clients perform their jobs. The company's experience is second to none, especially in the Gulf of Mexico where it has provided services for more than twenty-five years.

With the help of Community Bank of Lafourche, the couple was able to purchase the 105-foot-class *L/B Lauren* and the 120-foot-class *L/B Maggie*. Mike, Annie, Gary, and Errol comprised the original office staff and ran their new business out of a shotgun house located in Galliano. With the vessel crews, the company had fewer than twenty employees in the beginning.

Twenty years prior to the opening of Offshore Liftboats, LLC, the *L/B Lauren* and the *L/B Maggie* were considered to be large vessels; however, in 2002, these vessels were not meeting Offshore Liftboats customers' demands. Those companies found that ever-changing work methods required more up-to-date liftboats with greater capabilities. Equipment had become larger and the smaller vessels of years past only allowed a limited amount of space for such equipment. With a vision to the future, Mike and Annie launched the New Build Program of Offshore Liftboats, LLC.

That year, less than eighteen months in business, they engaged Marine Industrial Fabrication of New Iberia to lay the keel for the *L/B Audrey*, Offshore Liftboats' first 175-foot-class vessel. Advancing to vessels of this size opened up a new customer base for Offshore Liftboats. This larger customer base allowed the company's New Build Program to continue to flourish. When Mike and Annie signed a second 175-foot-class vessel, the *L/B Annie*, to be delivered in 2003, it became apparent that Offshore Liftboats needed to increase its office staff as it was quickly outgrowing the current office space.

Mike and Annie began working on plans for a state-of-the-art office building, and in December 2003, Offshore Liftboats moved its headquarters into a newly constructed office complex, which is built to withstand Category Four hurricane winds, and is also equipped with a backup generator capable of operating the entire facility should another disaster of major proportions hit the area again. Prior to the completion of the new office building, Mike's eldest daughter, Vanessa Pierce, had joined the Offshore Liftboats' staff as a receptionist. By this time, Offshore Liftboats had also employed a runner to help keep up with the increase in crew members and supplies needed for a four vessel fleet. For Offshore Liftboats to remain competitive in the industry, it was also necessary to launch a safety program and employ a fulltime safety manager, which they found in Vanessa's husband, Craig Pierce.

A new office building, three new staff members, and the completion of Offshore Liftboats' second 175-foot-class vessel was a lot to comprehend at one time, but it did not stop the company from forging ahead. At a staff meeting, it was unanimously decided that Offshore Liftboats, LLC would sign contracts for two additional 175-foot-class vessels. In preparation for an extension of this magnitude, Mike and Annie decided to sell Offshore Liftboats' original vessels used in the start-up of the company. In 2004 the *L/B Lauren* was purchased by Mike's brother, Reggie, followed by his purchase of the *L/B Maggie* in 2005. Purchasing these vessels afforded Reggie the opportunity to get back into the liftboat business and he founded Triumph Marine, Inc. John, Jr., also entered the liftboat business when he partnered with Dale Mitchell to open Mitchell Liftboats in 2005. Today, all of Johnny's children are in the marine industry.

The vessel sales allowed Offshore Liftboats to focus on building additional larger vessels so they could keep up with the growing demand of the liftboat industry. At that time, the industry was experiencing increasing activity of Plug-and-Abandonment work, which required the use of the larger vessels mainly due to the deck and crane sizes.

Both, the company and new technology in the industry were growing fast. To keep pace, Mike says, "Between 2004 and 2005, Offshore Liftboats had yet another 175-foot-class construction scheduled for delivery at the end of 2005, which meant our third new build within a three year period. To have experienced so much growth that quickly proved to be quite challenging for the company; especially, when it came to manning the vessels. Here, at Offshore Liftboats, we have always prided ourselves on promoting our crews through the ranks. We believe that recognition of employee craftsmanship, dedication, and loyalty has enabled us to keep a very low employee turnover. Today, we have quite a few captains and mates that started their careers here as deckhands. We like to train new employees at lower levels, and let them demonstrate to us that they are willing workers who are motivated enough to better themselves. This allows them an opportunity to advance with our company because of the aggressive building program we have undertaken," says Mike.

Above: Offshore Liftboats, LLC's first vessel to ever be built, L/B Audrey.

Below: Offshore Liftboats, LLC's L/B Joni.

Above: Offshore Liftboats. LLC's office in Cut Off, Louisiana.

Below: Mike and Annie Melancon with their granddaughter Janie Pierce and grandson Alex Pierce for the christening of L/B Janie.

In 2005, Offshore Liftboats signed a contract to build its fourth 175-foot-class liftboat, with a projected delivery in the third quarter of 2006. The delivery date of the vessel, however, was delayed until the beginning of the fourth quarter due to the worst natural disaster in the history of Louisiana, which was followed by another major hurricane. The latter, Rita, caused tremendous flooding at the site of the vessel construction, while Hurricane Katrina caused wide-spread flooding and damage throughout southeastern Louisiana. Besides Katrina's impact and the tremendous loss of life, it also did wide-spread damage to facilities located offshore.

The offshore damage caused by Hurricane Katrina wreaked millions of dollars of damage throughout the area; and boosted the boat industry. It created a high demand of work for all offshore areas.

Offshore Liftboats experienced an influx of work, thereby increasing industry-wide day rates. Because of the influx of work influenced by the hurricane, Offshore Liftboats was able to secure a one-year contract on L/B Janie before the 175-foot-class vessel was even completed. The increasing demand for work created a lot of capital for Offshore Liftboats, and set the groundwork for a continuing New Build program. During the past ten year period, Offshore Liftboats built four 175-foot vessels and three 200-foot vessels in an effort to meet the demand for vessels of these sizes. Their fourth 200-foot-class vessel is scheduled to be delivered during the first quarter of 2013.

With all of the current vessels, Mike and Annie have introduced a new generation to their business. Their daughter, Vanessa, is the current general manager and their daughter, Lauren, is office manager. Vanessa has been employed by Offshore Lifeboats for ten years, beginning her career in the family-owned business as a receptionist. She has worked her way up to general manager.

Lauren is a graduate from Nicholls State University and spent her high school career working for Offshore Liftboats as a receptionist. She became the office manager upon her college graduation in May 2011. The two sisters look forward to the future of their family business.

Mike and Annie have two other daughters who contribute behind the scenes to the company. Their daughter Michelle is a stay-at-home mother who has worked part-time in the office in multiple departments, including sales and safety. Daughter Johnette is currently employed by the company as Vanessa's assistant. Cameron, Mike and Annie's only son turned ten years old in 2012; it will be some time before he can become active in the family business but he enjoys spending time on the

vessels and at the company's office. With their five children at their sides and multiple grandchildren nearby, Mike and Annie are confident that Offshore Liftboats, LLC will continue to flourish in future generations.

Today the company, with more than sixty employees, is engaged in construction, plugging and abandoning wells, wire line and electric line services, coiled tubing services, core sampling, dive support, and snubbing services. Its revenue has grown more than 200 percent in ten years.

Offshore Liftboats, LLC strives to provide a workplace free of recognizable and preventable safety hazards. The management of Offshore Liftboats, LLC believes that all employees and subcontractors, both within and outside the boundaries of the job setting, share a responsibility of accident prevention. It is expected that individuals share accident prevention knowledge with all customers, competitors, and fellow employees for the benefit of all within the industry in which it participates.

Top, left: Mike and Annie Melancon's daughter Michelle Christen breaking a bottle on the leg of L/B Michelle during a boat christening.

Top, right: Offshore Liftboats, LLC's L/B Michelle.

Below: Offshore Liftboats, LLC's staff and crew gathered in prayer during a boat christening at Marine Industrial Fabrication in New Iberia.

FRANK'S CASING CREW

Above: Frank Mosing.

Below: Frank's Casing Crew's first location on Surrey Street.

In 1938, Frank Mosing founded Frank's Casing Crew (Frank's) out of his garage in Lafayette, Louisiana. Seventy-five years later, Frank's is known in the oil and gas industry as Frank's International and is one of the largest privately held oilfield service companies in the world. What began as a husband and wife team working with a single casing crew is now an international company with over 4,000 employees located in 40 countries. However, the central point for operations in the United States still resides in Lafayette where Frank Mosing's legacy began.

Born in the Oklahoma Indian Territory before Oklahoma was a state, "Mr. Frank" as he was fondly known by his employees, began his career in the oilfield in 1932. In 1937, Mr. Frank and a five-man crew were sent to run casing "down the bayou" in Raceland, Louisiana. After several months of being on the job, the company he was working for could not pay him or his crew, so Mr. Frank and his crew left. In October 1938, with promises of jobs to come and $2,000 in savings, Mr. Frank started his company in Lafayette and began working out of his garage with his wife, Jessie, as dispatcher. Local oil companies familiar with Frank's work ethic were great supporters of Mr. Frank. They wanted to work with someone they could depend on who was honest and reliable.

Mr. Frank's commitment to providing a quality job at a fair value soon became a trademark of how Frank's conducted business. It was not long before the oil and gas industry learned that using Frank's resulted in jobs being completed safely and efficiently.

As time went by, more orders came in, more jobs were completed and Frank's grew steadily. In less than three years, Mr. Frank had three crews working. Business was booming until the attack at Pearl Harbor. Within a few weeks, Frank's was back to only having one crew. Since orders continued to be called in, the lone crew worked incredibly long hours; however, Mr. Frank remained focused on providing a quality job.

When reflecting on this time in his life, Mr. Frank recalled, "Once I went to Ville Platte and ran three strings of pipe before I came in. We laid down the drill pipe, changed the rams, ran the casing, and dumped cement on two of those jobs. On the last job, the tool pusher came over and said, 'Frank, we'll lay down the drill pipe if you'll come and run the casing.' I replied, 'Okay, that'll give us time to get a bite to eat.' We went to a little café nearby and ate, then went back out there and ran the casing. When it came time to add the cement, the tool pusher could see how exhausted we were, so he told me that they would dump the cement—for us to go home. Right then, I felt like he was the best friend I ever had."

In 1950, at the age of forty-six, Mr. Frank stabbed his last string of pipe. However, his experience and expertise still kept him in the field to solicit and run the business. Under his leadership, the company flourished, and one of the most important keys to that prosperity was the addition of a new employee. Mr. Frank's eldest son, Donald Mosing, began working for Frank's after graduating from the Southwestern Louisiana Institute (now the University of Louisiana at Lafayette) with a degree in mechanical engineering. In the years to come, Donald's influence with his constant search for the perfect equipment would be profound.

One of Donald's first innovations helped Frank's bring to market an adjustable stabbing board. This board replaced a wooden plank high in the derrick and made the job of stabbing much more efficient. Donald later redesigned the adjustable stabbing board into an electrically powered board much like the units still in use today.

An important innovation to the oil and gas industry was the introduction of the hydraulic power tong in 1955. Mr. Frank called the introduction of hydraulic power

tongs the most significant change in the casing business. With deeper wells, companies needed tighter casing connections and faster installations. Power tongs were the answer, and Frank's was one of the first companies to put them into service.

Above: Donald Mosing, a Southwestern Louisiana Institute graduate.

Below: A stabber balanced carefully on an adjustable stabbing board platform inside a derrick.

Over the next twenty years the hydraulic power tongs proved to be a great addition. In 1978, Donald became disenchanted with the reliability of hydraulic power tongs manufactured by other companies. With a newly opened engineering department, Frank's was soon engineering and manufacturing its own hydraulic power tongs, setting the standard for safety and reliability in the industry. Manufacturing thousands

Right: Frank's Casing Crew's power tongs now available!

Below: A diesel hammer.

of hydraulic power tongs at Frank's plays an integral role in the continued growth of the company.

Innovations associated with the electrical stabbing board and hydraulic power tongs were the start of an extensive list of products that Donald would engineer over his long career at Frank's. To date forty-two patents at Frank's are attributed to Donald, and under his guidance and innovation Frank's became a leader in the design and manufacturing of casing and completing running equipment.

In the early 1960s, Frank's entered the conductor driving diesel hammer market. Driving conductor pipe is the first step in the drilling process. When Frank's initially purchased a D-12 hammer, their casing crews began driving conductor pipe for the operators—no drilling, no cementing, and a lot less work in half the time. As diesel hammers were added to Frank's inventory, the company entered a period of rapid growth, especially as it applied to a growing number of employees, products and services. Over the years Frank's has become one of the largest hammer operators in the industry and continues to benefit immensely from this advancement.

In 1965, Frank's added still another service when they began to sell conductor pipe. Donald's reasoning was simple. "We supplied the hammer to drive the conductor pipe, and our customers wanted us to supply both the hammer and the pipe." This gave Frank's the opportunity to inventory conductor pipe, and what began as a small inventory carried to fulfill customer requests has now grown into a global, multimillion-dollar-a-year business.

For twenty-seven years, from 1951 to 1977, Donald was the only engineer working at Frank's, and it was Donald who was instrumental in setting up Frank's engineering department with impressive results. In 1977, Donald hired his first engineer. Within two years, the engineering department had become a permanent fixture at Frank's as more and more engineers were hired. Today, as a major research and development center in the oil and gas industry, Frank's holds over 100 U.S. patents and currently carries more then than 150 different products, most designed and manufactured in Lafayette, Louisiana.

In addition to Donald, Mr. Frank had two other sons who played significant roles in building and expanding Frank's while working for their father. The second oldest son, Billy Mosing, attended college then enlisted in the United States Air Force. After his enlistment ended in 1955, Billy joined his father and Donald at Frank's where he became a salesman calling on land rigs and inland water rigs, often hitching rides on crew boats to barge rigs in the marsh. Soon thereafter, Billy took flying lessons and upon completion of his training, Frank's purchased a Cessna 180 amphibian so he could make sales calls on inland water rigs.

Through the years, Billy's flying and sales ability became real assets to Frank's where he eventually became vice president of sales, a position he held until his retirement.

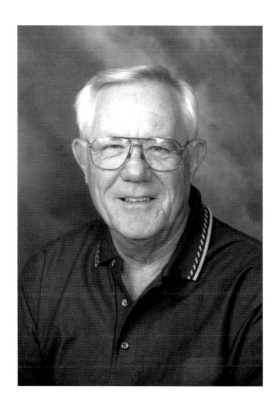

Larry Mosing, the youngest of Mr. Frank's three sons, is a United States Air Force veteran as well. After serving four years as an aircraft instrumentation instructor, he went to work at Frank's with his father and two brothers. Larry started as a dispatcher, but as the business quickly grew, he soon began to take on multiple responsibilities that included running casing crews, managing office personnel, and overseeing accounts payable. This was truly Larry's job description, one man working at many jobs. During his tenure at Frank's, no job was too small or large for him, even as he served as secretary-treasurer, a title he held until his death in 2012.

As the oil and gas industry expanded in the region, Frank's grew as well. The first branch office opened in Houma, Louisiana, in 1960. The success of that office led Frank's domestic operations to expand dramatically. During the next twenty years under the direction Keith Mosing, Donald's son, Frank's established offices in Alvin, Texas, in 1974, Corpus Christi, and Kilgore, Texas, in 1979, and Bryan, Texas, in 1980. Others were

Left: Billy Mosing.

Right: Larry Mosing.

Above: The Mosings (from left to right):
Donald, Frank, Jessie, Larry, and Billy.

Below: The Port of Iberia facility.

opened in Oklahoma City, Oklahoma, in 1980 and Laurel, Mississippi, in 1981. In 1981, Keith formed Frank's International and boldly expanded the business around the world.

Later, when the United States oil bubble burst in the mid-1980s, weak demand for oil curtailed domestic exploration and production. Companies in Louisiana and all across the nation began to scale back their operations. Frank's used this opportunity to purchase equipment and entire companies. Much of this equipment was reconditioned at Frank's facility in Lafayette before being shipped overseas where new markets were opening up. Today, with Keith as chairman and chief executive officer of Frank's International, the company now has offices and operations facilities in more than forty countries worldwide.

In the early 1990s, Frank's growth came closer to home when a deepwater fabrication facility was developed and built at the Port of Iberia south of Lafayette, Louisiana. When it opened, Frank's became the first top tension riser fabricator with access to the Gulf of Mexico. Now it is one of the largest fabricators of riser strings, providing support for deepwater projects for some of the largest exploration and production companies in the industry.

Throughout the history of Frank's, innovation and safety have always been linked together. In fact, in the 1950s a drilling rig collapsed when Donald was on the job. While observing the rig collapsing, he learned an invaluable lesson about safety that remained with him. At the time, Donald was quoted as saying, "While quality and service keeps Frank's ahead of its competitors, we must also try to measure the risk we encounter in this business so that safety is part of the decision making process." For Donald, it was not enough to make a tool work better; it had to be safer, too.

Over time, with a sustained focus on safety, Frank's gained a reputation for safety innovation that encompassed three key components: a long-term workforce, quality training, and technological innovation. Forty- and 50-year veterans as well as second and third generations of families are common among Frank's employees. This longevity in the workforce

contributed to remarkable safety and quality performances when new employees were matched with experienced crews.

Even today, Frank's training includes highly technical instruction that offers skilled training on drilling rigs set up for training and testing purposes at the Lafayette, Louisiana, and Aberdeen, Scotland, yards. These fully operational rigs allow new and experienced crews hands-on-training as well as to test casing and tubing equipment. This has ensured that safety principles have been and will continue to be learned and applied because Frank's is committed to incorporating safety solutions with operating procedures so crews can operate equipment safely.

Although Frank's is known around the world for its high quality services and equipment, it is still a family owned company that is extremely competitive. Keith, Ernest & Young's *Entrepreneur of the Year* in 2003, is now the force behind Frank's competitive drive. As chairman and chief executive officer, Keith's leadership and vision resonates throughout the company in what is commonly known as the "Mosing" way. For example, when asked how Frank's survived the wave of acquisitions of independents by major service companies, Keith confidently countered, "How do you know I'm not going to take them over?"

This entrepreneurial spirit is rooted in a legacy that began with "Mr. Frank", was carried on by Donald, and continues today with Keith. For seventy-five years Frank's has operated under the creed of providing a quality job at a fair value that has earned the company the reputation for being straightforward, reliable and honest. That has not changed. Today, Frank's continues to grow and excel by meeting the challenges and exceeding the expectations of an ever-evolving energy industry.

Above: Donald Mosing discussing a new connector designed by Frank's Casing Crew.

Left: Chairman and Chief Executive Officer Keith Mosing.

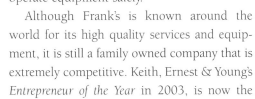

COASTAL PIPE OF LOUISIANA, INC.

Above: Coastal Pipe was started by N. J. "Buddy" Yentzen, Jr., in 1957. This photograph was taken after ten years of growth in 1967. The large pipe sign was used as a landmark by travelers on Highway 167, now I-49.

Below: Coastal Pipe sold the original yard in 1980 and opened a new "state-of-the-art" plant in 1987 at the new location across I-49. The company has steadily grown over the years as this 2012 aerial shot confirms.

N. J. "Buddy" Yentzen, Jr., was a forward-thinking man fifty-five years ago, long before others realized the potential versatility of their businesses. He began buying discarded or "used" pipe from major oil companies, selling it as used pipe for structural or construction applications. The vast offshore fields produced these large supplies of used tubing. Eventually, though, he took his sales of pipe to another level, developing methods to recondition the used tubing for reuse in the oilfield by small, independent operators.

To brand his sales of refurbished pipe to the oil industry, he founded Coastal Pipe of Louisiana, Inc., in 1957. One might say he started the business on a shoestring with one big deal. CLECO (Central Louisiana Electric Company) approached Buddy for 1,000 feet of 20-inch plain end pipe for road bore casing. Buddy purchased the used casing for $3 per foot and re-sold it for $4 per foot. He celebrated with $1,000 profit, considering it the "mother lode" in those days.

The late Orel Bridges, Jr., a friend and colleague, played a major role in Buddy's success, financing Coastal Pipe and others to get started in the business. He was one of the forerunners of reconditioning used pipe, and had the foresight to assist numerous people in the used pipe business. Orel, it is reported, kept track of all loans and payments between Buddy and himself on a calendar hanging on his wall. No banks were involved—it was an agreement sealed with a man's word and a handshake. Even with the uncertainty of the oil and gas business, Buddy knew he was in for the duration. He knew that there would be a demand from independent operators to purchase premium used tubing at fifty cents on the dollar as compared to new API tubing prices.

In 1981, Yentzen sold the established company at the peak of the oil boom. Within four years the new owners closed the doors because of the worst down turn ever in the industry. The severe recession wreaked havoc not only in the used pipe industry, but throughout the oilfield.

Undaunted by the recession, in 1985, Yentzen designed and constructed a modern pipe reconditioning facility across the highway from the location of his original yard. Drawing from thirty years of experience in the pipe cleaning field he developed and organized an assembly line process utilizing the latest technology available to recondition used pipe. The plant greatly reduced the labor needed to clean, drift and test the tubulars. The mechanization and computerized equipment also reconditioned the pipe better than the original manual methods; thus reducing the price of reconditioned pipe further.

Refurbishing and reselling used tubing, Buddy soon learned, would be the "meat and potatoes" of his business. He knew if he approached the business with the right emphasis, his service would appeal to industry operators. When major oil companies replaced tubing in a well, they found it too expensive to sort and rework it so they put in all in a scrap or "junk" pile. Used dealers such as Coastal Pipe soon realized they could make more profit from separating the used tubing and casing and placing them in the market for sale. Coastal Pipe was one of a handful of original pipe yards to start in the late fifties, and one among few who have survived and thrived. Later, Coastal Pipe improved the pipe handling process by using articulating forklifts.

The process was difficult, laborious and hard. It entailed unloading and loading the pipe onto trucks by hand with handmade runners and roller sticks. Frequently, it took more than half-a-day to load pipe onto a truck. Eventually, the companies could afford forklifts with transformed carriages (that were fabricated wider) to handle the 30- to 40-foot lengths of pipes. Originally, all pipes were sorted by hand and drifted and tested by hand. Soon Coastal Pipe manufactured its own tools for this use. They joined a round wire hose with an air powered reaming tool to clean the inside of the pipe, and used a forty-two inch API full length drift attached behind the pneumatic reaming tool so that two tasks were performed at one time. Threaded plugs were screwed on either end and water was forced

inside with pressure up to eighty percent of American Petroleum Institute (API) standards at 6,000 to 10,000 pounds per inch (PSI).

The pipe was also run through an electro-magnetic inspection to confirm body wall thickness and locate flaws. The combined effort of all these pipe reconditioning procedures insured the used pipe was in premium condition for downhole use.

Development of second-hand used tubulars and casing industry came of age in the late 1950s, and Coastal Pipe was making news as an industry leader with such efforts. It was understood that Buddy and his company had exactly what the onshore oil industry needed—and, at a cost they could afford. However, it was not long until the major players in the industry took notice.

At the time, they used only new pipe. The tubing laid down after a work over would end up as structural pipe only. Eventually, the specialty market evolved out of necessity and the ability to create methods to clean the inside and outside of pipe and test for pressure, etc. CS Hydril was created in the 1960s. There were forty-five hundred drilling rigs working during this time; and each company came up with its own needs for used pipe. A major determining consideration for the used market was the fact that used tubing is not manufactured; it is

Above: Doug Yentzen and N. J. "Buddy" Yentzen stand in front of the new office in 1989. The father-son team worked together to position the fledgling company for tremendous growth in the new and used pipe markets.

Below: Doug Yentzen and N. J. "Buddy" Yentzen stand in front of their new API casing inventory in 2013. The team has opened the door to new API and premium used oil country tubular goods markets.

takes pride in meeting the API standards and specifications. According to Douglas M. Yentzen, who went to work with his father in July 1987, thirty years after Buddy founded the company, "We take used tubing and casing and put it through a rigorous reconditioning process at our state-of-the-art plant at the crossroads on I-49 and Highway 182." The material is thoroughly brushed inside and out with a propriety system of wire brushes. Then, we hydrostatically test it to see if it withstands the pressure set by industry standards." Finally, he adds, "it goes through an Electromagnetic inspection that satisfies customer well inspections. It is then labeled with the stencil of its testing. Pro Pipe Services, Inc., a division Coastal Pipe, founded in August 1996, provides logistical support, trucking and EMI (Electromagnetic inspection) inspection services." Pay Oil and Pay Ventures are independent oil-producing divisions of the parent company. Pro Pipe was founded in August 1996, Pay Oil in 1994 and Pay Ventures, ten years later.

Other members of the Yentzen family have joined Douglas in the business. While Douglas is credited for growing the company to its present-day size, Tanya, his wife joined the company in August 1999 as office manager. She used skills learned on previous jobs to hire talented people that helped her update the office, increase sales, and expand the yard. Along with Doug, she helps him feel the pulse of the company and monitor market conditions.

Rounding out the third generation of the Yentzen family business, Doug's oldest son, Jonathan, joined the company in 2006; and Jake, the second son, began working at Coastal Pipe in 2008. The youngest son, Jordan, joined in 2011. The three young men have added sales skills and technology to the equation, and poised the company for the next level to meet the challenge of new-age technology in the industry. All procedures and techniques of buying, reconditioning, and selling used pipe has been passed on from father-to-sons. Doug laughs when he says, "There were no classes in college offering 'Used Pipe 101'. Many of our innovations were created through the years from experience and necessity, or as some would say, 'trial-and-error.'"

created from existing pipe. The availability of it depends upon the reconditioning of wells where companies lay down existing material as it comes out of the wells. Coastal Pipe fabricated and bought its first computerized hydro-testing machine in 1982 from Hub City Ironworks.

Coastal Pipe, a family-owned and operated business, today buys and sells premium used and new API tubing and casing. The company

Coastal Pipe is positioned for future expansion with the purchase of thirty-three acres adjoining the present property. The company has recently purchased a state-of-the-art internal blasting machine that will be in operation in 2013 along with a brand new threading machine. That means that smaller companies will no longer have to wait in line in Houston to get a string of pipe threaded.

Coastal Pipe will soon be a "one-stop" shopping facility for new and used pipe. It has educated and trained its sales team with cutting edge information in the field of steel and pipe manufacturing. It has joined forces with the industry's leading association—National Association of Steel and Pipe Distributors (NASPD) to constantly educate and inform its sales force following that organization's guidelines. A membership in LOGA (Louisiana Oil & Gas Association) keeps the company abreast of regulations, legislation and the direction of the oil and gas industry in Louisiana. Coastal Pipe has beefed up its yard capabilities by adding more testing and inspection areas. The company's physical location is close to everyone in its service area near the crossroads of I-10 and I-49.

End users need only to make a phone call to purchase the new API OCTG (Oil Country Tubular Goods), premium used tubing and casing, line pipe, and structural.

Pro Pipe Services (logistics) continues its growth to supply reliable trucking services and forklift services in the field. Its business plan is to continue to grow in the pipe reconditioning arena, including electromagnetic inspection (EMI) of tubulars. In addition, internal blasting of tubulars to remove coating, scale and foreign material, threading, bucking collars, full-length drifting hydro-testing, visual thread inspection (VTI), and special end area inspection are, and will be performed and improved upon.

Opposite, top: Tanya and Doug Yentzen stand in front of their decoy collection at the office on I-49. Tanya, the office manager, was instrumental in hiring the office staff to keep the business on its growth track.

Opposite, bottom: Doug Yentzen's three sons, Jonathan, Jake and Jordan, are a vital part of the company's growth. All three young men have achieved their business degrees and have helped position Coastal Pipe of Louisiana, Inc., to grow to the next level.

Above: The new offices were built to accommodate the expanding growth of the company. A replica of the old "landmark" signage was displayed on the new offices to brand the company's logo.

Left: The new state-of-the-art pipe reconditioning facility has enabled Coastal Pipe of Louisiana, Inc., to increase and improve their inventory of premium used tubing and casing.

Pay Oil, LLC and Pay Ventures, LLC continue to drill oil wells to increase production and perform thorough evaluations of properties and drill prospects. Doug and his sons, along with their field supervisor, Robley Richard, maintain the properties according to OSHA standards while producing gas and oil.

Today, all of Coastal Pipe and its subsidiaries employ approximately fifty people. The companies have averaged more than a thirty percent growth over the past ten years, even with the 2008-2009 industry down turn. The company prides itself on its mission statement: "Exceeding customer expectations

Above: The recent discovery of shale oil and gas fields and the constantly evolving and improving fracking procedures will ensure that Coastal Pipe of Louisiana, Inc., will continue to grow in the years to come to keep pace with the expected demand to produce these shale plays.

Left: Doug Yentzen and Randy Williams oversee Kendle Brown and Jerren Malbrue confirm the wall thickness on the tubes in four spots with an ultrasonic test.

Below: The cost savings and quality of the used pipe have combined with new API pipe sales to fuel the continued growth of Coastal Pipe of Louisiana, Inc.

through teamwork, flexibility, quality products, and customer service." Based on that, it enjoys a loyal customer base including land well owners and shallow water well owners that have trusted it for over fifty-five years. Anyone can learn more about Coastal Pipe by visiting www.coastalpipeofla.com.

The owners and employees of Coastal Pipe are community conscious, participating in and giving to various charitable organizations. Among them are the American Cancer Society, the Breast Center of Acadiana, MG20-20 (a charitable military organization), the RCAF (Ragin Cajun Athletic Fund), the University of Louisiana Scholarship Foundation, numerous high schools and sports organizations throughout the south, rodeo clubs, and individuals with special needs.

DELTA GULF RENTAL TOOLS COMPANY LOUISIANA/ TEXAS

Grandpa and dad, 1947.

For more than seventy-five years, the McClanahan family who entered the offshore, barge, land, and drilling and workover rig and rental tool business in Louisiana, continues to implement innovative techniques that provide ease-of-use and other advancements within the oil and gas industry.

The stock market crash of 1929 placed financial and employment constraints on many Americans for the years that followed. However, in 1937, Helen Edith and Felix McClanahan managed their private resources to start a small business, creating jobs for many along the Gulf coast who had been among the unemployed. At twenty-three, they became entrepreneurs when they formed a drilling rig and rental tool venture. That venture has metamorphosed through the years; and now, includes several ventures, all of which are oil-and-gas-related. Service Contractors and AWI (and its spin-off endeavors, Delta Gulf Rental Tools) continues the beliefs and goals of serving the oil

and gas industry begun by their parents and now, grandparents.

Originally, the young couple was involved in land, drilling rigs; and had a full oilfield rental tool business, providing a full complement of rigs and rental tools necessary to the oil and gas industry. The rigs and rental tool concept was, and still is, a viable alternative to other companies' investments in purchases of such equipment. In the fall of 1938 or 1939, the federal government confiscated Helen's and Felix's company, and never paid them for the company.

Dedicated to making a good living for his family, in 1946, Felix went to work for Jimmy Gray, who owned American Iron Machine and Foundry Company, setting up pipe yards throughout the country. The last pipe yard he set up was in Harvey, Louisiana. Once that was completed, he began operations of that yard. Subsequent generations have continued, while engaging in other enterprises.

In 1949, Gray informed Felix that he was disposing of the small pipe yard and machine shop, and offered to sell it to him for a nominal price. Knowing Felix was trustworthy, Gray gave him the option of paying cash when he had the money; or said he could set up an installment plan to pay him. At that point, the McClanahans were back in business, this time with the pipe.

Across the street from the McClanahan's pipe yard was a small machine shop owned by Brigham Young and Earl Elkins. The three good friends merged the businesses with each owning a one-third interest. A year later, the McClanahan's started another business, called American Casing Crews, Inc., and began running casing crews, along with the pipe yard and rental business. In the early 1950s, Young and McClanahan acquired Elkins' interest in the machine shop, and split the companies into two separate entities. During the first part of 1956, the managers of their casing crew were recipients of the entire company as a gift via the McClanahan's generosity.

Felix' uncle, also a McClanahan, worked for California-based Standard Oil Company. In 1956 the elder McClanahan invited his nephew to visit in California. It was there, that the older McClanahan told Felix that he was going to sell all the rigs that were operating under California Company, a division of Standard Oil, which worked exclusively in Louisiana. He wanted Felix and Helen to have all the rigs by buying them; and then, leasing them back to that company. In addition, he wanted Felix to take over the carpenters, electricians, roustabouts, boat skippers and other contract personnel.

The rigs, at the time, were primarily barge and offshore rigs. "That transaction laid the groundwork for my parents to grow the business by building several rigs," says Jack, Felix and Helen's son, who heads the rental

tool business today primarily involving workstrings and related tools, along with his daughter, Kelly (McClanahan) Yeager. In 1961, Jack's parents built their first offshore rig that could work 30-, 40-, and 45-foot skid beams. The engineer, at the time was Ed Dressel. Two years later, his father sold all of the drilling rigs that were working for the Humble Company to Rube Mayronne.

Employing his knowledge of the industry (and being the entrepreneurial man he was), Felix invented the short key way by turning the rig around on the barge. Throughout his career, along with Jack, he developed the four-posted substructure and built the first pre-fabricated buildings on barges.

Jack and Chris.

The founders' son literally "grew up" in the business. In 1964, they helped Jack form American Workover, Inc. (Well workover is the process of performing major maintenance or remedial treatments of an oil or gas well. In many cases, it implies the removal and replacement of the production tubing string after the well has been declined and a workover rig has been placed on location. This operation saves considerable time and expense.) Jack acquired one offshore concentric tubing unit (CTU) and started the building of four barge rigs over the next several years. In 1970, they merged American Workover, Inc., into Duquesne Natural Gas, and owned thirty-eight percent of Duquesne, which was a public company at that time. Service contracting was still retained by the McClanahans.

Felix passed away in 1972, but Helen and Jack continued operations, greatly building the business into a viable operation, especially in southern Louisiana and south Texas oil and gas drilling areas. Jack was just as focused on the ventures as his father had been. Felix is remembered as one who worked hard during his lifetime; but, enjoyed a few laughs along the way. Jack recalls several instances in the 1950s: "In those days, there were very few places that oilfield people felt welcome. Things were somewhat segregated in restaurants and bars. There was one place in Harvey—Phil's Place— where all the oilfield personnel hung out. My father was in the back playing cards with a few other gentlemen. History has it that he was losing the game, and became a little upset with the music blaring from the juke-box. My father approached the owner and asked that he kindly turn off the jukebox.

The man told him he couldn't because other customers are playing it, and wanted to hear the music. Felix, then, went to the telephone, called his office, and asked that a wench truck come to Phil's Place. 'Back it up to the front door,'" he said. "When the truck arrived, my father got up, put his gloves on (that he always carried in his hip pocket) and hooked the wench line through the door to the juke box. He told the driver to 'haul ass' and pull the juke box out the front door and down the street," says Jack. "He did!"

Another instance happened at insurance renewal time. Jack had taken the representative to visit several rig sites via a float plane so the man could tour the equipment. While there, he served lunch. Upon return, McClanahan asked how he liked the tour. The man's comment was that it was nice and interesting, "But on Rig No. 8, where we ate, the best thing was the upside down pineapple cake."

"Without saying a word, my father got up, put on his hat, walked out the door, got in the car and drove off. Later, though, he came back. My father had gotten on the float plane, went out to the jobsite and fired the cook. When asked why he did it, my father said he didn't want any more cakes. They can have cookies. They can put cookies in their pockets and eat one while working. With cakes, they have to stop working..." laughs Jack.

A story written shortly after Felix's death summed up the well-known oilman. "...Few men have enjoyed the genuine love and warmth with which he was regarded by many hundreds of people—employees, business associates, and those he had known through religious, civic, and social activities.

"He was a very human individual—a man who often hid his concern for others behind a rough exterior. He had a high regard for the dignity and worth of the individual and no person or problem was too insignificant to merit his attention and sympathy. He stood for the principles of fair play, honesty, trust, and the value of a man's word—principles that built his industry and country, but that are often forgotten in the computerized age..."

The year 1973, with part ownership of Duquesne, the McClanahans acquired the barge rigs of Service Contracting (SCI). By 1976 the newest company was ready to expand again, splitting AWI from Duquesne Natural Gas. The McClanahans then, disposed of the remainder of Duquesne Natural Gas, forming different entities consisting of gas compressors (that pull natural gas from a well in single or dual stages, and compress it into a gas-gathering system, which goes into a gas pipeline), truck lines, and Duquesne also had subsidiaries of vacuum trucks, reclamation plants, and pump manufacturing.

During the years, 1978-79, the family built several more barge rigs including twin barges named after Felix—the *Barge FE* and *Barge Sarge*. These super barges can handle thirty thousand feet, where others can only handle 10,000-12,000 feet. Still growing in 1980, the McClanahans acquired Mayronne Company's four barge rigs. A year later, another acquisition provided fifty percent ownership in Matagorda Drilling, with thirteen barge rigs. By 1982, they were ready to expand their holdings again and began a production company under the name of Aransas Drilling & Workover. Ten years later, in 1992, they sold part of AWI to investors; but continued to enlarge the production company through acquisition of several wells, and the drilling of several more.

In 1994, Jack merged AWI into Energy Ventures Company, continuing family involvement. Today, Jack is president and director, Kelly Yeager is in charge of operations, and Elizabeth D. McClanahan is a director. Kelly's responsibilities have her traveling between the home office in Corpus Christi, Texas, and Louisiana every week. Jack

helped his son, Jack C. at twenty-five, negotiate and work out the financing for the purchase of a small rig company in 1996, which now flowed to third generation involvement. Since then, Jack C. has built the company into a land and barge company.

As president, Jack has continued many "firsts" as his father did. He put the first treatment unit on barges, put the first remote station, was first with flood lights and mercury vapor lights on rigs, first with self-powered pumps, first with two-tiered head-ache racks, and first with blow out preventers (BOP) catwalks.

When Helen Edith McClanahan passed away in 1999, it left a void in the multi-generational enterprises. Yet, the next generations were up to the challenge because the founders had been the greats of the oil and gas industry. Today, they carry on the legacy left them from truly dedicated, responsible, and intelligent parents and grandparents.

While directing the McClanahans' business, Jack has been heavily involved in environmental issues such as protecting wetlands as they pertain to the gas and oil industry. As secretary of natural resources, his exit (or white paper), prepared for the State of Louisiana and signed by The Honorable Edwin W. Edwards, governor, said the loss of the state's coastal wetlands is a national catastrophe.

"At the present loss rate, we will, within fifteen years, start relocating coastal communities inland with dramatic socioeconomic impacts to the state. While restoration funds have been available since 1990, they are declining," he states.

In the 1995 document he proposed a number of major policy initiatives. Among them are:

• Develop the state's gameplan—The State should undertake a unified, sustainable economic development, coastal restoration plan with its primary focus on the restoration of the natural land building process.

• Assume leadership for fiscal responsibility—Fiscal responsibility must be a prerequisite in the building of restoration projects. Unlimited cost overruns should not be allowed to deplete the State's Wetlands Trust Fund.

- Generate additional funding mechanisms—Additional state funding must be obtained to use for a federal matching grant. This applies to all potential federal funding sources, including the Coastal Wetlands Planning, Protection, and Restoration Act (CWPPRA). He cited this is mandatory in order to gain the public's confidence and support necessary to increase state funding.

- Refine the state's administration—The Department of Natural Resources (DNR) should address any shortcomings in its operations and make the necessary staff, infrastructure, and contractual changes to establish an efficient project management Process. He proposed other state agencies working together to resolve land rights and oyster lease issues.

- Revise the project screening, evaluation, and selection process—With limited resources, the state will stick to the phased approach of its Gameplan and resist pressure from special interest groups to further their own projects. To counter this, he proposes that the state develop detailed scientific and engineering-based project selection criteria. He further suggests that all projects undergo this project.

- Secure funding for maintenance of Federal Navigation Banks—Separate federal funding streams for the maintenance of federal navigation channel banks should be identified.

The family's industry involvement continues as it did in the early days. Jack is, or has been, a member of the Harvey Canal Industrial Association, International Association of Drilling Contractors, Jefferson Parish Coastal Zone Management Citizens Advisory Committee, Louisiana Association of Independent Procedures and Royalty Owners, Louisiana Oil and Gas Association (LOGA), Louisiana State Mineral Board, member and chairman; Louisiana Wildlife Federation, National Association of Manufacturers, Secretary of the Louisiana Department of Natural Resources, Greater New Orleans Chamber of Commerce and U.S. Chamber of Commerce, Texas

Independent Producers and Royalty Owners Association, and West Jefferson Levee Board, and Industrial Advisory Board at Rose Hulman College.

Other memberships include the Algiers Irish Association, Algiers United Methodist Church, American Scottish Association, Boaz Social Club, Delta Shrine Club, Ducks Unlimited, Jerusalem Temple New Orleans, Road Runners unit of Jerusalem Temple of New Orleans, Royal Order of Jesters New Orleans Court No. 36, Safari Club International, Saints John Lodge No. 153, Selective Service Board, Timberlane Country Club, and Valley of New Orleans Scottish Rite.

Jack continues the philanthropy that his parents began. "As of the 1990s, the McClanahans contributions have helped many deserving students gain an education in parochial schools and colleges. "We think it is important to give back to the communities that have been so good to us; but, we don't like to make a big deal about it."

Delta Gulf Rental Tool Company is located in Amelia, Louisiana, at 302 Ford Industrial Road and in Corpus Christi, Texas, at 130 Gilliam Street and operated by President Jack McClanahan and Vice President Kelly McClanahan Yeager.

Above: Delta Gulf Rental Tool Company is operated by President Jack McClanahan and Vice President Kelly McClanahan Yeager pictured above.

KNIGHT OIL TOOLS

In an industry known for big thinkers and even bigger personalities, you would find no better example than entrepreneur and eccentric Eddy Knight, founder of Knight Oil Tools. The history of Knight Oil Tools is one of risk, determination, and success that parallels the rise of the Louisiana oil and gas industry over the last fifty years. From humble beginnings to a multinational enterprise spanning a full range of oilfield-related services, Knight Oil Tools has grown and adapted to meet the needs of an ever-changing industry.

Eddy attended Louisiana Tech and graduated from Centenary College with a degree in commerce. The degree provided him with a well-rounded education of business, but it was his love and passion for this energetic industry that opened the door to his dynamic career.

Eddy entered the oil and gas industry as a sales representative for Midcontinent Supply Company. In 1962 he left that company after proving his competence in sales, and joined Drilco where he moved up the ladder to sales manager within nine years. There he was named "Outstanding Salesman" every year from 1962-1971. After fifteen years of successful business experience, he was determined to form his own company, doing so in 1972. Known as Knight Specialties, his auto became his office, with the family garage and backyard, his inventory storage areas. Later that year, he opened the company's first official stock point in Morgan City, Louisiana. A few years after becoming more established, he moved his young family to Lafayette, Louisiana, and the company's headquarters to the current campus on Evangeline Freeway.

He grew the business, and expanded operations into Texas in 1976 when he opened Knight and Philips Specialties in Houston. That same year, he formed Harmon Rentals in Kilgore, Texas, and Knight and Philips Rental Co. in Oklahoma.

All the while Eddy was concerned with growth and diversification, he never failed to share a laugh with his friends and neighbors. Out on Highway 90, in front of the company headquarters, those who passed by never knew what they might see next. He took pride in decorating company equipment, putting it on display for all to see. He painted annular blowout preventers to look like colorful Easter Eggs; and field tanks red, white, and blue with stars for the Fourth of July! Regular travelers on the highway came to expect a weekly update of Eddy's humorous oilfield observations, and they were seldom disappointed.

The growth of Knight Oil Holdings is a history of success. In 1983 he acquired Douglas Oil Tools in Louisiana, Point Blank Rental Tools in Texas, and American Rental Tools in Oklahoma. In 1984 he merged operations into what is known today as

Knight Oil Tools. The company continued to flourish, and in 1996, Eddy acquired Robinson Tubular Services. Also, he began Knight Fishing Services in 1999. During the next three years, he acquired Tri*Drill Services, Prideco Rentals, and Myco Rentals. Today, the operations for Rental Tool Services, Fishing Services, Well Services, Manufacturing, Tri*Drill Services, and Advance Safety share the umbrella of Knight Oil Tools.

Knight Oil Tools' Fishing Services business unit provides the industry with a complete line of fishing tools and services with advanced mills, cutters and casing exit systems, in addition to other fishing tools—many manufactured by Knight Oil Tools' Manufacturing business unit. This capability ensures quality outcome every time. That is due to the company's management and technical personnel who have a vast experience base, providing expertise from deepwater to land operations. Each member of the core management group has more than twenty-five years' fishing experience.

The company's manufacturing business unit consists of a team of well-trained machine specialists, extensive product capability and a commitment to service. Through the acquisition of Hub City Iron Works, it has a long tradition of providing innovative tools and solutions, with a commitment to excellence in quality and safety—all embedded in the culture of Knight Oil Tools. The unit fabricates tools used in drilling and workovers, including surface equipment, downhole tools, whipstocks, subs and various fishing tools.

The Tri*Drill Services business unit is a leading provider of non-destructive inspection and casing-friendly hardbanding for drill pipe, tubing, bottom hole assembly components and heavy lift and handling equipment. Along with inspecting and hardbanding, Tri*Drill Services also offers customers pipe maintenance and storage.

As a recognized leader in safety training and preparedness, Tri*Drill Services has implemented in-house training to prepare employees to safely handle every situation, from tool preparation to environmental issues, requiring AMSE Section Nine safety certification. The unit works hand-in-hand with Knight Oil Tools' Advanced Safety business

Opposite, top: The first stock point in Morgan City.

Opposite, bottom: Eddy and Ann Knight at the company's ten year anniversary party held at the Sheraton Acadiana Hotel, where 900 guests from ten states were greeted by mounted knights.

Below: The corporate office building ribbon cutting ceremony, March 2006. Mark Knight is second from left followed by Ann Knight, Kelley Knight Sobiesk, and Bryan Knight (second from right).

A truck being loaded with drill pipe at Knight Oil Tool's Lafayette pipe yard.

unit, which specializes in building custom safety and training programs, safety inspection, and comprehensive consulting services to meet customer needs in the oilfield, communications/tower, utility, construction, food, and manufacturing industries.

Knight Oil Tools' Well Services business unit provides plug and abandonment (offshore, land, and inland waterways) and services across the Gulf Coast. Offshore services include plug and abandonment (P&A) of wells, temporary abandonment of wells, removal of wells and structures, sidetrack preparation, slot recoveries, project engineering and management, flush and removal of pipelines, preparing and submitting state/federal permits, surface equipment removal and salvage, saw services and casing jacks.

Knight Oil Tools' inland water plug and abandonment equipment consists of a 30-by-120-foot self-sufficient P&A barge, *Miss Ann*, with a 10-by-18-foot keyway, 12-man living quarters with galley, 40-ton hydraulic crane with an 80-foot telescoping boom, and a satellite phone and wireless Internet.

Today, under the stewardship of Eddy's son, Mark, Knight Oil Tools is a growing worldwide company dedicated to excellence, integrity and leadership through safety and quality. The company-wide atmosphere creates value for its employees and clients through innovation, technology, and operational expertise. Knight Oil Tools is committed to excellence in quality and a major emphasis on safety in everything it does. It strives to provide the highest quality products and services to meet the requirements of clients through efficient use of processes and resources. All employees are involved in the Quality Management improvement system, its products, processes and services. According to President Mark Knight, "This promotes safety, quality, competency, leadership, and teamwork. Recordable incidents are far below the national average, and that's a fact of which we are extremely proud."

Knight Oil Tools' fully computerized inventory system allows for full accountability and global tracking of its equipment. With its unique Quality Management System, clients feel secure knowing that each tool has been tested and every employee has been adequately trained.

A major player in the success of Knight Oil Tools is Eddy's wife, Ann Rinchuso Knight. The couple wed in Shreveport in 1955 when Eddy first started working in the oil industry. They became the parents of Mark, Bryan and Kelley (Sobiesk), and the grandparents of seven. Because they felt that education was important to success, they established an education fund for employees' children, which continues today. No matter how new the employee, his or her child is eligible for a scholarship each and every semester of undergraduate studies as long as they are fulltime students. Today, more than $200,000 in scholarships has been awarded.

Knight Oil Tools and the Knight family continue the tradition begun forty years ago by Eddy. The changing demands of the oil and gas industry have been instrumental in defining the focus of the service companies—from the single business line of yesteryear—to the multi-service lines of today. To remain current with demands of the industry, the company continually broadens its abilities and technologies, both domestically and internationally, through internal growth, well-executed acquisitions, and the enhancement of its manufacturing capabilities. Remaining constant throughout the company's growth is its commitment to providing zero failure equipment and service.

In 2013, Knight Oil Tools will be servicing oil and gas operators on six continents through facilities in North America, South America, Europe, North Africa, Middle East, Asia, and Australia.

The company's forty-year-history is quite impressive. Below is a timetable showing the growth of Knight Oil Tools:

- February 1972, Knight Specialties opened in Morgan City, Louisiana.
- March 1975, Knight Specialties moves to Lafayette, Louisiana.
- February 1976, Knight and Philips opened in Houston, Texas.
- June 1980, Knight and Philips opened in Alice, Texas.
- February 1982, Knight celebrated its tenth anniversary.
- September 1984, Knight Oil Tools is founded.
- February 1987, Knight Oil Tools celebrated its fifteenth anniversary.
- February 1997, Knight Oil Tools celebrated its twenty-fifth anniversary.
- September 1997, Knight Oil Tools opened in Farmington, New Mexico.
- November 1998, Knight Oil Tools opened in Odessa, Texas.
- April 1999, Knight Oil Tools' Fishing Services business unit was founded.
- April 1999, Fishing Services opened its Gulf Coast facility.
- October 1999, Fishing Services expanded to Permian Basin.
- January 2000 Fishing Services expanded to the San Juan Basin.
- January 2001, Fishing Services expanded to Rocky Mountains.
- May 2001, Knight Oil Tools opened in Vernal, Utah and Rock Springs, Wyoming.
- June 2001, Knight Oil Tools opened in Riverton, Wyoming.
- May 2003, Knight Oil Tools Well Services introduced Foam Units.

- February 2004, Well Services launched the *Miss Ann*.
- April 2004, Fishing Services celebrated its fifth anniversary.
- June 2004, Fishing Services expanded to Hobbs, New Mexico.
- June 2004, manufacturing developed quite/cleaner pipe cleaning machine.
- July 2004, Fishing Services introduced Knight Oil Tools Advantage.
- November 2004, Knight Oil Tools opened new Rock Springs, Wyoming facility.
- April 2011, Knight Oil Tools acquired Cool Group, Ltd in Aberdeen, Scotland.
- January 2012, Knight Oil Tools International launched.
- July 2012, Knight Oil Tools acquired Tri-State Tools & Inspection.

Eddy was an active leader in his church, community and industry. In fact, Knight Hall at Our Lady of Fatima Church in Lafayette was dedicated to the Knight family in appreciation for its continuing generous support of the parish. He served on numerous boards and committees, and was instrumental in raising more than $500,000 as chairman of the Bishop's Charity Ball. In addition, he was an Eagle Scout in the Boy Scouts of America, and was awarded the Boy Scouts' Beaver Award in 2001. He also helped build the first Boy Scout camp in Acadiana. In 2008 his wife, Ann, was named the Lafayette Civic Cup recipient as one of the city's most influential leaders. The Knight family continues philanthropy begun by its founder. Eddy passed away in 2002, but his legacy is carried on by the twelve-hundred-plus employees who today call the South Louisiana-based company home.

The corporate headquarters in Lafayette.

MONCLA COMPANIES

The oil industry was just beginning to thrive when, in 1942, Cecil Guinn moved his family from Monroe, Louisiana to begin a career in that state's famous oilfield in Jennings.

Clockwise, starting from the top:

Cecil Guinn in front of a pickup truck, rig, and a swab truck at the Pelican Well Service Facility in Lafayette, 1961.

Virginia Guinn with a brand new 1,000 hp twenty-four hour workover rig on display at the 1981 Louisiana Gulf Coast Oil Exposition (LAGCOE).

Cecil and Virginia Guinn with their grandson, Mike Moncla at the Pelican Well Service office in 1972.

When WWII broke out, he, and his identical twin brother Carl, wanted to sign up for active duty. Carl ended up in the Air Force; however, due to Cecil's perforated ear drum, he could not pass his entrance physical. He was upset about not being able to fight for his country, but another brother Earl, pastor at the First Baptist Church in Jennings, consoled Cecil, convincing him that the war efforts needed oil to support tanks and planes, and that the oilfield would make him feel a part of the war effort. Earl found Cecil a job with National Supply where he worked for five years in Jennings before being transferred to Houma.

While in Houma, he accepted a sales position with Garret Oil Tools, which later became Otis Oil Tools. After spending three years in Houma, he was transferred to Lafayette by Otis. It was in Lafayette that he saw an opportunity as an entrepreneur to own his own business. In 1957, Cecil bought his first workover rig and named his business Pelican Well Service after Louisiana's state bird. A workover rig, unlike a drilling rig, is more mobile and much smaller. While drilling rigs drill new wells for oil companies in hopes of finding oil or gas,

workover rigs work on the oil companies' existing wells that, for one reason or another, has either declined in production of oil and gas, or the oil or gas has totally stopped flowing. There are several types of well site jobs that workover rigs perform: workovers, completions, rod jobs, re-entries, sidetracks, and plug and abandonments.

Pelican's reputation was second to none in servicing the oil companies of Louisiana, and by the mid-70s Pelican had grown to ten land rigs and two swab trucks. In 1971, Cecil hired his son-in-law, Charlie Moncla. Charlie assumed by the family relationship, that he would have a nice office job, but upon arriving on his first day of work, Cecil pointed toward a hard hat, steel-toe boots, and a pair of coveralls. Cecil stated, "The best way to learn this business is by working on the rigs." Charlie spent about two years working on the rigs, before moving into safety, and later, sales. Cecil always described the workover rig business as "the janitors that had to go clean up wells, to make them flow again."

In 1977, Cecil was diagnosed with cancer and passed away shortly thereafter. His wife, Virginia took over as president of the company with, Charlie Moncla moving up to vice president. From 1977-1987, Virginia grew Pelican to four 1,000 hp 24-hour rigs, one 24-hour barge rig, 11 daylight rigs and two swab trucks, and employed 200 at its highest point. Virginia Guinn was a true pioneer as a female in the oil business, running a rig company through the ups-and-downs of the late 70s, 80s and early 90s before selling the rigs in 1992.

In 1984, Charlie Moncla went out on his own buying one rig, and by his tenth year in business, was running seven rigs. Charlie never liked the connotation of Cecil's janitor example, so he passed down to his children that, "we are the doctors of the oilfield, and our rigs fix broken and sick wells!" In 1993, Charlie hired his son Mike to handle sales and marketing. Three years later, and after adding three more rigs, Charlie hired his brother, Buck, and his second son, Marc (Spook). For the next 11 years (1996-2007) Moncla added 43 rigs. During that time, Charlie also added his brother Cain, son Matt, and nephews, Andrew and Ben. It became a running joke that every time Charlie added a new family member to the company; he had to add four or five rigs to pay for their cost. Also, in the same fashion as Cecil had done to Charlie, each family member had to work a week on each rig to learn the equipment and meet the entire rig personnel. The family members that came later than others jokingly complained that they had to work longer on the rigs, since so many more rigs had been added. There were a total of eight Monclas in the business, but all employees were considered family, to which the Moncla successes can be attributed. During those 11 years of growth, Moncla Companies made 11 acquisitions of local companies, and became the largest independent workover rig company in the United States. Moncla was headquartered in Lafayette, with offices in Sour Lake, Texas, and Sandersville, Mississippi. The Sour Lake yard was acquired through the purchase of Petroleum Well Service, and the yard covered the Texas Railroad District Three area. Through several acquisitions, Moncla became the largest workover company in Mississippi, marketing 14 rigs out of the Sandersville yard and covering the Mississippi, Alabama, and Florida areas. In Louisiana, Moncla was known for its fleet of 1,000 hp rigs that handled deep workovers, and their ability to work smaller daylight rigs on a 24-hour basis. Through the years Moncla also accumulated 40 rig hauling trucks that moved rig equipment from well-to-well. The company also diversified into other facets of the oilfield as part of that growth.

The demand to put land rigs on keyway barges for customers was tremendous, in some years having five land rigs on barges the entire year. So, in 2001 they constructed and christened their first fully fledged 24-hour inland barge rig, *The Stingray*, which accompanied *The Moccasin*, a daylight barge rig Moncla acquired from the acquisition of Harris Well Service (Harris had been a competitor since the Pelican days of the 1950s). By 2007, this subsidiary, Moncla Marine, also became the largest in the U.S. with eight workover barge rigs, all named for indigenous reptiles or fish of south Louisiana.

In 2003, Moncla acquired Louisiana Swabbing that catapulted them into the swabbing business. This subsidiary was named Brother's Oilfield Service & Supply (BOSS), and it furnished swab trucks, tubing testing units, hot oil trucks, anchor trucks, power swivel rentals and mud system rentals. In 2005, the company also started Moncla Drilling and converted two of its 24-hour workover rigs into drilling rigs and signed long-term contracts in the Barnett Shale near Fort Worth, Texas, and southwest Mississippi.

Above: Charlie Moncla on the cover of Well Servicing *magazine as he served as the 2002 national president of the Association of Energy Service Companies.*

Below: "The Moncla Boys" from left to right, Mike, Matt, Marc, and Buck in 2012 at their new facility on the Breaux Bridge Highway.

Moncla's yard on I-10 north near the University exit in Lafayette, was a familiar landmark with a huge American flag painted on the roof of the trucking building. It was at this twenty-acre facility that Moncla drilled a training well down to 4,000 feet, and began a new hire training school called the "U of Krewe". Here, hundreds of new employees were able to learn, in not only a classroom setting, but in actual on-the-job training, the safest and best way to be a part of a rig crew.

Moncla's most important asset was its loyal employees, many who dated back to the Pelican days. It was only by the expertise of the employees that Moncla was able to handle the many high profile jobs from sidetracking wells in the Florida Everglades, to high pressure completions 100 yards away from I-10, or from working for the U.S. government at the strategic petroleum reserve, to working in environmentally sensitive Federal Game Reserves. Due to the proximity to the Mississippi River, several large industrial plants transport products via ships from the Baton Rouge and New Orleans areas. These plants also have injection wells and storage wells that commonly have to be tested and worked on by workover rigs. Probably the oddest job in the history of workover rigs was done by Moncla in the early '90s when a fire at a Baton Rouge plant melted away the standard derricks atop of the 150-foot coke battery (see photograph). The Moncla rig was lifted by crane, set on a platform above the battery, and used to wash out these batteries, so that the battery could be disassembled and rebuilt for future use.

In 2007, at the peak of Moncla's growth, the family felt the time was right to sell the business. In November of that year, Moncla sold to Key Energy. Key was the largest workover company in the world at the time, and Moncla's reputation, its 53 rigs, and its 1,000 employees was a perfect fit to Key Energy's southeastern U.S. division. Charlie worked for Key in the corporate office in Houston throughout the transition period, while Charlie's family remained in Lafayette to run Key's southeastern division. After about two years of working at Key Energy in Lafayette, Mike, Marc, Matt, and Buck approached Key management about buying the barge fleet and the BOSS Company back from Key Energy. Negotiations were concluded and "the Moncla boys" (which is how they were mostly referred) bought back Moncla Marine and BOSS in May 2010. The third generation had successfully rejuvenated the family workover rig business that their family had been in for nearly six decades. "The rig business is just in our blood", said Mike Moncla. In the same timeframe as their purchase, the oil industry was suffering through its worst environmental disaster in history, the famous BP Macondo blowout and spill. Luckily, the inland water

activity was increased as the Obama administration's ban on offshore drilling, shifted oil companies' budgets to inland waters and land projects. In opportunistic fashion, "The Moncla boys" also went international for the first time in the family's history sending a drilling rig to Belize, Central America. Learning from their previous experiences in growing a business, the Monclas were soon on the same growth path as before acquiring the barge rig fleet from Tetra Technologies in 2012, adding to Moncla's fleet as the largest workover barge company in the U.S. In their first two-year span in business, they purchased 10 land rigs at auctions in preparation for getting back into the south Louisiana land market, opening Moncla Workover & Drilling in May of 2012. Also in December of 2012, Moncla diversified into the electric wireline market opening Moncla E-Line Services. Then in 2013, they signed the first long-term contract in their family's history and entered the offshore platform rig market in Alaska, creating Moncla Offshore. The Moncla companies were headquartered on the Breaux Bridge Highway.

The family, synonymous with workovers in Louisiana, awaits the arrival of the oncoming fourth generation to take over its legacy...

Opposite, top: Charlie Moncla Christening The Redfish Barge Rig #106 in 2005 in Abbeville, Louisiana.

Opposite, bottom: Perhaps the oddest job in the history of the workovers! Moncla Rig #8 in 1993 in a Baton Rouge plant atop a coke tower 150 feet high.

Above: The Gator Barge Rig #103 working in Quarantine Bay in 2012.

VERMILION RIVER TOOL & EQUIPMENT CO., INC.

VERTECO

The VERTECO crew.

One young boy from the south shore of Ohio's Lake Erie, which he refers to as the most industrialized area on earth at the time, grew up surrounded by technical and industrial surroundings. Today, that man—David L. Sipos—has switched locations and career paths while still embracing his first love: tool design.

He is now CEO, CCO, and board chairman of Vermilion River Tool & Equipment Co., Inc., better known in the gas and oil industry as VERTECO. Sipos recalls his earlier life, prior to the days in the energy field. "I grew up with the smell of machine shops in my nose and metal chips stuck to the soles of my shoes. Tool design was my first vocation, and continues to be my first love," says the father of six and grandfather of seven, who never finished college, yet has accumulated twenty-seven patents with more pending. When it comes to tools, if the best does not exist, he designs it himself.

His early exposure to tool design came naturally. His father was also an innovator,

designing tools for his employers. His mother was an artist. Sipos combined the inherited talents of both parents and came out a winner in his own right. His father taught him how to work on cars and guns at an early age. Even though he has made his living in the design of tools for the oil and gas industry, he continues his love of fine cars, as well as a fifty-year appreciation of guns. In fact, his gun collection today includes a variety of firearms from Smith, Colt, Winchester, and Browning. An early knowledge of and respect for automobiles was passed on to Sipos by his father. His vehicle collection today includes what he terms as "future classics."

As a self-taught tool designer, he went to work fresh out of high school as a draftsman and tool designer. He says he was so busy doing what he loved that he never had time for college. He taught himself and learned on the job while working for various companies, primarily factories, in Ohio. His first patent was for a hand-held shower head, designed for Moen in the late 1960s.

He admits to always having a "latent desire" to move to a warmer climate. Having read about the oil and gas industry, he became enamored with the South's petroleum country. That industry eventually lured him to Texas, where he spent fifteen years in "Oil Patch Houston." Eventually, though, he migrated to Lafayette, Louisiana to continue his oil tool design trade. He spent the rest of his career there, working for Reed Rock Bit, Peck-O-Matic Tongs, Bowen Tools, Hydra-Rig, Franks Casing, and even operated a business of his own—Tasmanian Tool Co. before his retirement in 2004.

In Lafayette, he designed and built the world's first 1,000-ton Flush Mount Spider (FMS), a tool used to grip large casing strings in deep water oil and gas exploration. He also developed a unique gripping die configuration known as the "Shallow Vee" Die. His oil and gas clients call him "the Einstein of flush-mounted spiders," a designation noted in a recent opinion of the Louisiana Third Circuit Court of Appeals (a designation of which he is quite proud).

As many individuals do, Sipos was looking forward to early retirement and the leisure it afforded. After selling Tasmanian Tool Co., Inc., which he founded in 2001, even with hobbies of fine automobiles and an extensive gun collection, he was bored. "After three weeks of retirement, I thought I would go nuts. I knew, then, that I was happiest when I was busy."

After talking with several friends, they decided to start a company to design and build custom oil tools, Thus, Vermilion River Tool & Equipment Co., Inc., better known as VERTECO was born in 2004. He and Preston Guidry were the original founders but were later joined by Alvin Meche, Jr., and Jesse Fike, with whom Sipos had worked in

the past. Each brought their area of expertise to the company table. Meche, who is known as "Junior" provided the sales contacts that allowed VERTECO to be in business, and Guidry contributed his solid business planning experience.

"With the industry knowledge and expertise of Meche and Fike's," Sipos says, "We got off to a good start very quickly. Another friend, Harry Webb, did the computer-aided design (CAD) work, purchasing, vendor interface, the assembly and painting. He did just about anything else that came up," Sipos says, reminiscing.

He says these oilfield tools VERTECO designs are the first for the industry in the twenty-first century. "Every tool for the past fifty or more years has been a copy of the original which are out-of-date designs. We are developing new designs based on the special needs of customers in the oil industry. As their needs change, so do the tools they need. That's where our design expertise comes into play."

This is a photograph of the original employees, left to right: Dave Sipos, Harry Webb and Alvin Meche, Jr.

Harry was the first full-time, permanent employee. He was joined shortly thereafter by Dr. Mike Elsayed, a University of Louisiana at Lafayette (ULL) professor. He is responsible for all of the engineering review and finite element analysis (FEAs) from day one. "The role he plays, like those of Harry and Junior, cannot be overstated," adds Sipos. "Without Junior's contacts in the 'Oil Patch' and Preston's invaluable business acumen, we may never have made it as a fledgling business." Sipos refers to himself as the chief creative officer as well as the CEO. "But, we each have significant input into the design process."

year law suit brought by a former employer. In the end, though, we prevailed. Today, our tools have an enviable reputation in the industry marketplace for original design, strength and durability."

When VERTECO got its first customer, Sipos decided not to replicate the original designs. Instead, he told the customers if they wanted VERTECO to build tools for them, "It will be the best tool I know how to build." And, that is what he does. Sipos custom designs every tool with a specific purpose in mind. "It can take as little as a week, or as long as a year," he adds.

500 TON / 2.25 S.F.

Thirty days after opening the office, which was provided gratis by Guidry, Offshore Energy Services (OES) gave us our first order. "While we were off to a good start, our progress was marred somewhat by a five

Initially, the first tools produced under the VERTECO banner had some glitches; so Sipos and Webb worked around the clock to get them running properly. He and Webb did just about everything from basic design to painting to testing once they received the customer's purchase order until they delivered the tool. The usual time, though, is two to twelve weeks.

Originally, VERTECO relied on local shops to supply parts. Since then, several vendors were founded to meet the company's needs. Occasionally, VERTECO purchased machines for, and leased them at a low rate, so some suppliers could meet the demand for parts. Recently, though, all shops are busy; and, with deadline pressures, VERTECO has started its own shop—Industrial Parkway Machine Works.

In eight short years, VERTECO has grown into a profitable company, with clients throughout the United States and abroad. Even with a tough global economy, neither VERTECO nor Sipos show any signs of slowing down. Located on Lafayette's Industrial Parkway, VERTECO continues to grow with eleven employees. The first year the company recorded sales of about $90,000. Before the Gulf was shut down, it had revenues of $15 million. Sipos says that domestic sales continue to grow and foreign sales are increasing.

He sees his beloved "oil patch" as getting busy. That is good for the company and good for Sipos. Neither seems to be slowing down, he says. "When business is good for VERTECO, it is good for Acadiana. VERTECO has eight satellite machine shops that build the company's tools. Seven of the shops are in the Acadiana area. He points out that ninety percent of VERTECO's business is located in-and-around the Acadiana area. "This is where I live. This is where the money stays," he adds, "Even though we could make more money overseas, I think it makes good business sense to keep the work here. When we keep work here, that means jobs are here for the people who reside here. It is a two-way street: They are good for the company and we believe in helping those who are loyal to the company. We do that by supporting local charities such as the Lafayette Community Health Clinic and the Skyliners, a swing band, which performs at the Petroleum Club."

While Sipos is not working, tinkering with his cars or guns, he and his wife of more than thirty years, Donna, are enjoying dining out or traveling. Their children are scattered around the United States so traveling takes up a good bit of his life. He admits that, while not born in Lafayette, he has found it to be the "land of milk and honey" for him, his wife and his new company.

Previously, VERTECO's emphasis has been on off-shore tools. Currently, with the new company, it has added premium smaller tools for the land market. "We plan to expand our machine shop to meet customers' needs. As we become better known in our field, we expect growth rates of thirty to fifty percent per year for the foreseeable future. We continue to include as much local content as is possible in our tools. Historically, local content has been more than ninety-five percent," Sipos concludes.

VERTECO is located at 157 Industrial Parkway in Lafayette and on the Internet at www.vermilionrivertool.com.

Surviving founders: Preston Guidry, Dave Sipos, and Alvin Meche, Jr.

VALVEWORKS USA

After a successful seventeen year career in the oil and gas (O&G) products business, Richard "Rick" Roberts founded Valveworks USA in 1994. The former cost accountant entered the O&G business when he joined WKM Wellhead Systems, one of the top three wellhead companies in the industry (along with Cameron and FMC). Until 1982 he had worked primarily in the plant and field services group which allowed him to gain valuable experience in the wellhead business throughout the nation.

In 1977, in the heart of the first O&G boom, he witnessed product backlogs for up to three years duration. Then, when the industry experienced the crash of 1981, and Penn Square Bank failed due to bad loans made without the proper collateral within the industry, he took note. He says that seventy-five percent of all employees within the industry lost their jobs. "That was a difficult period for many of us. Oil reached a low of $8 per barrel." It was then, however, that Rick made up his mind to change gears and became the controller of a small, independent multi-division wellhead service company—Custom Wellhead Services—where he fought the industry downturn.

Within the next two years, business for service companies was extremely limited, and inventories were ten times what anyone required. Because the supply was greater than the demand, Rick determined that it would be more lucrative to wholesale the excess inventory to friendly competitors than

it would be to compete for business where there was not enough to go around. Sadly, with growth in the new wholesale business and demand for machinery and capacity amidst strict banking policies and restructuring, the newly organized wholesale company fell prey to bankruptcy in 1991; and, the company was the target of a takeover by outside entities in 1993, leaving Rick to start over with zero assets—but zero debt.

When Rick began Valveworks as a valve parts wholesale company, it was initially a one-man operation. He drew upon his customer base during his seventeen year tenure with Wellhead Systems. Primarily, he was engaged in the repair of the huge volume of used equipment being refurbished during the oilfield downtimes. At this time, the service, support and attention paid to the needs of the struggling companies generated much-needed business, which grew rapidly on a daily basis. Attention to profit-and-growth (P&G) allowed the business to prosper without outside influence or debt. A huge helping hand was lent by Ron Holtby of Holtby Enterprises in Shreveport, who gave Rick space to operate and serve his customer base. Ron's support and encouragement to Rick's efforts proved "invaluable," he says.

During this difficult time in the oil and gas industry, many companies moved to Houston, Texas, but, Rick thought that his success would come from staying close to the support of his wife (he and Sherry Spataro have been married thirty-six years) and family and the

Bottom, left: Valveworks-India.

Bottom, right: Hydraulic fracturing using big-bore high-pressure Valveworks valves.

Louisiana area with which he was familiar. The decision to stay home in Louisiana, helped Valveworks achieve the success it would come to enjoy.

In 1994, Ed Stinson joined Valveworks USA as its first employee. Ed began working for Valveworks without the assurance of pay just the promise if the company generated revenue, he would receive compensation. Ed remains with the company today. Rick's brother-in-law, Kirk Spataro, who had worked in the wellhead service business since 1993, was a crucial addition. He, too, is still with the company.

In 1998, Brian Furqueron from Plain Dealing, Louisiana, the son of Rick's sister Donna Furqueron, joined the company as Rick's right hand, and later, became vice president of marketing and played a vital role in the expansion and success of Valveworks USA.

Todd and Lauren Roberts.

Gwen Sanders from local Sibley, Louisiana, joined Rick, adding to his work ethic, providing a hands-on service to customers. Together, their efforts proved that hard work pays off when Valveworks moved into a 175,000-square-foot property at Swan Lake Road, Bossier City, Louisiana. Recently, the company added a 155,000-square-foot warehouse at 5007 Hazel Jones Road in Bossier City. The addition increases the company's total operating areas to four hundred thousand square feet. The Hazel Jones Road facility is approximately 1.5 miles from the company's Swan Lake Road location. The facility is being used for receiving operations, special processes, and the warehousing of Valveworks' extensive levels of inventory. "It is a valuable addition to our operations as we expand and increase our overall business. It is especially helpful for our frac valve product line by giving us more space to store and inspect product, and stage production jobs for our Swan Lake Road assembly plant," says owner and president, Rick Roberts.

The valve parts success of Valveworks and the size of its inventory, led to the success of the company's ability to provide a quality of complete gate valves with a range not available by other competitors and customers who produce their own valves. Valveworks covers every size, working pressure, temperature class and trim class within the API 6A range of products.

Rick's son, Todd, a graduate of Louisiana Tech with a mechanical engineering degree, joined Valveworks in 2010, and changed the Valveworks' product line from old school to a proprietary engineered, verified product, proven throughout the world within all conditions. Rick's daughter, Lauren, is an economics major at Louisiana Tech scheduled to graduate in May 2013. Advance plans are that she will secure a master's degree at Louisiana State University (LSU).

Valveworks USA recently earned the PED accreditation from TUV SUD Industries Service GmbH (a pressure equipment directive notified body) and is certified to "CE" mark gate valves and safety valves up to, and including, Category III. The certification allows Valveworks USA to expand its reach into more specialized European markets where CE markings are required along with API 6A requirements. Valveworks USA is working diligently on a daily basis to meet the needs of its customer base; and listens carefully to their requirements.

Rick attributes the success of Valveworks to the company's objective of staying ahead of the competition on quality. When Valveworks was founded, the downturn of the oil and gas market had brought about a total usage of manufactured, refurbished, old, and used equipment. The risk and liability associated with the use of this equipment was a major issue for the higher end operators. Higher quality standards for equipment were becoming much more important, along with full tracability to prove the quality of each component. Therefore, the initial corporate name for Valveworks was American Certified Equipment, Inc., founded by Rick, and displaying the important qualities for certified, tracable, quality-assured products.

With strict adherence to American Petroleum Institute (API) 6A regulations and product control, Valveworks maintains the highest standards of quality control in the face of global competitive low/cheap prices. Of the three high requirements of the O&G industry: price, delivery, and quality, he says, "You can only have two. You cannot have all three. Longer than any other independent, wholesale producer, Valveworks utilizes a strict quality control of global production with USA assembly, test, and quality assurance to produce a globally-competitive product with the highest standard of quality.

"To achieve the highest standard of quality within all of the Valveworks valve components, all key processes are performed in house by Valveworks including grinding and lapping of gates and seats, hardfacing, HVOF tungsten carbide of gates and seats, Inconel cladding for HH-NL specified valves and full assembly and testing."

With the global expansion of Valveworks, the increase in the price of oil, and the natural gas production growth using hydraulic fracturing requiring a larger size valve with higher pressures by 2012, Valveworks became a

$150-million-per-year company—and growing. Now, with Valveworks-India manufacturing operations, Valveworks-Wisconsin, Valveworks-China, and Valveworks-Canada, Valveworks USA is proud to have remained in Louisiana and have the support of its local family, employees, and supporters.

Valveworks is dedicated to a quality policy that will achieve customer satisfaction by consistently producing products in conformance to specified products; and, maintaining a full stock for all company-manufactured valves and industry common WKM and Cameron® style valves, including gate valves, manifolds, frac stacs, and Christmas tree wellhead components.

Rick and Sherry are lifelong residents of Bossier Parish, Louisiana, and children of families with lifelong roots in Bossier Parish. Rick graduated from Hauton High School in 1971, and studied accounting at Louisiana State University-Shreveport. Sherry is a 1974 graduate of Airline High School.

Rick Roberts in China.

S3 PUMP SERVICE

In 2005, with thirty-five years of experience in the oil and gas (O&G) industry, Malcolm H. Sneed, III and his wife, Linda, decided it was time to form their own pump service company, making their knowledge and expertise available to companies throughout the Ark-La-Tex region.

Malcolm, a fourth generation oilman, and Linda, were the first two employees during the start-up phase. With only one pump, he was the pump operator, and she was his rigger for the first six months of operation.

Together, they founded S3 Pump Service that, today, has more than seventy-five employees and realizes more than $40 million in annual revenues. It is also recognized as the largest independent pump down company in the United States. The company has experienced annual growth of forty-five percent since its inception.

The high-pressure pumping service provides oil and gas customers with all their pumping requirements from the 600-horsepower pump with a variety of capabilities for testing casing, acid or mud pumping, and pumping various fluids, to the 2,250-horsepower pumps with a rating of 15,000 pounds per square inch (psi), to its top-of-the-line units with 2,500 horsepower and a rating of 15,000 psi. The company's goal is to provide professional employees who are trained and knowledgeable in maintaining the day-to-day pumping operations for its clients.

S3 Pump Service first began working in the Vernon Gas Field in North Louisiana and then in the popular Haynesville Shale. The owner is a fourth generation oilman with a wealth of knowledge and experience in the oilfield to help him realize that relationships with employees are vital to the company's

overall objective. As owner of the family business, he takes pride on cultivating that relationship not only with employees, but with clients, as well. "It is imperative that we hire and train knowledgeable people who will do a good job for customers. That keeps customers coming back and spreads word-of-mouth promotion of our capabilities throughout the O&G business," he says.

S3 Pump Service works hand-in-hand with its clients to develop on-site techniques, constructing complete pump packages for multi-sized projects. The company takes pride in being available for customers around the clock whether it is repairing equipment such as engines, transmissions and other related equipment; or, fabricating the pump packages.

"If someone has a problem with a pump, they know they can call us for maintenance or repair any time of the day or night. We'll be there for them," says Malcolm. "And, we will make sure that our professional staff provides the best quality service possible. We are dedicated to quality and safety in the field. We convey that to our customers upfront, and we follow through with that pledge." (The S3 owner believes that each employee, including himself, should supply the client with one hundred percent of the company's ability and knowledge, in a safe working environment.)

All of S3 Pump's equipment is checked daily and maintenance performed on a regular basis. Keeping the equipment in top-notch shape is beneficial to client and company employees, as well.

S3 Pump Service has exceptional experience with pump downs in the Haynesville Shale of Northwest Louisiana. They performed over 250 pump downs last year in Louisiana and over 500 pump downs last year in Southeast Texas.

In 2012, S3 Pump Service started pump downs in West Texas and will continue to be a presence in this area.

The company's mission is to serve the oilfield industry with quality and excellence, both in its equipment and employees.

As a locally owned business, S3 Pump Service believes in giving back to the community, and helping those in need. S3 contributes to many local children's charities and public service organizations throughout the Ark-La-Tex area.

S3's corporate office is located at 1918 Barton Drive in Shreveport, Louisiana. A Department of Transportation (DOT) shop is headquartered at 412 Hamilton Road, Bossier City, Louisiana and the Dilley office is located at 2120 West FM 117 in Dilley, Texas. S3 Pump Service is also located on the Internet at www.s3pumpservice.com.

WASHBURN MARINE SHIPYARD, LLC

Stephens Shipyard in the 1970s.

In 2006, Darby Washburn of Morgan City, Louisiana, had a unique opportunity before him. After working as a subcontractor in the shipyard industry for almost fifteen years, he had often contemplated starting his own shipyard. That year, he seized an opportunity to purchase the old Stephens Shipyard on Front Street in Morgan City. That was the beginning of his new venture that would later become Washburn Marine.

He saw it as investment property; but, still was not sure what he was going to do with it. "All I knew was that I wanted to start my own business and that property was at a great location."

It was an extensive undertaking to clean up the old property to make it usable. It required over six months of concentrated, laborious effort. Rusty old barges, an outdated home-made drydock constructed of railcar tanks, scrap, debris, and old dilapidated buildings covered the property. It was a hard job, to say the least.

Washburn put on his work clothes, rolled up his sleeves, and got to work. "We cut up and scrapped the old barges, sold the old dry dock to the scrapyard, sold off the components of an old machine shop that hadn't been in use for years. Then, we hauled off the debris and trash, tore down the old buildings, and even removed the two marine ways rail systems that had hauled out hundreds, if not thousands, of vessels over the years for Stephens Shipyard. We completely gutted the yard and got rid of everything that didn't work, or that we didn't have a use for," he added. "Fortunately, the scrap market paid well, and the revenues from the scrap kept Washburn financially afloat for a while."

Washburn had always dreamed of opening his own shipyard, and he was about to realize his dream. Once the property was cleared, the picture of a shipyard came into his mind; and the real possibilities of his dreams were closer than ever. Especially so, when he found a 150-ton capacity Marine Travelift® in San Diego that was affordable, and would be a perfect fit for the property. He purchased the Travelift, had it refurbished and moved to his property in Morgan City.

He drew upon his experience from working in the oilfield for the past fourteen years, practically in the shipyards in Morgan City, and all across the Gulf Coast. His experience as a former Marine served him well. A Desert Storm Veteran, where he served in the first Gulf War in 1991, his experience has been valuable in all of his endeavors. "My service in the United States Marine Corps is one of the most valuable experiences of my life. The Marine Corps taught me how to get things done efficiently and effectively, and not to back down from the difficult challenges in life," he said.

Darby Washburn founded Washburn Marine Shipyard, LLC in January 2008 and began offering haul-out services, steel and

aluminum repairs, and dockside services. It was a very busy time for the shipyard during his first year in business, he reflected. The first year of business, Washburn Marine hauled out 152 vessels ranging from 10 tons, with up to 165 tons being the heaviest; and handled over 20,000 tons using the Travelift.

The numbers were quite impressive for a 2.5-acre shipyard, considering most of this was done by Washburn, along with four or five employees. "Keeping our startup company lean and mean was my goal," he commented. To do that, his close attention to not incurring any unnecessary overhead was paramount to the first year's success. "I was determined to make this company successful," Washburn said. "Nothing mattered more than staying in business." Washburn's former employer said of Washburn, "When Darby makes up his mind; he makes a total commitment and remains focused. That's a rare quality in young people today. He is close to his people and they are close to him. How many shipyard owners do you know who are out there every day managing and supervising each job," he asked.

From 2008 to 2013, the present Washburn Marine Shipyard has lifted or hauled out over 700 vessels, and the combined gross weight of these vessels is over 85,000 tons—an accomplishment of which Washburn is proud. During this time, the yard has also worked on or repaired almost one thousand vessels.

In 2011, Washburn hired Bill Miller to be the administrative manager for the company. Bill is a longtime friend with a background in finance and business management. He came on board as part of an effort to structure the company from a management perspective. Miller has been a huge part of the company's growth and success. He brought a level of dedication and diligence not often found today. Miller's duties include accounting, finance, and oversight of all administrative functions of the company.

In 2012 the company hired Bubba Nini and Joe Prejean. Nini and Washburn have been friends for more than twenty years, and have worked together extensively over the years. Nini's duties include serving as shipyard operations manager and sales. Nini has over twenty years of experience, was born and raised in Morgan City, and is very well known throughout the industry. Prejean joined to assist with the continued structuring and organizational efforts of the company.

Mr. Joe, as Prejean is known, is the shipyard superintendent, a position he has held with various shipyards for over forty years. "Mr. Joe brought a level of experience to that company that is truly amazing. I have worked with him since I came to Morgan City in 1993, and he has taught me so much about the business and continues to do so. We are lucky to have him on our team," Washburn said.

Washburn Marine Shipyard today.

Pat Smith is another of Washburn's mentors. Smith like Prejean, has been in the industry for over forty years, and was instrumental in helping the company to get up and running. "We have put together a team of experienced people that have a common goal, which is to help the company grow and realize continued success. Mr. Pat has been a huge part of that for the company, and for me, personally."

In addition to those with experience now on the Washburn team, Darby's son, Alex, came on board at the beginning of 2013 and is learning the ropes from the more experienced teammates. Washburn said, "Alex is a very bright and intelligent young man who will have a brilliant future here for many years." Washburn is also hopeful that his daughter will join the company following her college education. "I see everyone who works here, and all of our friends that help, as family. I would love to see everyone achieve their goals and dreams through working at Washburn Marine. I wake up excited about it every day. It couldn't be any better having my closest friends and family involved," he added.

In 2013 the company purchased a drydock and is currently refurbishing the dock and upgrading its length, giving it more capacity. When completed, the drydock will have a twelve-hundred-ton capacity and will serve larger vessels in the area. Additionally, the company plans to upgrade the marine Travelift to 220-300 tons. Washburn hopes to grow into new construction of inland push boats and barges. "I have always wanted to start a new construction division, and have been waiting for the right time and right management support before moving forward with the idea.

"I believe next year will be the perfect time, once we have the drydock operational to support our efforts. We will be equipped to assist our customers with the new regulations from the Coast Guard concerning inland towing vessels. We are capable of repairing and upgrading our customers' existing vessels, and also will have the capabilities to build new vessels," he concluded.

Washburn Marine Shipyard is located at 1631 Front Street in Morgan City, Louisiana.

Opposite, top: M/V Bryelee.

Opposite, bottom: M/V Dixie.

Below: Aerial shot of Washburn Yard.

PHI, Inc.

Since its inception in 1949, Petroleum Helicopters, Inc. (PHI) has left an indelible mark on the industry it birthed as well as the companies, nations, and communities across Louisiana, the United States and the globe that it has served.

Above: One of the early PHI Bell 47 helicopters.

Right: The EC135 Air Medical helicopter.

In the early 1940s the South Louisiana marshland had become the nation's lifeblood for the oil and gas industry (O&G); and the only mode of transportation for seismograph and pipeline crews were cumbersome, unreliable and treacherous marsh buggies. At the time, helicopters, not yet considered for commercial use, were used solely for military or experimental purposes. But, visionary leaders in the late 1940s recognized the potential to use the helicopter to serve the emerging offshore oil and gas industry with greater speed, efficiency, and safety, for both workers and the environment.

On February 21, 1949, with three Bell helicopters, $100,000 in capital, seven employees and unwavering dedication to safety and service, J. E. (Jack) Lee, Robert L. (Bob) Suggs, and M. M. (Dookie) Bayon founded Petroleum Bell Helicopter Services, Inc. The company's formation was a landmark event in aviation history and an industry was born.

Within five years of its inception, the company changed its name to Petroleum Helicopters, Inc., when it began to acquire helicopters from Sikorsky as well as Bell. In less than a decade, the company had already established a dominant international presence, providing helicopter service to a variety of industries throughout the world.

With headquarters in Lafayette, Louisiana, PHI's mission was simple—to provide safe, reliable transportation to the offshore oil and gas sector. Now, more than sixty years later, helicopters are the most recognized form of offshore transportation to the industry on a global scale.

Suggs, considered as the father of commercial rotary-wing transportation, led PHI to providing a safer means of transportation for the oil and gas industry. With safety and customer service as the company's highest priorities, this "PHI Standard," as it became known, remains the standard by which the entire industry is judged. Suggs' entrepreneurial vision guided the company to establishing new markets, including the air medical business, providing helicopter ambulance services to hospitals across the nation. At the time of the air medical introduction,

few were aware of the profound impact PHI would have on that industry and the many lives it would positively impact.

Following Suggs' death in September of 1989, his wife, Carroll Wilson Suggs, assumed the duties as chairman of the board, president and CEO of the company, where she oversaw many safety advancements and guided the company through challenging times. She maintained her duties until current PHI, Inc. CEO and Board Chairman Al A. Gonsoulin, took over the company's reins in 2001.

In September 2001, Gonsoulin purchased a controlling interest in Petroleum Helicopters, Inc., assuming the titles and, with them, active roles as chairman and CEO of PHI, positions he currently maintains. Gonsoulin continues to place extraordinary emphasis on safety in operations, customer service and personal growth—the ideals that made it the "Total Helicopter Company." He also placed significant focus on restructuring the financial sector of the business as well as upgrading its assets and the infrastructure of the fleet and base facilities—ensuring the most modern fleet, model and protocols in the business.

PHI has grown to become the leader in support of deepwater oil and gas exploration in the Gulf of Mexico, serving installations as far as 200 miles offshore in 3,000 feet or more of water. Driven by the vision of improving safety for the offshore worker, PHI continues to introduce many industry advances, including the first dedicated deep-water air medical transport system, which saves lives and reduces recovery time for injured offshore workers in the Gulf. The revolutionary S-76C++ helicopter, with its extraordinary clinical capabilities and expertise was a joint undertaking between PHI's oil and gas and air medical groups.

Above: The revolutionary S-76 helicopter.

Below: PHI Air Medical personnel loading a patient.

Above: The S-92 helicopter.

Below: The AW-139 helicopter.

Outside of the offshore environment, PHI is a leader in providing critical care transport in partnership with many prestigious health-care systems, governmental entities in other countries, as well as emergency responders and communities across the nation through PHI Air Medical, a wholly-owned subsidiary of PHI, Inc. PHI Air Medical is one of the pre-mier and highly respected air medical providers in the world, and has built upon PHI's rich history with its many industry firsts, safety advances and leading practices.

Since the company's inception in 1949, PHI has operated and maintained virtually every model of Western-built helicopter, from early Bell 47Gs to the world's first and largest fleet of Sikorsky S92s. In fact, the company's pilots and crews have flown more helicopters under a greater variety of conditions over a longer period of time than any other civilian helicop-ter company—only surpassed by the military of the United States and former Soviet Union. In its more than sixty-year history, PHI has emerged as the industry leader in maintenance, technology, safety, and overhaul operations. The first-class overhaul and maintenance site, based in Lafayette, Louisiana, is considered the premier facility of its type in the world because of its advanced technology and highly trained, experienced employees.

PHI is renowned for its relentless pursuit of safe, reliable transportation to the domestic off-shore oil and gas, international, air medical, and technological service industries. With over eleven million flight hours on record to date, one of the most expansive and advanced fleets,

and one of the best safety records in the indus-try, PHI, Inc., is a world leader in commercial helicopter operations. The company continues to provide service to the foremost oil and gas companies, governmental entities across the globe, leading healthcare systems and commu-nities across the U.S. while having operated in more than fifty countries worldwide. Each year, PHI safely transports more than one million passengers and 30,000 patients.

The same story of entrepreneurial vision and courage, bold innovation, and unyielding commitment to excellence that defined PHI's inception are what drives PHI today. As the company continues to evolve and innovate, the one constant is its steadfast pursuit of its mission: To provide worldwide helicopter services that are unsurpassed in safety and customer satisfaction; we are a team dedicat-ed to continuous improvement in an environ-ment that promotes trust, personal growth and mutual respect. The company, born more than sixty years ago, continues to shape, transform, and lead the industry it started.

RENÉ J. CHERAMIE & SONS, INC.

René J. Cheramie acquired the fishing vessel *Brother in Law* in 1929 and started his own marine business. The vessel was powered by a 2-cylinder, 12-horsepower Alex engine. In 1937, he purchased M/V *Marine Pride*, powered by a 4-cylinder, 30-horsepower Fairbank Engine. When the United States entered WWII, it expropriated M/V *Marine Pride*, resulting in René working for wages at Delta in New Orleans.

After the war, the government paid René market value for his vessel, allowing him to purchase M/V *Midshipman* in 1946, powered by a 6-cylinder CAT, producing 120 horsepower and the second M/V *Midshipman* in 1952, powered by 6-cylinder CATs producing 500 horsepower. He continued expanding; purchasing his third M/V *Midshipman* in 1957. It featured 6-110 Detroits, producing 600 horsepower.

The October 17, 1960, edition of the *Oil & Gas Journal* shows, "How Gulf set a new drilling record". Dixie Drilling Company's Rig 3 is towed by tugs *Midshipman* and *Reed* toward Gulf Oil Corporation's state lease 1773 in Timbalier Bay, Louisiana. A month before in a nearby well, it set a record of 5,412 feet in one day. Captain René J. Cheramie and deckhand A. R. "Tony" Cheramie worked on tug *Midshipman* to make this happen.

René contracted with Main Iron Works in 1965, building tug *Maria Cheramie* and powered her with 16 V71 Detroits, producing 920 horsepower. René and Tony contracted with Houma Welders in 1972, and built tug *Aggie Cheramie* and chose D379 CATs at 1,200 horsepower for propulsion.

Tony assumed leadership of the company, constructing tug *René J. Cheramie* in 1974 at Houma Welders and powered the vessel with 8-645 E2 EMDs at 2,100 horsepower. René passed away in 1985. Tony contracted with Main Iron Works constructing tug *Ann T. Cheramie* in 2003, and working with Crimson Shipping Company in 2011 to build tug *Crimson Victory,* both powered by 3,516 high-displacement CATs producing 4,750 horsepower. Tony worked with the Towing Safety Advisory Committee in 2004. The Coast Guard's partnership with TSAC aids in managing the risks present in the towing industry and resolving problems of mutual concern.

Third generation René A. Cheramie joined the family business in 1993 when he resigned his commission as an Army captain after participating in Operation Desert Storm. The business was not new to the former soldier because he went on his first rig move in 1975, at age nine. He gained first-hand experience aboard tug *René J. Cheramie* working through various subcontractors. René currently lives in Lafayette where he is the president of A. R. Cheramie Marine Management, Inc. The company operates, maintains and manages offshore tugs and barges for various owners.

Above: M/V Marine Pride.

Below: Tug René J. Cheramie.

ARIES MARINE CORPORATION

Dwight S. "Bo" Ramsay, a geologist, was engaged in the exploration of oil and gas. In Louisiana and, especially in Texas, he discovered one of the largest gas fields, which has produced several trillion cubic feet of gas. That success provided the financial base to form several industry-related businesses in 1981, among them, Aries Marine Corporation (Aries).

During a review of the liftboat business in the Gulf of Mexico, he found few boats could work in water depths greater than eighty feet. The boats had small cranes; deck load was limited, as was crew and guest worker accommodations. It was determined that over three thousand platforms in the Gulf could be serviced by larger liftboats.

Aries is a privately-held Louisiana corporation, operating self-elevating work boats and supply vessels. The self-elevating work boats, also referred to as liftboats or jack-ups, provide mobile, yet stable work platforms, with crane capabilities, and living accommodations for crews working on wells and production platforms. The supply boats, primarily associated with drilling operations, transport tubulars, drilling fluids, and other equipment, and provide Aries with a diverse business mix.

Ramsay custom-ordered seven boats initially, with four to be delivered in 1981, and three in 1982. A shipyard salesman inquired about the owner's name of the company building the boats. The company name had not been established yet; so he suggested a competition be held among the workers to come up with a name and logo. Ramsay was to establish a bar tab for the workers and an award. The salesman, of course, won the award. He related "Ram" in Ramsay to the astrological sign, Aries. The name was born!

Knowing little about the marine business was a risk. That was overcome by the employment of Richard Johnson, an experienced marine manager. With the company from the beginning, he has witnessed the company's growth, now operating 16 liftboats and 12 large supply vessels.

W. D. "Butch" Bazer, who had operating experience and was able to organize the workplace and people, joined Johnson, and has been a loyal employee of the company since 1981. Earl Verrett was in charge of the supply boats and brought a world of experience to that division.

In the 1970s, supply boats (OSVs) were attractive tax shelters but became less so with the 1982-1988 oil business collapse. Available through banks and mortgage holders during that collapse, OSVs were ripe for Ramsay to pluck for pennies on the dollar. So, he started a fleet with older boats and later added new construction. The most recent additions are the new 292-foot Tiger Shark Class, largest purpose built OSVs, working in the Gulf today. Once again, thirty years later, Aries stepped out to lead the industry into more advanced vessels.

Times were difficult during the early years of the business. Day rates barely paid for upkeep of the vessels and debt was almost impossible to service. T-shirts often record the history of companies, and Aries' retirement of early debt was memorialized in one famous T-shirt. It depicted "Bo Owes" with a red line through it. In 1990 the company was finally out of debt!

Financing is necessary, however, and in 1994 Courtney, Bo's son, soon secured a deal with a local shipyard for two new DP2 vessels. This new positioning technology allows vessels to integrate with GPS in order to hold station. New to the industry in the early 1990s it is now standard equipment on most OSVs. The company was back to square one and owing the bank once again!

During the life of a boat company one learns from mistakes. To have a vessel under forfeiture to the government for a $125-million drug run via a bareboat charter was a sobering experience. W. F. C., Inc., part of Aries Marine, was a foolish name, meaning "Who Flipping Cares" and owned the *M/V Allison*. The name caused a moment of crises when the DEA, the Coast Guard, the Port Authority and FBI asked Ramsay, as a suspect, "What does W. F. C., Inc. mean?" Without hesitation he replied, Worldwide Floating Consortium." "Worldwide" sounded better to the authorities than the actual name. The vessel was released and returned to Aries Marine and is now working in the Gulf today.

The journey that the company has traveled has been one of high risk, great returns, challenges, and successes. Maritime business is as exciting as jumping from an airplane—thrilling and dangerous.

Aries' mission is providing safe transportation for men and materials to and from work locations in the Gulf. Company owners believe well-maintained vessels improve safety at sea, efficiency in operations, and job completion by its customers on time and budget. Aries' record of service was built on service to all major (and most independent and service) companies operating in the Gulf.

The Ramsay family—Bo, Courtney, and Allison—share the company's good fortune throughout the community. They helped found Episcopal School of Acadiana, and provided land and financial aid to Bridge Ministries. Father, son and daughter are active in many organizations and serve on various charity boards.

Aries Marine's corporate headquarters is located in Lafayette, Louisiana, with an operations office in Youngsville, Louisiana.

Above: The crew of the M/V Ram X.

Below: The M/V Kylie Williams.

SOUTHERN PETROLEUM LABORATORIES, INC.

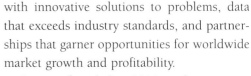

Established in 1944, Southern Petroleum Laboratories, Inc. (SPL) was one of the first entities to serve the oilfield exploration and production, petrochemical, refining, pipeline, and retail markets with petroleum and environmental testing expertise. Built on family values, innovative ideas, accuracy, and exceptional customer service, SPL is well-positioned to sustain its leadership position in the highly competitive oilfield services industry. SPL's leadership team and dedicated employees have a clear focus on providing customers with innovative solutions to problems, data that exceeds industry standards, and partnerships that garner opportunities for worldwide market growth and profitability.

SPL was founded in 1944 on the entrepreneurial spirit of W. A. "Dubb" Frier, a chemical engineering graduate of Texas A&M. While working for various companies, Dubb gained experience in market research and laboratory operations—and watched the fast-paced growth and expansion of the natural gas industry in Texas. As chief chemist for Saybolt, Dubb fielded calls from natural gas producers procuring the services of commercial testing labs. The Texas Railroad Commission had recently set up regulations and testing procedures for well testing, and many production companies chose to outsource these responsibilities to commercial labs. Dubb recognized the business opportunity, but was not able to convince his employer to purchase additional equipment or train staff to specialize in natural gas well testing. Dubb was sure there was a market for the services he had in mind and he decided to try it on his own.

Dubb built a trailer, installed a small separator and other measurement devices needed to perform the various test requirements, and, using the family car to tow it all, set out to test his first wells. This trip was the beginning of the W. A. Frier Company. His wife, Lillian, assumed the role of secretary and office manager, helping Dubb assemble, type, and report testing results. Dubb's clientele expanded quickly and he soon set up his own lab facility in Houston. He added a business partner, Edward Patterson, to manage all laboratory functions, and in 1945, the company changed its name to Southern Petroleum Laboratories, Inc. Patterson sold his company shares back to Dubb a year later, and he quickly hired the firm's first two employees—one to manage the laboratory and one to work with him as his first field assistant.

By 1957, SPL was in full-scale expansion mode, having established permanent facilities in Houston, Texas; Carthage, Texas; and Lafayette, Louisiana. Another Texas A&M graduate, H. R. "Herb" Brown, joined the company in 1957 to manage facilities in Carthage, and later in Lafayette. SPL was incorporated in 1958 with Dubb, Lillian, and their daughter, Natalee, assuming key leadership positions. Natalee inherited a breakthrough personality from her parents and set several gender precedents during her life. She served as chairman of the SPL board for over thirty years, until her death in 2006. Her business interests took her to roles outside the SPL boardroom as well. She became the first woman to serve on the board of directors of the Petroleum Club of Lafayette in 1989; founded MidSouth Bank in Louisiana; and was responsible for anchoring the revitalization of Lafayette's Oil Center into a retail corridor when she relocated her own design and decorative accessories boutique, Natalee Interiors, to its current location.

During the 1960s, SPL continued to expand geographically and added services as the oilfield industry continued to grow exponentially. In 1966, SPL developed its first measurement and production allocation project for the Sugar Bowl Pipeline Company. This project helped SPL's employees gain expertise in liquid measurement, meter calibration and repair, allocation, and auditing services. By the late 1960s, SPL began offering environmental services in response to the U.S. Department of Interior's enforcement of water discharge regulations in the Gulf of Mexico.

In the following decade, SPL's service offerings continued to expand to meet market demands. Following Dubb's death in 1972, Herb Brown was appointed president and CEO of SPL. Herb continued on the path of growth and success by leading SPL to new heights. New facilities were opened in Belle Chasse, Louisiana, in 1976, Traverse City, Michigan, in 1981 and, in recent years, SPL has expanded into Laurel, Mississippi; Carencro, Louisiana; Pearland, Texas; and Venus, Texas.

In 2010, SPL sold its environmental laboratory division to focus more precisely on the oil and gas industry. The following year, the company expanded its service offerings to include production data management through accurate web-based remote monitoring. SPL's most recent expansion was opening a new facility in Pleasanton, Texas, in late 2011, where they now service the oil and gas production companies, midstream operations, plants, and pipelines in the Eagle Ford shale area.

Until his death in 2012, Herb's guiding hand continued to reinforce SPL's reputation as one of the premiere hydrocarbon analytical and measurement companies in the United States.

With a total of ten facilities in Texas, Louisiana, Mississippi, and Michigan, SPL is truly a one-source service company and is recognized globally as the industry leader in third-party measurement and analytical needs for the oil and gas industry. Now, SPL is a third-generation family business led by Herb Brown's children: Mark Brown, Kimberly Noble, and Christopher Frier Brown. SPL continues its success by employing some of the same business success fundamentals that Dubb followed from the start. With over sixty-eight years of accurate analysis experience and exceptional customer service, SPL has proven that it is a sustained leader in the industry.

The Brown Family, clockwise, starting from top left, Christopher Frier Brown, president and corporate shareholder; Kimberly Noble, corporate shareholder; Mark Brown, chairman and corporate shareholder; and H. R. "Herb" Brown.

RELIABLE PRODUCTION SERVICE, INC.

Reliable Production Service's (Reliable) fortieth anniversary on October 31, 2005, was a milestone in the life of its founder, James L. Moore, more lovingly referred to as Mr. Jim.

This anniversary was memorable for Mr. Jim in many ways. It not only marked the date in 1965 when he founded the company; but, he felt the love and camaraderie of employees who joined the celebration to further express their heart-felt thanks.

Left to right: Founder and President James L. "Jim" Moore and James R. Moore, vice president of operations. The photograph was taken in the early 1980s at the office in Frisco, Louisiana.

Collectively, they had written a letter to their employer, detailing their gratitude to him as an individual and to the company. They understood the fortitude it must have taken to form a company and manage it as Mr. Jim did. "…He was a hardworking, man of humility with an incredible vision. He took a risk and realized a dream." They said he had given them a job, and with it, a wonderful quality of life for them and their families. "He has survived the bad times and expanded during the good; and the future looks bright for the next generation of employees. That is important to all of us," the letter concluded. The employees were right with their comments of the January 2005 letter. Mr. Jim was (and still is) a man of humble means. He believes in working hard, maintaining a safe environment, providing training and maintaining strong work habits. By focusing on that, Reliable will, in fact, protect its employees from personal injury, reduce loss of property, and protect the environment.

"Our operations policy is succinct—but on the money: "production with safety," not "production and safety," he says.

Reliable began as a one-man, local pumping service operating out of a converted grocery store in Livonia, Louisiana. The company operated out of that office until 1998 when it relocated to Port Allen, Louisiana. It was not long, though, until the geographical working range covered a three-state area, and the name "Reliable" would come to represent one of the most complete well-servicing and workover operations in South Louisiana. The company remains a family-owned and family-structured company. Mr. Jim upholds his belief that the company's family atmosphere provides for a great working environment, stating, "No one works for me; we all work together."

Reliable maintains a fleet of seven mobile rigs with the capability to handle a wide range of jobs covering everything in completion and maintenance work in the oil and gas industry. Among those capabilities are injection well jobs, and plugging and abandoning projects. The rigs are recognized as the best, most up-to-date rigs on the market, with a superior selection of support equipment.

Mr. Jim was born James Lavoy Moore on August 29, 1938, in Vasthi, Texas, to Samuel and Jewel Chapel Moore. He grew up on his parent's farm, helping with chores until age fifteen, when he began to "get his feet wet" in the Texas oil patch. At nineteen, he went to work full time for Ramey Well Service in Wichita Falls. When the owner of that company moved to Louisiana in 1961, Mr. Jim, and his young family, went with him to begin a new life.

The disciplined work habits he learned from his parents and his drive to succeed was evident to key people in the industry. Milton Adams of American Trading struck a fifty-fifty partnership with him; and the relationship proved to be very beneficial, and long lasting, allowing Mr. Jim to branch out into other oil-field services. Early on, W. E. Tally sold him his chemical business and showed him how to develop his passion into a money-making enterprise. Tally was a great business manager who taught him a lot about finance and

accounting. Earl E. Wall was most influential when it came to production and the overall knowledge he possessed in the oil and gas business. There were many other key people who helped in the early formation, people like Howard Ramey, B. M. Hester, Buck Chustz, Billy Parks, Joycelyn Newton, and Earl Parks, his first full-time employee. Joycelyn and Billy joined Mr. Jim in 1970, and are still employed some forty-three years later. The family atmosphere has made Reliable a desirable place to work, many second-generation workers are employed with the company.

In the 1970s, Reliable began to develop its full potential. Mr. Jim sought investors to raise more capital and, in 1976, formed Liberty Oil and Gas to explore the drilling side of the oilfield. From 1976-85, Liberty drilled or participated in the drilling of more than 125 wells; and, at one point owned interest in and/or operated over 200 wells. That company, although located in Livonia, was aggressive in Jackson and Natchez, Mississippi; Cortez, Colorado; Houston, Texas; and New Orleans, Louisiana, in the 1980s. Prior to the bust, Reliable was a thriving oilfield service company with the main office located in Livonia, Louisiana, and support offices located in DeQuincy and Vidalia, Louisiana. At one point, Reliable boasted 15 workover rigs, 1 barge for inland operations pump trucks, a swab truck, wire line unit, hot oil trucks, 5 roustabout crews, 10 mechanics and 15 pumpers. Additionally, Reliable owned and operated a saltwater disposal site, taking in non-hazardous oilfield waste water, and a solid waste landfill on an adjoining facility.

In 2009, Reliable received an "Impact Award" from the Greater Pointe Coupee Chamber of Commerce for its commitment to the economic well-being of the parish and its dedication to the welfare of the citizens. Many local people are employed with Reliable. As such, Reliable feels that it is necessary to support local businesses and to give back to the community by supporting many charitable causes, as well as, nonprofit clubs and organizations. Tens of thousands of dollars have been donated to help improve the lives of others. A huge amount of financial resources are dedicated each year toward public education, religious works, individual needs, fundraising efforts, as well as, promoting sports programs and a number of community based projects. Reliable has been home to many high school and college students who spend their summers and holiday breaks earning some cash to help them through school.

Today, Mr. Jim has entrusted the day to day operations of Reliable to the next generation, handing down his knowledge and expertise to his son, James Randall Moore, who is no stranger to the oilfield. Randy began his career at the age of fourteen, working as a roustabout for his dad. He worked his way through the ranks in nearly every job in the company to his current position as vice president of operations. Randy has spent over forty years of his life in the service sector. The company's foundation was set solid by Mr. Jim. The present operations have produced beneficial results under the direction of Randy and the future looks bright as the third generation grandson, Charner Moore, works his way through the ranks, hopefully preparing for the time when he, too, will lead the family business.

As Reliable looks toward the future, one word is ever present on the mind of those guiding the process. That word is "expansion." New plans are being formulated that will allow Reliable to continue for decades to come as the company grows in size and scope of operations.

An aerial view of Reliable's new office (left) and shop (right) located on Highway 190 in Livonia, Louisiana. The facilities were built in 2008.

UNITED OILFIELD SERVICES, INC.

Above: Present-day employees.

*Below: Left to right, Mac Royer, heavy
equipment operator; John Fontenot, crew
supervisor; Bill Schysm, operator; Max
Barrow, shop supervisor; Steve Schysm,
crew supervisor; and Butch Royer, owner.
The photograph was taken in front of the
new shop building in Industrial Air Park.
We still operate there today.*

Ray (Butch) Royer could easily have been
the inspiration for G. Harvey's painting,
Drifting through the Oil Patch.

Butch followed his older brother Charles
into the oilfield, where he began rough-necking at seventeen to work his way through
college. He pursued an animal science degree
at LSU, and worked summers and holidays
for nearly every drilling contractor in south
Louisiana. Butch met Buttons Boyer while
working for Jamison Drilling in his hometown
of DeQuincy. Buttons, a pioneer in oilfield

swabbing and wireline operation, became a
good friend and mentor.

Following graduation, Butch's first job
was managing a hog farm in Mississippi. Still
single and homesick, after a couple of years
he quit and moved back to DeQuincy. For the
next few years, Butch found himself working
at several menial labor jobs, getting married,
and even teaching school for three years
before he found himself back on a drilling
rig, rough-necking for Pernie Bailey Drilling.
By then, the Occupational Safety and Health
Association (OSHA) became a force in the oil
patch and he was offered the position of safety director for the company. Butch leveraged
his experience to advance to a loss control
manager for United General Insurance, an
up-and-coming company in Katy, Texas, that
insured workover rigs. By 1982 the crude
oil surplus combined with a downturn in
industrial development saw his job dry up.

Butch gladly accepted an unexpected
severance check and moved his family back
to DeQuincy, where he started a farm and
resumed the country life he had loved before.
With the assistance of his older brother,
Charles, and brother-in-law, Wallace Clark,
both working as pumpers, he put together a
crew truck and began an oilfield construction
company, christened United Oilfield Services
(UOS). The company struggled through
several lean years, all the while operating out
of Butch's home. His biggest
expansion came when he talked
to the assistant bank manager
and talked him into a $10,000
loan to buy an old Ford flatbed
truck with missing back win-
dows, an antique backhoe, and
a homemade trailer.

Butch, at thirty-five, had
never been on a backhoe, dozer,
or any other heavy equipment,
but on-the-job training got him
by. He soon became proficient
as a dozer and backhoe operator. His wife, Jimmie Lee, served
as the accountant and cook,
making lunch for the crews
during the week and passing
out checks every Friday.

In 1991, Butch built a new barn for his horses and cattle, with a small business office in the upstairs loft. The loft served as United Oilfield Services' (UOS) headquarters for several years. It was there, in September 1993 that he partnered with Bob and Steve McDaniel on a new business venture. They began Midstates Petroleum Company, an oilfield production company. With Steve's guidance, Midstates' growth culminated in an initial public offering (IPO) on the NYSE in April 2012.

In 1995, United moved its headquarters from the barn loft to a trailer house near the barn. That facility served as the main office until 1998, when Butch purchased a site in the industrial park in DeQuincy. Today, that site still serves as the UOS office, shop and headquarters.

UOS is a small, family-owned and operated company that continues to serve in Southwest Louisiana in the same capacity it did over thirty years ago. Over the years, it has worked for major companies including Tenneco, Murphy Oil, Unocal, Conoco, Hunt Oil, Sonat, Mitchell Energy, CXY, Wagner & Brown, Phillips, Swift, and many other independents.

Butch never dreamed of a livelihood in the oil industry, with no education in the field or training in that discipline. "In fact, I refer to myself as the least likely to succeed. I have roustabouts with more knowledge than I," he says. "I never liked the oil patch; it was just a means of making a living for my family. My success has been achieved wholly through my faith in God. Through all the struggling years, He provided just what I needed at just the right time. He brought the companies and people into my path to keep me going when there was little hope of another job or making payroll for my crews."

In addition to God, Butch attributes much of his success to his wife, Jimmie, and children, Mac and Dana. As children, Mac and Dana spent many days following their dad to remote oilfield locations and pitched in becoming part of the labor crews and, eventually, management. Mac now owns heavy equipment, and handles all the jobs for United that require dozers, backhoes, and similar equipment. Dana manages the office and is in charge of finances. Butch adds, "There have been so many helpful people along the way that I sincerely thank, and to whom I will have a lifelong indebtedness and friendship."

Above: The barn with the loft. This location served as the headquarters of United Oilfield Services, Inc., and the first office of the Midstates Petroleum Company.

Below: Butch Royer's daughter Dana at age sixteen, hot oiling.

J. D. FIELDS & COMPANY, INC. (JDF)

At an early age, Jerry Fields knew that he wanted to own his own business someday. His ambition was more than a pipe dream. It was the pipe that was his dream—literally!

Following graduation from high school, Jerry worked with his father in the oilfields to earn money for college. Once he obtained his degree from Southwest Texas State University, he joined a company that sold steel pipe related to the oil and gas industry (O&G).

In 1985, Jerry left the company to start J. D. Fields & Co., Inc., (JDF) a steel pipe company, along with three partners from a competing firm. Eventually, he bought out the other partners, and the company is now fully owned by the Fields family. In fact, the second generation is now serving in key positions. Jay Fields is president of the company with primary responsibility for the pipe business, and Pat Burk serves as president of the construction products division.

A year after the founding of J. D. Fields & Company, it opened an office in New Orleans as a supplier to the O&G and construction industries. Since then, the company's presence is recognized throughout the south Louisiana market, which has been critical to the firm's overall growth. The Louisiana office of J. D. Fields & Company, Inc., has provided pipe to all major and independent U.S. oil and gas companies as well as offshore fabricators along the Gulf Coast.

J. D. Fields & Company, Inc. is a material supplier providing the American Petroleum Institute (API) line pipe to the oil and gas industry, and steel piling for deep foundation applications. It is a unique and diverse organization that has proven viability through cyclical markets, while remaining a leading source to both industries.

The company is aligned with domestic and international producers to offer one of the broadest ranges in piling. It is a top tier supplier of U.S.-manufactured "H" piles, beams, and pipe piles, as well as a complete line of hot-rolled and cold-form sheet pile solutions.

Jerry admits that achieving his dream of owning a company was not as easy as it seems. His father and mother were uneducated and married at an early age. His father was an oilfield worker, traveling wherever he could to find work. Jerry says he changed schools thirty-two times, always being the new kid in class. Through the family's hard times, though, he persevered and graduated high school in 1963 in Midland, Texas, where he began working in the O&G fields with his father. It was while he was in rehabilitation for a back problem that he met and married Linda Gregg of San Marcos; and shortly after, went to work for a company that sold steel pipe related to the O&G industry. He was hooked, and left that job to realize his dream of ownership.

The company's corporate headquarters is located in Houston, Texas, with additional offices in Mandeville, Louisiana; Pittsburgh, Pennsylvania; Dallas, Texas; Denver, Oklahoma; Brea, California; St. Louis, Missouri; Plymouth, Massachusetts; and Central Florida. The company stocks inventory at strategic locations across the country.

Growth has been phenomenal since JDF's founding twenty-eight years ago. Sales have grown at a compounded annual rate of eleven percent since 2004; and, for the past five years, the *Houston Chronicle* has recognized J. D. Fields & Company, Inc., as a "Top 100 Private Company." In fact, it is a North American leader in API line pipe supply, carrying over one hundred thousand tons of revolving inventory throughout the nation. The differentiating quality between JDF and its competitors is the range of both domestic and international material it stocks, along with the experience and knowledge of its sales staff.

The company operates a unique business model. Jerry was outsourcing before outsourcing was cool! With thirty-five to forty employees, JDF has sold more than $2 billion of product since 2004. All non-sales functions are outsourced to third parties, including yard operations and freight. This allows the company to focus its capital toward inventory acquisition and the sales function.

J. D. Fields & Co. has long been active in community affairs with employees serving on numerous boards and committees of charitable institutions. In the past five years, the company has donated almost $15 million for charitable causes such as colleges, the Ronald McDonald House, hospitals, healthcare organizations, and other philanthropic organizations.

Jerry says the Fields family and the company are especially focused on helping to find a cure for cancer. "No one in my family had ever had cancer before, but when an employee and fraternity brother died from the disease, I bought a $5,000 table at the Houston Cattle Baron's Ball. Later, I was visited by the woman, a cancer survivor, who had organized the ball. I had already planned to give at the $50,000-level; but have made it a priority since I lost my mother-in-law, father, the woman who started the Ball, and many good friends to cancer. I consider my contributions to the American Cancer Society to be seed money that will have a multiplier effect."

Estis Compression LLC/ McClung Energy Services

Dennis Estis.

Dennis Estis left Production Operators in Houston in 1976 seeking a better career opportunity at a small gathering system in North Louisiana, however, that opportunity quickly fell through. That was the impetus he needed to start his own compression business.

He formed Ouachita Energy that same year, and for twenty years thereafter, the company operated larger compression equipment in Louisiana, Texas, Oklahoma, Mississippi, and Kansas. But, like many other small compression companies, Ouachita Energy went through the "compression roll-up," and in turn, merged with one company, later selling to Hanover.

Following the sale of Ouachita Energy Corp, Dennis decided to take an active role in a small compression fleet located in North Louisiana. The fleet was comprised of approximately twenty-five units. At that point, he began to re-establish relationships from the Ouachita Energy days, and began building a company that was a viable alternative to the larger companies that dominated the market.

Competing with the larger companies in the area, it soon became apparent that small horsepower compression (500 horsepower, and below) was not a major priority or concern. With the recognized lack of attention to the smaller projects, Dennis identified a niche that would become the core business of what would eventually become Estis Compression, formed in 2002.

Dennis says that his company was so small "that we had no office or shop. All our major repairs were completed in the field or, if we were lucky, in a Quonset hut that was leased by one of our major customers. Eventually, we rented a small office in Ruston that was about seven hundred square feet. From there, we continued to build the fleet though the acquisition of used equipment we found throughout the oilfield." One of the company's first jobs was replacing a competitors unit on a location that he had previously worked on in the 1970s.

The affiliation with McClung Energy was initiated by Odis McClung, a close friend. Odis helped Dennis find equipment and, in turn, rebuilt it for Estis during the fledgling years. As the Estis and McClung companies grew, Odis, began packaging units. The majority of the Estis fleet was packaged by McClung Energy Services. When Odis tragically died in a plane crash in 2007, his company went on the market for sale. Originally, there was a buyer for McClung; however, when the sale fell through, Dennis made the decision, based on his relationship with the company, to purchase the company making it a "sister company" of Estis Compression. He knew it would be a perfect fit because the companies complemented one another.

The company's goal was to secure a good market share in its operational region of northern Louisiana with a fleet of 100-150 units. That has been realized via operations in Texas, Louisiana, Mississippi, and Arkansas with a fleet in excess of four hundred machines. Most of the company's expansion into new operating areas developed through existing customer requests. For instance, Estis Compression may have a customer in one area, and because of the business relationship they share, is invited to work for them in a new area.

The growth has been phenomenal in the ten years from 2002-2012. Estis employs forty people, has a fleet of 425 units, and operates in six geographic regions. It started with a customer base of four, and has grown to over sixty; with some one-person outfits to major E&P companies. McClung boasts forty employees who package and sell units for domestic and international use in Mexico, Turkey, China, Columbia, and Canada.

With Estis Compression headquartered in West Monroe, Louisiana, and McClung Energy Services headquartered in Longview, Texas, the companies are strategically located to secure the market they seek to serve. Key people at the beginning of Estis Compression have grown along with the company and have been instrumental in the company's success. Dennis is grateful for many former Ouachita Energy employees who have chosen to work there. Ouachita Energy/Estis Compression/McClung Energy Services have employed up to three generations of families. "We have had fathers and sons (and even younger ones) who have ties to one of the three companies," says Dennis. "That speaks volumes for our companies and the services we provide, as well as to the loyalty of our employees. They're dedicated, and we are just as dedicated to them and their families."

Estis strives to become the highest quality service provider in its region of operations; and its business plan is the same as it has been through the years. It plans to continue offering excellent service to customers, and a comfortable place for its employees to make a living. Dennis believes that if someone is willing to work hard, communicate effectively (and enjoys what he does), the company will flourish. He believes that each employee is as responsible for the company's success as the next person. "We all eat out of this trough, so we all make sure we help one another to the best of our abilities," he concludes.

PROLINE SYSTEMS, INC.

Proline Systems, Inc., gives new meaning to the popular saying, "It's in the bag!" For the company it IS the bag—literally!

Proline, founded in 1995 by Kenneth Boutte and Ban Green, began experimenting with, and evidentially developing, an innovative bag patented to provide dry bulk drilling mud additives to the oil and gas industry (O&G) drilling operations in the Gulf of Mexico (GOM) and Brazil. The company was begun during a low economic point in the industry; however, it is the leader today in providing fifty cubic feet, nylon and PVC-coated bags.

The company, headquartered in New Iberia, Louisiana, manufactures and maintains the recyclable Proline Bulk Bags that replace the fifty pound paper sacks traditionally used on a typical offshore rig. "The footprint of these sacks is tremendous. Our bags are durable, recyclable and save trees from being harvested to make paper bags. They (Proline Bulk Bags) have streamlined the industry," says Boutte.

Proline bags are delivered empty to the respective drilling fluid company, which fills the order from the rig-based mud engineer, and ships the full bags to the rig or platform. Once the bags are emptied, they are returned to Proline for cleaning, inspection, and repair—if necessary—before being stored to await the next order. Proline has expanded its marketing reach from New Iberia and the GOM to O&G locations throughout the world, providing a unique system that allows for greater safety and efficiency in adding materials while eliminating waste packaging and, therefore, reducing the overall environmental impact.

When the two began their business, deep-water drilling was just starting in the GOM and Brazil. Traditional methods of mixing chemicals were inadequate to meet the needs of this new drilling frontier. Both men had been involved in the oilfield business for years and, therefore, recognized the problem. That is when they decided to start Proline Systems, Inc., to solve the problem.

After spending months of research on bulk bags used in the industry throughout the world, they soon decided upon a design. A large operator in the GOM with imagination and foresight provided the test site. The first test was ten bags filled with material destined for a floater 120 miles offshore; however, in route to the rig, the supply boat sank. During rescue and salvage they found the bags were still floating and watertight. These qualities, along with other unique features, "opened everyone's eyes to the future of the Proline bags," adds Green. "Bags were manually lifted onto wash racks on a ladder, washed, inspected, and then laid on the shop floor for repair. That was a lot of work for two 'older' guys," he admits, laughing.

In 1997, two years since the company was founded, the same operator experienced a close call, averting an accident when a traditional poly bag tore out of its slings and fell through a laboratory house. The next morning, the operator called Proline and asked the company to supply all their rigs with Proline Systems Bulk Bags. That meant the company had succeeded and was ready to devote fulltime to manufacturing, marketing, and repairing its product. At that point, Proline grew from the 2 principals to its present-day workforce of 12; and from 100 bags to 5,000 bags. Proline employees average twenty-two years in the O&G industry.

The Deepwater Horizon disaster in 2010 put a damper on Proline (as it did all oilfield service companies). With little-to-no activity occurring in the GOM, only the overseas business allowed Proline to remain open and in production. During that period, Proline kept all employees at full pay—a fact of which it is proud. That philosophy remains today: regardless of the hardship (or downturn), it makes every effort to retain valued employees.

The early Proline bag had a safe working load of 4,000 pounds and a 2:1 safety factor. With today's safety concerns, operators demand an 8:1 safety factor. Proline was able to meet, and even exceed the requirement. It remains the only bag that meets the industry standards. Proline continues to offer new ideas to the O&G industry with two patents pending, and other projects/products in the

works. The Arctic drilling in the future invites special challenges, requiring new material handling methods. Proline is at the forefront.

The company mission is: To provide the highest quality service by continuous improvement, and through the skillfulness of our most valuable asset—our employees. The company is focused on zero accidents, believing all injuries and occupational illnesses are preventable. "No job is so important that we cannot take the time to do it safely," adds Boutte. "We take pride in maintaining employee retention and minimizing turnover."

In a 2012, *The Environmental Report* (CNN and FOX) with former football great Terry Bradshaw, recognized Proline "For changing the way we do things to help preserve and protect our world for the future…"

Boutte and Green, president and vice president respectively, are long-time supporters of the ARC in Acadiana, The Boy Scouts of America, and Girl Scouts of America. The Beaver Club and Salvation Army are beneficiaries of Proline's community generosity.

FALCO ENERGY

It has been said more than once that the energy business is one that defines the American dream. In the same vein, the history of Falco is a history of humble beginnings, vision, and enduring prosperity born of consistency and fruitful collaboration. With its roots in 1950s Louisiana and a current presence felt strongly throughout the south and northwest, Falco is a name that continues to be synonymous with the trade and transportation of American Crude Oil.

In the years that followed WWII, a young man named J. E. Fowler was working on the refinery truck rack at Shreveport Producing Co. (currently Calumet Refining Co.) While unloading crude oil and loading product, he saw an opportunity before him. His first unit of "rolling stock" was a tank in the back of a pickup truck. When the 1950s unfolded, so did the first legal liabilities climate. With major oil producers looking to reduce transportation risks, J. E. quickly assessed his willingness to take ownership of crude and condensate, and the birth of Falco, Inc. was the result.

Through the next three decades, J. E. grew his fleet of trucks, becoming the largest oil products transporter in Louisiana by 1970. It was an era of prosperity for a hardworking, tenacious "trucker" with an eye for opportunity, and the will to succeed. He became a strong presence in North Louisiana, and

served under Governor John McKeithen as the Louisiana representative to the Interstate Oil and Gas Compact Commission. The year 1979 brought tremendous loss to many when J. E. died tragically, along with his granddaughter, and pilot Cotton Jeter, as they attempted to land at his beloved hunting camp in south Texas.

By the time of the accident, J. E. was retired, and Clair S. Smith was president and CEO of what had become P&O Falco. The prior period in Falco's evolution began when J. E. hired Clair in 1971, and initiated an era of growth that defined the company. Fresh from his early years of acquiring and scheduling crude for Monsanto, Clair would soon lead Falco into full-dimension trading to complement the companies' solid roots in transportation. Although Clair brought a new perspective to J. E.'s company, the two men were quite similar in many respects. Raised in working class families, they were both guided by basic principles of right and wrong, fairness, and hard work. They also shared a great passion for the outdoors, and spent a good deal of time fishing and hunting, with a particular fondness for the bobwhite quail of South Texas. They were said to be hard-nosed bosses, who were also notably kind, compassionate individuals.

In 1974, with a fleet of 125 trucks moving crude oil, Falco's growth potential sought the influx of additional capital, and Clair negotiated the company's sale to Devon Energy' and later to the high-profile mainliner, Peninsular and Oriental Steam Navigation Company of London. With the support of an impressive balance sheet, and a rapidly expanding oil market as a result of the first embargo, Falco flourished. With Clair at the helm, Falco built terminals and pipelines, entered into refinery processing arrangements, and developed a large refined products marketing operation. Led primarily by Clair's gut instincts, the company carefully navigated the early crude oil trading days where inventories were difficult to gauge and track, much less trade.

With no transparent futures market to hedge risks of inventories, and a less than high-tech communication system, it was a challenging environment to say the least. There was no "futures price" provided by a

market, so the "majors" set their own "posted price." Never a man to mince words, Clair once said: "some days I feel like a one-legged man in an ass-kicking contest." This was particularly applicable since he was, in fact, an amputee who lost a leg to an accident early in life. A significant challenge was not unfamiliar territory to him, and like most difficult things, he saw the inherent possibilities it provided. While enjoying continued prosperity, P&O Falco became UPG Falco, and in the early 1980s it was reorganized to become Enron Oil Trading and Transportation (later merging with other companies to become Plains All American Pipeline Company.)

In 1990, Clair re-entered the oil trading and transportation business using the brand he helped establish. Having received the rights to the Falco name years earlier, Clair formed Falco S&D, along with his son, C. Scott Smith, and the Davison family, of Ruston, Louisiana. The company was sold to Genesis in 1999.

What followed was another example of fortunate timing and good collaboration for Falco. As Scott carefully eyed the market, his friend, Jackie Heckman, urged him north with just the opportunity he awaited. Two months before Clair's death in December 2007, his son, Scott, proudly raised the familiar flag; launching seven trucks in the Rockies. Today, with Scott as president and CEO, Falco Energy enjoys continued growth with a fleet of almost 100 trucks and over 200 employees.

In the seven decades since Falco was formed, the world has seen the most significant technological advancements in history, and the energy business has been transformed along with all areas of life. However, the mission of the company remains consistent. Falco energy offers the same flexibility and efficiency clients have come to expect, while providing a safe, reliable, and timely source of transportation of crude oil products.

Falco continues to respond and adapt as the industry requires, yet it maintains the awareness that some things are never meant to change. The Falco Flag is more than a company logo. The current flag represents the evolution of an industry; while the familiarity of the traditional symbol stands as a reminder of the superior level of service provided, wherever the flag flies.

ACTION INDUSTRIES, INC.

Michael J. Medine, Jr., knows firsthand, the benefits of diversification. The president and CEO of Action Industries, Inc., had a hunch that his father's company would produce higher revenue if he expanded his portfolio by providing additional services to a variety of clients in the oil and gas (O&G) industry.

Action Industries is the parent company of two original companies—Action Oilfield Services, Inc., begun in 1982, and Shelby J. Gaudet Contractors, Inc., founded in 1981. Elmar Consulting, LLC, was started in 2001; and Action Environmental Services, LLC, was created in 2011.

Action Oilfield Services, founded by Michael J. Medine, Sr., remained primarily local, serving South Central Louisiana until the late 1990s. After college, Mike, Jr., became more involved in the day-to-day operations in and out of the office. He saw the growth potential and purchased the business from his father on August 2003. He could see the oilfield "shrinking" on a local scale and realized the company needed to diversify by securing new clients, offering additional services, and covering a wider geographical base. Today, under the umbrella of Action Industries, the company's various divisions continue to provide construction, maintenance and operational services, not only locally, but throughout the Gulf Coast Region. The company's mission is to provide professional, cost-effective services to the oilfield and related industry sectors.

"After paying back my original corporate loan (2010), I focused on reducing other equipment debt and upgraded older equipment. Just about when that was going on, I had a phone call from Shelby Gaudet concerning a possible buy-out opportunity for me. After serious consideration, it was a signed deal, giving the company additional diversification opportunity," says Mike, Jr.

Action's Industries' growth and core values have remained constant. According to the CEO, "Careful decision making, personal responsibility, accountability and leading by example, have served us well in developing and providing additional services to many well-known clients."

To demonstrate the company's diversification, Action Industries is recognized as a leader throughout the O&G industry for piping services, well blowout/oil spill response, field management, production and process operations, vegetation management, environmental services, project management, rig welding, general plant maintenance and construction.

"Since our last business venture in 2011, we have more than doubled our workforce, employing over 125 people. Our revenues have increased substantially," he adds. "We continue to serve industries in which we've diversified, and are expanding into other geographical areas.

"Our goal is to provide clients with services that will allow them to be the best in their respective fields, and deliver results that directly impact their bottom lines."

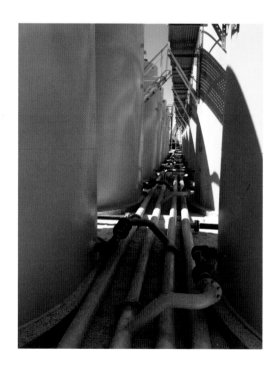

Action Industries is headquartered in Belle Rose, Louisiana, with branches in White Castle and Lafayette.

STRIC-LAN COMPANIES, L.L.C.

Above: Multi-well pad site, post frac flow-back, Marcellus Shale.

Below: Company founder Ronald Landry.

For more than forty years, Stric-Lan Companies, L.L.C. has tested the most challenging oil and gas (O&G) wells under the most diverse conditions. Stric-Lan can test any well, anywhere! They have performed outstanding services in depths of over 3,000 feet of water on a floating deepwater rig; and at an elevation as high as 3,000 feet on a multi-well pad in the Marcellus Shale. Stric-Lan's extensive fleet of equipment is unmatched in the industry for their capacity, innovation, adaptability, and unparalleled maintenance standards.

Stric-Lan was founded in 1972 as a production well-testing company by Ronald J. Landry and Jim Strickland in Lafayette. In 1973, Ronald Landry, a registered petroleum engineer, designed the first "super separator", the SL Super Separator™—a vessel well-adapted to cleaning up and enhancing the testing of O&G wells. A unique oil burner, the SL Super Burner, was designed in 1975. Landry purchased the interests of Strickland in 1978 and developed them into the largest, privately-owned well testing company in the Gulf Coast region. Landry was principal owner until his passing in November 2002. The company is currently owned and managed by two of his children, CEO Karen Landry-Oertling, and President Gary Landry.

In 1978 it opened an office in Shreveport with operations in Victoria and Alice, Texas. In 1982, a full-service slickline company was established in Lake Charles, with sales offices in Houston and New Orleans. SCORE, an electric wireline company specializing in data acquisition and interpretation services, and a gas lift operation were founded in 1984. Two years later, market conditions prompted downsizing, with the company reorganizing and consolidating as a single company headquartered in Lafayette. The assets of Dubco Wireline and Proline Wireline were purchased in 1997. All wireline operations were sold in 2003. The first company to provide Ultra High Volume separators to the pipeline industry in 1999, Stric-Lan opened its first separate pipeline operations group in Tulsa in 2006. This on-line separation service is trademarked as the Total Containment® Package.

Today, Stric-Lan Companies, L.L.C. is a diversified energy and oilfield service company specializing in production well testing and flowback services, DEEPTEST™ deepwater testing, pipeline services including cleaning, pigging, hydrotesting, drying, filtration and separation, turnkey SCADA services from concept-implementation, electronic data acquisition, and reservoir engineering to a wide base of clientele. The company has grown from a handful of people in its infancy to more than eighty people since 2007.

Stric-Lan is one of the few well test companies providing the additional engineering needed in today's oilfield. From complete test design to data acquisition and analysis, they offer their clients the latest in computerized reporting, wireless well test data acquisition and satellite transmission of critical data. Its expertise, innovation, and state-of-the-art equipment have distinguished it as an industry leader.

Stric-Lan maintains the most stringent safety and training requirements in the industry. Its employees are highly trained and experienced in all aspects of safety including job safety analysis, incident prevention and reporting, and behavioral safety. Working in diverse markets demands the company's dedication to accurate measurement, timely data, quality personnel and equipment for flowback, well testing, SCADA and pipeline work.

Stric-Lan has built an unparalleled reputation as a company that delivers the highest quality services to its clients in diverse service applications and is recognized as a "Best in Class Service Leader." A focus on detail and a determination to go the extra mile have been among the core values of Stric-Lan since its beginning. The challenging and dynamic nature of the O&G industry have not deterred the company from maintaining the highest standards for each service it provides in each region, and on each job.

Stric-Lan has based its operations out of Lafayette for more than forty years, and currently has offices in Conroe, Texas; Pleasanton, Texas; Coraopolis, Pennsylvania; and Monroeville, Alabama. Its Lafayette main office allows for coverage in South and Central Louisiana and the Gulf of Mexico, where it performs well testing, flowback, pipeline, and SCADA services. The company's Texas operations in Pleasanton and Conroe allow for special attention and services required in the Eagle Ford, Woodbine, and Texas Railroad Districts 1, 2, 3, 4,

and 6. There, Stric-Lan focuses on delivering flowback, SCADA, and pipeline services. The Coraopolis office was opened in 2009 to facilitate flowback services in the Marcellus and Utica Shale regions. Stric-Lan's Monroeville office focuses on the South and Central Alabama and Mississippi regions where it is the dominant holder of market share of SCADA services.

The company's mission is providing specialized equipment and services to the energy industry—both domestic and international. It positions itself as the service leader to continually improve its professional services through teamwork and innovation in a safe and environmentally sound manner.

Above: Mr. Ronnie, *250MMCFD separator, one of the largest true separators available.*

Left: DEEPTEST™ *deepwater testing operations.*

Below: Cajun Express 400 *and* Challenger *working a pipeline job in California, flowing 1.2 BCF gas.*

WET TECH ENERGY, INC.

Wet Tech Energy (WTE), begun in 1999 as a small dive and navigational company in the Gulf of Mexico (GOM) region, has since grown into a diversified company offering customized solutions for a wide range of floating and fixed aids to navigation, including platform navigational lighting, horns, navigational buoys, and mooring systems.

Because of the highly competitive diving market, the stockholders in 2000 decided to consolidate by spinning off the company solely as a navigational company. That proved to be a wise move because each year since, WTE has experienced phenomenal growth, adding new products and services.

Don Carl, founder and chief operating officer of the family-owned company previously worked as a pioneer in the offshore navigational industry, first utilizing solar panels offshore. His early experiences positioned him well for owning and operating companies that performed anchor handling services in the 1970s and 1980s.

With the oil bust in the 1980s, Don did not want to give up the ship, so to speak. That is when he joined Exxon. Upon his retirement from Exxon, he worked as a

company representative for several other oil companies where he gained invaluable experience prompting him to realize that the timing was right to form his own company. Wet Tech was incorporated in August 1999, with his wife, Jayne; son, Todd; and daughter, Tonya, joining him. The three have continually worked alongside him to assure the success of the company.

Although each family member has carved a particular niche for themselves in the business, Don continues to play a major role in the day-to-day operations, and says that, "Each passing day has been another notch in the belt for the company, family, and our loyal, experienced employees who helped the business grow and diversify. I have learned to delegate more; but admit that I'm the first in the office in the mornings—and, the last to leave."

As WTE has grown, expanding its operations with supply, providing offshore services for installation and inspection/repair of systems in the GOM and beyond. It maintains a full fabrication department that fabricates the buoys and navigational skids; and, also works with a wide-range of leading companies providing custom fabrications in aluminum and steel. As part of Wet Tech's fabrication services, it maintains a full-scale sandblasting and coatings department that is charged with coating all steel assets. In addition, it shares its experience with many other companies.

In addition, Wet Tech Energy provides equipment and marine fenders globally, including anchor chain and all fittings for connections. It also caters to the wire rope and sub-sea industry by providing rental spooling machines and operators for spooling umbilical lines and wire rope for spools, some weighing up to seventy thousand pounds.

The Carls founded Wet Tech Safety and Rentals in November 2012 as a subsidiary of the parent company. It focuses on providing clients with cost-effective safety solutions executed with professionalism, quality equipment, and the highest level of communications— all completed in a timely manner.

Since the first day of operations, Don's family has been instrumental in the development of Wet Tech. Jayne serves as president and CEO; Tonya Carl Anderson is secretary and treasurer; and Todd is vice president of South Texas Operations.

Jayne has been there for her husband during the ups and downs of the company and O&G industry. Her responsibilities include the financial and administrative operations. The couple has been married for forty-seven years and, aside from day-to-day operations, look forward to the many events the company holds for staff each year, from employee-family picnics, to holiday gatherings. These activities build teamwork and incorporate family attributes within the company.

Tonya has been in charge of payroll and all financial/insurance administrative duties since the company started. While raising three children, she projects a positive image with her smile and warm nature, which is contagious throughout the organization. Her husband, Paul, joined the company in 2003 and became vice president in 2007.

Todd has worked in most of the operational capacities that WTE offers. He leads the company in many of the newest product and service lines, and reaffirmed his role into the new business subsidiary in South Texas where Wet Tech Safety and Rentals has begun to grow with compliance testing, employee training, safety equipment, rental equipment, and a wide range of products and services through the three locations in South Texas (Cotulla, Carrizo Springs, and Karnes City).

While conditions during the first years of WTE existence were challenging and educational, the team has adapted to the cyclical nature of the offshore industry, balancing a business with a wide range of inventory and a full array of services while adapting to varying marketing conditions. Many of those changes were induced by hurricane devastation in the GOM that began in 2001 with Lili, and continued through the storms of 2005 and 2008. These storms have enabled WTE to tackle problems for their growing client base, including preset mooring systems for construction, salvage operations, multi-point mooring systems, and marine equipment for a wide range of market activities domestically and abroad.

RAY OIL TOOL
COMPANY

Right: Ray Mikolajczyk.

Ray Mikolajczyk believes in family values. And, he believes that family history has been the contributing factor to his success in the oil and gas (O&G) industry.

As owner of Ray Oil Tool Company, he only remembers his grandfather's funeral; but, it is the deceased man's work ethic that has inspired him. "My grandfather was a successful farmer and rancher who began his own business with six acres of land and flowing water well," says Ray. "He was a hard-worker who was able to leave his five children 500 acres each, complete with house, water well and cattle," he adds. "I want my children to remember me just like I remember grand-daddy-kind, conscientious, hardworking, focused, and dedicated to what I do."

Ray's own father, while leaving him property, also encouraged him to attend college and get a degree that would prepare him for a successful career. Living in Louisiana amid the land that was ripe in petroleum, it was natural that Ray felt drawn to the industry. He graduated with a petroleum engineering degree and a knack for problem solving. Young Ray was always challenged, hoping to find a better or easier way to do something. He admits to always being on the lookout for ways to make operations faster and better. And, he has succeeded, with several patents for oil field tools.

He designed a measuring device that indicates exact drill bit depth at all times. He

chose not to pursue a patent for the device because it required a specialist to install and service it. "I realized that service people are expensive," he says.

In 1984, however, Ray had an idea to change life-and-well completion technology. "I was a consultant drilling manager on an independent producer's well. We had a good bore and everything was in perfect condition. We used the mud sweep in front of the cement to make sure it was not contaminated. We wanted a good cement across our productive interval. Still, the logs showed poor bonding across the sandstones that constituted the life of the well.

"A few days later, the company ran a cutting-edge composite log. The new composite log told the entire story-caliper of the shale and sandstone formations, washout of the shale formation, near bit size across the sandstones, sandstone formations supporting the casing resulted in poor cement bonding, and shales washed out with poor bonding. It was like the light bulb went off. I instantly realized that we needed to combine the logs."

At that point, he realized the industry's standard, flexible, bow-type centralizers were ineffective. "They did not have the strength to support the casing off the side of the well bore throughout the productive sandstones. That's when I developed a centralizer that was strong enough to hold it off."

His theory explained a longstanding oil patch mystery as to why certain wells that seemed properly drilled and completed inexplicably degenerated from water coning. "When the gauger swabbed the well back onto production, he encountered mud and then water. That is a direct indication the mud came from somewhere that was never cemented," he adds.

He says that when drilling through sandstone, the bit and drill string are never plumb-bob straight vertical, but leans to one side. "The hole is not perfectly round, so the worn section has a notch cut. If everything isn't properly centralized, the wear-area channel will not get proper cement."

His revelation set the industry standard that a solid centralizer constitutes a better oil field. "It's easy to install; it's just a matter of having the rig crew slip it on the casing. It has stop rings to keep them separated, and set screws in the blades, which attach it to the casing and keep it moving."

With Ray's years of drilling experience, his friends and workers in the oilfields were obvious targets for his products that make drilling more efficient, easier, and safer. In the years since his epiphany, his centralizers have become the industry standard, although others have now gotten into manufacturing.

"It doesn't matter who is manufacturing them, think I could not have designed a better tool for the oil industry."

By 1988, he applied for a patent that was later issued for a centralized float shoe and a centralized float collar. With his inventions, secondary cementing is almost passé. The company sold its first float shoe in August 1990; and, after more than 600 jobs, primary cementing has proven sufficient more than 99 percent of the time. Other innovations have been a spiral solid casing centralizer, in-line casing centralizers, and well-splitters.

Ray Oil Tool has grown because of Ray's innovations, and his belief in building a company with dedicated employees, some of which are his family. His daughter, Aleta Richard, oversees the company's financial picture, while son, Raymond, Jr., manages the daily operations. His stepson, Robbie Robbins has been with the company since start-up and is vice president of sales. Third generation Jake Mikolajczyk just started working and has a degree in industrial technology. "Whether we're family or not, our employees focus on quality. Nothing ruins a relationship quicker than product failure. We aim to avoid that—and, keep our customers happy, too."

SLICK CONSTRUCTION CO., INC.

Do not be fooled by the name on the door. Slick Construction is professional in every sense of the word. "Our name is actually derived from the first owners," says Vice President Ginger Smith Rozas.

Rozas, representing the third generation of the family-owned business, adds that her grandfather, Douglas D. Smith came to Louisiana from Texas with Brown & Root Company.

In 1956, with knowledge and experience in the oil industry, Douglas, along with C. M. Click, Paul Montgomery, and Drew Cornell, decided to form their own service company. At that time, they bought the Y. M. Yarbough Co. assets. They merged the names Smith and Click, forming the name Slick, as the company is known today—a name they felt people would remember

During the early years, Slick was primarily engaged with board roading and well hook-ups. During 1957-58, when oil dropped to $3 per barrel, the business reached a low point. That is when Click, Montgomery, and Cornell resigned and sold the company to Douglas.

In 1959, Douglas' son, Clifton (Buz) joined the company on a full time basis. Sherald Reeves, joined the company in 1962 when she married Clifton. At that point, most of the work was performed for Mobil Oil and consisted of hook-ups as well as board road installations. At that time, Slick purchased Hub City Construction's Eunice property at 1101 East Ardoin Street, which remains their office today.

In 1965, Clifton expanded the business to include gas processing plants construction and maintenance, and some limited pipeline work for companies such as Union Texas Petroleum, Texas Pacific Oil and Ashland Oil at the LSU field.

In 1988, Ginger, Clifton and Sherald's daughter, joined the business. Slick expanded its pipeline work to include such companies as Exxon-Mobil Pipeline, Columbia Gulf Transmission, Gulf South Pipeline, Crosstex Energy and Targa Resources, as well as many others.

Slick Construction remains a family-owned business specializing in construction and maintenance in the oil and gas industry. With over fifty-seven years of service, Slick provides years of knowledge in pipeline, gas processing, compressor and metering stations, concrete and right-of-way work. Their span of work spreads from Louisiana to Texas, Mississippi, and beyond.

Originally, as the old timers in the oil industry can remember, Slick conducted business with a verbal agreement and a handshake. Today, work includes lengthy contracts, strict safety regulations and detailed record keeping. Slick remains a woman-owned business that strives to achieve its customers' high expectations. They credit their success to God's blessings, their wonderful long term work force of dedicated employees and their faithful customers.

Slick Construction Company takes pride in its mission statement: safety, quality, and integrity…it is how we do business!

Above: Douglas D. Smith at an oilfield location.

CBC Services is a family-owned business that was started in 1996 by Delton, Jeff, and Greg Caskey from Goldonna, Louisiana. For the Caskeys, welding was in their blood. Their desire to weld was passed down to them from their father and uncles.

For years, Delton, Jeff, and Greg worked as welders all over the United States. Most of the time, at least two of the brothers were working together. While working for a construction company in California, they decided they wanted to start their own company. Though the Caskey brothers tried relentlessly, the business never came together.

After leaving California, the brothers found themselves working in different cities in Florida. A year later, the idea of starting a business was brought up again because the brothers wanted to work closer to home. Delton, Jeff, and Greg met at Grady's restaurant between Orlando and Tampa to discuss the idea once again. The business plan was written on a napkin and it was decided that each brother would invest $10,000. The company would be named CBC Services, which stands for Caskey Brothers Construction Services.

Greg came back to Louisiana to start the process of getting the license for the business. Since funds were limited, CBC saved money whenever possible by purchasing used equipment. Work for CBC picked up in the summer of 1997 when the company got a few small contract jobs with only a few employees. The owners worked as welders during the day. Their nights consisted of working on equipment and doing paperwork. Their first office building was a 12-by-24-foot portable building. They later built their home office.

For years, CBC did municipal work along with pipeline jobs. In 2004 the owners decided to stop municipal work to focus on the gas industry. In 2005, CBC took an offer to help with clean up in South Louisiana after Hurricane Katrina.

Upon returning home from the Katrina clean up, CBC received work in the Vernon Field. They also worked in the Haynesville Shale in 2009. In a year, CBC nearly quadrupled in size. During this time, the owners also started CBC Pipeline, LLC to handle larger operations.

In addition to the home office, CBC has an office in Ohio where they have work in the Utica Shale. With the success of CBC, the owners have stayed true to their family roots. Though CBC continues to grow, it is still a family business, which now includes a second generation of Caskeys. Delton, Jeff, and Greg work closely with their children to ensure continuing success of CBC Services and CBC Pipeline.

CBC SERVICES

NGE TECHS

In an effort to keep equipment in South Louisiana's oil and gas industry running properly and safely, many onshore and offshore companies have come to rely on the services of Natural Gas Engine Techs (NGE Techs).

Founder Bill Adams opened Compressor Engineering, the forerunner of NGE Techs in June 1999. When he retired in 2004, he gave the company to Ed Pickett, mechanical supervisor, and the other employees who had worked for him. That group changed the name to Natural Gas Engine and Compressor Services, Inc., which was strictly a mechanical service company. Pickett decided to retire in July 2010. The CPA of Natural Gas and a silent partner purchased the company from Pickett and NGE Compressor Services was formed.

NGE Techs is dedicated to repairing and maintaining natural gas and diesel engines and compressors onshore and offshore. She says that the company "provides instrumentation and electrical crews and technicians for panels and production location hookups." In addition, NGE Techs provides production operators and valve technicians. "We pride ourselves on quality—not quantity," says the CEO. Because the owners of the previous company wanted out,

rather than having all the employees search for jobs, Joanie decided to step up and form the company as woman-owned.

"In the early days, we operated on a shoestring, providing all parts and repairs in our shop and offshore. I ordered and delivered parts to all locations from Venice, Louisiana, to Cameron, Louisiana, docks and heliports. I was on call 24 hours a day—7 days a week—365 days a year, in addition to keeping the books and answering the phones. I was the 'lifeline' for the customers as well as the employees looking for parts or for someone to talk to or to get in touch with their homes. The mechanics did diesel and natural gas work and Brent Duhon was shop foreman, but was also a call-out and overhaul mechanic. It was up to us to make it happen for our customers," Joanie said.

Today, NGE has 20 employees, 15 customers and $2.5 million in revenues.

What is on the table for NGE Techs in the future? The company wants to grow to a maximum of fifty employees; however, it plans to remain at the 5011 Port Road location in New Iberia. "Our motto is, "The Good Lord led us to it; He will get us through it; and He only gives His hardest battles to His strongest warriors." Joanie adds that NGE Techs is focused on quality not quantity. "That is vital to our small and diversified company."

Above: Joanie Edgar.

Today, as the world's oil and gas reserves are found in more difficult geologic settings, they require increasingly better technology to facilitate oil and gas recovery.

Flotek Industries, Inc., headquartered in Houston, Texas, has come to play a vital role in the innovative and technological advances in the extraction of oil and gas resources from the earth's more difficult geologic settings.

Flotek was founded in 1985, with the original Petrovalve as the primary product. The company joined forces with CESI Chemical, Inc., in 2001, and has continued to grow through acquisitions including centralizers, downhole tools, drilling motors, Teledrift directional drilling surveys, along with stimulation and production chemicals. As a result, Flotek has become a leading force in the technology-enabled revolution within the oil and gas industry. And, while each technology requires unique technical expertise, all of our products and services share the commitment to our vision to provide best-in-class technology, cutting-edge innovation to address the ever-changing challenges of our customers and to provide exceptional customer service.

Flotek plays an important role in the entire lifecycle of a well through our three product lines (Chemical and Logistics, Downhole Tools and Artificial Lift). In the drilling process, our Downhole Tools division provides a variety of equipment used in the drill string including drilling jars, shock subs, drilling stabilizers, roller reamers, and mud motors. Flotek also provides real-time MWD directional surveys through our Teledrift subsidiary.

In addition, Flotek furnishes a number of drilling chemicals and products that enhance the drill bit penetration rate. Once drilled, Flotek assists clients in their primary completions with cementing float shoes and our casing centralizers, including bowsprings, turbulator centralizers, and polymer centralizers to ensure an easier entry for the casing and better cement integrity. Flotek also provides cement additives to ensure that the cement quality is adequate for zonal isolation.

Once the primary completion is accomplished, then Flotek is heavily involved in providing environmentally friendly stimulation chemicals such as our Complex nano-Fluid™

suite of chemistries, which enhance the production rate and reserves obtained through hydraulic fracturing operations. After the well is drilled, completed, and stimulated, Flotek's pump services division provides electrical submersible pumps (ESPs) and our patented Petrovalve for our client's artificial lift needs. And further along in the life of the reservoir, Flotek's chemical group provides various chemistries for conformance control and other improved oil recovery (IOR) applications.

Flotek is known throughout the industry as a global supplier of critical well services and equipment that enhance recovery. To maintain leadership with the technology, Flotek has invested in client-centered research, which promotes building relationships and bringing products and services to market quicker and more efficiently.

With all of Flotek's innovative and technology driven products, there is now only one question to ask, "IS FLOTEK IN YOUR WELL?"

FLOTEK INDUSTRIES, INC.

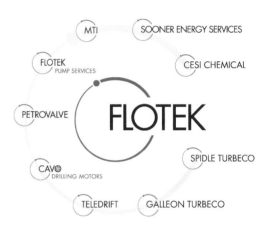

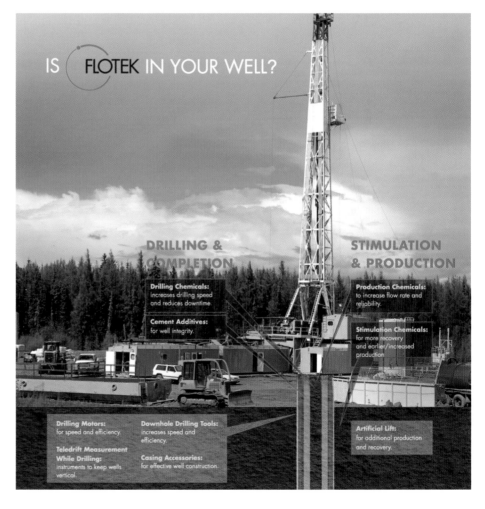

SUPPORT SERVICES

PHILLIPS ENERGY PARTNERS

Christopher Phillips.

Christopher Phillips is quick to give praise where it is due. As president of the company that he started in 2006, Phillips Energy Partners (PEP), he emphasizes the contributions and value of the three generations who played vital roles in the family's earlier businesses. "From Sam Sklar, my grandfather, who started the first business, the torch has been passed for them to carry the rest of the family businesses forward.

"PEP is an evolution of three generations and three different company names. With each generation came a new company name with each of three generations' contributing to the core values. 'Mr. Sam,' as my grandfather was known, was a dedicated, hard-working, frugal man who passed those values on to the rest of us," Phillips said.

In the early 1920s, Sam Sklar and his wife, Ida, set sail from Russia immigrating to the United States in search of the American dream. The couple worked their way south to Shreveport, Louisiana, where they started a small scrap metal company during the Great Depression. The company, Louisiana Iron & Supply enabled Mr. Sam to trade scrap material to increase his income as he worked toward the East Texas oil boom.

Sklar Production Company was the outgrowth of the scrap business he had started. It soon grew into one of the largest oil and gas (O&G) companies in the Ark-LA-Tex area. Like many of his generation, Mr. Sam's life was more about opportunity than it was about the frills and thrills that success often brings—and that future generations would come to enjoy. He proved himself with his business acumen, deriving extreme joy in his work. That joy was shared by Ida and their three children—Albert, Fred, and Betty.

Mr. Sam, it has been said, was tight with a penny. In fact, one story handed down through the years is about Mr. Sam and Gus Erickson, his landman and future vice president, stopping for coffee on their way to a site. Gus asked if he could get Mr. Sam a cup of coffee, and Sam replied, "No thanks, but I will take the nickel!"

In the early days, Mr. Sam often rode to various locations with Gus. Together, they checked out wells and discussed business.

Gus played a major role in helping to grow Sklar & Phillips, along with geologist S. A. Womack, among others.

When Fred was killed during WWII, his death took a toll on the family. Following his death, Albert went to work with his father, and Betty attended the University of Texas. She married Leonard Phillips, who had just acquired a law degree from the University of Denver. It was his law degree that proved valuable in the O&G industry when he joined Albert and Mr. Sam in forming Sklar & Phillips Oil Company.

Albert and Leonard brought a new dynamic to the company. Mr. Sam continued to accompany the pumpers to check the wells, resting assured that the company was in good hands with the two younger men who worked to develop relationships throughout the industry. At that time, Shreveport was a hub to many of the major oil companies, as well as large independents. This wealth of opportunity now gave Sklar & Phillips many advantages to participate in prospecting, develop prospects, nurture relationships in return for farm-outs, which required additional help.

Albert and Leonard were polished gentlemen, but real oilmen at heart. They were men of their word, and time proved their word was as good as a contract. During this time, Albert and Mariam had three children—Judy, Suzy and Howard. Leonard and Betty were the parents of Sandy and Fred.

Albert and Leonard, along with their wives, not only became partners, but best friends, as well. They shared a unique bond. Times for them were interspersed with glamorous summers spent in LaCosta, California, attending the races at Del Mar that attracted other O&G executives, people from other industries, and Hollywood stars. In fact, among Betty and Leonard's good friends in the Hollywood jet set were John Wayne and William Holt. They often wintered in Acapulco. They enjoyed their free time; but, they loved the conservative business that Mr. Sam had grown only out of cash flow and never with the utilization of debt. In a boom or bust business, this company philosophy and virtue provided them with an advantage when times were tough and geologists they knew could bring Sklar &

Phillips a prospect and if they liked it, they could count on being paid on time.

Betty remained interested in the business, especially when Freddy, her son, assumed more responsibility after his father died from cancer in 1987. She felt it was her role to ensure what her father, husband, and brother had built. A petite blond, she was still socializing at seventy years old. She knew everyone in town—and, they knew her. Leonard's death left Fred and Albert to manage the business. The relationship proved challenging, but effective. Albert's son, Howard, returned to Shreveport after receiving degrees from Massachusetts Institute of Technology (MIT). His father, Albert, died in 1997, and Fred and Howard continued to operate as Sklar & Phillips for several years before splitting the company. Although sad, they both agreed it was better to split the company in order to accommodate each side's growing families, and to allow each to pursue their individual agendas.

Freddy was the first to return to the family business after obtaining a business degree from the University of Colorado. While there, he developed a love for flying, race cars, was married, and had his first child, Christopher. He later attended Tulane where he received a MBA in finance and spent twenty years before being joined by his cousin, Howard, Albert's son. Fred, not quite as frugal as his grandfather, enjoys life to the fullest, becoming a world class race car driver, representing the United States in Europe for the Kimberly Cup, and winning the Formula Atlantic Championship back home. His second son, Cassidy, was born in New Orleans just before he moved back to devote the rest of his life to Sklar & Phillips, which would later become Phillips Energy, Inc. (PEI).

Fred, also known by family members as Freddy, initially focused on the real estate of the family while gaining knowledge of the oil business. He spent twenty years working with his father and uncle, gaining the experience that he could not acquire from textbooks. The hands-on experience enabled him to develop a keen sense for deals, but also helped him transition into a more conservative businessman later in life, always recognizing the responsibility to pass along what he had inherited. He has, in turn, shared his expertise, knowledge, and contacts with his own son while heading his own company, PEI. "I value all he has taught me about the O&G industry. He has impacted my life in more ways than I can count, and remains a great mentor, today," says Chris.

Through his initiatives, Freddy helped change the landscape of southern Shreveport after the family donated the land where LSU-Shreveport is located. The college has proven beneficial to the city in terms of developing infrastructure, revenue and increasing traffic. He was instrumental in developing three hospitals, the original shopping centers, and a theater in what was once three cotton fields. Most of the first structures in southern Shreveport were developments and tenants he encouraged to move there. Today, the area is a high concentration of traffic, retail, hospitals, lodging and restaurants.

In addition, Freddy invested in a start-up company led by Kelsey Warren after Kelsey sold Cornerstone Natural Gas (previously Endevco), a company he brought out of bankruptcy to El Paso. The Energy Transfer Co. went public in the late 1990s, and is now

one of the largest Midstream/Pipeline MLPs in the country. If that were not enough, he started an aviation company to manage, own and maintain Arkla Gas' flight department, which was later acquired by Arkla.

While Freddy was dedicated to the family business, like his parents, he likes to have fun; being more of a thrill-seeker. He continues to fly his own planes and is type-rated to fly everything from small aerobatic airplanes to big jets. He, too, had friends in Hollywood, including Paul Newman, who raced in the twenty-four hours of Daytona. *Esquire* magazine quoted Newman about hanging out with Freddy in Shreveport while filming the movie, *Blaze*. He said he took along a couple of beers when the two were flying in one of Freddy's aerobatic planes above the Red River. Freddy set the beers on the dash, then began rolling the plane upside down without the beer falling.

In 2000, Phillips Energy, Inc. (PEI) was formed. By then, Fred was remarried with three more children—Collin, Sue, and Alexa. His sister, Sandy, also had three children—Gregory, Kimberly, and Randolph. These six, along with Christopher and Cassidy, comprise the fourth generation to enter the O&G business. Betty passed away in 2010, resulting in each of the others becoming shareholders in PEI, and each being involved with the business and family in some definite way. Betty played a very dear

and important role in her children and grandchildren's lives.

Christopher learned many of the values implemented within Phillips Energy when his grandfather, Leonard, allowed him to sit in on prospect showings and staff meetings. Christopher recalls his grandfather teaching him to read stock quotes in the newspaper, drilling reports, and even racing forms. After his grandfather passed away, Betty, his grandmother, played an important role in encouraging young Christopher to develop his ability to network with all types of people, building his confidence, "sometimes with tough love," Christopher admits. "She always told it like it was, but exuded a love for life."

Christopher "Chris" Phillips, today, the chief executive officer of Phillips Energy Partners (PEP), owes the company's success in the oil and gas industry (O&G) to the integrity and reputation built before him. "As a youngster growing up in Shreveport, the only thing I knew was oil and gas. After all, both sides of my family had been in the industry for three generations before I came along."

The love of the industry grew on him; and, when it was time to decide on a career, it was natural that he turned to the one thing he knew and cherished: oil and gas. He attended the University of Mississippi during one of the "bust" times, graduating in 1992 with a bachelor's degree in petroleum land management. At that time, the university was one of only four schools offering Petroleum Landman degrees. "I just assumed I would work for the family, and spent a year back in Shreveport working in the family business, which was still Sklar & Phillips at the time."

With diploma in hand, "I was lucky to be working with others who shared my enthusiasm of the oil business. By then, my grandfather had passed away and my father, Fred, and uncle, Albert Sklar, ran the business." During that time, Christopher recognized that he could utilize the vast knowledge and experience of those working with his father and spent countless hours picking the brain of one of several great mentors. "I owe a lot to Scott Stroud, the company's geologist, who, eventually, formed his own successful company. He taught me so much about exploration." (Scott's successful company today is Stroud Exploration.)

Christopher tells how his own company came to be formed. "In 1992, Sklar & Phillips made a significant discovery in Limestone County, Texas, called the Oletha Field. While the discovery was being developed, Endevco emerged from bankruptcy and approached us about building a pipeline and gathering system. Kelsey Warren, the new president of that company was challenged with restructuring and building. After Kelsey made his pitch to us, I asked if I could speak with him. I explained my interest in his company, and told him if there was ever an opening, I would be interested in a job regardless of the pay. He took my offer seriously."

After Endevco's bankruptcy, the name was changed to Cornerstone Natural Gas. That's when they offered Christopher a job trading in natural gas. It was during the early days of deregulation and transparent futures contracts in natural gas. By late 1993 he moved to Dallas and rode one of the biggest waves in the energy industry, which was the development of the trading business, including Enron, among others. Although public, Cornerstone Natural Gas was a small-cap company, which gave him the opportunity to undertake many different responsibilities working closely with

everyone including a man by the name of Kelsey Warren with whom his father had worked. Christopher refers to Kelsey as his friend and early mentor who would ultimately prove to be one of the best deal makers in the O&G industry. Eventually, Kelsey formed Energy Transfer, one of the largest pipeline companies in the country, where he remains CEO and chairman today.

When Cornerstone sold to El Paso in the mid-1990s, Christopher decided to join Lacy Williams, an acquaintance who had just begun his own trading company, Texla Energy Management, a well-known and highly respected mid-sized gas marketing company in Houston. "Like me, he was from Shreveport and his family had roots in the oil and gas industry. We represented over one hundred independents and ultimately endured the bankruptcy of Enron, which led to continued growth." The company has grown to over thirty employees today and continues to market and trade over a billion cubic feet of natural gas per day (bcf/d).

PEP's CEO reflects on the trading business where he learned many helpful lessons, saying, "The ability to assess risk and the potential reward is not always intuitive. Trading has a unique way of developing that skill. It is a skill that can be applied to many different facets of business and life and is imperative to success in trading. Those lessons provided a wealth of knowledge and along with the many valuable contacts, have played one of the biggest parts in molding my future." Enron had helped grow the trading business into one of the highest profile businesses and sectors of its time. Hundreds of mid-20 to mid-30 year-olds had moved to Houston to participate in the boom. Movies were made about friends and their unknown involvement in the Enron Scandal. Downtown Houston developed and embraced the culture of the traders at that time, huge bonuses were paid, and lofts full of traders sprang up in the downtown area.

"I lived next door to the old Cotton Exchange in the Herman Building, a seven-story structure where everyone there was involved in some way with energy, and everyone knew everyone else. It was truly an once-in-a-lifetime period in Houston, which made it seem like everything revolved around the trading of oil and gas commodities. Young, well-educated, extremely well-paid, fast-paced traders were everywhere, and resulted in a "fraternal" close-knit group. The story of Enron ended as more of a tragedy. Watching a company achieve such a high level of success only to come crashing down is something you can only believe possible by witnessing it.

"Lacy (Williams), too, played a significant role in the development of my career and my approach to business. With his expertise in the business, we became highly successful

(Texla remains so) and had a great time doing it. While I enjoyed helping him build that company, I still had the desire to start my own business. I resigned as executive vice president of that company with the idea of pursuing a new business model somewhat void in the oil and gas sector.

"Shortly after making that decision, I was visiting home and reviewed some of the Phillips family investments, when I noticed a royalty acquisition that my uncle Albert had made when he purchased some of Atlantic Richfield's (ARCO's) minerals during one of its restructurings. The investment was yielding more revenue than when it was acquired some fourteen years earlier, had paid out twice, and had a net asset value greater than that when first acquired. That prompted me to do some serious thinking—and called me to action. That's when I founded Phillips Energy Partners, LLC, which initially stemmed from the investment of the cash flow generated exclusively from trading," he adds.

He began by buying small royalties her and there, and soon recognized an opportunity to employ his skills, which previously had been under-appreciated and undervalued. It offered him exposure to energy and the only thing he really knew, while limiting the risk. There were not many companies in the space. He was nearly forty by then, and had built a reputation capable of raising enough money to get started in 2005. Christopher raised a fund from among family and friends, to form an investment pool of one million dollars. In 2007, one of the largest private energy equity providers offered significant capital, and has since committed over $200 million.

He says that the shale revolution enabled the company to grow quickly with the ability to expand acquisitions, including non-producing minerals without the typical geologic risk, and led to the potential to grow significantly. "Prior

to that," adds Christopher, "we primarily acquired producing minerals/royalties on a discounted rate of future cash flows. The shale plays, however, allowed us to take on a little more risk and, in return, provide years of inventory/cash flow/exposure to our investors at a very low cost of entry. All of this "new risk" was, of course, balanced with producing assets and acquisitions to supplement the near term cash flows, thereby, minimizing the potential of not being able to provide a return."

Today, Phillips Energy Partners, LLC is focused on acquisition and management of minerals in nineteen states throughout the United States. The company continually develops and applies strategic portfolio management methodology for minerals with the intent of capitalizing on a niche space within the energy industry. Christopher's hope is that well-engineered portfolios can be molded into investment products, which are perfect for the institutional investor to individual investor looking for exposure in real assets, inflation hedges, and a simpler energy investment with less risk.

Christopher finds it interesting that PEP is active in the same basins as his family was in the early days of the O&G business, beginning with his great grandfather when he entered the industry. "It is quite likely my grandchildren will want to work these same areas and make a living off oil and gas produced through new technologies in these hundred-plus-year fields for years to come. I am hoping my guess is correct that they will take advantage of the family legacy, and will carry on the family tradition."

DARNALL, SIKES,
GARDES & FREDERICK, CPAs

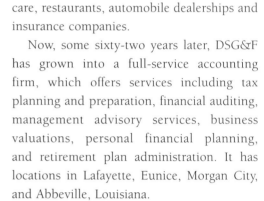

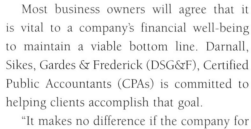

Above: Eugene H. Darnall.

Most business owners will agree that it is vital to a company's financial well-being to maintain a viable bottom line. Darnall, Sikes, Gardes & Frederick (DSG&F), Certified Public Accountants (CPAs) is committed to helping clients accomplish that goal.

"It makes no difference if the company for which we provide services is well established or in start-up mode. We strive to provide all clients with the best advice to help it succeed," says Larry Sikes, partner.

Darnall, Sikes, Gardes & Frederick was founded in 1950 by Eugene H. Darnall, who, after serving in the Pacific Theater in WWII, came home to attend what became the University of Louisiana at Lafayette. There, he obtained his degree in accounting and, after working a couple of years for a local sole practitioner, he decided to set out on his own by establishing his practice. Even in the early days of the firm, innovative ideas were developed to help the firm's clients succeed in the various industries they represented. The development of the firm took a significant advancement in 1989 when the original

Darnall firm joined forces with the Sikes, Frederick firm, which was located in Eunice, Louisiana, creating one of the largest firms of its type in the southwest Louisiana area. Today, the firm services clients throughout Louisiana. The client list includes a wide variety of industries such as oilfield service companies, banking, construction, health-care, restaurants, automobile dealerships and insurance companies.

Now, some sixty-two years later, DSG&F has grown into a full-service accounting firm, which offers services including tax planning and preparation, financial auditing, management advisory services, business valuations, personal financial planning, and retirement plan administration. It has locations in Lafayette, Eunice, Morgan City, and Abbeville, Louisiana.

The CPA firm has been instrumental in the development of its clients' businesses by providing them with valuable and thoughtful planning through tax and management consulting services. In fact, DSG&F understands that when individual companies handle their financials internally, it can sometimes become overwhelming and challenging. The firm's team of professionals has the knowledge and expertise to help companies conquer these challenges by providing accounting support services that allow clients to concentrate on their business without sacrificing control.

Darnall, Sikes, Gardes & Frederick has a host of services to offer its clients. Its consulting experts can help with business and financial consulting, mergers and acquisitions, investment advice, investment banking, litigation support and forensic accounting, and fraud investigation, as well as risk management.

It has a strong team of tax professionals who are hundred-percent tuned into clients' needs. With its longevity and combined experience, it offers comprehensive tax planning, preparation, and consulting solutions to help clients meet their goals. The company is responsive to clients' needs because no two clients are alike. DSG&F listens to clients, understands their objectives, and leverages its own industry experience to shoulder the burden of tax compliance while helping with tax reductions, projections and tax savings strategies.

As its mission statement indicates, Darnall, Sikes, Gardes & Frederick is committed to its clients and dedicated to its employees. The company views growth as opportunity to explore new ideas and technologies, pledging to be the leaders in innovation by staying abreast of all changes within its profession.

The mission further includes the provision of the highest quality and timely service to clients while providing an environment in which company professionals can grow and expand professionally and personally. DSG&F's responsibility is to enhance clients' opportunities for growth by providing innovative concepts that challenge them and ensures their own resources are focused on the future. Darnall adds that the firm will concentrate its energies to maintain the most technically advanced and forward-thinking services possible. The firm provides its entire professional staff with innovative continuing education resources so they can feel confident that they will be up-to-date on the current tax and accounting standards.

It steadfastly embraces a philosophy, which promotes a positive, enriching atmosphere where employee morale is high, where the individual is valued and respected, and where real opportunities for personal growth in the areas of health, education, and professional development are provided. It encourages a high level of openness among employees, promotes communications, and develops a cooperative spirit that fosters teamwork. The firm is proud of its mentoring program that assigns every accountant a mentor who, with their experience in the accounting industry, can help guide the younger accountant as they grow within the firm.

Darnall, Sikes, Gardes & Frederick accepts responsibility to maintain the integrity and enhance the image of its profession. To do that, it strives to be a good community citizen by supporting various charities and organizations, and promoting growth of all the communities within which its employees live and work. DSG&F encourages its entire professional staff to become involved in professional organizations, especially the state organization for CPAs known as the LCPA.

DSG&F is proud of its sixty-two year history of serving its clients with the very best accounting services available and the partners look forward to continuing to strive to be the most innovative and service focused accounting firm in Louisiana.

BRAMMER ENGINEERING, INC.

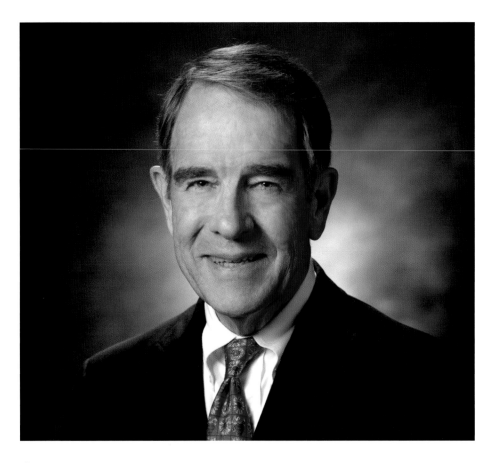

Bob Brammer.

As a petroleum engineer for Franks Petroleum Inc., in the mid-1960s, L. R. "Bob" Brammer, Jr., saw a niche in the oil and gas industry and thought often about filling it.

The native Oklahoman had come to Shreveport in 1954 after earning his engineering degree from the University of Oklahoma (Boomer Sooner!) and serving his country in the Marine Corps in both WWII and Korea. Bob was an intelligent, hard-working professional who had a tremendous capacity to manage multiple complex projects simultaneously. Coupled with his strong work ethic was a very admirable business ethic and integrity that won the trust and confidence of many a person and client.

With experience under his belt, a love for his profession, a reputation widely admired in the Shreveport area, and the support of his mentors like John Franks and Ralph Gilster, Bob left Franks Petroleum and formed Brammer Engineering, Inc. (BEI) in September 1968. His partner and first client was his former boss and close friend, John Franks. The company,

as Bob envisioned it, would be a contract operating firm to service local independent oil and gas operators in the ArkLaTex. The goal was to provide value-added, high-quality engineering and operational services at competitive prices. He further saw the company as a vehicle that would enable many independent oil and gas people in Shreveport to control and operate their own deals and properties. His vision became reality in spite of the fact that Bob was out sick his first week in business and his wife, Dot, was left to answer the phone in his absence.

Today Brammer Engineering, Inc., provides services not only domestically, but around the globe. It is a full-service operating, property management and consulting firm that provides a wide-range of operational and administrative services. Among them are drilling, completion, facility and pipeline construction, procurement, well-site supervision, production management, operations, land, accounting, regulatory, oil and gas marketing, health, safety & environmental services, compliance & reporting, and risk management & insurance services.

Bob felt that many small exploration geologists neither had the resources nor the activity to justify their own staffs. He understood the need for, and created a company built on the "outsourcing" concept a few decades before it became commonplace in the oil and gas world. For the first fifteen to twenty years of the company's existence, the ArkLaTex, and later the South Louisiana market, were the primary areas of Brammer Engineering's activity.

Early clients were Franks Petroleum (John Franks), Goodrich Oil Company (Henry Goodrich), Grigsby Oil and Gas (Jack Grigsby) and Harvey Broyles. These men were all Shreveport independents and personal friends of Bob's. By aggregating multiple accounts of business, Bob could support the staff necessary to drill, complete and operate properties, and supply quality service at a reasonable price.

By the mid-to-late 1980s, oil and gas properties began to change hands frequently. One of those transactions, SONAT's acquisition of Franks Petroleum's North Louisiana properties, proved to be a seminal moment for

Brammer Engineering. Because of that sale, one of Brammer Engineering's clients, Kelley Oil and Gas Corporation, acquired operations on approximately 200 of those wells and hired BEI to contract-operate them. This new piece of business more than doubled the size of the company in a very short period of time and helped position Brammer Engineering for new growth opportunities in the future.

While Shreveport had been a thriving hub for large and small companies in the 1960s and 1970s, that changed in the 1980s as the domestic energy business suffered through a very tough period. Many of those companies had begun relocating to Houston and, as the 1990s arrived, it was evident that BEI's future growth opportunities were primarily with E&P companies headquartered outside of the ArkLaTex. The company began targeting potential clients in Houston and elsewhere. Those efforts provided the growth that carried Brammer Engineering into the twenty-first century.

On New Year's Day 1995, Bob retired from the company, turning the reins over to Keith Evans. Keith was a petroleum engineering graduate from LSU who started his career with Shell and joined the company in 1982. The new management team, which included Keith's partner, Tad May, realized that maintaining the high standards that Bob had set during his forty plus year career were vital to the company's continued growth and success. They also clearly understood that the legacy that Bob left both personally and professionally was the principal foundation for the company's success in the future.

One of the many sales trips to Houston in early 1996 was a visit to a friend at Amoco. The timing was right and thinking "out of the box," Amoco hired BEI to drill three wells in North Louisiana that summer. The success of that first project led Amoco to name Brammer Engineering as project manager for its East Texas drilling program a year later. The relationship continued through the merger with British Petroleum (BP) in 1998. Since that time, Brammer Engineering has drilled and completed hundreds of wells for BP in East Texas and BP remains one of BEI's largest clients.

Brammer Engineering continues to develop strong relationships with numerous large and small independents in both the domestic and international markets. The new millennium prompted continued growth and more opportunities as the outsourcing model became more widely accepted within the industry. The emergence of private equity into the domestic E&P world in the 1990s has fostered exceptional growth opportunities as well. Many relatively small E&Ps, funded by private equity, are a perfect fit for Brammer Engineering's business model.

In January 2005, two longstanding Shreveport oil and gas companies, Anderson Oil and Gas and Franks Exploration Company, purchased interests in the company. Evans remained with the company as the managing partner, and soon after ownership was extended to several employees of the company. These transactions have made the company even stronger and have been mutually beneficial for all involved.

The BMR Consulting subsidiary, begun in 2009, focuses on the consulting side of the business. The venture has added a multi-million dollar line of business to the company's revenues since its inception.

Brammer Engineering, Inc., is headquartered in Shreveport, with offices in Lafayette and Arcadia, Louisiana, and a satellite office in Houston, Texas. BEI currently has operations in many producing regions of the lower forty-eight and its subsidiary, BMR Consulting, has consultants placed domestically and around the globe.

"We recognize that we are truly blessed and that we stand on the shoulders of a giant as we move towards our fiftieth anniversary," says Evans. "Bob left our company and this industry a great legacy that we will continue to preserve, protect and build on well into the future."

Bob and his wife Dorothy "Dot" Brammer.

LOUISIANA GULF COAST OIL EXPOSITION

Louisiana's Gulf Coast region has always been rich in petroleum, and the people living there are respected for their dedication to the exploration and production of the world's energy needs. For those reasons, it is fitting that the Louisiana Gulf Coast Oil Exposition (LAGCOE) is located in Lafayette, right in the heart of America's energy corridor.

In 1953 a group of local oil men and women came together, with the support of the Greater Lafayette Chamber of Commerce, to create a showcase for the services and technologies of local oil and gas related businesses. The inaugural "Lafayette Oil Show" featured service company exhibits in the parking lot of the Lafayette Petroleum Club. There was even a parade through downtown Lafayette with volunteers and exhibitors throwing Mardi Gras beads. The show was such a success that the organizing group incorporated as the Louisiana Gulf Coast Oil Exposition, Inc. The first "official" show under the LAGCOE banner was held in 1955 at Blackham Coliseum on the grounds of the Southwestern Louisiana Institute, now the University of Louisiana at Lafayette.

Throughout the history of LAGCOE, perhaps no personality has been more identified with the show than Founder Gloria Patton Knox. Gloria was recognized by the Smithsonian Institution as the world's first woman "landman" and her image was part of a Smithsonian exhibit for many years. She served on LAGCOE'S Executive Committee from 1955-2005 and was honored as "LAGCOE Looey" in 2001. Founder Granvel Salmon played a key role in the show's early years, serving as show chairman in 1969 and executive director and treasurer from the late 1970s until 1994. The roster of founders and early organizers also includes Jack Hayes, Dobbin Cloninger, Leo Franquez, George Petrie, Kaliste Saloom, Jr., and Rose Martin.

In 1995, LAGCOE moved to its current home, the Lafayette Cajundome and Convention Center, where it hosts 400 exhibits and welcomes more than 14,000 visitors during the three-day event. Industry professionals from almost every U.S. state and twenty-six countries attended LAGCOE in 2011. In order to ensure maximum exposure to decision makers from a critical energy hub, charter jet service was implemented in 2003 to provide transportation from Houston to LAGCOE.

A highlight of each biennial show is the awarding of the coveted golden hardhat to "LAGCOE Looey," the honorary Ambassador of LAGCOE. Looeys are chosen based on their prominence in the oil and gas industry and their contributions to the Lafayette community. Recent LAGCOE Looeys include Bronc Foreman, Charlie Milam, Donald Mosing, William J. (Bill) Doré, Gloria Knox, John Chance, Paul Hilliard, Frank Harrison, and Dwight S. (Bo) Ramsay.

The very early expos were directed toward rig and production personnel in the field—the roughnecks, toolpushers, and drilling superintendents who work the rigs—and thus LAGCOE became known as "the working man's oil show." As the industry changed, the show became more technical, attracting CEOs, executive and mid-level management, engineers, geologists, and other professionals from both operating and service companies. Today, LAGCOE provides a platform for the industry's innovators to present cutting-edge technologies, equipment, and services for both onshore and offshore markets. In addition to traditional exhibits, LAGCOE Technical Sessions feature industry leaders addressing current technologies, issues, and trends from across the nation and around the globe.

LAGCOE has been held in odd-numbered years since 1955. A small full-time staff coordinates over 250 industry volunteers who serve on 21 committees. The organization is led by a board of directors, who appoint a rotating slate of three officers who oversee each show. LAGCOE leadership is an honor and trust granted to those who are respected within the oil and gas industry, but the show would not be possible without the tireless dedication of those hundreds of volunteers.

Within LAGCOE, workday competitors pull together with pride and enthusiasm for the betterment of our oil and gas industry and our community. The show celebrates the entrepreneurial spirit and resourcefulness of the people in south Louisiana—the birthplace of oilfield technologies used across the globe. Attendees from around the world savor the hospitality they experience in Lafayette, voted one of the most optimistic cities in the U.S. In addition to a warm welcome, they enjoy award-winning cuisine, culture, music and entertainment. LAGCOE is known as the hospitable energy exposition, which offers state-of-the-art equipment, services, and solutions for the world's continuing quest for energy.

LISKOW & LEWIS

Above: Founder Cullen Liskow.

Below: Founder Austin Lewis.

For nearly eighty years, the law firm of Liskow & Lewis has been a leader in energy law, and in the process, has served many of the companies in the oil and gas (O&G) industry in Louisiana.

It was the early 1900s when a young Cullen Liskow began his legal career as a secretary in the law firm of Pujo and Williamson while studying law in their office. He was admitted to the Louisiana Bar in 1917, in the midst of World War I, and entered the service shortly thereafter, serving in the Army for the remainder of the war.

He returned from service and practiced law alone until 1935, when he associated with Austin Lewis, and they practiced under the name of Liskow & Lewis. Two years later, Richard Gerard joined them. Liskow was known for his courtroom work, and his knowledge of the existing mineral law of the state made him a recognized authority in the field. In fact, in 1950, as a public service, he represented the state before the U.S. Supreme Court in an effort to defeat the federal claim to the Louisiana tidelands, an offshore area rich in mineral production. While the state did not win the case, Liskow actively participated in the preparation and passage of the Submerged Lands Act by which Congress restored parts of the lands to the state that it had lost in the suit. In the Tidelands case, *United States v. Louisiana*, the Supreme Court enjoined the United States and the State from leasing or drilling in the disputed area pending further orders of the court, "unless by agreement of the parties." After months of negotiation, Lewis prepared the famous "Interim Agreement," which created zones allowing mineral operations to move forward, but with revenues derived from the disputed zones to be escrowed pending final determination of Louisiana's seaward boundary.

In the 1930s, and thereafter, Cullen Liskow and Austin Lewis, as well as others who joined the practice, participated in many landmark cases that helped shape the mineral law of Louisiana. For instance, it was Liskow and others with the firm who handled *California Company v. Price*, a landmark decision of the Louisiana Supreme Court regarding the ownership of water bottoms in the state. Other important cases handled by Liskow & Lewis

include *Vincent v. Bullock*, which established the rule of prescription for mineral royalty rights; *Fontenot v. Magnolia Petroleum Company*, which created a rule of strict liability for damages from geophysical operations, even though the activities were done with reasonable care and in accord with accepted methods; *Richard v. Sohio Petroleum Company* and *Sohio v. Miller*, which were key cases establishing the law concerning the reasonable development obligation of a mineral lessee; *Gueno v. Mdlenka*, which determined for the first time the ownership of delay rentals paid by a mineral lessee of land subject to a usufruct; *Freeland v. Sun Oil Company, et al.*, which determined for the first time the value of lessor's royalty on gas and products where gas was processed in a plant owned by a third party; and *Henry v. Ballard & Cordell Corp.*, which answered for the first time the open question as to the "market value" for lessor royalty purposes of natural gas produced and sold by the lessee under a long term gas sales contract.

Austin Lewis was known as an authority on the conservation of Louisiana's natural resources, particularly in the area of well spacing to avoid the waste involved in the drilling of unnecessary wells. He was instrumental in the drafting and passage in 1941 of Louisiana's conservation statute which was the model for forward thinking conservation legislation in the mineral producing states across the nation. As the foremost practitioner in administrative hearings before the Louisiana Department of Conservation, Lewis drafted rules of procedure that were made mandatory by the Department to shorten lengthy hearings and assure fair play to all.

The firm continues to be at the forefront of practice before the Commissioner of Conservation. Moreover, the firm became very involved in pipeline right of way acquisition and expropriation (condemnation) and an early leader in the expropriation of underground storage rights in Louisiana in such cases as *Trunkline Gas Company v. Rawls* and *Southern Natural Gas Company v. Poland*. And of course, the firm throughout its existence has been very active in the examination of mineral lease and production site titles and the preparation of basic and sophisticated contractual documents utilized in the O&G industry.

The firm has represented and continues

to represent some of the world's largest O&G companies on a statewide, regional, and national basis. It also has represented many independents and smaller O&G companies. Advancement of the young firm and its practice in the early years was provided by Richard E. Gerard, Arthur J. Shepard, Jr., and William M. Hall, Jr. Shortly thereafter, William M. Meyers, Charles C. Gremillion, Robert T. Jorden, Gene W. Lafitte, and Billy H. Hines joined the firm. Many, like both Liskow and Lewis, served the country in the armed forces. Austin Lewis went on to win national acclaim and served as president of the American College of Trial Lawyers in 1974, and Gene Lafitte served in the same position in 1985. The firm's reputation and representation in the O&G industry became national in scope largely as a result of congressional legislation affecting the industry and which instigated important administrative and court proceedings in other jurisdictions where the firm was employed.

Since the founding by two partners, the firm has experienced substantial growth and now has 121 lawyers (75 in New Orleans, 20 in Lafayette, and 26 in Houston, along with support staff to assist the lawyers and manage the firm). Growth has been steady and Liskow & Lewis has diversified to cover areas outside its traditional O&G work.

During its nearly eighty years of experience, Liskow & Lewis has tried cases throughout Louisiana and Texas, and in other jurisdictions, handling matters from the trial courts to the U.S. Supreme Court. It also is active in administrative

hearings and practice and in a broad variety of office or business practices. While its primary business continues to be derived from the O&G industry, it also has an extensive business and regulatory practice. Today, its core practice areas, in addition to the O&G field, include antitrust, appellate practice, aviation, banking, bankruptcy, construction, corporate and business, employee benefits, environmental regulation and litigation, federal income tax and state and local taxes, insurance and indemnity, intellectual property, labor and employment, maritime, product liability defense, professional liability defense, real estate, securities, and toxic tort and occupational disease, among others. Liskow & Lewis is well-known for its commitment to excellence, integrity, and the ability to identify and resolve key issues in a timely and cost-efficient manner.

According to Lafitte, a long-time member of the firm, "At Liskow & Lewis, we believe that the practice of law comes with a responsibility to represent and protect not only our clients, but our community as well. When feasible, we do that by providing pro bono legal work and involving ourselves in community activities. Such work is a win-win situation. It helps our community, and it helps our firm.

"We recognize and celebrate that our firm's culture is enhanced by the diversity of our employees. Liskow & Lewis has a history of actively recruiting, mentoring, and promoting lawyers and staff members with diverse backgrounds and life experiences," adds Keith Jarrett, another firm member and the firm's president.

The firm's earliest members. Top row (from left to right): Bob Jordan, Gene Lafitte, Billy Hines, Charles Gremillion, Bill Meyers, Thomas Hardeman, and Jim Pelletier. Bottom row (from left to right): Will Hall, Dick Gerard, Cullen Liskow, Austin Lewis, and Arthur Shepard.

G&J LAND & MARINE FOOD DISTRIBUTORS, INC.

Above: Left to right, Mike and Erik Lind.

Gerry and Eileen Lind, owners of a retail grocery store in Seattle, Washington, in the early 1950s, were receptive to opportunity when it knocked on their door. It was Galley Supply/Universal Services in South Louisiana hoping to recruit Gerry to join their food services operation.

After five years working for Galley Supply/ Universal, Gerry and Eileen decided to branch out on their own, forming a food distribution business to specifically service the offshore oil industry. They founded G&J Land & Marine Food Distributors, Inc. in Morgan City, Louisiana in 1964.

Their son, Mike, who literally grew up in the business joined G&J in 1974, becoming president in the early 1990s. Today, as owner of the company, he continues to hold that title. His son, Erik, a graduate of Texas A&M University, joined the company in 2007 and is vice president. Mike's son-in-law, Cleve Boudreaux, a graduate of Louisiana State University, joined the company in 2010 and is involved in Operations and Purchasing. Together, they carry on the tradition of a family-owned business that has grown from 10 employees to more than 100 and from 3 trucks to over 20.

G&J Land and Marine Food Distributors, Inc., is a full-service food distributor that provides several services in the transfer of goods to the offshore oil industry in the Gulf of Mexico.

It operates a federally inspected warehouse facility that is strategically located to deliver grocery and janitorial items, as well as other items pertinent to the O&G industry, such as bedding, blankets, pillows, towels, washcloths, etc., as well as small wares, galley and restaurant equipment such as fountain machines and CO_2 tanks for use with fountain/drink dispensers. In other words, their inventory includes just about anything a work crew might require while working on a rig in the middle of a water- or land-based operation.

To assure delivery of food items in a safe manner to those who work on the rigs offshore, it is vital that the company comply with rigorous federal and state food safety regulations. Its warehouse and delivery trucks are inspected regularly to ascertain that they do, in fact, meet all safety requirements established by the U.S. Department of Agriculture (USDA), U.S. Department of Commerce (USDC) and the Federal Drug Administration (FDA), as well as other agencies. In addition, G&J maintains its own team of employees who monitor product recall alerts from the USDA on a daily basis. They do that by using the Federal Government identification (established by number) system. Retrieval of a recalled product is performed expeditiously as required by industry guidelines.

G&J draws upon its network of strategic partners in the catering business in the Gulf of Mexico (GOM) and overseas to provide food for serving meals on the rigs and platforms offshore. And, when customers request special items that are not routinely stocked by G&J, the company goes to great lengths to locate the requested products and deliver them offshore in a safe and timely manner.

In transporting goods to various sites along the Gulf Coast, G&J complies with Occupational Safety and Health Administration's (OSHA) regulations, as well as other state and federal regulations governing the enforcement of safety. In fact, it requires all employees to attend monthly meetings where it deals with safety issues and enforcement.

The programs focus on safety topics, including proper handling of food to lifting to driving. All employees, including drivers, warehouse employees, and office employees, attend. Mike says that, "With everything we do, safety is paramount. That's imperative to our livelihood and the well-being of our employees and customers." He adds that the safety programs further take into consideration such topics as driver training/qualification, vehicle inspections, drug and alcohol testing, and hours of service log auditing. "These guidelines results in safer drivers, and better management controls across our entire operation."

Since inception in 1964, customer satisfaction is top priority at G&J Land & Marine Food Distributors, Inc. A core value in achieving customer satisfaction is reliability. The company's customers know they can depend on G&J to deliver quality products when they need them—where they need them—twenty-four hours a day, seven days a week.

After almost nearly a half-century of servicing the Gulf of Mexico, customer loyalty and service remain the company's core principals. The Lind family goes to extremes to ensure that the G&J team works together to provide an enjoyable experience to its customers. No doubt, those principles have contributed to the company being recognized as a leader in its field for nearly fifty years.

Erik says it does not matter if a company needs to feed a two-man platform, a 250 person drill ship, or a remote land site of 1,000, G&J is ready to assist them with the food and janitorial supplies they might need on the job. "Their remote location is not a challenge for us. We have everything to provide for the distribution of quality products safely and efficiently."

C. H. FENSTERMAKER & ASSOCIATES, LLC

Above, left: A close view of team members conducting pipeline surveying.

Right: Team members conducting pipeline surveying.

Below: C. H. Fenstermaker, Jr., is the founder of the company.

In the early 1900s, surveyor Charles H. Fenstermaker, Sr., provided professional services in New Iberia, Louisiana, never dreaming that he was paving the way for a family business that would become a thriving twenty-first century company. Today, C. H. Fenstermaker & Associates, LLC, is a multidisciplinary consulting firm that offers survey and mapping, engineering, environmental, and advanced technology services. Headquartered in Lafayette, Louisiana, the firm has additional offices in Baton Rouge, New Orleans, and Shreveport, Louisiana; Houston and San Antonio, Texas; and Montrose, Pennsylvania.

The company was founded in 1950 by Charles Fenstermaker, Jr., who was also a professional surveyor. Back then, it mainly served the oil and gas industry in the New Iberia area. His son, Bill, became the third generation to join the family business, taking over as president and CEO in 1980. Bill's brother, John, currently oversees survey operations in both the office and field. R. J. Boutte, a thirty-six year Fenstermaker veteran, is presently senior vice president.

In 1964 the business moved into a two-story building at 1538 Pinhook Road in Lafayette, and the Charles Street location in New Iberia eventually became a warehouse for boats, vehicles, and other field equipment. Ten years later, Fenstermaker added an engineering

department, providing civil engineering services to government agencies and private developers. In 1981, following rapid progress, Fenstermaker's headquarters in Lafayette moved to 135 Regency Square. That year, the company diversified further, implementing an environmental department.

In 1988, noticing these new developments, the U.S. Army Corps of Engineers awarded Fenstermaker a $5-million contract to map the entire Atchafalaya Basin. The project created additional jobs and greater diversification with two promising areas of expertise: information technology and special projects. The company remained focused on emerging technology and new methods in survey and mapping. Fenstermaker was an early adopter of automated mapping, introducing smart maps and advanced computer mapping techniques during the inaugural days of Geographic Information System (GIS) software and applications.

The company's reputation for quality work continued and, in 1990, Bill won the Entrepreneurial Success Award presented by the Louisiana Department of Economic Development. Three years later, C. H. Fenstermaker, Jr., was presented the Surveyor of Excellence Award by the Louisiana Society of Professional Surveyors. Fenstermaker continued its momentum by adding offices in Baton Rouge and New Orleans, as well as remodeling the Lafayette headquarters. To support and promote future growth, a business development team was formed.

The company's success continued with a team of talented members focused on hard work, innovation, positive leadership, and a commitment to customer service. In 1998, Fenstermaker opened a Houston office and made another strategic decision in 2005 by appointing former Secretary of the Louisiana Department of Transportation Kam Movassaghi, PhD, P.E., as the company's president. A well-respected expert, teacher and leader in civil engineering, Dr. Movassaghi's prominent career highlights his dedication to the engineering profession.

Under Dr. Movassaghi's direction, Fenstermaker broadened its market reach and regional ambitions in 2007 with a Shreveport location and the creation of the advanced technologies department. Two years later, the advanced technologies team, incorporating underwater acoustic services, high definition surveying, intelligent 3D modeling, and dimensional control, won the Louisiana Transportation Excellence Award at a special engineering conference. The following year, Fenstermaker's survey and environmental teams began working in Texas' Eagle Ford Shale area. In 2011, Fenstermaker teams entered the Marcellus Shale area in Pennsylvania. The company's consistent progress and expansions have resulted in annual revenue growth reaching $40 million in a recent year.

Currently, Fenstermaker employs over three hundred team members dedicated to making the company a vital partner in the success of its clients. Management stresses the importance of promoting the company's core values and principles, which include adhering to the highest ethical standards, being courteous, leading in technology, and focusing on innovation and coordination of effective services. According to Dr. Movassaghi, "In achieving our corporate mission, we commit to acting in the best interest of our clients by delivering services on time, within budget, and in accordance with established quality standards. When we do that and make a fair profit, we know we have done our job right."

Bill and Dr. Movassaghi believe in not only the business side of Fenstermaker, but also in the areas in which the company operates. Both men make community involvement a priority by participating in various programs that strengthen the local culture and future community prosperity. Both have provided leadership for the Greater Lafayette Chamber of Commerce and promoted industry-related activities, continuing education, and community organizations.

Bill is currently the chairman of IBERIA-BANK Corp. and a past chairman of Lafayette General's Medical Center. Additionally, both he and Kam have raised millions in scholarship donations for the University of Louisiana at Lafayette. In 2011, Governor Jindal selected Bill to serve on the State of Louisiana's Board of Regents.

Above: Team members out in the field for surveying work.

Below: Wendell Levy, a party chief in Survey Field, doing general surveying work.

T. Baker Smith, LLC

Kenneth Wm. Smith is determined to carry on the tradition begun by his grandfather a century ago. As president of the firm that bears his grandfather's name—T. Baker Smith, LLC (TBS)—his aspiration is to provide Superior Integrated Professional Solutions across a broad spectrum of markets in multiple geographic regions.

In 1913, upon graduation from Tulane University, T. Baker Smith, returned to his home in Houma to begin his profession. His appreciation for the community and the outdoors allowed him to help build the early infrastructure in Lafourche, St. Mary, and Terrebonne Parishes, which included roads, bridges, and utilities systems. He became an expert at the accurate reconstruction of U.S. government surveys dating back to the late-1800s along the south Louisiana coast between the Mississippi and the Atchafalaya River. He was a national pioneer who developed techniques, grounded on irrefutable empirical evidence, that have become professional benchmarks. His original and reconstructive surveys have withstood the test of time for accuracy, impartiality, and legal viability.

From the beginning, TBS clients were among the industry's largest and most successful pioneers, including Fohs Oil and the Texas Company. As a result, from the industry's infancy, these exploration companies, and the large landholders that allowed drilling on their property, developed an enduring partnership that relied heavily on the firm's surveying expertise, and, for more than eighty years, the company that bears the founder's name has been actively involved in staking out leases, mapping pipeline rights-of-way, managing permits, and resolving numerous other regulatory issues.

Baker's son, William Clifford Smith (Kenneth's father), succeeded him in the business, expanding operations to include integrated solutions in urban planning, environmental science and regulatory compliance, and land development. As the oil and gas (O&G) industry became more developed, he pursued near and offshore surveying; civil, structural, and coastal engineering; as well as program and construction management. Kenneth joined the family business in 1980, and after becoming president/CEO in 2001, he soon welcomed Geographical Information Systems (GIS), hydrographic surveying, and oyster assessment services to expand and further develop the firm. Beginning in 2002, he expanded the firm geographically as well by adding TBS office locations in Thibodaux, Lafayette, and Baton Rouge, Louisiana, and Houston, Texas, and more recently adding Shreveport, Louisiana, and San Antonio, Texas.

Today, Kenneth says that, "We help our strategic clients with the entire life cycle of their developments. Every project is different and every solution is, too. We do not take a 'one-size-fits-all' approach to the services we provide. At TBS, we aim to be a true partner to help clients become successful no matter how complex or unique the challenge. Plain and simple: We do what it takes to get the job done." He adds that while it may mean collaborating with stakeholders across locations and practice areas throughout the entire project life

cycle to tailor a solution for clients, "We do it with the same, creative spirit we've used to make clients successful since 1913."

TBS has built its reputation on professionalism, turning ideas into reality and building relationships one project at a time. The TBS team consists of more than three hundred professionals and support staff members, including urban planners; environmental professionals; professional land, near, and offshore surveyors; civil, coastal, and structural engineers; hydrologic and 3D modelers; oyster biologists; air and water professionals; project managers; and CADD/GIS technicians.

As technology changes the industry landscape, TBS changes techniques and technology to keep pace. TBS owns and operates all of their own equipment. Its internal resources consist of over 30 three-man land/nearshore survey crews, numerous marine survey vessels and barges, an offshore survey vessel, airboats, all-terrain vehicles (ATVs), global positioning systems (GPS) total stations, laser scanners, and gradiometers/magnetometers. The knowledge, equipment, and talent of team members at TBS is compatible with a number of markets, including pipeline, O&G exploration and production, industrial infrastructure, land development, and public works.

TBS continues to be modeled on Baker Smith's precision, ingenuity, and integrity. In fact, it has experienced five hundred percent growth since 2000. Kenneth says, "We want to develop mutually beneficial relationships with key clients that allow our three hundred-plus professionals and support staff to grow and develop professionally. We will continue developing key professional and niche services and expand our geographic footprint all while staying true to our corporate culture."

Between 1913 and 2013, TBS developed and grew from a one man surveying and civil engineering operation "into one of the top 500 engineering, architectural, and environmental design

firms in the United States," according to *Engineering News Record*. TBS received the 2012 Best Architect/Engineering/Contractor (A/E/C) Employer Award from PSMJ, a national industry consulting firm, and was recognized as one of LSU's 100 fastest growing tiger businesses.

Year in and year out, TBS has helped countless clients with well locations, flowlines, facilities, and pipelines from the Rio Grande to the Piney Woods of North Louisiana to the deep blue waters of the Gulf of Mexico. Rooted in tradition and providing cutting edge solutions, TBS is proud to celebrate a Century of Solutions. Additional information is available at www.tbsmith.com.

Opposite, top: Founder T. Baker Smith in the field.

Opposite, bottom: A portrait of three generations (from top to bottom) T. Baker Smith, Wm. Clifford Smith, and Kenneth Wm. Smith.

COMFORT SUITES
OIL CENTER

The management and staff of Comfort Suites Oil Center—Lafayette, Louisiana, say, "Bienvenue" (welcome). Just over a year old, and located in the Oil Center and Cajun County, the modern, three-story hotel plays host to business and leisure travelers.

In the Heart of Acadiana, and near the University of Louisiana at Lafayette and the Lafayette Regional Airport, Comfort Suites makes an ideal lodging spot for those visiting students at the university, or others flying into town for business or pleasure. Even family vacationers looking for a fun place to break up

their travels, visit, and sightsee, find Comfort Suites Oil Center to be a great location.

Nearby are Girard Park, the largest public park in the city, the Cajun Dome and Convention Center, a seventy-two-thousand-square-foot venue where the red carpet is rolled out for world-renowned musicians and festivals, the Acadian Cultural Center with special educational programs on the origins and culture of the Acadians (Cajuns) who were native to the area, along with a junior ranger program for children.

Comfort Suites Oil Center opened May 2011 and features eighty suites with microwave, refrigerator, hairdryer, coffeemaker, iron, and ironing board. All rooms have either one king-sized bed or two queen beds with a queen sleeper sofa. Rooms are tastefully decorated; with padded leather headboards and all with deluxe pillow-top mattresses for a restful night's sleep. Rooms have luscious spreads and matching drapery. "All rooms feature flat-panel televisions and complimentary wireless and wired Internet connections. It is actually a 'home away from home' for those who want amazing guest service and a family-type atmosphere. Comfort Suites Oil Center cares about the people it serves and treats guests to true southern hospitality," says General Manager Anne Gros.

Upon entering the canopied hotel, a sleek modern look welcomes visitors. "We provide training for staff to assure that visitors' receive a warm welcome and exceptional service during their stay." Anne adds.

Comfort Suites Oil Center features all the modern-day amenities in each room, including a recharge station on each desk for your cell phones, iPods, laptops and all your portable, electronic gadgets.

For local businesses and associations that need extra meeting space, Comfort Suites Oil Center has just the right solution, complete with banquet facilities. The spacious conference room can be arranged in various designs to accommodate up to fifty persons. It also offers catering for business lunches and dinners.

Business individuals traveling will welcome the convenient Business Center designed just for them. There, they can take advantage of a computer, fax machine and telephones to conduct business while on the road.

A full, hot buffet breakfast awaits all guests, giving them the option of eggs, meat, waffles, yogurt, fresh fruit, cereal, and much more. When guests have to leave early, the "Your Suite Success™" breakfast to go is available two hours prior to the breakfast buffet. Offered in a "Grab & Go" bag, it includes a breakfast bar, fresh fruit, and bottled water. The hotel also offers a fitness facility where guests can continue their health regimen. There, they will find a mini-gym, complete with treadmills, elliptical, and nautilus machines. When water is the sport of choice, individuals can take a refreshing swim in the pool or laze poolside. Enjoy cooking out? Try out our gas grill at the poolside gazebo.

Located near downtown and within close proximity to many of Lafayette's fine restaurants, visitors are drawn to the local cuisine because of the Cajun heritage and culture of the area. Located near Lafayette General Medical Center, University Medical Center, Heart Hospital Womens and Childrens Hospital, Zoo of Acadiana, and the Mall of Acadiana, there is always something to do and see while visiting the Acadiana area.

Comfort Suites Oil Center says come visit us and "Laissez les bon temps rouler!" (Let the good times roll)!

DON BRIGGS, PRESIDENT

LOUISIANA OIL & GAS ASSOCIATION

Over forty-five years ago, Don Briggs, a Miami, Florida, transplant began his career in the oil and gas field right here in Louisiana. He got his start at Owens Drilling Company and worked there through college graduation at USL in Lafayette. After many years in the field and ultimately becoming president of Aztec, an oil and gas service company, Don stepped away to answer a need. He saw a gap in the armor of the industry: very little representation at the state capitol.

Left: Don Briggs in the early 1960s as a roughneck for Owens Drilling.

Right: Don Briggs as the president of the Louisiana Oil & Gas Association in 2013.

In 1992, Don started the Louisiana Independent Oil and Gas Association (Now LOGA). Don knew that if the industry was to survive under the onslaught of the many bureaucratic state and federal agencies, the industry needed representation in Baton Rouge.

Bob Meredith, an early LOGA Chairman, was at the table when LOGA was conceptualized. Meredith says that there was a true need for oil and gas representation and Don stepped up to the plate to run the show. He continued by stating, "I'm sure there are others who could have run LOGA, but no one could have matched Don Briggs for these past twenty years. It's impossible to have done better." Meredith continued by saying, "Don knows how to relate to the producers, the service sector, the politicians, and the public. He has never underestimated what we could achieve. His passion is LOGA."

Don desired to give a voice to each aspect of the industry. Therefore, LOGA, at its roots represents most of the exploration, producing and service sector companies operating in Louisiana. His goal was and still is today to make Louisiana a state where the oil and gas industry can prosper and enjoy the fruits of its hard work and at the same time be in harmony with the environment and state government.

Jim Cole, a longtime friend and colleague of Don, says that dating back into the 1970s, Don has been "fun to work with and a great salesman." But Cole's compliments did not stop there. Cole continued by stating, "Don Briggs' maturity in his handling of good times and bad at LOGA is quite remarkable. He is a man of true integrity and is a great leader."

LOGA has developed into the oil and gas industry's resource for advocacy within Louisiana. With over twenty years of experience, there is very little LOGA has not seen. From the 2010 oil spill, to bad and good legislation, to parish ordinances, LOGA is the trusted advisor for local, state and federal oil and gas issues.

There is no doubt about it, Barry Hebert and Thomas LaSalle were looking for a niche in the oil and gas (O&G) upstream sector to provide environmental compliance and consulting services. They found it in 1994 with the formation of HLP Engineering.

In 1990 the Clean Air and Clean Water Acts underwent significant revisions after the Exxon Valdez Spill. The amendments reregulated government environmental regulations previously established. Today, the laws establish the basis for many environmental regulations being promulgated.

Hebert and LaSalle previously worked for a company specializing in O&G surveying, where environmental consulting was also offered. They saw the burden imposed by the multitude of regulations being passed. Even though other environmental consulting firms existed, they realized a unique need for a professional engineering service company dedicated to the field of environmental compliance within the O&G upstream sector.

Starting from ground zero and with minimal financial backing, it was imperative to set the bar for excellence, maintain efficient services, and contain costs. "Operating 'ultra lean,' in the early years," says LaSalle, "meant we used a single computer and took turns answering the phone. We had little marketing experience, so we knocked on doors to sell our services." Their perseverance paid off, and they began to see small jobs trickle in. HLP Engineering became a "breath of fresh air" at a time when many such consultants were frowned upon by industry. That philosophy helped HLP to grow market share and broaden its service sector base.

HLP proved to be the perfect fit for small independent operators not staffed to keep up with the ever-changing regulations. Projects bid upon by HLP were usually successful. As the company's client base of small independent O&G operators grew, its quality reputation spread. In early 2000, HLP began landing larger customers via referrals. Companies such as Phillips Petroleum (now ConocoPhillips), Anadarko Petroleum and Apache Corporation, inquired about HLP. As such, HLP's clientele and dedicated, experienced staff continue to be the most important element of its growth and existence.

The evolution from an unknown entity to a common name has brought welcomed growing pains for HLP. From ensuring that new staff members understand and uphold the company's core values, to addressing needs of improving systems and efficiency in order to keep up with workloads, the challenges continue. But HLP will continue to provide the quality of service that has earned their customers' confidence.

Hebert and LaSalle feel blessed by the company's success, which positions them to support the area economy by contributing to various charities, hiring area professionals, and sponsoring an HLP Engineering Scholarship at University of Louisiana-Lafayette.

HLP Engineering, Inc. is located on the Internet at www.hlpengineering.com.

PETROLEUM ENGINEERS, INC.

Founded in 1970 by Don Claxton, Skip Kimball and Al Bellaire, Petroleum Engineers, Inc. (PEI) has grown to one of the oil industry's most respected engineering firms.

Above: Don Claxton, Skip Kimball and Al Bellaire.

The three were former colleagues at Drilling Well Control (DWC). They left DWC to pursue a niche they believed would provide the industry with professional engineers, well site supervisors, and technical services. They also envisioned providing these technical services at a moment's notice anywhere in the world!

Success was slow to come, but they persevered. According to Bellaire, now president, "Employees at DWC thought we were crazy to leave there because the rig count was at an all-time low. They were partly correct because we had difficulty finding work. The first two wells we supervised and drilled filed for bankruptcy, and we were several years getting paid for our services. With no income for about the first three months, we went back to the drawing board—and the bank."

Then, they did what they had to do: They tapped businesses with which they had provided services. At DWC, they had drilled wells for Willard Randolph of the LVO Corporation in Tulsa. Understanding their financial situation, Randolph engaged them to drill five wells. He suggested getting five rigs and drilling them simultaneously; or, getting one rig and drilling wells in succession. They chose the latter to "stretch out" the income, and ease the bank's mind. That was the beginning of their success!

Bellaire and Kimball remained in the field until 1978, when the oilfield "boom" began. Challenged with planning and management supervision, they rode the "boom" into 1981, when business improved. By 1989, however, there was only one rig running with seventeen employees. They discussed relinquishing the company in August; however, Claxton asked Bellaire to stay. "If business hadn't improved by September, we would throw in the towel. As luck had it, the business turned around and we had four rigs running," Bellaire said. "In an effort to survive, we formed partnerships with contractors doing offshore and foreign work. That allowed us to pay off our debts."

PEI sold to a group of investors in 2005, and the investors relinquished the business to venture capitalists—The Hamilton Group including Hamilton Engineering, Atlantis, and PEI. Claxton and Kimball have since retired.

Today, PEI, with offices in Houston, Texas, and Lafayette, Louisiana, has 30 employees, 250 consultants, and clients around the world. It continues to grow the partnership with Hamilton, and is further developing the Houston office to offer deepwater and international services.

Albert Reid Wherritt served in the U. S. Army during World War I and was wounded by mustard gas in the fields of France during the Battle of the Argonne Forest in the fall of 1918. Hospitalized in Europe, Reid eventually returned to his home in Pleasant Hill, Missouri, to recover.

By 1919 oil wells were being drilled in the Caddo Pine Island Field in North Caddo Parish on the John J. Dillon land, which had been acquired in the mid-1800s. The Dillon heirs asked their cousin from Pleasant Hill, Missouri, to go down to Louisiana to "look out after the oil," initiating his career.

Mr. Wherritt established himself in Shreveport, thirty miles south of the Caddo Pine Island oilfield and married Lucille Sibley of Shreveport. He would drive to the field daily on dirt roads before the highways were paved, sometimes traveling four hours each way when it rained. Soon Mr. Wherritt understood the oil business well, and he also knew the major players in the Shreveport area. He was much too conservative to buy the oil leases and drill the risky wells that many of his friends were busy doing, so he began to buy and sell producing royalty interests….no dry holes for him! He would hire brokers to seek out the landowners who owned the minerals and royalty in the major fields being discovered all across the Upper Gulf Coast. With his business relationships in Shreveport and Dallas, he could then make a market for the producing royalty and minerals as well as speculative minerals in the surrounding area. He would always keep a few royalty and mineral acres for himself in each trade, thus started his fifty year career of buying, selling, and acquiring minerals and royalty.

His expertise in the growing exploration and production business along with his personal friendship with the owners and officers that headed the independent companies that were finding the oil and natural gas across Texas, Louisiana, Arkansas and Mississippi fueled his success. Eventually, he came to own many thousands of acres in thirteen states from Texas to Florida and as far north as the Dakotas. To anyone who would ask about his success in the oil and gas business Mr. Wherritt would gladly share "People are the key to this business, you have to know people."

Mr. Wherritt's properties are now owned by his daughter in the VWM Properties Partnerships and by his grandchildren in the ARW Properties Partnerships. His many personal and professional accomplishments continue to positively affect new generations of his family.

A. R. WHERRITT
1896-1982
ROYALTY AND MINERAL TRADER

Albert Reid Wherritt.

SPONSORS

About the Author

WILLIAM D. REEVES

William Dale Reeves was born in New Orleans in 1941. He received a B.A. from Williams College, and a Ph. D. from Tulane University in 1968. He worked for eight years in a real estate investment trust and as president of an insurance company. Since 1990 he has been a full-time contract historian. His books include *De La Barre: Life of a French Creole Family in Louisiana* (1980); *Historic City Park: New Orleans* (1992); *Westwego: From Cheniere to Canal* (1996); *Manresa on the Mississippi: for the Greater Glory of God* (1996); *Paths to Distinction: Dr. James White, Governor E. D. White and Chief Justice Edward Douglass White of Louisiana* (1999); *Historic Louisiana: An Illustrated History* (2003); *From Tally-Ho to Forest Home: The History of Two Louisiana Plantations* (2005); *Le Pavillon Hotel: A Century of Triumph* (2008); *Hotel Monteleone* (2011); His publications include an article on the Public Works Administration in the *Journal of American History* (1973); "A Transitional Plantation House in Louisiana Architecture" in *Arris, the Journal of the Southeast Chapter of the Society of Architectural Historians* VIII (1997); and "Two Hundred Years of Maritime New Orleans: An Overview" in *Tulane Maritime Law Journal* (Winter 2010).